WINSTON CHURCHILL'S WORLD VIEW

WINSTON CHURCHILL'S WORLD VIEW

Statesmanship and Power

KENNETH W. THOMPSON

Louisiana State University Press   Baton Rouge and London

Designer: Roderick Parker
Typeface: Linotron Sabon
Typesetter: G and S Typesetters, Inc.

Library of Congress Cataloging in Publication Data

Thompson, Kenneth W., 1921–
Winston Churchill's world view.

Includes index.
1. Churchill, Winston, Sir, 1874–1965—Views on
international relations.   2. International relations.
I. Title.
DA566.9.C5T39   1983   327.1′01   82-4699
ISBN 0-8071-1045-0 (cloth)
ISBN 0-8071-1419-7 (paper)

Louisiana Paperback Edition, 1987
10 9 8 7 6 5 4 3 2 1

To Beverly C. Thompson

CONTENTS

Introduction   1

PART ONE   *A Philosophy of International Politics*

chapter one   Prevailing Illusions and Enduring Principles   11

chapter two   Contemporary Theories and Churchill's Philosophy   25

PART TWO   *The Man and His Philosophy*

chapter three   The School of the Statesman   61

chapter four   The Roots of Churchill's Approach to Politics   78

PART THREE   *Statesmanship, Public Opinion, and Politics*

chapter five   The Tradition of Statesmanship   113

chapter six   Public Opinion and the Dilemma of Realist Foreign Policy   119

chapter seven   Progress, Politics, and Leadership in the Western Tradition   162

PART FOUR   *War*

chapter eight   The Nature of War   175

chapter nine   Three World Wars   194

PART FIVE   *Peace*

chapter ten   A Survey of Historic Approaches   223

chapter eleven   The Balance of Power as Law or Alternative   229

chapter twelve   The Disarmament Dilemma   251

chapter thirteen   The World State and International Law   270
chapter fourteen   International Organization: The United
                      Nations   295
chapter fifteen   New Insights on "Old Diplomacy"   332

                      Index   361

WINSTON CHURCHILL'S WORLD VIEW

INTRODUCTION

On the eve of World War II, Winston S. Churchill wrote: "The modern world presents the extraordinary spectacle of almost everybody wishing to prevent or avoid war, and yet war coming remorselessly nearer to almost everybody. Surely this will be the great mystery which future generations will find among the records, and perhaps the ruins of our age."[1] Historians will ask themselves how Western societies comprised of vast numbers of well-educated and for the most part virtuous men and women fell victim to the grim perils of war. The answer according to Churchill will be: "They had no plan."

Churchill's terse statement of what is required to stop war is as timely today as it was in the years before World War II. It is puzzling why leaders who came after him, including present-day heads of state, have shied away from his prescriptions for peace. The fact that Churchill spoke with such clarity on the prerequisites for the maintenance of peace offers an invitation to return to his life and works. Because he held, as he put it, "to a fairly consistent line of thought" on foreign policy, his philosophy may even now serve as an example for others including American presidents.

For Americans in the postwar era, it has become fashionable to say that peace depends on the United Nations or international law, or each nation's resisting aggression, and these worthy objectives have been pursued as ends in themselves. Alternatively, other leaders have maintained that pragmatism offers the best guide to foreign policy. In the absence of a plan, Western leaders have proceeded case by case out of a conviction that each successive crisis was unique. Yet in the final analysis, modern leaders have grounded their policies on unacknowledged theories, hidden assumptions, and inarticulated premises. They have proceeded on the basis of un-

1. Winston S. Churchill, "How to Stop War," *Step by Step, 1936–1939* (New York: Putnam's, 1939), 25–26.

examined propositions. Some have said the sole determinant of successful foreign policy was strength and have made military preparedness the guiding principle of policy. Being number one as a world military power or attaining strategic superiority has become the supreme goal for the nation without asking "number one for what?" Others have proposed, without first examining the consequences for national security, the negotiation of universal disarmament and, failing that, some form of unilateral disarmament. If it is true as Lord Oliver Franks has argued that "the most prevalent single cause of misunderstanding and suspicion . . . [is] failure to communicate the assumptions of a proposal,"[2] then critical analysis and comparison of these views is essential.

Churchill's importance in twentieth-century statecraft, especially before and after World War II, in part derives from the twin pillars on which he sought to base foreign policy: strength and negotiations. From 1936 to 1939, he wrote fortnightly letters commenting primarily on crucial issues of foreign policy. He set forth his views in the most simple and straightforward language. No plan, he wrote, had any value unless it had behind it force and the resolve to use force. Imperialism had not been turned back without a Grand Alliance founded on the combined efforts of nations threatened by such imperialism, whether the threat was Philip of Macedonia setting out to conquer the Greek city-states or Napoleon and Hitler overrunning Europe. Peace had to have its constables; the scales of justice would have no influence lacking the sword. Not only one nation confronting an aggressor but all nations whose security was jeopardized had to join together. However, history demonstrates that the call for united strength, so obviously sound in the abstract, went largely unheeded. Nations who faced a common threat were lulled into believing they could escape the sacrifices required by a common defense effort; they sought security by making a deal, retreating into isolation, or relying on their own strength.

While Churchill understood the essential nature of the common defense, he also recognized the different perspectives from which

2. Oliver S. Franks, *Britain and the Tide of World Affairs* (London: Oxford University Press, 1955), 34–35.

nations viewed threats to peace. The aggressor appeared in different forms to different countries. For some the danger was near, for others less immediate, and for still others far off. Theorists of collective security maintained that peace was indivisible and each nation should join every other: "Who touches one, touches all." To demand that nations act without regard for their particular interests, however, was to ask more than mankind in its present stage of development could sustain.

Therefore, in giving content to his plan for strength, Churchill called for zones of responsibility and regional structures. He wrote: "In the front line, pledged to all the necessary measures, well-equipped, strictly combined, stand those who dwell nearest to the Potential Aggressor; in the second line those likely to be next affected, or indirectly affected, by his aggression. Farther off, and least heavily committed, will be the states who, while they do not fear this particular Potential Aggressor, nevertheless realize that some day . . . their turn may come." [3] It would be divorcing practice from reality to expect nations in the three zones to respond to each successive threat as if it touched them equally and in the same way. To weave together the varied regional and national interests into one worldwide organism, Churchill maintained, was the inexorable task of world statesmen. If some states were by virtue of their interests and power destined to take the lead, others according to their respective interests and power must band together. The alternative was to be destroyed one by one. In Churchill's words: "A series of regional pacts included in a Grand Alliance or League offers . . . the sole hope of preventing war or of preventing, if war should come, the ruin of those who have done no wrong." [4]

Yet Churchill's plan for peace, in contrast with those of a multitude of contemporary leaders, was not exhausted in his appeal for strength. It rested as well on a strategy of diplomacy. What he offered the world was a framework for understanding the relationship between strength and diplomacy, between power and negotiations. On the one hand, no one is more deserving of the title "defender of

3. Churchill, *Step by Step*, 26–27.
4. *Ibid.*, 27.

freedom." Churchill stands supreme as the father of the doctrine
that security depends on strength, that the appetite of an aggressor
feeds on success. Often forgotten, however, is the fact that in perhaps his most famous speech, at Fulton, Missouri, rallying the West
to the defense of freedom against Soviet expansionism, he also declared: "What is needed is a settlement, and the longer it is delayed,
the more difficult it will be and the greater our dangers will become." On December 10, 1948, Churchill addressed the House of
Commons, saying: "I have frequently advised that we should endeavour to reach a settlement with Russia on fundamentally outstanding questions. . . . I believe that in this resides the best hope of
avoiding a third world war." On December 14, 1950, he dealt specifically with the view that negotiations meant appeasement: "The
declaration of the Prime Minister that there will be no appeasement
. . . commands almost universal support. It is a good slogan for the
country. It seems to me, however, that . . . it requires to be more
precisely defined." Churchill, as leader of the opposition, went on to
explain: "What we really mean, I think, is no appeasement through
weakness or fear." It was weakness not strength that led Chamberlain into appeasement at Munich, and Churchill came to office
to rectify that error. But in 1950, he linked strength with diplomacy,
saying: "Appeasement in itself may be good or bad according to circumstances. Appeasement from weakness and fear is alike futile
and fatal. Appeasement from strength is magnanimous and noble
and might be the surest and perhaps the only path to peace."

Churchill's plan for peace constituted a "theory," a doctrine or
a set of organizing principles of foreign policy. No leader could deal
with the contingencies of world politics without such a theory. In
his words: "Those who are possessed of a definite body of doctrine
and of deeply rooted convictions upon it will be in a much better
position to deal with the shifts and surprises of daily affairs."[5] In
this sense, the "right" political decision is the outcome of a powerful and creative mind possessed of a body of doctrine comprehending the varied dimensions of a given political situation. Wisdom in-

5. Winston S. Churchill, *The Second World War*, Vol. I, *The Gathering Storm*
(Boston: Houghton Mifflin, 1948), 210.

volves an evaluation of all the intractable elements in a complex situation. Clarity of vision depends on a scaffolding of thought founded on certain bedrock principles concerning man, politics, and society. To paraphrase the poet T. S. Eliot, without a philosophy or a plan, wisdom will be lost in knowledge and knowledge in information.

Churchill's philosophy and thought, grounded in certain historic views of man and politics, represents a counterforce to the prevailing trends of the times. Contemporary culture is endlessly tempted to cope with its problems by piling facts on facts. The age is the era of the computer. Statistics are more complete; we have more accurate records of birth rates, death rates, and emigration rates. Elemental factors responsible for the growth and prosperity of nations are better understood and more subject to control. Yet while knowledge has increased, so have the factors that must be identified and evaluated. In place of once isolated rivalries, we face struggles that involve directly or indirectly the whole habitable globe. Our problems have become so vast and interconnected, their solution so painful and uncertain, and the weight of contingencies so overwhelming that wise statesmen are needed as never before.

Withal, the essential character of problems in international politics is not new. However much we speak of change, men and states have confronted one another in the past across vast expanses of geography embracing values and interests that persist for generations. The continuity of foreign policies is a reality because national interests in broad outline persist and the suspicion of state for state has survived. Political movements that are alive only to change, not continuity, flounder in the international arena. Writing of his own Labor party, Denis Healey could assert: "Because the Party as a whole lacks any systematic theory of world affairs, it has too often fallen victim to the besetting sin of all progressive movements— utopianism. In particular it tends to discount the power elements in politics, seeing it as a specific evil of the existing system rather than a generic characteristic of politics as such."[6]

6. R. H. S. Crossman *et al.*, *The New Fabian Essays* (New York: Frederick A. Praeger, 1952), 161–62.

Churchill approached foreign policy in terms of power and diplomacy. For the most part, he resisted the temptation to set aside his doctrine in practice. In a debate in the House of Commons he declared: "Foreign policy is not a game, nor is it an academic question, and . . . not an ideological question. . . . Foreign policy is in fact a method of protecting our own interests and saving our own people from the threat of another war, and it is against that criterion that the foreign policy of any government is to be measured."[7] A doctrine provides guidelines, but the statesman must be flexible in its application. It can be said of foreign policy as Churchill wrote of warfare: "The best plan of acquiring flexibility is to have three or four plans for all the possible contingencies, all worked out with the utmost detail. Then it is much easier to switch from one to the other as and where the cat jumps."[8] With flexibility, the leader is not shackled; the doctrine is not a straightjacket. The alternatives are never ideal cases for applying a principle, and they conflict with one another in various ways. In one context, the Soviet Union is the threat, but, confronted by Hitler's Germany, Churchill declared bluntly he would make a pact with the devil to stop Germany's expansion. On October 18, 1951, Churchill defended Britain's policy in the Middle East against its critics: "Our own self-interest demands that we take cognizance of the Muslim world, its legitimate aspirations, and try to help out."[9]

Churchill's firm grasp of world politics was rooted in history. His conception of the Grand Alliance was based on the lessons of the coalition that resisted Louis XIV. His historical masterpiece, *Marlborough: His Life and Times*, was written during the decade of "the gathering storm," about which he warned not *ex post facto* but as the first signs of dark clouds appeared on the horizon. As Marlborough was the linchpin of the first Grand Alliance that thwarted France's attempt to dominate Europe, so Churchill led in marshal-

7. *Parliamentary Debates* (Hansard) House of Commons, Fifth Series, Vol. 427, October 23, 1946 (London: His Majesty's Stationery Office, 1950), 1706.
8. Winston S. Churchill, *The Second World War,* Vol. V, *Closing the Ring* (Boston: Houghton Mifflin, 1951), 162.
9. London *Times*, October 19, 1951, p. 5.

ing the resistance to German expansionism and again at Fulton, Missouri, in calling for unity to oppose Soviet expansion. Yet resistance was not an end in itself. By the 1950s, Churchill had called on no less than forty occasions for an approach to the Russians based on peaceful settlement. Fifteen months after the Fulton speech he declared before Parliament: "It is idle to reason or argue with the Communists. It is, however, possible to deal with them on a fair, realistic basis, and, in my experience, they will keep their bargains as long as it is in their interest to do so, which might, in this grave matter, be a long time, once things were settled."

Churchill's plan was not always followed and, when followed by his successors, was not always applied with the same wisdom and skill he might have employed. Because he had a plan based on twin pillars of peace—strength and negotiation—he pursued a steady course. For that reason, a study of Churchill's philosophy can provide lessons for presidents and prime ministers as well as statesmen in many lands. With this objective in mind, we propose to study the origins of his approach to international politics, its evolution over time, and its application to the great issues of war and peace.

PART ONE

A Philosophy of International Politics

"I try to pursue, as it seems to me, a steady theme and my thought as far as I can grasp it, measure it, is all of one piece."

CHAPTER ONE

Prevailing Illusions and Enduring Principles

On February 28, 1945, a young Conservative member of Parliament, Captain Peter Thorneycroft, destined in 1951 to become the youngest member of Prime Minister Churchill's cabinet, addressed the House of Commons. The speeches up to that point had been limited to the immediate, concrete issues arising from the Polish settlement drawn up at the Crimean conference by Churchill, Roosevelt, and Stalin and incorporated in the so-called Yalta agreement. Reports of its political and territorial provisions stirred opposition. Despite the well-known British realism and sangfroid, the moral and political ambiguities of the Yalta agreement as early as 1945 had begun to inflame segments of British public opinion. In the minds of most speakers who addressed the Parliament that day, Yalta was a question that called for judgments of right or wrong, good or evil, black or white. It was in the popular mind a simple problem in morals.

In contrast, Captain Thorneycroft was representative of a small group of extraordinarily able members who framed their comments in the language of well-considered principles of international politics. Thorneycroft seized on the occasion of the debate over Yalta to lay bare the intellectual roots of two kinds of foreign policy. What he said with such force and clarity serves a dual purpose. His words are directed essentially at a crucial and fundamental aspect of foreign policy, particularly American foreign policy. Because the speaker was one of the prime minister's faithful disciples, his language offers a clue to the nature of Churchill's thought on foreign policy. At the same time, his formulation, when contrasted with Churchill's statement, introduces a recurrent dilemma of democratic foreign policy.

The debate had ranged far and wide as some members denounced the prime minister for yielding too much to the Russians while others condemned him for claiming too much for Britain's postwar role. Thorneycroft chose the occasion to cast his specific comments on Yalta in the framework of a more general statement on foreign policy which raises certain pressing questions with which we must be concerned:

I believe the real difficulty in which my hon. Friends find themselves is not so much Poland at all. I believe it is in the apparent conflict between documents like the Atlantic Charter and the facts of the European situation. We talk to two different people in two different languages. In the East we are talking to the Russians. The Russians are nothing if not realists. . . . I believe that the Russian Foreign Office is perhaps more in tune with the advice which would be given to the Tsars than to the potentates of the twentieth century. In such circumstances we talk in language not far removed from power politics. In the West we are faced by the Americans. They are nothing if not idealists. To them we talk in the polite language of the Atlantic Charter. Somehow or other we have to marry those two schools of thought. If I could persuade the Americans, particularly in the Middle West, to have something of the Russian realism in international relations, and persuade the Russians to have the idealism that exists on the East Coast of America, we might get somewhere, but let us face the fact that the process will be a long and painful one. You do not move suddenly from a world in which there are international rivalries into a world where there is international cooperation. It is the world we are in that the Prime Minister has to deal with. We could not come back from Yalta with a blueprint for a new Utopia. . . . The rights of small nations are safeguarded by a mixture of diplomacy and military power.[1]

On the other side of the Atlantic, the most learned American diplomat speaking to a distinguished audience about foreign policy set forth a theme remarkably similar to the text by the British "Tory." In 1951, less than a year before his appointment as ambassador to Moscow, George F. Kennan concluded a series of five lectures at the University of Chicago with this statement:

As you have no doubt surmised, I see the most serious fault of our past policy formulation to lie in something that I might call the legalistic-moralistic approach to international problems. This approach runs like a

1. *Parliamentary Debates* (Hansard) House of Commons, Fifth Series, Vol. 408, February 28, 1945 (London: His Majesty's Stationery Office, 1950), 1458–59.

red skein through our foreign policy of the last fifty years. It has in it something of the old emphasis on arbitration treaties, something of the Hague Conferences and schemes for universal disarmament . . . something of the League of Nations and the United Nations, something of the Kellogg Pact . . . something of the belief in World Law and World Government. But it is none of these, entirely. Let me try to describe it.

It is the belief that it should be possible to suppress the chaotic and dangerous aspirations of governments in the international field by the acceptance of some system of legal rules and restraints. This belief undoubtedly represents in part an attempt to transpose the Anglo-Saxon concept of individual law . . . and to make it applicable to governments as it is applicable here at home to individuals. It must also stem in part from the memory of the origin of our own political system—from the recollection that we were able, through acceptance of a common institutional and juridical framework, to reduce to harmless dimensions the conflicts of interest and aspiration among the original thirteen colonies. . . . Remembering this, people are unable to understand that what might have been possible for the thirteen colonies in a given set of circumstances might not be possible in the wider international field.[2]

And Kennan concluded:

It is the essence of this belief that, instead of taking the awkward conflicts of national interest and dealing with them on their merits with a view to finding the solutions least unsettling to the stability of international life, it would be better to find some formal criteria of a juridical nature by which the permissible behavior of states could be defined. . . . Behind all this, of course, lies the American assumption that the things for which other peoples in this world are apt to contend are for the most part neither creditable nor important and might justly be expected to take second place behind the desirability of an orderly world, untroubled by international violence. To the American mind, it is implausible that people should have positive aspirations, and ones that they regard as legitimate, more important to them than the peacefulness and orderliness of international life.[3]

These two strong expressions of a British and American viewpoint on the nature of foreign policy are significant because of the

2. George F. Kennan, *American Diplomacy, 1900–1950* (Chicago: University of Chicago Press, 1951), 95–96.
3. *Ibid.*, 96.

light they throw on two opposing theories of international politics in the West. The counsel of Mr. Kennan and Captain Thorneycroft is that of traditional political realism. For the political realist, rivalry and some form of strife in politics and world politics in particular are the rule and normal state of things and not a mere accident of an archaic past. There are harmonies as well as disharmonies and cooperation as well as conflict in international life, but the failure of every past scheme for world peace must be sought in the conditions which underlie these disharmonies. In all social groups, whether in states or in smaller, more intimate communities, rivalry and a contest for influence and power go on unceasingly. On the international scene these rivalries are uncontrolled by effective law or government. Under the constraints of present international society, the business of statesmanship and diplomacy is to limit the struggle and contain it through establishing effective balances of power and rough equilibrium among the contending parties. Accommodation requires mutual recognition that an equilibrium exists or can be established. The realist strives to mitigate the inescapable rivalries among nations through checks and balances and compromise and bargaining. In the adjustments or compromises that are worked out, abstract moral principles may be the ultimate object and purpose, but an abstract principle is not an essential part of the bargain itself. Realism would prepare the student of international politics for the possible moral discrepancy of means and ends. It accepts as the guide and premise of its thought the permanence of the struggle for power. At the same time, it strives unceasingly through every means at its disposal to contain and limit concentrations of power and to compose and relieve tensions that might lead to war.

By contrast, the utopian philosophy of international politics has little in common with political realism; nor has it shown much patience or understanding for it. Utopianism chooses deliberately to abjure the toils of power politics since at most they are considered an abnormal and passing historic phase of international relations. With the creation of one universal society, a primitive and barbaric form of international politics, if not politics itself, will be eliminated. Political realism, it is claimed, is a crude distortion and a cynical corruption of the true meaning of history. The spokesmen of political idealism maintain that if there have been group controversies throughout history, the struggle has centered not in political rivalries for influence and power but in the clash between incompatible ideals and principles. A concrete example is the aggression of fascism against democracy. When fascism and other philosophies whose ruthless aims and policies make conflict inevitable are permanently destroyed, power politics and war will disappear.

Historically, utopianism has offered three alternatives for moral nations faced with the threat of aggression and the practical problems of survival in a world of archaic power politics. Ultimately, power politics must be eliminated through instituting one world government. Practically, it will be abolished when its main exemplars, the totalitarian states, have been erased from the face of the earth. Provisionally, its evil influence will be progressively and decisively undermined by the example of moral and upright nations forswearing relations with corrupted, power-seeking nations, pursuing instead policies of neutrality and abstaining from all forms of traditional power politics. In practice, nations of good will who have accepted the philosophy of utopianism have pursued policies reflecting precisely these alternatives. Not by accident, the United States as the nation which in recent decades has been especially vulnerable to the precepts of utopianism has pursued a foreign policy that has vacillated between the three possibilities. Utopianism accounts for the neutrality policy of the United States before both world wars. In each prewar period, America tried to abstain and withdraw from the impure and corrupted power politics of the European continent. Any concession in the form of territorial guaranties against German expansion would have been unworthy of the philosophy espoused. Any intervention in the affairs of Europe for the purpose of bolstering and strengthening the Weimar Republic would have weakened our moral position.

When at length, however, America was driven by the inherent logic of utopianism to justify its role in World War II, we turned from neutrality to a holy crusade against the evil incarnate in fascism. When through no fault of our own war became unavoidable—for we had meticulously avoided any political actions that might invite the conflict—we gave unsparingly of resources and principles. We engaged in the world struggle not selfishly or for political advantage but in order to end conflict in Western society and destroy and eliminate once and for all those evil men and ideas who alone were responsible for all the strife and carnage. Such wars were not ordinary struggles for mere territorial adjustments, new balances of power, or specified political gains; they were crusades for advancing the spread of democracy. They became holy wars of "unconditional surrender" against solitary infidels and troublemakers. Evil men had caused the catastrophes; with their elimination, aggrandizement and rivalry would disappear.

The third stage in the utopian journey, however, has been for America the most fateful and far-reaching. After the war, we declared that it was essential that what had been achieved in war should be sealed and perfected in peace. The agents of power politics lay mortally wounded; the climate in which their nefarious policies had thrived must be cleansed and transformed, democracy with free elections substituted for authoritarian and totalitarian practices, and international organization put in the place of politics. In a new commonwealth of man, the problem of power would disappear. What this meant politically was that the status quo with its prevailing lawfulness based on the relative satisfaction of the victorious powers must be made permanent through the regularized procedures of new international organizations. Thus, through neutrality, moralistic crusades, and the substitution of organization for anarchic world politics, America has consistently pursued, in recent times at least, the aims of political idealism. This threefold development provides an instance in which philosophy determined action. Philosophy was more than some set of arid, academic questions and issues. The political consequences of utopianism are clearly and unmistakably discerned in the aftermath of World War II.

Yet, if utopianism has shaped foreign policy, its assumptions have been thrown into question by postwar events. The adequacy of simple idealist answers has been challenged if not refuted by developments since 1946. Observers, whatever their perspectives, agree that the efforts to eliminate Germany and Japan from the international scene created conditions favorable to Russian expansion. The presence of gaping political vacuums at the heart of Europe and on the fringes of the Far East removed traditional obstacles to historic Russian expansion. In order to restore the political situation in Europe, the United States took the lead in the reconstruction of Europe. To succeed, Americans were driven to reexamine slowly, awkwardly, but resolutely the philosophies of American foreign policy.

Engaged in such self-examination, the wisest analysts on the American scene have found in the words and political action of Winston Churchill the prototype of one conception of foreign policy against which to measure contemporary policies and objectives. Almost alone among postwar Western statesmen, he seized on the precepts of political realism. For latter day American statesmen who have sought to rediscover the wise principles of foreign policy which guided the founders in the early days of the republic, Churchill's philosophy, paradoxically enough, is more in harmony with their thought than with that of latter-day innovators.

Nonetheless, Churchill remains the despair of those who would label him in the popular terms by which we pigeonhole most public figures. For one thing, his political rise and fall was meteoric. In the domestic affairs of England, his sudden ascents to power were matched by the abruptness with which political power was taken from him. The line from a Gilbert and Sullivan operetta "Every little boy and girl who is born into the world alive, is either a little Liberal or a little Conservative" is disproved twice over by Churchill, who campaigned under both banners. In 1901, as a twenty-four-year-old hero of the Boer War, he was elected to Parliament as a Conservative. Later he became a Liberal member of Parliament from Manchester only to return to the fold as a Conservative. On more than one occasion he found supporters in "the party opposite" at the same time that his own group was divided in support of him. He served constituencies from Oldham, Manchester, Epping, and Woodford as shifts in opinion, including his own, sent him in search of new communities for which he might speak in the national interest. There is only one sense in which he can be considered a conservative. That is as conservative spelled with a small *c*. This aspect of his philosophy merits some measure of scrutiny and study before we go further in our discussion.

Throughout Western civilization, liberalism and conservatism have vied with one another for authority down to the present day. Liberalism has for the most part been motivated by a high sense of justice, but its programs have often lacked a decisive and realistic understanding of power. Conservatism, by contrast, whatever its sense of justice, has, particularly in its traditional forms in Western Europe, been rich in insights and wisdom on questions of political means and political power. If liberalism has been acutely aware of the ends and ideals toward which mankind should be tending, conservatism has understood more profoundly the nature of the crude and ambiguous instruments of power through which political ends are pursued. Especially in foreign affairs, where international society is only partly organized and integrated and contests of power are more brutal and less hidden and obscured, the traditional conservative mind has generally proved better equipped to comprehend and employ the instruments of power.

Present-day conservatism, as formulated in the rationalizations of the business community which rose to prominence in the nineteenth century, is a departure from historic Western conservatism. Among modern statesmen, Disraeli and Theodore Roosevelt were exponents of traditional conservatism, while Neville Chamberlain was the archetype of bourgeois conservatism. Both in theory and practice, bourgeois conservatism has tended to be spurious and ossified. It stems not from an integral aristocratic tradition, well schooled in the use and the limits of power; it is derived from a decaying liberalism under whose colors the businessman in the nineteenth century achieved his now precarious eminence. The conservatism of Chamberlain, while not blessed with liberalism's passion for justice domestically, possessed the weakness of liberalism internationally. As a result, it consistently underestimated its country's global responsibilities while at the same time overestimating its moral authority. It drew on the resources of liberalism at points of greatest weakness. It oscillated in the policies it espoused from the myopia of isolationism to the excesses of a crusading imperialism. It imagined that politics was merely an extension of commerce and that negotiations entailed the simple mathematics of finding what price an antagonist would pay. In these terms, negotiation became not an art based on adjusting the resources and objectives of the two participants in world politics but a geometrically rational transaction in which reasonable businessmen sought to beguile one another confident that every man had his price.

Conservatism in this form became a decaying liberalism bereft of that movement's original strength. The conservatism of the business community retained for itself only the husks of slogans such as "liberty and freedom" which had been the battle cry of a truly revolutionary movement in the nineteenth-century struggle against feudalism. At the same time, the permanence of the struggle for power was concealed and disguised by emergent forms of economic power and the nice balance maintained in a perfectly equilibrated competitive market theoretically unspoiled by overt force and violence. Not only has contemporary conservatism concealed the complexities of power within the economic orbit by its moral, sometimes sentimental, and often cynical descriptions of competition, but it imagined that all social relations were rational and calculable. Since the brutal realities of power were invisible in the economic cosmos of the businessman, they also remained obscured and misunderstood by him within the sphere of contemporary world politics.

These deficiencies of contemporary bourgeois conservatism which blinded American conservatives who, heedless of strategic interests, would withdraw today and intervene tomorrow at any point on the globe, left Churchill's views relatively unaffected and untouched. It was no accident, therefore, that his country's deepest crisis called him forth from enforced political retirement. As Britain began to feel the pull of the stern winds of the "gathering storm," Chamberlain demonstrated his incurable illusions in confronting the torrent of forces which only a deeper and stronger historic conservatism was capable of resisting. "Tory" tradition having lived by the precarious and judicious control of power and having suffered less disillusionment and dismay over the abrupt and violent reappearance of barbarism and violence, was better able to meet the threat by organizing resources of power against predatory foes. In the sense that he belonged to traditional Western conservatism enriched by an aristocratic heritage long acquainted with the brutal facts of power and the unending rivalries among nations, Churchill was a classic conservative. The sentimental if hypocritical conservatism of the twentieth-century bourgeois variety was at least as alien to his approach as that form of crusading liberalism which would abjure the responsibilities of great power to safeguard its untarnished virtue.

However, the problem of determining Churchill's place in the mainstream of the West's history and philosophy is not at an end when we have identified him as a conservative in the ancient and respected Western tradition. Indeed, conventional standards and criteria are used in such utterly divergent ways by his critics and admirers that a serious analysis must look beyond popular criteria and guides. Some critics characterized Churchill as a bold, but impetuous buccaneer, long on character but short on judgment. If judgment is a matter of abstract consistency and of a slavish adherence to conventions, Churchill was found wanting. If one measures Churchill's political career in the mirror of conventional political behavior in England, it does not correspond to well-accepted patterns. If rigid conformity is the sign of good Conservative or Liberal standing, Churchill was indeed recklessly unpredictable and unreliable. However, the picture of the prime minister as a soldier of fortune, an adventurer and a troublemaker was misleading. Its persistence gives a clue to the unwillingness of British opinion to accept Churchill unreservedly for more than a few climactic moments in history; it hardly does justice to the mainsprings of his approach. In this connection, it may be helpful to recall some of the estimates of Churchill by certain prominent contemporaries.

A few of his critics, among them Harold J. Laski, refused outright to examine the underlying basis of Churchill's political approach because they said he had no systematic philosophy. Regarding this proposition, it is obvious that few statesmen have elevated their beliefs into complete systems of moral or political philosophy and Churchill was no exception. Yet the unbridled contempt for the roots of his thinking which the following polemic illustrates leaves his philosophy of politics exactly where Laski found it, essentially unexamined and unexplored. The Socialist political theorist characterized the prime minister as follows:

> Mr. Churchill has not a speculative mind; with him a theory begets not interest but suspicion. His habits of thought have been formed in the House of Commons, where the men on the front benches argue either to keep power or to achieve it. Even his books are nothing so much as speeches; and his vast life of Marlborough cannot be judged unless it is regarded as a massive reply to a vote of censure.[4]

Laski's views were uncritically supported by other able Britishers at various points on the political spectrum. In almost every case, Churchill's unwillingness to espouse the professed principles and standards of his critics led them to charge that his politics were bereft of any operative political standards. Since he had not adopted the popular phrases and guides of others, he was declared to be a man without principles.

No less persistent was the notion that Churchill was a warmonger possessing a tragi-heroic conception of war, because of which he, more readily than others, would plunge the world into conflict. It was argued from his own achievements that he had a kind of preternatural capacity for finding happiness in unending struggles with danger and adversity. The "happy warrior" would be less likely to keep the peace because he embraced courses of action that were not safe and predictable. The opposition exploited this view with vigor when, as in 1951, Herbert Morrison declaimed: "I cannot but feel alarmed at the thought—if he had been Prime Minister since 1945, supported by a hysterical band of backbenchers—of what would have happened to the world and, in particular what would have happened to the British."[5] Churchill's career, with its mountain peaks of political success coinciding with recurrent peri-

4. Harold J. Laski, "Winston Churchill in War and Peace," *Nation*, CLVII (December 18, 1943), 726.
5. Herbert Morrison, Speech at Bellingham, London *Times*, August 6, 1951, p. 2.

ods of grave stress and crisis, lends support to the indictment. But during the autumn campaign of 1951, *The Times* of London in an editorial entitled "Peace and Solvency" registered a sharp dissent maintaining: "It will be seen by historians as an extraordinary perversion that Mr. Churchill should have to come to be regarded by so many critics and opponents in politics as a man eager for war and a crusted Tory. Perhaps because so much of his fame and character has been made—with uncommon zeal and gusto—in the midst of world carnage, his thought has always been, between the wars, upon the means of making peace among the peoples."[6] This latter interpretation is reinforced and gathers strength from Churchill's repeated postwar assurances that war was not inevitable and peace could be gained through strength joined with a political settlement. Someone who possessed only a passion for war would hardly have been as tireless in exploring the narrow paths to peace. No one who was incurably a warmonger would have been willing to pay so high a price for peace.

There is a third judgment, equally unfavorable to Churchill, which was sounded by liberals on both sides of the Atlantic immediately after World War II. It was expressed in attacks on his old-fashioned conception of world affairs. For those who imagined that Anglo-American legal and political institutions could simply and quickly be transferred to the world scene, Churchill's insistence on regional unions as pillars of any world government was nothing more than hidebound reaction. From one side of the Atlantic, Laski cried out: "Mr. Churchill is one of the great anachronisms of our time."[7] From the other, Norman Cousins in the *Saturday Review of Literature* spoke for American liberals when he charged: "It is this counter direction, this retrogression, this reliance upon devices which have never before succeeded, that characterizes the general nature of [Mr. Churchill's approach]."[8] Stubbornly resistant political and social forces were not the obstacles to a brave new world.

6. "Peace and Solvency," London *Times*, November 10, 1951, p. 7.
7. Laski, "Winston Churchill in War and Peace," 724.
8. Norman Cousins, "Blood, Sweat, Tears and Iron Curtains," *Saturday Review of Literature*, XXIX (March 30, 1946), 27.

Instead, Churchill as the personal devil of liberals was the deterrent to progress. The severest attack on Churchill came from what was then the popular mouthpiece of simple, unambiguous American liberalism, the *New Republic*. The burden of its editorial comment was that two worlds were represented by two princes of the cities of darkness and light. The prince of darkness was Winston Churchill, a passionate Tory capitalist whose idolatry for royalty and authoritarianism had betrayed him into uttering "bitter words of hatred for Soviet Russia. As well expect an African witch doctor to perform a delicate surgical operation as to expect such a man to take the lead in creating a better new world."[9] In Churchill's city, the regnant forces were power politics, spheres of influence, and evil. Happily, new paths of light and hope pointed toward the bright and shining city which the princes of liberalism were helping to erect. World government now would usher in a new kind of international relations. From self-righteous moral outposts, the editors of the *New Republic* indignantly sniped at the entrenched imperialism of Churchill's world: "The world today stands at a crossroads. Mr. Churchill's path leads to power politics, imperialism, spheres of influence and more and more war. The other path leads to democracy, peace and freedom. It is for peoples of good will throughout the world to fight, and fight hard, for the second road."[10]

The knight-errant of evil met the most virtuous of all his foes when in 1947 Henry Wallace took the field against him. In the mind of the former vice-president, Churchill had been indelibly stamped by his Fulton speech as the Mephistopheles of alliances and power politics. The reversion to alliances and blocs of nations taking shape against other peaceful world powers was a fatal counter-beat to the progress of the Atlantic Charter and the formation of an embryonic world state at San Francisco. To meet this perversion of principle, the imperatives of a brave new order had to be dramatized and defended against the cynicism of hardened imperialists like Churchill. For this reason, in numerous public statements and especially in one

9. "Back to Power Politics," *New Republic*, CXI (December 25, 1944), 852.
10. "The Churchill Tragedy," *New Republic*, CXI (December 18, 1944), 821.

particularly strident editorial, Henry Wallace castigated "the Fulton philosophy," proclaiming:

Few public addresses in the history of the world have been so loaded with dynamite as Churchill's Fulton Iron-Curtain, Anglo-American-alliance speech. The American people were shocked and staggered by its content. . . . Many accepted the idea of an Iron Curtain imposed by Russia and the idea of Russia's implacable hostility toward the Western world. Some Americans, war-weary but tense, began to move dangerously toward the thought of an irrepressible conflict. My speech of September 12 helped to blow away some of the fog Churchill had created.[11]

Churchill to many critics, then, was an impetuous soldier of fortune, a prima donna, a warmonger and a power-crazed imperialist. His impetuousness was deduced from his resistance to the swiftly changing tides of public opinion and to simple adherence to conservative or liberal dogma. His reputation as a warmonger was born when the nation's destiny hung in the balance and was perpetuated when he refused to disassociate foreign policy from power. His standing as arch-imperialist was a response to his conviction that the gulf separating the old and new in international relations could be spanned only by applying wise principles of traditional international politics until the new society came into being. Criticisms were rooted in the critics' standards, not those he applied. If it proves possible that the nature of international politics can be transformed overnight, then he was indeed the high priest of evil and depravity. If the ancient wisdom of Roman statecraft endures—*Tempora mutantur et nos mutamur in illis*—then Churchill spoke for the ages.

11. Henry A. Wallace, "Churchill's Crusade," *New Republic*, CXVI (January 13, 1947), 22.

CHAPTER TWO
Contemporary Theories and Churchill's Philosophy

Optimism and Pessimism

There have been many attempts to establish new and contemporary theories of international politics. Some theorists have invoked the categories of optimism and pessimism to judge a statesman or theorist. It is often argued that one group of statesmen and philosophers are optimistic and sanguine about the present and the future. They have faith in man's perfectibility. They look to new social forms and institutions and are persuaded that only the law of change is unchanging. History is an account of mankind's infinite and irresistible linear progress. Human nature possesses the capacity for unending growth and development. Man through reason can control nature and himself. The business of educators and statesmen is to inculcate and inspire new faith in the limitless horizons of the future. Opposed to this viewpoint, the pessimist sees trouble ahead and is ready to accept man as he is. The pessimist rests content with the management and control of problems and difficulties. The optimist condemns men who surrender to unreasoning impulse or the blind rush of events; the pessimist maintains that a fatuous devotion to the mystique of progress can destroy more than it saves. The optimist is hopeful; the pessimist is cautious.

Such distinctions can be carried to absurdity, as in the assertion that the optimist looks to the future and the pessimist to the past. Optimism and pessimism as guides to statecraft share at least three practical difficulties. To call someone an optimist or a pessimist refers to expectations which are never verifiable at the time. They are categories that lack objective criteria. Secondly, optimism and pessimism are weighted down with emotional content. For example, optimism in popular usage bespeaks a positive and dynamic outlook while pessimism is seen as mere negativism. Yet one man's affirmations are oftentimes denials of another's viewpoint. The question thus becomes who is being positive and who negative. *Optimist* or *pessimist* refers to opinions, not judgments based on the best available evidence.

Thirdly, pessimism and optimism are not fixed quantities but are shaped by events. In 1945, Churchill's insistence that the United Nations must rest on regional groupings of states appeared pessimistic in the extreme. Who but a pessimist would fail to see that a world organization was supplanting the sovereign nation-state? By 1952, the optimists of an earlier day were plunged into deep gloom as nations looked outside the United Nations to regional security organizations in the Pacific, the Near East, and the North Atlantic. On the inevitability of war, the supreme pessimist in 1947 was Churchill at Fulton, Missouri, warning of the grave perils of Russian imperialism. By 1951, he had raised his voice against mounting fatalism over the inevitability of war. The same British leader who announced he had not become prime minister to preside over the dissolution of the British Empire declared in 1950: "Outside this island a vast and formidable world has come into being dwarfing our calm Victorian days."[1] For the leader called on to guide the nation through hours of triumph and tragedy, pessimism and optimism are poor ways of describing international relations. The political situation, and not individual temperaments, should concern us. In the kaleidoscopic movement of politics, situations change and require the statesman to chart a steady course in the face of an ever-changing flow of events. On March 4, 1942, in a letter to the dominion secretary, Churchill observed:

I do not see much use in pumping all this pessimism [appreciation of the situation in the Far East] throughout the Empire. It is the fashion here; but it will do great harm wherever else it goes. Has it gone? Altogether there is too much talk. A very different picture and mood may be with us in a couple of months.[2]

1. London *Times*, February 15, 1950, p. 4.
2. Winston S. Churchill, "Prime Minister to Dominions Secretary," March 4, 1942, *The Second World War*, Vol. IV, *The Hinge of Fate* (Boston: Houghton Mifflin, 1950), 847.

Thus a simple-minded division of world statesmen into pessimists and optimists is likely to prove fundamentally defective. It becomes almost meaningless when applied historically. Those who seek enduring principles to evaluate leaders must look to other standards and criteria. Optimism and pessimism have limited value in characterizing the position of Churchill or any other world leaders.

Isolationism versus Internationalism

In the United States at one time, the practice of distinguishing foreign policy perspectives as *either* isolationist *or* internationalist had broad acceptance. It became the single most popular form of describing and evaluating the views of leading political figures. The isolationism that America pursued throughout the nineteenth century was seen as having ended with World War I. Up to that time, isolationism was a reflection of America's international position and of the world balance of forces. By the Spanish-American War and the First World War, it had hardened into a dogma. President Woodrow Wilson campaigned for a better world and the transformation of American thinking from isolationism to internationalism. Controversy has persisted in different forms; policies have been opposed or accepted, politicians defeated or elected on the grounds that they were internationalists or isolationists. Internationalists have justified their policies in terms of the nation's global responsibilities; isolationists have defended themselves in the language of patriotism. Both sides exhibited political skills and adroitness in wielding shibboleths and slogans. Internationalists made political capital of the argument that the new form of international relations would do away with alliances, secret treaties, and the balance of power. Since public opinion had been educated to believe that alliances and secret treaties were causes and not symptoms of a profound international malaise, internationalists appeared to stand for light against darkness, for good against evil.

Abroad, crusading internationalism manifested itself in Europe and on the British political scene. On November 7, 1945, the leader of the Liberal party, Clement Davies, declared: "We cannot rely any longer upon treaties, understandings, or alliances, or any of the old methods of the past which were supposed to guarantee peace but never did so. The new problems cannot be settled by secret diplomacy. . . . They can be solved only by the united peoples of the world."[3] In the same debate, a Labor member of Parliament spoke out against the policy of the Conservatives, identifying them with nationalism and arguing that the only policy which offered hope was internationalism. He called for substituting international organization for nationalism and charged that "Honorable Members opposite . . . need . . . an excuse for the policy which led to the war . . . a policy precisely the same as that they are advocating today . . . the policy of nationalism, the policy of . . . preferring this alliance or that alliance according as the needs of power politics prompt them."[4] Statesmen and peoples possessing such a version of internationalism have consistently underestimated the influence and the problem of power. It is tempting to proclaim that nations must participate as equals in international relations and that the same rights of speech and action enjoyed by individuals within democratic societies are essential for sovereign states. On November 23, 1945, the British foreign secretary, Ernest Bevin, gave expression to this viewpoint in a foreign affairs debate: "If an ambassador, or representative, or a foreign secretary visits me to discuss a matter between his nation and ours, I cannot allow myself for one moment to consider whether he represents a great nation or a small one."[5]

The three expressions of internationalist sentiment by prominent British political leaders quoted above seemingly support the division of foreign-policy thinking into internationalism and isolationism. Even the "old Tory," Churchill, advanced a thought illustrative of internationalism. A popular belief after both world wars was the idea that war was caused by the ignorance of peoples of one another's culture and customs. By multiplying contacts through cultural exchange programs, information would replace ig-

3. *Parliamentary Debates* (Hansard) House of Commons, Fifth Series, Vol. 415, November 7, 1945 (London: His Majesty's Stationery Office, 1950), 1304.
4. *Ibid.*, 1349.
5. *Parliamentary Debates*, Vol. 416, November 23, 1945, p. 762.

norance and understanding would take the place of national rivalries. On May 15, 1946, Churchill appeared to embrace this belief when he proclaimed in New York: "Misunderstandings will be swept away . . . if the British, American and Russian peoples are allowed to mingle freely with one another and see how things are done in their respective countries. No doubt we all have much to learn from one another."[6] In another context, however, Churchill warned that superficial international contacts, such as those produced by tourism, might also generate misunderstandings if not outright hostility.

Clearcut distinctions between internationalism and isolationism as guides in foreign policy break down when applied more generally to Churchill's thought. For one thing, he struggled to understand and explain traditional American isolationism. In three articles written in 1947, he observed:

I understand and have never underrated the weight of arguments of former days in favour of American isolationism. If my father had been an American citizen instead of my mother, I should have hesitated a long time before I got mixed up with Europe and Asia and that sort of thing.

Why, I should have asked myself, should my forebears have gone across the Atlantic Ocean in little ships with all the perils of wind and weather to make a new home in a vast, unexplored Continent? Why should they have left class and feudal systems of society, or actual tyrannies which denied them religious freedom to encounter the unknown?

Why, then, I should have asked myself, have I got to go back to Europe and to Asia, just because they showed me maps of these continents when I was at school? Are not the oceans broad and have we not got one on each side of us? It would have taken me a lot to get over this.[7]

For Churchill, the new climate of postwar American public opinion less hostile to foreign contacts could not explain the shift from isolationism to internationalism. Nor had the new institutions of international organization induced the change. The real cause was the elevation of the United States to a position of world leader-

6. New York *Times*, March 16, 1946, p. 2.
7. London *Daily Telegraph and Morning Post*, April 15, 1947.

ship and the responsibilities of world power suddenly thrust upon it. He wrote: "It would have taken me a lot to get over this [isolationism]. However, there has been a lot, and it is needful to look around upon it all. The United States has become the most powerful force in the world, and at this same moment all the ancient nations and races of Europe and Asia, except only the Union of Soviet Socialist Republics and Great Britain and her Commonwealth, have been for the time being exhausted in the aftermath of their horrible struggles."[8] If the balance of power in Western Europe were to be maintained and preserved and the new threat of imperialism countered, the United States inevitably would have to be at the center of a stream of world politics. A genuine humanitarian interest expressed for the world was one practical form in which national interest was expressed. While such internationalism envisaged that nations were equally concerned with events anywhere on the globe, this vision for Churchill led inevitably to an interest in everything in general and nothing in particular. World-mindedness had to be informed by a realistic perception of national interests around the globe. Churchill's internationalism became in practice a function of perceiving the true national interest. Internationalism could serve as a guide to foreign policy only when there was a confluence between broad goals and concrete national interests. The indignation of some internationalists with the moral shortcomings of the techniques of international politics was absent from Churchill's principles. Thus classifying of people as internationalists and isolationists had limited value. It could not be said that Churchill was an internationalist or an isolationist within the popular meaning of these terms. To understand his world view and principles, we must turn, therefore, to other classifications.

Constitutional Idealism, Legalism, and Moralism

Constitutional Idealism. It was not surprising that in 1952 the Americans who were nominated for the Nobel Peace Prize, including Clarence Streit and Giuseppe Borgese, were constitutional ideal-

8. *Ibid.*

ists. They were men who had championed constitutional changes, whether universal or regional, of institutions in international affairs. One peculiarity of American thinking on international politics is the marked preference which important segments of public opinion have displayed for grand designs. The American people have been drawn to peace plans through which national rivalries undergo sudden and drastic transformation. Important changes in international society come about through universal conventions or charters.

In the immediate postwar years when world government received serious attention, popular response to the problems of creating a world state was widespread. Proponents appealed to the moral force of constitutional conventions. If nations merely came together in world assemblies, they would be shamed into conforming with a majority of good and world-minded nations.

Whatever the abstract merits of these proposals, the creation of new institutions have generally followed certain broadly defined stages of development. In the first stage, institutional development reflects utopian visions and proposals. The mysteries and perplexities confronting a people are resolved or disposed of in imaginary or radical transformations of the cultural or social order. As knowledge and science make inroads, the utopian phase yields to more realistic thought and action. Men learn to live with and to manage problems instead of seeking to remake or legislate them away. Young countries pass through a stage of strong preference for constitutional change as the only panacea. In Anglo-American experience, the strong impetus toward constitutionalism derives from the uniqueness of national existence. In both nations, conflicts of interest have long been reduced to harmless dimensions by common constitutional and institutional frameworks. Success fired English-speaking people with the conviction that national structures were transferable to the wider international arena. For Americans, the infinitely variable yet fundamental problems of the present limited world community and the overweening political ambitions of sovereign states were seen as obstacles no more formidable than those which separated the thirteen original states. Yet these states had many fewer long-standing goals and ambitions to sacrifice as the price of union than those possessed by national communities with respected and honored traditions. Furthermore, national aims exceed legal restraints because nations interpret the law not on its merits but from the standpoint of what the law ought to be if national security is to be assured. Thus nations are driven inevitably to place their interests beyond universal constitutional commitments and in practice the most faultless legal charter will be abandoned if it proves incompatible with the national interests of its signatories.

Public opinion in England, with a tradition of over one hundred and fifty years of imperial policy, has found simple constitutionalism less beguiling than has America. The British constitution is not a codified body of principles and rules. It is the result of an organic growth through centuries, and Churchill's approach was an outgrowth of this experience. By comparison, in the United States, men like Streit and Borgese were influenced by the American constitutional experience and mistakenly believed that international problems would be resolved through written covenants. Churchill demonstrated little sympathy for constitutional idealism. The political philosophy by which he was guided assumed that governments were more the result of underlying community than of premeditated design. In simple language, they grow and are not made. Out of the nature and life of a people and stemming from instincts, traditions, and common cultural circumstances, fundamental institutions emerge. To superimpose on a people institutions unrelated to their common life is vain, futile, and illusory. Political contrivances which clash with a people's feelings and interests are unlikely to survive.

What aroused Churchill more than the belief that new governments could be manufactured like ploughs or tractors was a corollary still more misleading. It was that new institutions in themselves could assure that problems would be settled once and for all. In an address at the Massachusetts Institute of Technology on March 31, 1949, commemorating a century of advance in the physical sciences, he openly exposed this illusion:

> Human beings and human societies are not structures that are built, or machines that are forged. They are plants that grow and must be tended as

such. Life is a test and this world a place of trial. Always the problems, or it may be the same problem, will be presented to every generation in different forms.[9]

Churchill lived by the rule in politics that the forces which determine constitutional practice are more important than legal content. The gloss on compacts and constitutions may be more important than the letter of the law. He was fond of paraphrasing Napoleon, who said that a constitution should be short and obscure. Grave emergencies require changes. He referred to one such change when he assumed an added dimension of wartime responsibility during the Second World War: "In calling myself, with the King's approval, Minister of Defence, I had made no legal or constitutional change. . . . It was, however, understood and accepted that I should assume the general direction of the war."[10]

The differences between Churchill's views and those of constitutional idealists were manifest in other areas. One concerned the drafting of national constitutions. With the spread of movements for national independence and self-government around the world, Englishmen and Americans in the twentieth century found themselves taking responsibility for the drafting of new constitutions. In some occupied countries, the process was euphemistically called advice and assistance. In point of fact, charters and constitutions for occupied countries were often drafted and produced out of whole cloth in London and Washington. Churchill criticized postwar British policy in India, saying that an alien constitution was being imposed on them from the outside: "There was the attempt to formulate a Constitution and press it upon the Indians, instead of leaving the Indians, as had been promised, the duty of framing their own proposals."[11] Quite possibly and for the same reasons, he along with certain American critics was anxious about the document that was "made in the United States" for the establishment of Japan's postwar government.

9. New York *Times*, April 1, 1949, p. 10.
10. Winston S. Churchill, *The Second World War*, Vol. II, *Their Finest Hour* (Boston: Houghton Mifflin, 1949), 15–16.
11. *Parliamentary Debates*, Vol. 434, March 6, 1947, p. 669.

The most striking statement by Churchill on constitutional idealism concerned the formation of a Western European union. In England and the United States, the most vocal groups proposing solutions were federalist organizations. While endorsing their ends and
good intentions, Churchill wrote: "In our European Movement we
have worked with federalists. . . . Personally, I have always dep-
recated . . . our becoming involved . . . in all the tangles and in-
tricacies of rigid constitution-making, which appeals so strongly
to a certain type of mind."[12] He never wavered in his belief that
the tender plant of European unity must receive nourishment and
grow without being weighted down by premature constitution making. On May 8, 1948, he cautioned against "laboured attempts to
draw rigid structures or constitutions."[13] The foundations of union
would result from a multitude of acts based on common interests.
They would stem from the infinity of threads that bind people together. Later public officials with the authority of government could
build political structures. On November 17, 1948, he counseled:
"My advice is not . . . to define too precisely the exact constitutional form which will ultimately emerge. We do better to concentrate our united efforts on immediately practicable steps."[14] On
March 28, 1950, he instructed the House of Commons on evolving
a government, saying:

I have always held that the cause of united Europe would not be
helped, and might well be injured, by attempts to draw up precise and rigid
constitutions and agreements too soon or in a hurry. The first stage is to
create a friendly atmosphere and feeling of mutual confidence and respect. . . . Once the foundation of common interest and solidarity of sentiment has been laid it may well be that formal agreements would take the
form, not of hard bargains or weak compromises, but of setting down on
paper the living basic truths and thoughts which were in all minds. Then
difficulties at present insuperable might well become irrelevant.[15]

12. *Parliamentary Debates*, Vol. 476, June 27, 1950, p. 2156.
13. *Time*, May 17, 1948, p. 48.
14. Winston S. Churchill, "A Speech at the Dorland Hall, London," November 17,
1948, *Europe Unite*, ed. Randolph S. Churchill (London: Cassell and Company,
1950), 465.
15. *Parliamentary Debates*, Vol. 473, March 28, 1950, p. 196.

Finally, on August 11, 1950, he summed up his views on a United Europe: "I have always thought that the process of building up a European Parliament must be gradual, and that it should roll forward on a tide of facts, events and impulses rather than by elaborate constitution-making. Either we shall prove our worth and weight and value to Europe or we shall fail. We are not making a machine. We are growing a living plant." [16] Churchill spoke in the spirit of the architects of the coal and steel community and Euratom.

The public utterances of the late prime minister make clear his basic attitude toward constitutional idealism. At the same time, his criticism revealed something more than mere negativism. What was constructive and positive was the emphasis given to practical steps en route to wider unity. His *bête noire* was an over dependence on paper plans and schemes. His aversion to planning helps in part to explain the sincerity of some of his admittedly political forays against the Socialist government. It was his conception of politics, no less than his role as leader of the opposition, that stirred him to criticize Socialist designs for the nation and the world, as when on August 4, 1947, he charged that "the Government had the knowledge, but they had neither the sense nor the decision to act. They were too busy planning and making their brave new world of controls and queues, of hordes of officials and multitudes of regulations." [17]

Legalism. Contemporary thinking on international relations has also placed a heavy emphasis on the attainment of peace through international law. Respect for law and conventions, inspired by the Anglo-American domestic experience, was offered as the best means for controlling the restless and lawless behavior of nations. In Churchill's eyes, British municipal law comprised the aggregate common sense of centuries of British experience. The nation had charted its political course by British common law. British respect for law was ingrained in British national character.

16. Winston S. Churchill, "Consultative Assembly of the Council of Europe," August 11, 1950, *In the Balance*, ed. Randolph S. Churchill (London: Cassell and Company, 1951), 348.
17. London *Times*, August 5, 1947, p. 4.

An attitude and spirit of lawfulness is vital within national communities. It is a cherished goal for those who would move within sight of a world community. Here and now, it serves more as an ultimate precept than as a rule or directive of conduct for existing international society. Churchill put forward a threefold code for nations in his great work on Marlborough: "One rule of conduct alone survives as a guide to men in their wanderings: fidelity to covenants, the honour of soldiers, and the hatred of causing human woe."[18]

In practical terms, lawfulness can be inspired only when nations have a stake in the observance of a given law. Principles of international law and treaties are respected to the extent they are grounded in mutual national self-interest. When treaty observance is consistent with a nation's security and survival, treaties are more likely to be observed. Rules of land, sea, and air warfare are respected when they serve the nation's survival. In the early days of World War II, Churchill, in a letter of September 10, 1939, warned his countrymen against increasing all-out violence until English defenses against total war had been completed. Even if a nation recognizes the inevitable deterioration of warfare in more and more ruthless forms of combat, it may nevertheless adhere to rules of international law if thereby its security is temporarily enhanced. Churchill's comment was extraordinary for its candor: "It is to our interest that the war should be conducted in accordance with the most humane conceptions of war, and that we should follow and not precede the Germans in the violence. Every day that passes gives more shelter to the population of London and the big cities."[19]

Yet other issues of survival in the field of international politics cannot be so readily controlled by legal prescriptions. It is fundamental in war and politics that accident and chance create unforeseen problems and radically new situations. Battles and political

18. Winston S. Churchill, *Marlborough: His Life and Times* (6 vols.; New York: Scribner's, 1938), VI, 600.
19. Winston S. Churchill, *The Second World War*, Vol. I, *The Gathering Storm* (Boston: Houghton Mifflin, 1948), 453.

strategies are seldom guided effectively by lawyers or legal agreements. In Churchill's words: "There are all kinds of emergencies which arise from time to time."[20] In war the successful waging of the struggle takes priority over legal exactitude. In discussing the justice to be meted out to Mussolini after his fall, Churchill argued that justice or injustice was secondary to military and political concerns: "Some may prefer prompt execution without trial. . . . Others may prefer . . . confinement till the end of the war in Europe. . . . Personally, I am fairly indifferent on this matter, provided always that no solid military advantages are sacrificed for the sake of immediate vengeance."[21]

Even more significant was Churchill's point of view on the slaughter of 14,500 Poles in the forest of Katyn. Locating the guilt for this brutal act was not difficult. In Churchill's history of the war he found it significant that the Soviet government at the Nuremberg Trials made no effort to remove the suspicion hanging over it nor any attempt to fasten the guilt upon the German government. Therefore, the International Tribunal at Nuremberg in its final judgment passed over the issue of Katyn in the section which dealt with Germany's mistreatment of prisoners of war. Such an omission did not escape Churchill's attention. Yet, whatever his suspicions of Soviet guilt, Churchill in his history repeated the statement he made at the time. In it, he reaffirmed his unshakable conviction that in war, questions of right and wrong, as legalists define them, must be subordinated to military and political objectives. He wrote: "I had heard a lot about it from various sources, but I did not attempt to discuss the facts. 'We have got to beat Hitler,' I said, 'and this is no time for quarrels and charges.' But nothing I could say or do prevented the rupture between the Russian and Polish Governments."[22] Whatever the Soviet atrocities, Churchill believed the war against Hitler had to go on.

The postwar development which best illustrated the paramount

20. *Parliamentary Debates*, Vol. 441, August 8, 1947, p. 1803.
21. Winston S. Churchill, "Thoughts on the Fall of Mussolini," *The Second World War*, Vol. V, *Closing the Ring* (Boston: Houghton Mifflin, 1951), 58.
22. Churchill, *The Hinge of Fate*, 760–61.

importance of political in contrast to legalistic considerations for Churchill was his approach to the German problem. Fundamentally, there were two different approaches. According to one, the German nation deserved to be punished for its sins. The allies had a responsibility to force the Germans to cleanse themselves of their guilt by legal judgments against individual malefactors and by fair and evenhanded international justice. Nazism from this viewpoint was an alien and foreign growth grafted onto a healthy political organism. Once this cancerous growth was removed by legal surgery, the German problem would be solved. Those who held to the other view called for allied statesmen to lift their eyes beyond the crimes and tragedies of the past. They had to search for wise policies that would enable Europe and Germany to meet the urgent need for Europe's economic recovery. Revenge and retribution were destructive in the long run. Violence and hate feed on excess; they are strengthened when a whole people are demeaned and their national destiny held in suspense. Difficult as it may seem, the victors must draw a sponge across the crimes and horrors of the past. The goal should be not to enfeeble but to strengthen healthy forces within the German society. Germany because of its manpower and resources was destined to rise again. It was surprising that liberal internationalists who prided themselves on a vision of the future should have favored a comprehensive program for the punishment of all past war crimes. Traditionalists like Churchill were prepared to sacrifice legal designs and the unfinished processes of justice for policies less unsettling to the healthy revival of German influence and authority. On October 9, 1948, in Wales, Churchill summarized his attitude toward the German problem:

I deplore and condemn the stupidity which, at a time like this above all others, persists three and a quarter years after the war in endless trials of Germans who were convicted with the Nazi regime. . . . But how foolish, how inane—I might almost say insane—it is to make a feature of such squalid, long-drawn vengeance when the mind and soul of Germany may once again be hanging in the balance between the right course and the wrong. I trust that even now wiser counsels may prevail. On the general question of post-war vengeance I strongly urge our American friends to let bygones be bygones after three years have passed and the principal culprits have suffered the punishment they deserve.[23]

Yet thoughtful observers of postwar international politics point to another sphere in which legalistic thinking for good or ill has prevailed. The volatile character of world politics was expressed in the abrupt transformation of popular attitudes toward treaties. After World War II, many liberal and enlightened thinkers confidently believed that a supreme international organization would make bilateral and multilateral agreements obsolete. Crusading internationalists proclaimed that alliances and international government were incompatible. They assumed that the grouping together of nations in security arrangements organized on less than universal terms would progressively fade away and recede into the limbo of forgotten things. With the announcement early in 1947 of the Truman Doctrine for assistance to Greece and Turkey outside the United Nations, this expectation was shattered. As is so often the case, an earlier disdain for binding alliances was transmuted in a series of frenzied policies aimed at drawing every potential ally into the struggle with Russian imperialism requiring them, as it were, to sign on the dotted line. Successful efforts at extending the range and membership of multilateral security pacts were interpreted as a *bona fide* contractual guaranty that Russian expansion would be deterred. Because the supreme rule of modern international law, according to the legalistic approach, was the requirement "*pacta sunt servanda*" (treaties ought to be observed), nations would not endorse new regional commitments unless they expected to observe them.

Yet throughout history, security has been achieved through arrangements that were not dignified or formalized by treaties. The Monroe Doctrine was an executive declaration which defined the United States' supreme political interest in the Western Hemisphere. The British and the Russians in the Near East and Middle East recognized one another's spheres of influence in primarily political

23. London *Times*, October 11, 1948, p. 4.

terms. Legalistic commitments may sometimes be more a cause for
alarm than a reason for hope. Some observers argued that the North
Atlantic Treaty countries were included in or excluded from NATO
without regard for their strategic interests. For example, Spain was
geographically and strategically a part of a West European defense
system. Once regional arrangements had been hardened into sharply
defined ideological and legalistic molds, it was excluded. Greece
and Turkey were not part of the same strategic system as Norway
and Denmark but when security came to be based on formal legalistic commitments, the pretense of common interests had to be maintained. An obsession with formalism and legalism can lead to an era
of "pactomania"; treaties are signed reflecting few if any common
interests. They run the risk of becoming mere scraps of paper.

Churchill questioned an attitude which reposed too much faith
in formal commitments. He argued that real security could be found
in agreements less sweeping than far-flung multilateral contracts.
What was needed was best illustrated in Anglo-American relations,
of which Churchill wrote:

I have never asked for an Anglo-American military alliance or a treaty. I
asked for something different and in a sense I asked for something more.
I asked for fraternal association, free voluntary association.

I have no doubt that it will come to pass, as surely as the sun will rise
tomorrow. But you do not need a treaty to express the natural affinities
and friendship which arise in fraternal association . . . nothing can prevent
our nations drawing closer to one another and nothing can obscure the
fact that in their harmonious companionship lies the margin of hope of a
world instrument for maintaining peace on earth and good will to all
men.[24]

The true sources of strength in a partnership arise not from formal
papers of association but from mutuality of common interests. The
purpose of a treaty is to seal and reflect but not to create common
interests and outlooks.

In a similar vein, Churchill found in 1946 that: "Strong bonds
of affection, mutual confidence, common interest and similar out-

24. New York *Times*, March 16, 1946, p. 2.

look link France and Britain together. The treaty of alliance that has lately been signed merely gives formal expression to the community of sentiment that already exists as an indisputable and indestructible fact." [25] In a day when countries with long suspicion and antagonism to entangling alliances find security in "binding, legal commitments," it is well to be reminded by the arch-champion of alliances and power politics that "the British and American peoples come together naturally, and without the need of policy or design. No policies, no pacts, no secret understandings are needed between them." [26]

When we turn attention from alliances and treaty arrangements to three of the most vital contemporary diplomatic issues in the postwar era—the United Nations intervention in Korea, the Schuman Plan, and Britain's relations with Egypt—Churchill's philosophy and his preference for political over legal standards are further illuminated. In current evaluations of foreign policies, major emphasis is oftentimes placed on legal justifications. In fact, legal reasons have frequently supplanted political requirements as the foundation on which foreign policy is made. Both in legislatures and the popular press of many Western countries, the legal aspects of United Nations action in Korea received more attention than all the other aspects of the Korean problem combined. The most debated issue in the debate over Korean intervention was whether measures were being taken in accord with the United Nations Charter. Churchill's first statement in Parliament on Korea was exemplary for its restrained but unmistakable criticism of Prime Minister Clement Attlee's legalistic approach. While Churchill referred to the legal arguments set forth by the prime minister to justify action by the Security Council, he supported Britain's policy primarily on nonlegal grounds. [27] Anglo-American unity had been enhanced; this unity and not fidelity to the principles of the Charter made the action significant.

25. *Ibid.*, May 15, 1946, p. 11.
26. *Parliamentary Debates*, Vol. 415, November 7, 1945, p. 1294.
27. *Parliamentary Debates*, Vol. 477, July 5, 1950, p. 495.

   Churchill also found British policy at the outset of negotiations on the Schuman Plan indefensible. He had himself repeatedly maintained that Britain's freedom of action on the continent of Europe was circumscribed by British interests outside Europe. What he bewailed was Britain's excessively legalistic interpretation which excluded participation in the negotiations. While Commonwealth interests prevented full partnership in the Schuman Plan, this hardly ruled out discussions and talks in which no one was committed until formal constitutional consent was given. Churchill rose in Parliament to say: "I could not help feeling very sorry that our relations with France have been reduced to this long legalistic argument, making point after point with professional skill in order to reach and justify a deadlock." [28]

   Finally, wise policy may sometimes dictate that a nation go beyond the letter of its treaties or commitments. In 1946, Churchill maintained that if Britain had taken steps beyond the strict construction of its 1936 treaty with Egypt, it could have reassured the Egyptians that it had no intention to interfere in their affairs: "There is however one practical step which should have been taken by us. . . . The withdrawal of troops from Cairo and Alexandria ought to have been completed many months ago. It would have been a wise act of policy. . . . It would have been entirely in the spirit, and . . . beyond the letter of the Treaty of 1936." [29] Excessive legalism bound to the form and the letter of treaties and agreements may blind statesmen to wise actions. A statesmanship which weighs political requirements is more likely to transcend the constraints of legalism.

Moralism. The popular conceptions of international politics concerning the freeing of nations from international rivalries and the struggle for power by world constitutions and world law are given more general expression in moralistic philosophies of foreign policy. The tenets of moralism are simple. International life provides the

28. *Parliamentary Debates*, Vol. 467, June 27, 1950, p. 2145.
29. *Parliamentary Debates*, Vol. 423, May 24, 1946, p. 768.

opportunity for service to eternal principles of morality. Only the depraved mind with a preference for expediency over principle supports foreign policies that ignore principle. Foreign policy is perceived as a crusade to place truth upon the throne and condemn evil to the scaffold. Upright and moral nations ought to wage this campaign untiringly and remorselessly.

Churchill recognized the importance of morality in international and in domestic affairs. He was fully aware of the consequences which flowed from the absence of moral principles or their constant abridgment. On September 17, 1951, he observed: "A nation without conscience is a nation without a soul. A nation without a soul is a nation that cannot live."[30] If private ethics and international morality were readily equatable, Churchill would stand squarely alongside the moralists. Even in war when the gentler private virtues of pity and mercy seem erased by brutal conditions of conflict, he demonstrated extraordinary compassion and unflagging concern for the plight of England's soldiers. On April 29, 1941, he wrote to General Ismay: "I noticed that the parachutists who landed on Saturday several times had their knuckles terribly cut. Has the question of protecting their hands and [also giving them] knee-caps been considered?"[31]

As a young man, his early reactions to war and carnage were the product of a sensitive spirit tormented by all the brutality and injustice against subject peoples that he witnessed firsthand. His initial impulse was to embrace the underdog and defend his rights to liberty, self-determination, and independence. Revolutionary movements such as upheavals in Cuba stirred his sympathy. His political creed espoused in early writings and speeches was national self-determination. When his military duties turned him against the forces of change in India and Africa, he recognized instinctively the moral dignity of the enterprise in which the foe was engaged. While

30. London *Times*, September 17, 1951, p. 4.
31. Winston S. Churchill, "Prime Minister to General Ismay," April 29, 1941, *The Second World War*, Vol. III, *The Grand Alliance* (Boston: Houghton Mifflin, 1950), 761.

fighting to preserve Britain's rights and interests, he was conscious that he was present at the birth of new nations and people.

He also discovered in the League of Nations a moral dimension extending beyond political authority. In distinguishing moral from military force and pointing out their relationship, he traced the function of morality in a world of power politics, explaining that:

I look to the League as a great addition to the strength and to the safety of our country. . . . Since when can we afford to ignore the moral forces involved in the public opinion of the world? Moral force is, unhappily, no substitute for armed force, but it is a very great reinforcement, and it is just that kind of reinforcement which may avoid and prevent the use of armed force altogether. For five years I have been asking the House and the Government to make armaments . . . but I am quite sure that British armaments alone will never protect us in times through which we may have to pass.[32]

His early reflections depict a statesman with a deep awareness of the role of morality as one stratum within which man's common humanity is expressed. But Churchill's philosophy was seen in another more tragic light when he examined the moral problem not in general terms but in the context of practical problems which arise out of concrete political situations. The fundamental moral problem for Churchill and for all present-day statesmen arises from the fact that contemporary foreign policy is conducted not in the bright light of shared moral values but in the gray colors of disputed national ends. Nor are policies everywhere determined by objective moral standards and principles. Instead, relations are carried on in the murky half-light of unrestrained power politics. Morality must be construed in relation to the international environment. For the statesman to indulge himself the luxury of abstract ethical decisions without regard for the consequences for his nation's power and influence was unthinkable for Churchill. In commenting on the situation following World War I, he declared: "Although I should like to see European peace founded upon a more moral basis, I am very anxious that the present foundation should not be deranged until at

32. *Parliamentary Debates*, Vol. 330, December 21, 1937, p. 1838.

any rate we have built up something satisfactory in its place."[33] The moral foundations in a world of power politics are not the same as the foundations which would exist if this kind of world had been eliminated and transcended. The foundations that exist today have their center in divergent national interests and statesmen must act within such limits until something better evolves. In the cold war, "Moralists may find it a melancholy thought that peace can find no nobler foundation than mutual terror. But for my part, I shall be content if these foundations are solid, because they will give us the extra time and the new breathing space for the supreme effort which has to be made for a world settlement."[34] The quest for morality goes on in an immoral world.

Nothing is gained by obscuring the conflict that is tragic and unavoidable between ultimate moral prescriptions and the practical standards by which nations protect themselves and survive. Frequently this conflict imposes a choice between two political and military acts, both of which are evil and immoral. Thus the real issue with international morality is not what standards or principles a nation or people would like to pursue; it is rather what standards are in practice compatible with the nation's survival. A more eloquent demonstration of the conflict between the choices of abstract and practical international morality can hardly be found than in the morally hazardous decision by America to use the atomic bomb against Japan. In simple moralistic terms, this action can be condemned on almost every count. Yet moralists fail to perceive the dilemma of the tormented moral man making choices in an immoral world. The moral issue is never simply a choice between right and wrong but a choice between lesser evils. The moral dilemma in politics takes on its starkest terms in the perilous choices honorable men must make on the world stage. What were the standards by which Churchill was guided in approving the decision to use the atomic bomb? They were ethical to be sure, making reference to the preservation of human life. But human life was a factor primarily as

33. *Parliamentary Debates*, Vol. 265, May 13, 1932, p. 2353.
34. *Parliamentary Debates*, Vol. 473, March 28, 1950, p. 198.

it affected the self-preservation and survival of America and Britain. The ethical command to preserve human life had to be channeled and refracted through the prism of national self-interest. Churchill reflected almost sadly:

I am surprised that very worthy people, but people who in most cases had no intention of proceeding to the Japanese front themselves, should adopt the position that rather than throw this bomb we should have sacrificed a million American and a quarter of a million British lives in the desperate battles and massacres of an invasion of Japan. Future generations will judge these dire decisions, and I believe that if they find themselves dwelling in a happier world from which war has been banished, and where freedom reigns, they will not condemn those who struggled for their benefit amid the horrors and miseries of this gruesome and ferocious epoch.[35]

In an important sense, the main task of the true philosopher of foreign policy was to distinguish moral pretense and ethical practice embodied in the claims that nations are continually making. The speeches and words of the makers of foreign policy cannot be taken at face value but neither can they be entirely ignored. Ideologies are sometimes merely weapons used to deceive and soften the foe. This was true of Germany and Japan, whose ethical indictments of communism were rationalizations for their aggression, not moral principles. For the British leader: "these two great powers in opposite quarters of the globe use the pretext of their fears of Communism to proclaim an association the purpose of which, and the consequences of which, can only be the furthering of their national designs."[36] Yet other speeches and proclamations may provide an image, however faint and indistinct, of elementary ethical principles and standards that ultimately carry mortal men beyond themselves. However mixed with selfish interests, the principle of opposing tyranny and condemning bad faith was a clear moral precept in Churchill's credo. It was a sign of man's upward thrust toward fashioning a fundamental ordering principle for international life:

35. *Parliamentary Debates*, Vol. 413, August 16, 1945, p. 79.
36. Winston S. Churchill, "Germany and Japan," November 27, 1936, *Step by Step: 1936–1939* (New York: Putnam's 1939), 65–66.

We did not fight only in the sacred cause of self-defence, like the Russian patriots who defended their native soil with sublime devotion and glorious success. No one attacked us. We fought for a higher and broader theme. We fought against tyranny, aggression and broken faith, and in order to establish that rule of law among the nations which alone can be the shield of freedom and progress.[37]

In truth, then, there are some practical moral standards which are in context to be taken seriously, first, because of their "rightness" but more fundamentally because, from a practical standpoint, they are needed if international society is to operate even tolerably well. They have a constitutive function. Without some minimum assurances that states can rely on each other, society breaks down through mutual fear and distrust. Good faith or its practical and realistic equivalent is the oil that lubricates the relations between sovereign states. Mutual respect and trust provides the cement which holds the international order together despite all its centrifugal forces.

In this connection, what deserves emphasis is the contrast between prevailing trends of moralistic thought and the philosophy by which Churchill was guided. It is a fact that ethics and politics are in conflict wherever man acts politically. This is because the essence of politics requires men to choose goals and objectives which are fragmentary and limited and therefore equitable and just only for certain groups or nations. In practice what is done in the interests of labor will frequently work an injustice upon management. Only in pure thought can policies and actions remain uncorrupted and undefiled at the margins of injustice. The universal corruption of absolute justice whenever men enter the realm of politics finds its most outstanding expression in international morality. In international politics, my nation's justice oftentimes means your nation's injustice; the requirements for my nation's security appear as the cause of your nation's insecurity. The alliances, armaments, and spheres

37. Winston S. Churchill, "A Speech on Receiving the Freedom of Westminster," May 7, 1946, *The Sinews of Peace*, ed. Randolph S. Churchill (London: Cassell and Company, 1948), 124.

of influence essential to my nation's safety threatens your nation's security and that of others. The tendency everywhere present for ethics to be separated from politics reaches its culmination in international affairs. Three answers to this dilemma have been provided in modern thought. They are the answers of moralism, cynicism, and political wisdom.

First, it is always tempting to seek to bridge the gulf between ethics and politics and resolve these contradictions and discrepancies in simple moralistic terms. Moralism as a political philosophy maintains that at present men pursue a double standard of conduct in their private and public lives. Privately, man is honest and ethical; publicly he covers his acts with a tissue of lies and deception. His virtue in personal relations is seen as an outgrowth of the conquest of culture over barbarism and of a moral over an immoral age. At an earlier stage in man's evolution, his conduct in private affairs was equally corrupted by violence. Through reason he has progressed beyond this early stage. In the same way in international affairs, the cultural lag from which nations now suffer is being efficiently and rapidly erased. The forward march of history is carrying nations from a retarded condition into a new and enlightened era when private standards will become public rules. The same conception of ethics which determines the conduct of individuals will henceforth influence the behavior of nations in one universal society of nations. This was the faith of President Woodrow Wilson and of Secretary of State Cordell Hull. Moralism of this kind was decidedly lacking in Churchill's philosophy because for him man's ambition for power is inherent in his social existence and therefore not so simply set aside. Nations must continue in the old forms of international politics, until either they or their environments are radically changed.

If moralism is an unacceptable characterization of Churchill's political ethics, cynicism is often described as the most common alternative. According to cynicism, politics and ethics diverge because they are fundamentally different. Politics are means and ethics are ends. While means may be evil, good and worthy ends, to which means must be subordinated, can endow acts that are morally ambiguous with ethical content. Thus the dictum that the end justifies the means appears in politics to furnish a simple clue to solving the moral problem. Yet history teaches that men and nations universally justify every evil measure by claiming it serves an ethical goal. For Stalin the brutality of liquidating the kulaks found justification in communist eschatology; for Hitler the cremation of so-called inferior races was excused as a necessary hygenic measure if Teutonic virility were to continue unimpaired. Since nations in the present anarchic world society tend to be repositories of their own morality, the ends-means formula has prevailed as an answer to the moral dilemma; for it is undeniably a hidden but essential truth that nations tend to create their own morality. In its extreme form, this viewpoint has found nations accepting as ethical whatever redounded to their own material advantage and judging whatever proved detrimental to be immoral and evil.

In one sense, Churchill himself was bound by the limits of contemporary international morality. He was surely no exception to the rule that no Western statesman can be expected to approve broad humanitarian policies if they endanger the national interest. However, nations may cooperate in international arenas when there is no threat to their security, even though in so doing they may not advance national interests except in the long run. They may act from concerns lying beyond the national orbit. In these instances, national interests are not so clearly the basis for ethical evaluation. Churchill would seem to have departed from the view that only those acts that serve national ends can be viewed as ethical when he said: "But the British nation from time to time gives way to waves of crusading sentiment. More than any other country in the world, it is at rare intervals ready to fight for a cause or a theme, just because it is convinced in its heart and soul that it will not get any material advantage out of the conflict."[38]

From such evidence, we have reason to doubt whether Churchill's approach to political morality can be discovered either in simple moralistic theories or ethical outlooks in which moral principles are reduced to means-ends relationships. Instead, a better clue to his philosophy may be found in an honorable dictum of Salic law: "King thou will be if thou follow the law. If thou do not follow the

38. Churchill, *The Gathering Storm,* 183.

law, thou wilt not be king." Because of the nature of man and of
politics, statesmen and nations never wholly escape the judgment of
elementary ethical standards. The history of politics discloses that
no peoples have ever completely divorced politics from ethics. Philosophers are generally agreed that men are required to conform to
standards other than mere success. One sign that ethics are recognized in some form in most societies and cultures is the apparent
compulsion felt by political actors to justify their actions in moral
terms. This tribute to a moral order has its consequences both in
words and deeds. There is a striking dialectical movement of expediency and morality which has its impact on international politics.
Moves in practical politics must be articulated to pay tribute to
moral principles. However limited and particular, such acts of political expediency must seem to carry forward aims of justice and
the common good. Thus political morality forces the statesman
who would link expediency with ethics to choose political measures
so that the practical and moral march hand in hand.

Hans J. Morgenthau offered two guides for linking politics and
morality. It is political wisdom to act successfully in accord with the
interests of state. It is political and moral wisdom to choose the
most moral of several alternatives through which both expediency
and ethics may be served. The margin that separates cynicism from
political and moral wisdom may frequently be narrow but by that
margin the statesman is saved both from a fatuous moralism and an
unprincipled expediency.

Churchill's practical application of international morality is illustrated in a Parliamentary debate over South Tyrol. During and
after World War II, concessions were made to Italian claims for the
Austrian Tyrol on the grounds of expediency by the British. Arrangements were worked out with the coalition government of Italy
at the London Conference in September, 1945. The Socialist government of Britain insisted such pledges must be kept. The Honorable
Hector McNeil declared:

In the height of war, every nation, including our own, makes concessions
and undertakes obligations difficult to fulfill in the days of peace. War,
however arduous, is simple; its objective is to destroy the enemy. Toward

that end, in loyalty to allies, in generosity to hoped-for allies, in rage against enemies, in haste and in sentiment towards those who have fallen, settlements are made which are not too carefully thought out. Then, in peace, when prestige, long-term security and trade begin to point their complex and conflicting conclusions, difficulties about the settling of the bill begin to appear. The honeymoon of war, curiously, is over.[39]

However, McNeil concluded that his government had no choice but in all good faith to discharge its promissory notes. Churchill answered McNeil in a statement that is pregnant with political and moral implications. It illustrates how considerations based on both political wisdom and moral judgment can be joined. In his response he declared:

I could not feel any satisfaction when I read in the newspapers that one of the first points upon which they had all been able to come to a unanimous decision in Paris was to confirm the assignment of the Austrian Tyrol to Italy. . . . The sentence I myself contributed to the Atlantic Charter, about no transference of territory apart from the will of the local inhabitants, has proved, in many cases, to be an unattainable ideal and, in any case did not, in my experience, apply to enemy countries. But I know of no case in the whole of Europe, more than that of the Austrian Tyrol, where the Atlantic Charter, and the subsequent Charter of the U.N.O., might have been extended to the people who dwell in this small, but well defined region which is now involved in the general war settlement. . . . Is it not illogical to have one standard of ethnic criteria for Trieste and Venezia Giulia, and another for the Southern Tyrol? The Soviet Government are quite logical; they are willing to override the ethnic criteria in both cases. I think that we might try, in this case, to emulate their symmetry of thought. There are no grounds for suggesting that any decisions adverse to the restoration of the Southern Tyrol to Austria were taken by the Government of which I was the head. . . . It is possible that, in September, some further committments were made, but that is a matter for which the Government are responsible. I am obliged to the Foreign Secretary for giving me the material on which to check this point, which arose in his speech yesterday, by reference to official papers.[40]

39. *Parliamentary Debates*, Vol. 423, June 5, 1946, pp. 2109–10.
40. *Ibid.*, 2018–19.

It should be plain that this policy expresses not the simple moralism of the Atlantic Charter but Churchill's moral judgment informed and inspired by political and strategic insights. It presents, in a nutshell, the essence of his conception of international morality.

Realism versus Utopianism

We have seen how inadequate are some of the popular modes by which Western statesmen are classified and how partial and fragmentary are the truths they indicate. It would be difficult to show that Churchill was either optimistic or pessimistic as those terms are generally interpreted. Nor do internationalism and isolationism in popular American parlance give any clear picture of the pillars on which his philosophy was founded. If the viewpoints of constitutional idealists, legalists, or moralists are relevant at all it is in showing, from a negative viewpoint, what Churchill's philosophy *was not* rather than revealing what was positive in his approach. So all that remain among the keys to theories and philosophies of international relations are those introduced by Captain Thorneycroft and Ambassador Kennan at the outset of this discussion. Realism and utopianism, as two divergent outlooks on international politics, offer the last and most important means for distinguishing Churchill from his contemporaries. For they concern themselves with identifiable problems and concepts and proceed from principles and assumptions which are capable of analysis and study. In a word, these assumptions have to do with the permanence of national rivalries and the ubiquity of the struggle for power. For one school, these conflicts of will and interest are transitory and accidental; for the other they show every sign of continuing throughout contemporary history. It is important to know where Churchill stood on these questions and to discover whether he, along with the realists, looked upon international politics as a tragic predicament in which we must do the best that we can, or whether he ranged himself with the utopian school in awaiting the early transvaluation of nationalism into universalism and of political rivalries into international harmony.

In four respects it is evident that Churchill had little in common with the proponents of utopian philosophy. In the first place, he never imagined that the human condition could be transformed overnight, especially in international relations. He never proposed discarding the balance of power nor abandoning the formation of alliances to deter an aggressor. His concept of Anglo-American unity as an indispensable prerequisite for peace incited one outspoken utopian critic to declare: "I suggest—I have listened to hon. Members talk about Western and Eastern *blocs*—if we can use that organisation [the U.N.], it will be the finest measure possible to ensure that we never again resort either to Eastern, Western, or any other type of bloc. I believe it was Hitler who once said that an alliance which does not lead to war is senseless and worthless."[41] Churchill categorically rejected this view. It was inconceivable to him that nations should discard their traditional sources of security any more than an infantry soldier should dispose of his rifle in battle on the promise that newer and better atomic weapons were on the way.

Secondly, utopianism is generally obsessed with the future. Sometimes it has paid a price for this preoccupation in costly and tragic ignorance of unchanging values that shaped the past or present. No critic maintained that Churchill was ignorant of the enduring values of the past. His accusers claimed that he lacked a vision of the future. Some said he was a statesman who was never quite able to free himself from the shackles of an earlier age. Although he displayed qualities of courage and vitality, he was a nineteenth- rather than a twentieth-century leader. His words rang out in the sonorous declarations of the *agora* perpetuated in English schools with their passion for everything traditional. His deeds were reminiscent of the grand imperial style of the nineteenth century. His aims and principles became alien in his own country. Taken together, these criticisms add up to the charge that Churchill's concern for the past weakened him in facing challenges of the future. If this is true, his shortcomings were the very opposite of those of utopianism.

41. *Parliamentary Debates*, Vol. 416, November 22, 1945, p. 669.

Thirdly, the prevailing rationalism which accompanies utopianism was conspicuously missing in Churchill's philosophy. Certain analysts of international affairs, as of municipal and national problems, imagine that we can plan our way into utopia. If persistent international issues are precisely described and painstakingly set forth, then the rational operations and procedures of new world institutions will assure their solution. Yet the great peril and danger of planning is that proposals may be detached from the exigencies of real earthbound problems. The story is told of a shingler who found his immediate task so engrossing that on a foggy day he continued his shingling five feet beyond the eaves. Idealistic schemes of international organization and administration which reduce all political problems to self-contained systems are as illusory as they are appealing. In planning a "solution" to the problems of international existence, they ignore the vital management of problems and crises which has been the function of traditional diplomacy.

Finally, utopian proposals for resolving difficulties offer a single answer to the countless problems by which men have been plagued. For Churchill, monistic answers to troubles were false and unreal. On October 4, 1947, he rejected the notion of grand panaceas: "I must make it clear that we Conservatives do not believe there is a quack cure-all for the trouble and tribulations of human life."[42] The unfolding of the international situation is too profoundly a narrative of human conflict to validate the principles and predictions of utopianism. On balance, Churchill's philosophy squared only occasionally and by accident with the futurism, rationalism, and the simplistic and unpolitical way of looking at international affairs that has been called utopianism.

Therefore, in considering the fundamental nature and underlying sources of Churchill's thought, we come inevitably to the tenets of political realism. By enumerating the assumptions of realism and placing them alongside those of Churchill, we shall discover to what extent he can be considered a practical realist. Basically, the realist

42. Churchill, "Annual Conference of the Conservative Party," October 4, 1947, *Europe Unite*, ed. Randolph S. Churchill, 153.

ranks the quest for security and power at the top of the scale of political values. In international politics, the compulsion of every nation is to assure its survival. Power is essential to this end. However, the power of one nation inspires fear and anxiety in others for their own security. Because of a Hobbesian fear, nations in their quest for security achieve power and influence at the price of creating insecurity in other groups. Tragically, there is no alternative to the morally hazardous quest for security through strength. For Churchill it was axiomatic that: "Integral communities are dominated by the instinct of self-preservation. This principle is expressed in each generation by moral, logical or sentimental arguments which acquire the authority of doctrine."[43] As early as October 1, 1939, he put his finger on the wellsprings of Soviet foreign policy: "Russia has pursued a cold policy of self-interest. We could have wished that the Russian armies should be standing on their present line as the friends and allies of Poland instead of as invaders. But that the Russian armies should stand on this line was clearly necessitated for the safety of Russia against the Nazi menace."[44] For the same reasons, security for the West was a matter of power and the will to use it: "You have not only to convince the Soviet Government that you have superior force . . . but that you are not restrained by any moral consideration if the case arose from using that force with complete material ruthlessness. And that is the greatest chance for peace."[45]

The chief characteristic of some contemporary philosophies of politics in the West has been their denial of the central place of power and strength. Some of the culture's wise men have dreamed of a purely rational adjustment of interests in society or have seen the assuagement of rivalries and differences through scientific solutions or by sharp definitions and distinctions of justice and injustice. In consequence, a hiatus occurs between the shrewd concepts of practical men of affairs and the vapid speculations of philosophers

43. Winston S. Churchill, *The World Crisis, 1911–1918* (New York: Scribner's, 1931), 289.
44. Churchill, *The Gathering Storm*, 449.
45. Churchill, "New York: A Speech at a Dinner by Mr. Henry R. Luce at the Ritz Carlton Hotel," March 25, 1949, *In the Balance*, ed. Randolph S. Churchill, 39.

and theorists. The early American statesmen were imbued with the historical insight and political courage to set forth principles about the necessity and misuse of political power. It would be difficult to find a contemporary American or indeed a Western statesman who could declare with John Adams: "Power always thinks it has a great soul and vast views beyond the comprehension of the weak and that it is doing God's service when it is violating all His laws." Churchill was one of the exceptions, for he was preoccupied with the stubborn facts of power throughout his political career. Before the second great war he declared: "The scales of Justice are vain without her sword." [46] While speaking with great reverence and esteem of Eduard Benes, the ill-fated president of Czechoslovakia, he pointed to one fatal weakness in the former president's indifference to violence, saying: "He was a master of administration and diplomacy. He knew how to endure with patience and fortitude long periods of adverse fortune. Where he failed—and it cost him and his country much—was in not taking violent decisions at the supreme moment. He was too experienced a diplomatist, too astute a year-to-year politician, to realise the moment and to stake all on victory or death." [47]

Because power is so influential an aspect of international politics, a nation's foreign policy, to succeed, must express strength, firmness, and fortitude. Churchill believed a more aggressive posture toward Iran following World War II might have forestalled other shows of strength with Middle Eastern nationalist movements. "A firm and resolute policy in Abadan would very likely have saved, without bloodshed, not only our vital interests there, but might actually have prevented the bloodshed that is now taking place in Egypt." [48] Realist and utopian analysts look through different eyes at military considerations. Some outspoken moralists reject military preparation, reasoning from the standpoint of a perfectionist ethic. The military aspect of a nation's power is seen as morally inferior. Churchill reacted to the condescension expressed

46. Churchill, "How to Stop War," June 12, 1936, *Step by Step*, 26.
47. Churchill, *Closing the Ring*, 452–53.
48. London *Times*, October 18, 1951, p. 3.

in a report of April 20, 1950, by Emanuel Shinwell, minister of defense, at the eighth meeting of the European Consultative Council, who referred to the fact that European unity was not merely an alliance. To this Churchill responded: "May I ask him whether he would consider, on the first page of his statement, altering the word 'merely'—'not merely a military alliance'—to 'not only a military alliance,' because his statement deals almost entirely with military matters. 'Merely' seems, I will not say a disparaging, but an inadequate term to use."[49]

Yet the military element of national power is only one aspect of a nation's strength. Among those who say they oppose power politics there has been undisguised confusion on this issue. For some, a nation's strength is conceived solely in nonmilitary terms; for others it appears as completely a question of military strength. The great classics such as Clausewitz' *War, Politics and Power* are free of such confusion because they see war and diplomacy as a continuum. Churchill took his stand somewhere between the extremes of sentimentalism and cynicism. In defining national power, he maintained that military and political elements joined and that one could never be exclusive of the other:

> It is not possible . . . to divide military from political affairs. At the summit they are one. It is natural that soldiers should regard the military aspect as single and supreme, and even that they should speak of political considerations with a certain amount of disdain. Also the word politics has been confused, and even tarnished, by its association with party politics. Thus much of the literature of this tragic century is biased by the idea that in war only military considerations count and that soldiers are obstructed in their clear, professional view by the intrusion of politicians, who for personal or party advantage tilt the dread balances of battle.[50]

The true test of Churchill's realism will come in considering the great historic actions he took and his reasons for acting. It is evident, however, even from scattered examples, that he viewed international affairs primarily in political terms, that he judged broad

49. *Parliamentary Debates*, Vol. 474, April 20, 1950, p. 329.
50. Churchill, *The Grand Alliance*, 28.

affirmations of international purpose in the light of the interests of nations, that he looked upon world institutions as means and instruments and not as ends in themselves, and that he understood that peace can only be ensured through the tentative adjustments, territorial arrangements, political settlements, and spheres of influence which have kept an uneasy and precarious peace in the past.

PART TWO

The Man and His Philosophy

CHAPTER THREE

The School of the Statesman

When Winston S. Churchill became prime minister on May 10, 1940, he spoke of walking with destiny. As a young man, when his life was spared in war, he concluded that God must have a plan for him. At age sixty-six, he looked back on his life as a preparation for leading Britain. For six years, he had warned of an impending conflict. For more than fifty years, he had schooled himself in the classics and in speaking to the people. One biographer described his life as having been "a slow start—then fame at 21." His first twenty-six years were for him the school of the statesman.

Devotees of the psychoanalytical studies of politics would probably stress the circumstances of Churchill's birth and his early childhood, perhaps not giving sufficient weight to his own unique qualities of intellect and will developed over the years. On November 30, 1874, an announcement in *The Times* reported the birth of a son to "the Lady Randolph Churchill, prematurely." Lady Churchill was the daughter of a self-made American millionaire, Leonard Jerome, who gained his wealth through business investments and the ownership of famous race horses. Legend has it, that at age seventy-three Jerome entered the ring at a London circus incited by a strong-man's offer to pay fifty pounds to anyone who could last five minutes with him. Jerome beat his opponent into unconsciousness but soon thereafter died of a heart attack. Churchill's father, Lord Randolph Churchill, had proposed to the beautiful young Jennie Jerome forty-eight hours after having met her at a British seaside resort. Although neither of the parents were close to young Winston, he described his mother as a fairy princess, a radiant being of limitless riches and power. Lord Randolph was seldom home and considered Winston retarded and unfit for the study of law. Lady Churchill was more sympathetic but Winston rarely saw her. His British nanny, Mrs. Everest, raised him and he kept her picture at his desk through long years of tribulation. He spoke of her as his confidante and his most intimate friend. Young Churchill could remember only one extended conversation with his father, who determined, allegedly on seeing his son's skill in ordering and maneuvering toy soldiers, that he should go to Sandhurst Royal Military College, now the Royal Military Academy. Winston's father died in 1895 and his mother, who twice remarried, died in 1921. Before Sandhurst, Winston studied at Ascot, Brighton, and Harrow, being remembered most for his rebelliousness, unruliness, and poor record, especially in Latin and mathematics. His love of books asserted itself, however, and, while his classmates read Latin, he mastered the essentials of the English language. Yet he never rose above the lower form at Harrow. He failed the entrance examination for Sandhurst three times before being admitted in June, 1893. Then because of his intellectual powers and general knowledge, he graduated eighth in a class of one hundred fifty and on being commissioned a lieutenant joined the Fourth Hussars at Aldershot.

What followed was a series of military experiences molding his views of man and politics. On leaving Sandhurst, he turned for adventure to active military service. He joined in the fighting between independence forces and the Spanish in Cuba, writing for the *Daily Graphic* and coming under fire for the first time on November 29, 1895, near Trocham on the eve of his twenty-first birthday. In Cuba, he had a foretaste of contemporary guerrilla warfare over misty, tropical terrain. He wrote five reports of the war, which appeared in the London newspapers. He returned to England to find that his regiment had been ordered to India. Britain had ruled India for nearly three centuries, protecting economic interests and seeking to preserve the peace among quarrelsome Indian princes. Churchill landed at Bombay harbor and soon thereafter was transferred to Bangalore. There he excelled in polo, showed his courage, and used the afternoon rest hours to read the many books on history, philosophy, and religion which he had neglected in his formal education.

He employed a three-months' military leave to travel through Italy and Greece, and on returning to England, found that General Bindon Blood was leading a British force against the "wild Pathan tribes of India." He returned to India without an assignment, persuaded General Blood to accept him as a correspondent for the "Allahabad Pioneer," and traveled to Malakand in the mountains along the boundary separating India and Afghanistan. He joined Brigadier General Jeffreys at the entrance of the Mamund valley in a bloody struggle to subdue the cruel Mamund tribe. He came under fire and half his company were killed and mutilated. The British retaliated, emptying the reservoirs, burning the crops, destroying the houses, and leaving the valley devastated. For Churchill, war had lost much of its glamour and he asked in his dispatches if all the carnage was necessary to satisfy British honor. When the regiment returned to Bangalore, he wrote a book, *The Story of the Malakand Field Force*, which drew favorable reviews by learned authorities in England. He also wrote a novel, *Savrola*, that preserved his thoughts and reflections intermingling romanticism about war with a new realism.

In the novel, there were signs of an evolving view of the relation of ideals and force. The leading character, Savrola, whom reviewers identified with Churchill, asked himself whether the nation with the strongest ideals was not most likely to succeed in war. What if a people with lesser ideals but greater strength intervened? Strength is a form of fitness, Savrola commented, but lower on the scale than virtue. He concluded that political organizations imbued with moral fitness will ultimately rise above those whose only virtue is physical. In the novel, Churchill addressed himself to all the great issues raised throughout the classical tradition by Plato, the cynics, and the Stoics: honor, honesty, politics, customs, and society. In the novel two forces oppose one another in an imaginary land, Laurania. On one side are President Molara, his wife Lucile, his secretary Miguel, and a subaltern, Lieutenant Tiro, engaged in exploiting the people. Revolutionary forces under Savrola rise against them. In the struggle that follows, Savrola urges restraint even in revolution, while others call for immediate violence. The novel poses questions which must have been in Churchill's mind regarding revolution and man's most cherished values. One passage depicts the hero's room, the room of a man who appreciated all "earthly pleasures," appraised them at their proper worth, "enjoyed and despised them"—

again a vignette of the young war correspondent's unfolding personal philosophy.

In *The Story of the Malakand Field Force*, Churchill described that struggle as one example of the eternal warfare that went on at the outposts of civilization. The struggle involved a small band of soldiers and settlers armed with the resources of science, assailed by thousands of warlike and merciless enemies. The conflict was not only one between an empire and savage tribes but one in which Britain defended nineteenth-century India, threatened by imperialist forces from Russia and Afghanistan. As long as the borders between India and Afghanistan remained a buffer with a "great gulf" separating India from its foes, a balance would be maintained. If Afghanistan or Russia were to gain supremacy, India's survival would be imperiled. Britain's mission was to help India resist Russian domination along the border territories from which a dominant Russia would have gained the power to invade India at will.

The Story contained Churchill's first fragmentary thoughts on empire. The British Empire inspired in the Sepoys a dim, half-idolatrous faith in a distant, mysterious sovereign whose ideals restored their "fainting strength." In England, it was vital that patriotism be maintained, and Churchill warned of the consequences of its decline, especially among British intellectuals. The Queen's message in brigade orders to the troops fighting tribesmen in the Mamund valley on the Afghan frontier expressing sympathy with the suffering of the wounded and satisfaction with the conduct of the troops gave hope to British forces. Even native Indian soldiers noted with pride and exultation that their deeds were recognized by the august sovereign. Cynics and socialists, wrote Churchill, may sneer but the loyal sentiments of rulers and citizenry assured the essential solidarity of empire. Unborn historians with longer perspectives, Churchill prophesied, would trace the influence of a benign and mysterious power directing the progress of the human species and seizing opportunities to add to the liberties, happiness, and learning of mankind. Churchill's sense of empire, dimmed by his brief experience in Cuba, was strengthened through trial by fire in India. Yet he maintained certain reservations, especially about a policy of playing one brutal khan against his neighbors or mixing in the petty intrigues of border chieftains. Such practices were beneath imperial dignity, like a millionaire counting the lumps in a sugar basin. If Britain were to safeguard the Afghan frontier, its task was to act with strength in preserving its hegemony.

Conversely, Britain could ill afford to underestimate the qualities of its enemies. Never despise your enemy, as he wrote, was an old lesson which had to be relearned afresh year after year by every nation that was warlike and brave. Thus he set out to understand his Asian foe. Except at times of sowing and harvest, a continuous state of strife prevailed all along the Afghan frontier. Tribe warred with tribe. The people from one valley fought with those in the next. To the quarrels of communities were added the combat of individuals. Khan assailed khan, each supported by retainers. Every tribesman had a blood feud with his neighbor. Every man's hand was raised against the other and all against the stranger. Of the Umra Khan, Churchill could say he was a great man, which on the frontier meant he was a great murderer. In such a world, as Savrola explained to Lucile, the dictator's wife, honor has no true foundation, "no ultra-human sanction." Its codes are constantly changing with time and place. At one time, it was thought more honorable to kill the man you have wronged than to make amends. At another time, it is more important to pay a bookmaker than a butcher. And of the enemy's ferocity and of the action of Afghan troops who aided the tribesmen of the Mamund valley against the British, Churchill could say that it was no disparagement but to their honor that they were prepared to support with their lives those causes which claimed their sympathy. So a state of war persisted reflecting "deep-seated instincts of savagery" over which civilization casts but a "veil of doubtful thickness."

Churchill's account of the rise and fall of an ambitious Pathan warrior also reflected his attempt to achieve an evenhanded estimate of the enemy. He observed that the Pathan toils with zeal and thrift on a plot of land given him by his family. He accumulates a sum of money, buys a rifle, becomes feared, builds a tower in his house, dominates others in his village, and not being satisfied to rule his village, he persuades or compels his neighbors to join in an attack on the castle of the local khan. The attack succeeds, the khan flees, the castle is captured and the Pathan gives land to retainers who join him in conquering neighboring khans. In such a world, any external power is limited in controlling conflict and aggression. Savrola seemed to be expressing Churchill's concerns about the limits of British power when he declared that the military force of the Lauranian Republic was organized to protect its territory from invasion but was discouraged from vast schemes of foreign conquest or aggressive meddling in the affairs of neighboring principalities.

Nevertheless, Churchill saw himself and Britain carrying forward civilization. He described General Blood as a rare type of soldier-administrator schooled in the responsibilities of empire and unmatched since the days of the Roman proconsuls. Leadership and authority on the frontiers of empire would flow to political officers displaying force of personal character and strict adherence to regulations along with the right combination of individuality and uniformity. As long as the brigades dominated the countryside and appeared confident and successful, their communications would be secure and uprisings localized. However, at the first sign of a reverse or a retreat, powerful combinations would rise up against them on every side. Any sign of weakness was fatal. Churchill gave as an example of an action essential to preserving imperial prestige, an incident in which native tribesmen were pursued and forced to give up rifles taken when they broke their agreements. The captured rifles were worth little; the men and officers who lost their lives in the recovery were worth a great deal. These campaigns were unsound economics but imperialism and economics clashed as often as honesty and self-interest. An empire had to throw good money after bad in order to maintain its credit much as a businessman who cannot pay his tradesmen sends them new orders instead of settling his debts. Churchill in India increasingly portrayed imperialism with a sweep and breadth of thought rare among war correspondents. He found that individuals were carried along by history. Lord Elgin, viceroy of India in 1897, was for peace and retrenchment and fewer involvements with native tribes along the Afghan border. Yet his viceroyalty was marked by the greatest frontier war in the history of the British Empire in India, leading Churchill to remark on how little an individual, however earnest his motives and great his authority, can control the course of history.

Churchill was too clear-eyed and self-critical for the moral ambiguities of imperialism to escape him. Not only were Englishmen caught up in moral dilemmas but so were Pathan soldiers when required to suppress their countrymen. As he participated in the burial of soldiers at Inayat Kila on September 16, 1897, Churchill observed their shapeless forms, coffined in regulation blankets, men who had been the pride of race and the pomp of empire but now representing only the faint and unsubstantial fabric of a dream. He sensed "morality perplexed and reason staggered" and quoted Burke's memorable phrase: "What shadows we are and what shadows we pursue." Yet he answered those European critics who charged that Britain's use of dum-dum bullets was a violation of the Geneva Convention (bullets with a conical depression in which lead was inserted, which on striking a bone spread out tearing and splitting the body). He responded that no clause in the Geneva Accord forbade expansive bullets; the primary purpose of all bullets was to kill and the dum-dum variety merely did the job more effectively. In war, the objective was victory. Military success and all warfare had its share of moral ambiguity. Exhilaration was short-lived. General Bindon Blood, after a great victory at Chakdara and Castle Rock against native Indian forces of the Swat valley and Bajaur, must have experienced the rewards of long weary years of training and the fatigue and dangers of past campaigns. Yet, Churchill reported, there was no time for enjoyment. The victory had been won; it remained to profit by it. Churchill's dispatch concluded by noting that Blood sent four squadrons of cavalry after the retreating enemy.

What drove Churchill on in his personal intellectual and moral journey also inspired the empire in its march. In *The Story of the Malakand Field Forces*, he asked what motivated men and nations to face such great hazards. He answered courage, but continuing his inquiry, found the principal elements of courage to be preparation, discipline, vanity, and sentiment; and of all these, sentiment in the

end made the difference. Everyone clings to something he thinks is
high and noble, whether tradition, race, ancestors, or loyalty to his
regiment. Savrola asked himself if the struggle, sacrifice, and turmoil of revolution were worth it and for what end. He answered his
own question, pointing to the good of the people as his aim. But
this, he confessed, represented the direction rather than the cause of
his effort. Ambition was the motive force and he was powerless to
resist it. He appreciated the rewards of an artist's life or that of a
philosopher but knew he could not endure it. He would find rest
only in action, satisfaction only in conflict. His personal makeup
was vehement and daring. Yet even power or reputation was not
enough. Man needs a vision beyond himself to cling to in his hour
of need. That vision for Churchill in India was of the triumph of
civilization over barbarism. Rome declined because it had only its
sword. Modern civilization had higher values, scientific technology,
and superior fitness in things moral, physical, and mathematical.
Frontier wars were the surf marking the edge and advance of the
wave of civilization.

In India, Churchill learned other lessons in the school of the
statesman. One concerned the need for the statesman to make decisions in a context of indeterminism and uncertainty. He compared
the statesman with the historian, noting that the statesman must
cope with events that the historian merely records. The historian
constructs at his leisure theories or policies to explain successful opportunism by the statesman. All governments and rulers face the
same difficulty. None can pierce the veil or peer into the future.
However wise considerations of policies and principles or consequences and economics, they are all brushed aside by the "impetuous emergency." Statesmen must decide off-hand and on the spur
of the moment.

Churchill recorded two other lessons which were to persist
throughout a long career. One concerned the relationship of the political and the military and the other the relation between war and
religion. On the former, Churchill wrote that all British military
leaders in India from Lord Clive to the present (1897) had opposed
attaching political officers to military forces on grounds they would
encourage vacillation and interfere with military command. Church-

ill saw political officers as performing two vital functions, one that of negotiations and the other intelligence. He found the first to be valid and indispensable, requiring the study of foreign cultures through a lifetime. Local languages and customs, the power and influence of the khans, and the general history of the country were beyond the ken of the military officer. When an enemy ceases resisting and is ready to submit, the rough and ready tactics of victory and defeat are not enough. Men are needed who understand the whole question and all the details of the quarrel. They must have the capacity of putting themselves in the shoes of both the natives and the government. Churchill had serious doubts that such men could be found in an army. The demands of being a good soldier were sufficient to exhaust all the talents of the most accomplished men. His observation was that: "Civil officers should discharge diplomatic duties, and military officers the conduct of the war."[1] Years later, in response to Averell Harriman's criticism of the British parliamentary system, he responded that few men are so gifted as to understand the politics of their own country, let alone the politics of another.

Not surprisingly, in the conflict with the Pathans, Churchill found that Islam, a religion "which above all others was founded and propagated by the sword," produced a wild and merciless fanaticism in war.[2] On three continents, the tenets of Mohammedanism gave incentives to violence and slaughter. Several generations had passed since nations in the West had drawn the sword in religious controversy. Rationalism and human sympathy had overcome memories of a dark past. However distorted and degraded by cruelty and intolerance, Christianity now worked a controlling influence on men's passions and the more violent forms of political fanaticism. But, Churchill concluded, "the Mohammedan religion increases, instead of lessening the fury of intolerance."[3]

The young war correspondent returned to England famous overnight for his lively military writing. His reports stirred up indig-

---

1. Winston S. Churchill, *The Story of the Malakand Field Force* (New York: Longmans Green, 1898), 277.
2. *Ibid.*, 5.
3. *Ibid.*, 40.

nation in the highest military circles that a young lieutenant should have criticized the military operations of his superior officers. Wits renamed the book *A Subaltern's Hints to Generals*. Antagonism to his writings posed a troublesome obstacle to Churchill's next project. Concern in Britain over the Sudan was mounting. In 1885, the Sudanese under their most famous Mahdi, Mohammed Ahmed, had driven out the Turks and the Egyptians, killing General Charles Gordon in the process. The even more brutal tyranny of the Khalifa followed the Mahdi. The African Dervishes threatened Egypt once more as the Khalifa organized an army of ten thousand men in Omdurman, the capital of the Sudan. Sir Herbert Kitchener, commander of the Anglo-Egyptian army prepared to turn back the enemy. The young subaltern's first request that he join Kitchener's forces was turned down. Lord Salisbury, the Conservative prime minister had read and admired Churchill's *Malakand* book and invited the author to call on him. At the end of the visit, Churchill asked the prime minister to intervene with Kitchener but, despite Salisbury, the general's reply remained negative. Finally, Lady Randolph pleaded her son's cause with the adjutant general, Sir Evelyn Wood, and with his help Winston received an unpaid commission in the 21st Lancers. (He was required to accept a provision that if wounded or killed, his family would have no claim on army funds.) The *Morning Post* appointed him a correspondent and in the summer of 1898 he left for his fourth campaign on three continents. He arrived in time to take part in the battle of Omdurman and to write his second book, *The River War*.

As he began his account of the battle, Churchill sketched in a graphic picture of the scene: "level plains of smooth sand—a little rosier than buff, a little paler then salmon—are interrupted only by occasional peaks of rock—black, stark, and shapeless. Rainless storms dance tirelessly over the hot, crisp surface of the ground. . . . The earth burns with the quenchless thirst of ages, and in the steel-blue sky scarcely a cloud obstructs the unrelenting triumph of the sun."[4] For anyone who has ever watched the sun rise over that desert city, Churchill's words call up unforgettable memories: "It is

4. Winston S. Churchill, *The River War* (New York: Longmans Green, 1899), 2.

early morning, and the sun, lifting above the horizon, throws the shadows of the Khartoum ruins on the brimful wastes of the Nile. The old capital is solitary and deserted. . . . Across the river miles of mud houses, lining the banks as far as Khor Shambat, and stretching back to the desert and towards the dark hills, display the extent of the Arab metropolis. As the sun rises, the city begins to live. . . . a score of camels plod to market with village produce."[5] No one wrote military history with more vividness and flair than Churchill, although he himself drew an implied comparison with General "Chinese" Gordon's chronicle of the three-hundred-seventeen-day defense at Khartoum in 1884, saying: "No one will ever write an account which will compare in interest or detail with that set forth by the man himself in the famous 'Journals at Khartoum.'"[6]

In the summer of 1898, Churchill landed in Cairo, found that the troop he was to command had departed, followed them with tireless determination 1,400 miles up the Nile by train and steamboat, and joined the British forces encamped twenty miles from Omdurman. Sent ahead on patrol, he and six men and a corporal reported the advance of 60,000 fanatical and well-armed Dervishes. Churchill joined in the charge, cutting down Dervish swordsmen with a Mauser automatic and surviving the battle. *The River War* offered not only a masterful description of the tense and fast-moving battle which gave Britain the victory but contained severe criticisms of Kitchener for his vengeful treatment of the enemy (the fewer the prisoners captured alive, the greater Kitchener's satisfaction) and for the desecration of the Mahdi's tomb. Churchill's prose stamped him as a writer whom friends of Kitchener as well as ordinary Englishmen felt obliged to read, adding to his reputation. He wrote of the attack on Abu Hamed: "The outlines of the mud houses were sharply defined. . . . The Dervish riflemen crouched in the shelter trench that ran round the village. . . . Within this small amphitheater one of the minor dramas of war was now to be enacted."[7] Or "The line of advance [to Abu Hamed] lay along the

5. *Ibid.*, 86.
6. *Ibid.*, 50.
7. *Ibid.*, 194.

river; but no road relieved the labour of the march. Sometimes trailing across a broad stretch of white sand, in which the soldiers sank to their ankles, and which filled their boots with a rasping grit; sometimes winding over a pass or through a gorge of sharp-cut rocks, which, even in the moonlight felt with the heat of the previous day—always in a long, jerky, and interrupted procession of men and camels, often in single-file—the column toiled painfully like the serpent to whom it was said: 'On thy belly shalt thou go, and dust shalt thou eat.'"[8]

Churchill gleaned other lessons from his experience, some of which were to last for a lifetime. He learned the importance of common bonds with a military ally as with the Egyptian army of *fellahs*, for: "The British officers . . . who abused the *fellah* soldier were reminded that they insulted English gentlemen. Thus a strange bond of union was established between the officers and soldiers of Egyptian Service; and although material forces . . . accomplished much, without this moral factor the extraordinary results would never have been achieved."[9]

Churchill also appropriated some enduring political lessons from the struggle in the Sudan. During the war, he gave tacit approval, despite criticism in England, to Lord Salisbury's conciliatory policy toward Russia in China aimed at preventing a combination of Russia with France on the Upper Nile. That policy assured that when France (moving east from the Atlantic) and Britain (moving south from the Mediterranean) met, France would find itself alone. Military operations had gone on for fourteen years from 1884 to 1898. The war saw the deployment of an Anglo-Egyptian army with a British contingent of 8,000 and ended in the utter defeat of an enemy once numbering 80,000. It witnessed the reconquest of territory measuring 1,600 miles from north to south and 1,200 miles from east to west. It enabled Egypt to link up with South Africa through a network of railroads, telegraph systems, and waterways. It united territories and combined people whose futures were inter-

8. *Ibid.*, 191.
9. *Ibid.*, 92.

twined. Britain regained a vast territory whose political value was coveted by every great power in Europe.

Moreover, in the Sudan, Churchill observed the workings of the balance of power. In India, he had noted that when a Pathan leader grew too strong, surrounding chiefs and their adherents combined against him. In the Sudan, he learned that the Abdullah after Mahdi kept the relative power of various tribes and classes in balance. If a tribe threatened, it was struck down. For thirteen years, the Khalifa held the balance. Churchill acknowledged: "Such was the statecraft of a savage from Kordofan." Among Europeans, another balancing process was at work. On March 1, 1896, Italy was defeated by Abyssinia at Adowa, lowering the prestige of Europe and especially Italy. Her defeat had been assisted by arms supplied to the Abyssinians from French and Russian sources. The Triple Alliance was involved. Churchill concluded that only England had the power to restore the European balance if it would.

English contemporaries who possessed little understanding of the reasons Britain was in Egypt and the Sudan had no awareness of these truths. Yet England was strengthened twice over. Not only had she gained a vast territory, but France's influence in Egypt had been destroyed, though France retained the power to obstruct financial arrangements. Yet such influence unsupported by military strength was bound to crumble. The waters of the Sudan fed the Egyptian Delta and Egypt contributed to the development of the southern provinces. From 1819 to 1883, Egypt ruled the Sudan, but because of corruption and bribery its rule was a house of cards. "The rule of Egypt was iniquitous: yet it preserved the magnificent appearance of Imperial domain. The Egyptian pro-consul lived in state at the confluence of the Niles. The representatives of foreign Powers established themselves in the city. The trade of the south converged upon Khartoum. . . . An elaborate and dignified correspondence was maintained between Egypt and its great dependency." [10] Yet for Churchill reviewing the past, all was sham. Taxes were collected at the point of a bayonet. Egypt, though a member of the international

10. *Ibid.*, 11.

league against the slave trade, made money from it. The new order following the British victory at Omdurman promised a better life and this made the war worthwhile. It justified for Churchill Britain's response to the call of honor. Moreover, in the struggle great and small people had responded, and Churchill reminded his readers that "the applause of the nation and the rewards of the sovereign are bestowed on those whose offices are splendid and whose duties have been dramatic. Others whose labours were no less difficult, responsible and vital to success are unnoticed." [11]

In Churchill's reports from the Sudan, he began to contrast the ideal and the reality of imperialism. The ideal which justified Britain's efforts in Africa had never been more forcefully postulated: "What enterprise that an enlightened community may attempt is more noble and more profitable than the reclamation from barbarism of fertile regions and large populations? To give peace to warring tribes, to administer justice when all was violence, to strike the chains off the slave, to draw the richness from the soil, to plant the earliest seeds of commerce and learning, to increase in the whole people their capacity for pleasure and diminish their chances of pain—what more beautiful ideal or more valuable reward can inspire human effort? The act is virtuous, the exercise invigorating, and the result often extremely profitable." [12]

However, Churchill had seen too much to suppose that the ideal was matched by the reality. He went on: "Yet as the mind turns from the wonderful cloudland of aspiration to the ugly scaffolding of attempt and achievement, a succession of opposite ideas arises. Industrious races are displayed stinted and starved for the sake of an expensive Imperialism which they can only enjoy if they are well fed. Wild people, ignorant of their barbarism, callous of suffering, careless of life but tenacious of liberty, are seen to resist with fury the philanthropic invaders, and to perish in thousands before they are convinced of their mistake. The inevitable gap between conquest and dominion becomes filled with the figures of the greedy

11. *Ibid.*, 162.
12. *Ibid.*, 9–10.

trader, the inopportune missionary, the ambitious soldier, and the lying speculator, who disquiet the minds of the conquered and excite the sordid appetites of the conquerors. And as the eye of thought rests on these sinister features, it hardly seems possible for us to believe that any fair prospect is approached by so foul a path." [13]

Even as a young war correspondent and cavalry officer, Churchill grasped the truth that philosophers through the ages have struggled to understand. He recognized the fact that mankind possesses a moral sense which strives to relate sordid reality to noble precepts. Few writers have formulated with greater clarity the interconnectedness of ideals and reality. The young Churchill wrote:

> Few facts are so encouraging to the student of human development as the desire, which most men and all communities manifest at all times, to associate with their actions at least the appearance of moral right. However distorted may be their conceptions of virtue, however feeble their efforts to attain even to their own ideals, it is a pleasing feature and a hopeful augury that they should *wish* to be justified. No community embarks on a great enterprise without fortifying itself with the belief that from some points of view its motives are lofty and disinterested. It is an involuntary tribute, the humble tribute of imperfect beings, to the eternal temples of Truth and Beauty.[14]

Years later, the theologian Reinhold Niebuhr was to write in more terse prose that hypocrisy is the tribute vice pays to virtue.

Churchill also recognized the connection between revolution and ideals, saying: "The sufferings of a people or a class may be intolerable but before they will take up arms and risk their lives some unselfish and impersonal spirit must animate them." Not every people or nation is capable of such a spirit. "Ignorance deprives savage nations of such incentives. Yet in the marvelous economy of nature this very ignorance is a source of greater strength. It affords them the mighty stimulus of fanaticism." [15] Some link fanaticism with

13. *Ibid.*, 10.
14. *Ibid.*, 18.
15. *Ibid.*

moral crusades and military campaigns for a people's own peculiar version of righteousness. Churchill viewed with detachment another side of fanaticism and in his early book declared: "Fanaticism is not a cause of war. It is the means which helps savage people to fight. . . . What the horn is to the rhinoceros, what the sting is to the wasp, the Mohammedan faith was to the Arabs of Soudan—a faculty of offence or defence."[16]

Churchill went beyond the clarification of the relation between ideals and reality, however, to sound a warning note that was to echo throughout all his later years of statesmanship. "All great movements," he wrote, "every vigorous impulse that a community may feel, become perverted and distorted as time passes, and the atmosphere of the earth seems fatal to the noble aspirations of its people."[17] As a soldier in his early twenties, Churchill possessed a tragic sense of life. In particular, he appeared to foresee the rise of militarism and totalitarianism, writing: "There is one form of centralised government which is almost entirely unprogressive and beyond all other forms costly and tyrannical—the rule of an army. Such a combination depends not on the good will of its constituents, but on their discipline and . . . mechanical obedience."[18] Mutual fear prevails when mutual trust is destroyed. "History records many such dominations, ancient and modern, civilised or barbaric; and though education and culture may modify, they cannot change their predominant characteristics—a continual subordination of justice to expediency, an indifference to suffering, a disdain of ethical principles, a laxity of morals, and a complete ignorance of economics."[19] Militarism leads to a great centralized capital, to consequent impoverishment of the provinces, to oppression and want, to the ruin of commerce, to the decay of learning, and to ultimate demoralization even of the military order through overbearing pride and sensual indulgence.

The young Churchill appeared to sense that Britain as a Great Power was not immortal. Its paramount role, like that of all previous empires, was subject to the prospect of tragic decline. He rec-

16. *Ibid.*, 19.   18. *Ibid.*, 69.
17. *Ibid.*   19. *Ibid.*

ognized at the turn of the century that the world was tranquil and Britain rich and powerful. The Royal Navy was more than equal to the next two or three navies put together. England was the world's manufacturer; London was the unchallenged financial center. Almost sadly, he spoke of Britain being able then, with these great advantages, to pursue a steady and modest policy of avoiding foreign entanglements and only reluctantly accepting new possessions or responsibilities. He also understood that the future was indeterminate and that "every incident is surrounded with a host of possibilities, any one of which, had it become real, would have changed the whole course of events. The influence of Fortune is powerfully and continually exerted. . . . We live in a world of 'ifs.' What happened is singular; what might have happened, legion. But to try to gauge the influence of the uncertain force were utterly futile, and it is perhaps wise . . . to assume that the favorable and adverse chances equate, and then eliminate them both from the calculation."[20]

Soon after the battle of Omdurman, Churchill returned to London having obtained his discharge from the Fourth Hussars. He chose to run for Parliament from Oldham in industrial Lancashire, one of the largest voting districts in England. He ran as a Conservative sponsored by a senior Conservative member, Robert Ascroft, who died before Churchill's first speech to constituents. Churchill was defeated. In October, 1899, he sailed for South Africa to report the Boer War for the *Morning Post*. He was captured by the Boers, escaped, and gained more fame thereby than would have been possible in a dozen years of politics. But the main precepts of his philosophy were set through his early experiences which constituted for him the "school for the statesman."

20. *Ibid.*, 138.

CHAPTER FOUR

The Roots of Churchill's Approach to Politics

Though it is not given to all men to seize princely or royal power, yet the man who is wholly untainted by tyranny is rare or non-existent. In common speech the tyrant is one who oppresses a whole people by a rulership based on force; and yet it is not over a people as a whole that a man can play the tyrant, but he can do so if he will even in the meanest station. For if not over the whole body of the people, still each man will lord it as far as his power extends. (John of Salisbury, *Policraticus*)

An inquiry into Churchill's political philosophy and foreign policy must be concerned with the further evolution of his views on the nature of man, politics, international politics, and statesmanship. Taken together, his perspectives on these basic issues provide the pointers necessary to define his overall thought and philosophy. In dropping a plumbline to the roots of his approach to politics, we shall examine his thought on each of these fundamental questions.

Human Nature and Politics

A truism against which utopians in the Western world have protested in vain is that all politics is a struggle for power. It can hardly be denied that throughout society, and at every level of group life, men seek influence over the minds and actions of others. The most trenchant studies of politics and social relations provide overwhelming evidence of this truth. Whatever man's ultimate ends and goals may be, when he ventures into practical politics it is in quest of power, influence, and authority. Competition and rivalry, therefore, characterize the conduct of social and political groups whenever they or their members strive to implement aims and objectives politically. While this is widely recognized and accepted as an aspect of domestic politics, it has been supposed that the struggle for power internationally is a particular historical phenomenon, temporary in character, and bound to disappear when the conditions that occasioned it have been eliminated. Liberalism and Marxism have marched hand in hand to the militant beat of this utopian rhythm. Both philosophies assume the problem of power will be resolved through social transformation. To the liberal mind, power politics is an expression of a past aristocratic era. With the ascendance of an emancipated bourgeoisie to political and economic authority, these strange and evil forms of politics will inevitably pass away. A frictionless free-market economy will create a frictionless polity exemplifying freedom everywhere in the world. For Marxism, capitalist imperialism is the sole cause of power politics. The corruption of justice domestically, which is the outcome of the workings of a system of private property, has a larger and more tragic counterpart internationally in the corruption of universal justice by the violent collision of greedy imperialist nations. The struggle for power for Marxists and liberals, therefore, is nothing more than an unwholesome remnant of obsolete economic or political systems. With the replacement of these systems by liberal or communist economies, peace and concord will be assured.

No honest observer can deny that both the liberal and communist dreams of justice have been corrupted in the twentieth century. Yet for those who contend that rivalry is ubiquitous and power an inescapable reality in human experience, such deterioration is understandable. Men and states in every period of human history have found themselves engaged in contests for influence and power. The isolated and primitive communities in which rivalries are absent or concealed are as limited in numbers as they are localized in area. The nation in today's world who adopted their customs would run grave risks of national suicide. Our present critical situation in international society inspires a searching reexamination of the dilemma of power. When we examine and seek to explain the recurrence of the struggle for power, we are confronted once again, as we were at the outset of this study, with the assumptions of political realism. We are reminded that realism's supporters maintain that, far from comprising an accident of history, the will to power is an elementary bio-psychological drive common to all men at all times in much the same way that the drives to survive and to propagate are universal. As we have seen, utopian critics consistently dispute this fact. Where does Churchill fall in his views on this subject? This is the question we now turn to examine by tracing in detail what he has said on the problems of political power in relation to human nature.

From one standpoint, the wellsprings of human conduct are a more proper subject for philosophical inquiry than for comment by recent political figures. Yet Churchill was clearly guided by a conception of the nature of man which he more than once made explicit. For example, he wrote that it is a universal characteristic of men everywhere that: "Ambition, not so much for vulgar ends, but for fame, glints in every mind."[1] This ambition, as it is acted out in the human economy of limited material and psychological rewards, leads to rivalry and struggle. To the people of the brave little country of Norway he counseled: "I . . . urge you never to forget that life is one continuous struggle."[2] In peace as in war, he told his countrymen: "The struggle for life is unceasing. There is no easy or pleasant road."[3] Beyond the shores of Britain, he found in the national experience and history of other European nations evidence of the ubiquity of power. In commenting on France's political rivalries during World War II, he observed: "The struggle for power between de Gaulle [whom Churchill sometimes supported] and Giraud [whom Roosevelt favored] went on unabated as the weeks passed, and frequent clashes took place over both civil and military appointments. The fault did not lie always with de Gaulle."[4] He discovered the same process going on in postwar Greece where the Communists in Papandreou's cabinet were contending for political

1. Winston S. Churchill, *The Second World War,* Vol. II, *Their Finest Hour* (Boston: Houghton Mifflin, 1949), 15.
2. Winston S. Churchill, "Oslo: A Speech in the City Hall," May 13, 1948, *Europe Unite,* ed. Randolph S. Churchill (London: Cassell and Company, 1950), 333.
3. London *Times,* August 18, 1947, p. 2.
4. Winston S. Churchill, "Thoughts on the Fall of Mussolini," *The Second World War,* Vol. V, *Closing the Ring* (Boston: Houghton Mifflin, 1951), 183.

power, evoking from Churchill the remark: "Throughout, this has been a struggle for power. They [the Communists in the cabinet] were playing the game of the E.L.A.S. bands and of their Communist directors. While sitting in M. Papandreou's Cabinet, they were working in the closest combination with the forces gathering to destroy it and all that he and their other colleagues represented in the everyday life of Greece."[5]

Furthermore, in the same way individuals and political parties engage in the struggle for power, all nations, at one time or another, are involved in the competition for power. Even the righteous nations who stand for principles beyond the pursuit of mere selfish advantage are not immune, or as Churchill explained in Parliament: "The desire for glory, booty, territory, dynastic or national aggrandisement . . . are all temptations from which even those who only fight for righteous causes are not always exempt."[6] All nations strive for influence and power, Churchill concluded.

In return for his candor in confronting the issue, Churchill earned the epithets of imperialist and warmonger. It is of course true that armed force and the machinery of war, with all their potentialities for brutal conflict and violence, remain a vital element of a nation's power. The structure of contemporary international society has not outlawed war. Any nation of influence must be endowed with the sinews of war, inasmuch as the final arbitration of international conflict takes place in the tribunal of war. Speaking of the Communists and their respect for armed strength, Churchill concluded: "I have had some experience in direct contact with the highest authorities, under the most favourable conditions, and I can tell you that you can only do it by having superior force on your side and on the matter in question—and they must also be convinced that . . . you will not hesitate to use these forces, if necessary, in the most ruthless manner."[7]

5. *Parliamentary Debates* (Hansard) House of Commons, Fifth Series, Vol. 407, January 18, 1945 (London: His Majesty's Stationery Office, 1950), 402.
6. *Parliamentary Debates*, Vol. 473, March 28, 1950, p. 198.
7. Winston S. Churchill, "New York: A Speech at a Dinner by Mr. Henry Luce at

However, in Churchill's mind, force and strength bear an intrinsic relationship to politics not only in the conduct of war but as a primary deterrent of aggression. Power is important in the half-organized, half-anarchic international society because it provides nations with the capacity to organize and transmit the energy required to counterbalance both the "static" and "kinetic" energy by which a foe would do others harm. The compulsive effect of force is to deter the aggressor through the only terms of international control which all parties—even the evil ones—can recognize. Military power is the fist of the whole body politic of nations. To neglect it imperils a people's most direct and final means of defense. The real difference between power politics in the broadest sense and violence or warfare based on national power is in the nature of the relationship between violence or force and power. While the threat of political violence is a basic element of national policy and power in international politics, the outbreak of overt violence heralds the abandonment of political for military power. When the use of armed force is merely potential, the relationship between nations is political and psychological in character. When overt violence is employed, the relation becomes physical in character. The aim in both cases may be forcing the enemy to yield to influence and pressure. But the means and the techniques, and particularly their limits, are radically different in the two cases. The psychological relation between two minds is political; the physical relation between two bodies for domination is military in character. When war and violence replace power, the contest for political power has been transformed; indeed, it has come to an end.

In the early 1950s, *The Times* of London, with a long record of discriminating judgments in international affairs, editorialized on the differences between Laborites and Conservatives in their comprehension of the facts of political power. The editorial writer concluded: "The contrast in weight in foreign dealings or in defence matters between, on the one side, Mr. Churchill and Mr. Eden and, on the other, the Labour leaders hagridden by old doubts about the

---

the Ritz-Carlton Hotel," March 25, 1949, *In the Balance*, ed. Randolph S. Churchill (London: Cassell and Company, 1951), 37.

place of power in world affairs is so evident that the Labour spokes-man have belched out the smokescreen of warmongering to obscure it."[8] This same British journal five years earlier had characterized Churchill's concept of international cooperation as follows: "Mr. Churchill has never been one of those who believed that words could supply the place of action, and it was appropriate that he should have been insistent on the need for clothing international co-operation in the concrete forms of power."[9]

If some British journals appreciated the essential unity of Church-ill's thought on the nature of man and politics, the same could hardly be said for certain leading American journals, especially the more crusading liberal publications. The *Christian Century* in an editorial of March 20, 1946, found, following the fateful speech at Fulton, there was little to distinguish Churchill from Hitler: "Not even Hitler in the days of his power resorted to more naked military warnings than Churchill thundered forth in his Missouri speech."[10] In the most indignant terms, the editor declaimed against the nefari-ous balance of power system that Churchill and his ilk seemed bent on establishing:

England needs to be told in unmistakable terms that the American people no longer believe in the balance-of-power method of preserving peace. It was one of the more obvious cynicisms of the Churchill speech at Fulton that he declaimed against the balance of power principle and then went ahead to call for an Anglo-American world balance of power. . . . With Russia in possession of the all but impregnable citadel of the geopoliti-cians' "Heartland," and with the assurance of our scientists that common possession of the atomic bomb may be assumed by 1950, the people of this country do not believe that the sort of security Mr. Churchill talks about is any security at all.[11]

As the Second World War was drawing to a close, Churchill's name and the long British tradition of imperial policy became twin symbols of power politics. Especially in American eyes, the devil

8. London *Times*, October 23, 1951, p. 5.
9. London *Times*, March 6, 1946, p. 4.
10. "On Talking Tough," *Christian Century*, LXIII (March 20, 1946), 358.
11. *Ibid.*, 359.

theory of politics that had fixed on the munition makers as the in-
stigators of World War I, now singled out the British as the cynical
purveyors of a wholly un-American form of world politics. It was
argued that nations had the choice of taking or leaving power politics. A few evil men or a handful of sinister nations had a vested
interest in the evils of power struggles. Churchill, in his letters to
friends in America and in speeches before Parliament, gave evidence
of a deep sensitivity to many of these criticisms. He found it ironic
that his most outspoken critics were the citizens of the most powerful nation in the world. He spoke out on this issue in Parliament,
saying:

The expression of "power politics" has lately been used in criticism against
us in some quarters. I have anxiously asked the question, "What are power
politics?" I know some of our friends across the water so well that I am
sure I can always speak frankly without causing offence. Is having a Navy
twice as big as any other Navy in the world power politics? Is having the
largest Air Force in the world, with bases in every part of the world, power
politics? Is having all the gold in the world power politics? If so, we are
certainly not guilty of these offences, I am sorry to say. They are luxuries
that have passed away from us.[12]

In his long ordeal with American liberals, Churchill found a
comrade in President Roosevelt. While FDR was not a serious philosopher of politics nor a systematic thinker on the relevance of
principles of international politics, he grasped instinctively the great
issues and the enduring character of international politics. In foreign policy, he played by ear and more than once earned the acclaim
of his British wartime associates for his shrewd comments about
men and politics. Of FDR, the prime minister declared: "With that
marvelous gift which he has of bringing troublesome issues down to
earth and reducing them to the calm level of ordinary life, the President declared in his recent Message to Congress, that power politics
were the 'misuse of power.'" As for the British, Churchill explained:

We define our position with even more precision. We have sacrificed everything in this war. We shall emerge from it, for the time being, more

12. *Parliamentary Debates*, Vol. 407, January 18, 1945, pp. 425–26.

stricken and impoverished than any other victorious country. . . . We declared war not for the sake of our obligation to do our best for Poland against German aggression, in which aggression, there or elsewhere, it must also in fairness be stated our own self-preservation was involved.[13]

One crucial difference separated Roosevelt and Churchill. For Roosevelt, the question of power was almost entirely a matter of social engineering and control. Power had only to be harnessed to good ends and it would no longer cause concern. For Churchill, power was a profound moral problem, for: "The pursuit of power with the capacity and in the desire to exercise it worthily is among the noblest of human occupations. But Power is a goddess who admits no rival in her love."[14] These two perspectives illustrate, in capsule form, the difference between the buoyantly optimistic liberal conception of power and the soberly realistic outlook on politics. According to the former, the solution or transformation of power depends solely upon political and administrative techniques; spokesmen of the latter unashamedly confess helplessness in the face of conditions which can be managed but probably never transfigured. It is fair to ask whether the political and intellectual climate in America and Britain accounted in part for the emphasis of the two wartime leaders.

In the early postwar era, the general opposition to power politics centered in a widespread popular revulsion, especially in America but also in Britain, against the inequality of states and the practical implications inherent in this fact. For the members of a civilization for which a rough if imperfect justice presumably existed (within national boundaries), it was offensive to reason and justice that in world politics small powers should be subject to controls from which great powers were exempt. A Labor member of Parliament, one of two outspoken pacifists who were M.P.s at the time, raised an important question in 1945, in connection with the proposed United Nations. Rhys Davies asked Churchill if the proper interpretation of the various Dumbarton Oaks proposals would be that

13. *Ibid.*, 426.
14. Winston S. Churchill, *Marlborough: His Life and Times* (6 vols.; New York: Scribner's, 1938), IV, 171.

"if a great Power were guilty of the same kind of aggression there is no method of dealing with it at all."[15] In an answer that was remarkable for its realism and candor, the prime minister replied: "I am sorry that there should be a high degree of axiomatic truth in the fact stated by the hon. Member."[16] And he subsequently added an additional word of counsel:

We have made a perfectly voluntary agreement with the other two Great Powers gathered at Yalta, and it prescribes a differentiation between the greatest and smallest Powers. We may deplore, if we choose, the fact that there is a difference between great and small, between the strong and the weak in the world, but there undoubtedly is such a difference, and it would be foolish to upset good arrangements which are proceeding on a broad front for the sake of trying to obtain immediately what is a hopeless ideal.[17]

One of the great ironies of contemporary world politics is the fact that small states should exist only at the will and by means of the protection of the strong. In 1947, Churchill observed: "Norway is not a very powerful state and would not have been a state at all but for our exertions."[18] New international structures grow up and may ultimately protect and safeguard great and small nations from the threat of aggressors. For the present, however, international government is dependent in security matters primarily on the great powers. The postwar debate on whether power was a factor within the United Nations is reflected in Churchill's statement:

I do not take the view which was fashionable some time ago that the day of small States is ended and that the modern world can only adapt itself to great Empires. I trust that the new world instrument of the United Nations, upon which so many of our hopes are centered, will be strong enough and comprehensive enough to afford security and justice to large and small States alike. For this purpose however the help and guidance of the greatest Powers, as they now stand forth in the world, cannot be set aside.[19]

15. *Parliamentary Debates*, Vol. 409, March 15, 1945, p. 387.
16. *Ibid.*
17. *Ibid.*
18. *Parliamentary Debates*, Vol. 444, November 11, 1947, p. 210.
19. Winston S. Churchill, "Louvain University: A Speech on Receiving an Honor-

Churchill's convictions, then, about the disparity of the rights and duties of nations can be put in summary form if we say that he believed in joining power with responsibility. It is inevitable that the political arrangements of any international government should reflect differences in the political power of its members. One serious criticism of the League of Nations was that it neglected consideration of power both in principle and practice. The pretense was maintained by provisions calling for unanimity of voting on the assumption all nations were equal: one nation, one vote. Similarly, in negotiations the trend toward open diplomacy assumed that each nation has an equal stake in an issue even though all nations may not have made equal contributions. Churchill's uncertainty about the virtues of open diplomacy can be explained in part by his belief that since the stakes are not equal, nations who shoulder the greatest physical burden must transact in private among themselves the quest for vital political settlements. At some stage, the lesser powers must participate, but Churchill maintained that they need not be drawn in when the great powers are negotiating the terms of settlement. Following the Yalta conference, Churchill took note of:

. . . criticisms in this country that France was not invited to participate in the Conference at Yalta. The first principle of British policy in Western Europe is a strong France. . . . It was, however, felt by all three Great Powers assembled in the Crimea that, while they are responsible for bearing to an overwhelming degree the main . . . burden of the conduct of the war and the policy intimately connected with the operations, they could not allow any restrictions to be placed upon their right to meet together as they deemed necessary, in order that they may effectively discharge their duties to the common cause. This view, of course, does not exclude meetings on the highest level to which other Powers will be invited.[20]

The policies of liberal Western nations are often imperiled by public antagonism to the moral ambiguities of power politics. It has become customary for unfriendly powers to charge, with the aim of

---

ary Degree at the British Embassy, Brussels," November 15, 1945, *The Sinews of Peace*, ed. Randolph S. Churchill (London: Cassell and Company, 1948), 43–44.
20. *Parliamentary Debates*, Vol. 408, February 27, 1945, p. 1270.

arousing public opinion, that mutual assistance pacts are designed to create hostile power blocs organized against the complainant. Liberal societies are peculiarly vulnerable to these propaganda attacks and democratic peoples have consequently been the chief critics of certain defensive security arrangements. Churchill was frank to say that nations who strive to be so liberal and pure as to forswear all political arrangements may be inviting their own destruction. In 1946 as the West sought to unite to contain Russian imperialism, Churchill warned: "If the liberal nations of the world—the Western democracies, as they are called—are to be turned from their natural associations and true affinities by bugbear and scarecrow expressions like "bloc" and "ganging up," they will have only themselves to thank when once again they fall into misfortune."[21]

For Churchill politics among peoples and nations, then, was viewed as a tragic and unceasing struggle for power. Those who would survive must play the game in spite of their more delicate and sensitive impulses. It is the duty of moral men and nations not to grow weary, or, if weary, not to desist from the struggle, for the rewards are nothing short of national existence, human survival, and the chance to build stronger foundations for a peaceful world. Surveying the world after World War II and informed and inspired by such a philosophy, Churchill was led to say: "It is sad after all our victory and triumph and all that we hoped for . . . to find not peace and ease and hope and comfort but only the summons to further endeavour. But that is life!"[22]

From one standpoint, this conception of politics and history finds a different but important application in the sphere of economic life. Churchill's disapproval of the equalitarian creed of socialism is in a sense nothing more than a concrete application of his philosophy of power. In his words: "The ideas of Socialism are contrary to human nature. To maintain a robust and lively progress all adventurous and enterprising spirits should have their chance to try,

21. *Parliamentary Debates*, Vol. 423, June 5, 1946, p. 2022.
22. Churchill, "New York: A Speech at a Dinner Given by Mr. Henry Luce at the Ritz-Carlton Hotel," March 25, 1949, *In the Balance*, ed. Randolph S. Churchill, 38.

and if they fail try again."[23] In economic life, infinite variations and differentials express themselves among individuals and groups and these normally are registered in their competition with one another. Socialism for Churchill was against human nature since it dampened out struggles for position and authority and brought down the strongest and most productive to the level of the weakest in society. He announced: "In our view the strong should help the weak. In the Socialist view the strong should be kept down to the level of the weak in order to have equal shares for all."[24] Admittedly, as a political partisan, Churchill maintained that the policy of the Socialist government did not aim necessarily at the increase of justice or of production but specifically at the increase of political power. The program presented for the nationalization of steel was instituted "not because the Government wants more *steel* but because they want more *power*."[25] In the hands of the Socialists, the British steel industry would become an unparalleled weapon of political and economic warfare. The strategy of British socialism in general was dedicated to the increase of political power. This would be true of any political party, but in socialism's merging of economic and political power, Churchill found a particular corruption of an original dream of social justice:

British Socialists hope to get everyone into their power, and make them stand in queues for the favours which an all-wise and all-powerful governing machine chooses to bestow. To have power over their fellow-countrymen, and be able to order them about is the natural characteristic of any Socialist. He loves controls for control's sake. . . . We are the masters now, says the Attorney-General. I must say this rouses indignation in my heart.[26]

Moreover, for Britain's leading twentieth-century statesman the political leaders in the twilight of the Victorian era were persons of greater stature because, in his eyes, this was the golden age in the

23. Churchill, "Election Address: Leeds," February 4, 1950, *ibid.*, 178.
24. Churchill, "Election Address: Devonport," February 9, 1950, *ibid.*, 192.
25. Churchill, "Woodford Adoption Meeting," January 28, 1950, *ibid.*, 166.
26. Churchill, "Election Address: Leeds," February 4, 1950, *ibid.*, 176.

struggle for political office. Position was an earnest of high moral and political attainments and in his memorial to the Earl of Asquith, Churchill reflected:

But I must say that the statesmen whom I saw in those days seemed to tower above the general level in a most impressive way. The tests were keener, the standards were higher, and those who surmounted them were men it was a treat and honour to meet. They were the representatives of an age of ordered but unceasing movement. Liberalism had stricken the shackles off the slave and broken down the barriers of privilege. The road was open to those of the highest natural quality and ability to chose to tread it.[27]

If the facts proved less trustworthy than the principles he enunciated, it was noteworthy that Churchill conceived of political leadership as essentially the outcome of a profound political contest between men of great ambition and character.

The final test of the stateman's conception of the tragic international struggles for power and influence comes in his judgment regarding his own nation. Does he appreciate its role in contemporary power politics and can he evaluate its capacity to engage in the struggle successfully? Or is he so overwhelmingly the captive of its nationalism and patriotism that he interprets its fortunes and decline through the eyes of the lover of power and not of the statesman? Put to this test, Churchill emerged unscathed as preeminently the statesman guided and informed not only by his nation's mission and its historic grandeur but likewise by its present political decline. His judgment on the hazards of playing the game of practical international politics was rooted in a natural and shrewd understanding of his country's predicament and the limits of its power as well as the power of both friend and foe. The standards and measures of power politics must be applied to Great Britain as well as to other nations in international society. There is a note of profound pathos in his reflection that: "A mood of deep anxiety mingled with bewilderment oppresses the nation. They have tried so hard and they have done so well, and yet at the end of it all there is a widespread

27. Churchill, "Unveiling of a Statue to the Earl of Oxford and Asquith," December 6, 1950, *ibid.*, 443.

sense that we have lost much of our strength and greatness, and that unless we are careful and resolute, and to a large extent united, we may lose more still."[28]

The True Nature of Politics

While the Second World War was still going on, an American periodical published its sharpest indictments of Churchill and his wartime associates. It charged him with having sacrificed the principles of the Atlantic Charter for which the Grand Alliance had been formed. It convicted him of a blind and headstrong preoccupation with selfish political approaches while the great legal and moral questions involving all mankind were forgotten and bargained away: "The war is being lost. It is being lost in the reversion to power politics, in the cynical evasion of solemn engagements with the peoples who have poured out their blood and treasure, in the manipulations of boundaries and power blocs as substitutes for the protection of the weak and the establishment of a universal reign of law."[29] Churchill's critic succeeded in leaving the impression that the political problems of postwar Europe would settle themselves if only the Atlantic Charter were given a fair chance. The criticism concluded: "To men in authority in Britain and Russia, the division of Europe into power blocs and spheres of influence may seem like enlightened self-interest, but in the hearts and consciences of thinking people it is losing the war. The one thing that now makes the Atlantic Charter such a stumbling block to men like Churchill and Stalin and Roosevelt is that its principles were so practicable and clearly stated."[30]

At one stage in the war, Churchill appeared overwhelmingly concerned with immediate military and political issues. Throughout the war, inflamed by the spirit of battle, he had spoken in inspiring if unpolitical terms about the nature of the struggle, as when he exclaimed in 1941: "My one aim is to extirpate Hitlerism from Eu-

28. London *Times*, October 3, 1951, p. 7.
29. "Can the War Be Saved?" *Christian Century*, LXII (January 3, 1945), 6.
30. *Ibid.*, 7.

rope. The question is such a simple one. Are we to move steadily forward and have freedom, or are we to be put back into the Middle Ages by a totalitarian system that crushes all forms of individual life and has for its aim little less than the subjugation of Europe and little more than the gratification of gangster appetites?" [31] Such a clarion call for preserving freedom was scarcely the statement of a national political leader concerned primarily with the distribution of political power. Yet if we go back to the years before World War II and review the diagnosis he offered of the deteriorating international scene following World War I, his clear and steady perception of the urgent need for a stable equilibrium of power in the world is dramatically illustrated. At that time, the Wilsonian conception of national self-determination was widely heralded as a panacea for curing all international ills. It was said that the nations who had ignited the fuse of the world conflict should pay for their sins by the breakup of prewar empires and the redistribution of territory to emerging national groups. Critics of this novel but utopian illusion, among them Churchill, spoke forthrightly in opposition: "The doctrine of self-determination was not the remedy for Europe, which needed above all things, unity and larger groupings. The idea that the vanquished could pay the expenses of the victors was a destructive and crazy delusion." [32] The curse of Woodrow Wilson's noble dream of independence for every ethnic and national group was that it led to the fragmentation of the unity of Southeastern Europe creating many tiny rival national economies incapable either of cooperating effectively together or of surviving alone. The balkanization of Europe opened up a gaping political vacuum where formidable buffers to German or Russian expansion had once existed. Economic and political atomization became a source of future conflict; it afforded the pretext of enforced unification by the Germans and left a vast area prostrate before any would-be aggressor. In his history of World War II, Churchill wrote:

31. Winston S. Churchill, "We Will Not Fail Mankind," January 17, 1941, *The Unrelenting Struggle*, ed. Charles Eade (London: Cassell and Company, 1942), 38.
32. New York *Times*, April 1, 1949, p. 10.

[A] cardinal tragedy was the complete break-up of the Austro-Hungarian Empire by the Treaties of St. Germain and Trianon. For centuries this surviving embodiment of the Holy Roman Empire had afforded a common life, with advantages in trade and security, to a large number of peoples, none of whom in our own time had the strength or vitality to stand by themselves in the face of pressure from a revivified Germany or Russia. . . . The Balkanisation of Southeastern Europe proceeded apace, with the consequent relative aggrandisement of Prussia and the German Reich, which, though tired and war-scarred, was intact and locally overwhelming.[33]

Some students of international affairs have argued that little could have been done to prevent the emergence of Nazi Germany other than the very efforts that failed. The lenient terms of the peace and the magnanimity of the United States in not insisting upon the repayment of its loans were pointed to as evidence that Germany suffered no Carthaginian peace. But if the Treaty of Versailles and the peace treaties for Austria and the Balkans bore few if any resemblances to a conqueror's peace, they were politically stupid if taken in the aggregate. Contemporary journals of opinion in the West have a penchant for debating issues and policies in terms of the political actors' intentions. Yet intentions are less significant than the consequences that flow from concrete foreign policies. It is said that the cardinal sin for the diplomat is not dubious intentions, but that he blunders. For Churchill, it was a blunder not to bolster and shore up the Weimar Republic; failure to support it prepared the soil for Nazism. It was a blunder to approach the question of reparations in legalistic-moralistic terms instead of rebuilding and creating the strongest and most stable political situations possible in Germany: "Even when so much else had failed we could have obtained a prolonged peace, lasting all our lives at least, simply by keeping Germany disarmed in accordance with the treaty, and by treating her with justice and magnanimity."[34]

For these reasons, political problems should have been para-

---

33. Winston S. Churchill, *The Second World War*, Vol. I, *The Gathering Storm* (Boston: Houghton Mifflin, 1948), 10.
34. New York *Times*, April 1, 1949, p. 10.

mount in the minds of the postwar planners. In a word, there were grave risks inherent in the breakdown of prewar world empires. As infant states and former dependencies made the transition from colonies to statehood, the dangers increased that they would be overrun. In 1934, Churchill warned: "There are very special dangers to be feared if any Great Power possessing Dominions and connections all over the world falls into a peculiarly vulnerable condition. How many wars have we seen break out because of the inherent weakness of some great empire, such as the Hapsburg Empire or the Turkish Empire when they fall into decay? Then all the dangerous forces become excited."[35] Before Hitler began his march through Europe, Churchill proposed that the West reexamine the popular doctrine of opposition to every form of imperialism. Following World War II, Churchill, contemplating the consequences of the disintegration of the British Empire, urged over-sanguine liberals to ask themselves "what coherent theme will take its place? What would fill the void, for void there would certainly be? These are the questions which we must ask ourselves."[36] The threat in Burma and India and throughout the colonial world was that sinister forces would seize the opportunity created by chaos and confusion. About India in particular, he reflected: "No one can measure the misery and bloodshed . . . or [foresee] under what new power their future and destiny will lie."[37] Subsequently he expanded on these thoughts:

Hitherto they [India] have been protected from foreign aggression by the strong shield of our island power. Our policy, our influence among the nations, our modest military forces, our latent strength and that of the Empire and, of course, the Royal Navy, have protected India from foreign invasion.

Now this protection can no longer be given in any effective form. There is always the United Nations organization, but it is still struggling for life and torn with dissension. Moreover, in India the causes and signs

35. *Parliamentary Debates*, Vol. 286, March 8, 1934, pp. 2072–73.
36. Churchill, "A Speech on Receiving the Freedom of Westminster," May 7, 1946, *The Sinews of Peace*, 125.
37. Churchill, "Conservative Party Conference at Blackpool," October 5, 1946, *ibid.*, 209.

of a future internal war are already alive, and its portents multiply as the months pass by.[38]

Nowhere is the political problem seen more clearly in its elemental simplicity than in the postwar policy of the West for Germany and Central Europe. Wartime thinking and early postwar measures were derived from essentially unpolitical concepts and motives. On October 10, 1948, a New York *Times* release under the by-line of veteran foreign correspondent Herbert L. Matthews reported a speech by Churchill: "The British and American Governments should not have withdrawn their forces so quickly from Germany, he asserted. Hinting at an apparent disagreement with President Roosevelt, Mr. Churchill said it would have been wiser for the British armies to take Berlin and for the United States armies to enter Prague, as, he said, they could have done."[39] Other substantial differences surfaced with General Dwight D. Eisenhower, who maintained that Berlin, while psychologically important, was not the logical or the most desirable objective for Allied forces. In *Crusade in Europe*, Eisenhower declared: "The future division of Germany did not influence our military plans for the final conquest of the country." Eisenhower went on to say that Churchill "held that, because the campaign was now approaching its end, troop maneuvers had acquired a political significance that demanded the intervention of political leaders in the development of broad operational plans."[40] Yet neither the Roosevelt administration nor its military leaders were persuaded by Churchill's thinking. Nor was President Harry Truman, who rejected proposals contained in Churchill's cables of June 4 and June 9, 1945. In these cables, Churchill expressed profound misgivings over the forthcoming retreat of the American army in the central sector of Germany, "thus bringing Soviet power into the heart of Western Europe and the descent of an iron curtain between us and everything to the eastward." Churchill proposed to

38. *Parliamentary Debates*, Vol. 457, October 28, 1949, p. 250.
39. New York *Times*, October 10, 1948, p. 5.
40. Dwight D. Eisenhower, *Crusade in Europe* (Garden City, N.Y.: Doubleday, 1948), 396, 399.

delay the withdrawal of American troops until "the settlement of many great things which would be the true foundation of world peace."[41] It is an open question, of course, whether the available military alternatives were equally legitimate from a strategical standpoint, or whether certain alternatives that were politically desirable were militarily feasible. The crux of the matter is that the different viewpoints were inspired not primarily by personal preference for one military alternative or the other but by two divergent conceptions of international politics fundamentally at variance with one another. In retrospect what Churchill feared most was precisely what occurred: "The war had liberated Russia from her two preoccupations—Germany and Japan. . . . Now both have ceased to be . . . factors and the years that have followed our victory have brought enormous increases of power and territory to Soviet Russia."[42]

In the conduct of warfare throughout the nineteenth century, leaders undertook, at the same time that one threat was being repelled, to anticipate the next threat to the balance of power. British statesmen like Canning and Castlereagh refused concessions to Russian expansion at a time when the menace of Napoleonic France was being turned back. The advent of democratic diplomacy and total warfare in the twentieth century has made the task of looking ahead increasingly more difficult. Some of the twentieth century's wisest statesmen have failed when popular pressures became too great. Churchill confessed that his most egregious error was his action in initialing the Henry Morgenthau Plan for Germany at the second Quebec Conference. The Morgenthau Plan would have destroyed Germany's industrial capacity and returned the country to pasture land. It ran counter to every sound principle of international politics. Churchill's explanation of the conditions under which this mistake was committed illustrates the plight that confronts every statesman who must make decisions in the atmosphere of war. The British prime minister said of the Morgenthau Plan:

41. Winston S. Churchill, *The Second World War*, Vol. VI, *Triumph and Tragedy* (Boston: Houghton Mifflin, 1954), 523–24.
42. *Parliamentary Debates*, Vol. 481, November 30, 1950, pp. 1331–32.

I do not agree with this paper for which I bear, nonetheless, a responsibility, but when . . . fighting for life with a fierce enemy I feel differently towards him to what I do when that enemy is beaten to the ground and suing for mercy. Anyhow if the document is ever brought up to me I shall certainly say that I did not agree with it and I am sorry I put my initials to it. I cannot do more than that, but many things happened with great rapidity.[43]

After the conflict, Churchill implored his fellow Western leaders to choose policies which restored political stability in the West, drawing a sponge across the crimes and horrors of the past. He argued the West should continue the trials of German war criminals only so long as they were compatible with the creation of political stability in the heart of Europe. Neither retribution nor the claims of abstract justice but the birth of a sound and healthy postwar Germany was the standard against which every concrete action should be judged. He counseled Americans in particular: "I assure you you must forget the past. You must obliterate all parts of the past which are not useful to the future. You must regard the re-entry of Germany into the family of European nations as an event which the Western World must desire and must, if possible, achieve."[44] Old feuds and present retribution and justice no matter how clearly and simply understood must be secondary to the building of stable international political situations for the future. Europe could not live without a healthy and independent Germany; and if Europe continued in travail, the international society would be placed in serious jeopardy:

Here is the forward path along which we must march if the thousand-year feud between Gaul and Teuton is to pass from its fierce destructive life into the fading romance of history. Here are two men [de Gaulle and Adenauer] who have fought and struggled on opposite sides through the utmost stresses of our time and both see clearly the guidance they should give. Do not let all this be cast away for small thoughts and wasteful recriminations and memories which, if they are not to be buried, may ruin the lives of our children and our children's children.[45]

43. *Parliamentary Debates*, Vol. 467, July 22, 1949, 1597–98.
44. Churchill, "New York: A Speech at a Dinner by Mr. Henry Luce at the Ritz-Carlton Hotel," March 25, 1949, *In the Balance*, ed. Randolph S. Churchill, 35.
45. *Parliamentary Debates*, Vol. 473, March 28, 1950, p. 195.

Central Europe became the chief battleground of the cold war and in this struggle the West turned to its ancient foe as potentially its most important ally. Therefore, the ambiguities of contemporary international politics appeared in their starkest and most undisguised form in the new role Germany was required to play. In dealing successfully with a new imperialist power, memories of the brutal realities of an ancient foe could not be the primary determinant of policy. In 1948, Churchill called for unity in the West against Russian imperialism, saying:

I recognize fully that the British Government, like that of the United States, has followed a course of action based on combining all forces against Communist intrigue and Russian Imperialism. . . . We will not allow ourselves to be blackmailed out of Berlin by the inhuman efforts of the Russian Soviet Government to starve the two and a half million Germans who dwell in the British and American zones. They were our enemies in the war but we are now responsible that they should not be treated with cruel severity.[46]

However, the European political problem involved more than a new role for Germany in halting Russia. It likewise depended on balancing Germany's increasing power by strengthening France and Britain. If France and England were able to join one another, they would possess the power to move forward with confidence on the hazardous course of restoring Germany to its natural eminence in Europe. In Churchill's words: "Britain and France must stand together primarily united in Europe. United they will be strong enough to extend their hands to Germany."[47] Elsewhere in Europe, he called for a new balance among the powers. As early as May 22, 1943, as Britain's wartime leader, he warned: "It was important to re-create a strong France for the prospect of having no strong country on the map between England and Russia was not attractive."[48] And in the Southeast, Churchill understood that equilibrium required some

46. London *Times*, July 12, 1948, p. 6.
47. *Parliamentary Debates*, Vol. 472, March 16, 1950, p. 1288.
48. Winston S. Churchill, *The Second World War*, Vol. IV, *The Hinge of Fate* (Boston: Houghton Mifflin, 1950), 803.

substitute for the ancient Austro-Hungarian Empire: "I also hoped that in Southeastern Europe there might be several confederations— a Danubian Federation based on Vienna and doing something to fill the gap caused by the disappearance of the Austro-Hungarian Empire."[49]

Whether the policies the British statesman proclaimed were practical or impractical or simply difficult of attainment is not the question. Our intention is not in showing whether Churchill's proposals or prophecies were right or wrong in every case. What we can show is that he took his bearings from an approach which provided a common denominator for each of his proposals. It was Churchill's judgment that the political problem must always be seen as paramount. When he wandered from this guiding principle and path of duty in response to allied pressure, popular clamor, or military necessity, he did so with great reluctance. Sometimes, after the event he humbled himself to make public confession of his error. An unchanging political instinct unfailingly warned him, and through him his nation and its allies, that in contemporary international society profound political issues can be ignored only at great price.

International Politics: Tradition and Tragedy

A third dimension of Churchill's political approach set him apart and must not be overlooked. It concerns the nature of tradition and tragedy and the role they play in politics. For present-day prophets and planners who approach politics in purely rational terms, tradition and tragedy are dismissed as mystical and essentially meaningless for political analysis. Because these subjects constitute what Bismarck called the "imponderabilia" of politics, they are considered beyond scientific study or political analysis. Yet the uncommon sagacity of a handful of past leaders derives in part from an instinctive knowledge of people's tradition. Historical and political imagination is the product of rare genius but invariably is enriched when its roots are firmly planted in the past. Societies have not been

49. *Ibid.*

guided to their finest hours by visions of an imaginary future. Instead, heroic epochs have resulted from a vision of the past which
more or less faithfully portrayed a nation's history. Nations safeguard their future by judging the present through a deep understanding of the past. A people with a history is best able to judge
where it is and where it is tending. In Gladstone's cogent phrase:
"No greater calamity can happen to a people than to break utterly
with its past." For Churchill: "It is only by studying the past that we
can foresee, however dimly, or partially, the future. It may well be
that it is only by respecting the past that we can be worthy of the
future."[50]

Some contemporaries respond that history provides no firm terrain on which the statesman can take present bearings with anything like scientific accuracy. At best, the statesman is like the recon-
noitering soldier who estimates his position from the stars. Few
would deny that history has its unities and recurrences and that
events take place in a stream of observable actions and consequences. However, Anglo-American thought with its empirical bent
has for the most part avoided making generalizations about history
as such and has called up the lessons of history with caution and
circumspection. On December 1, 1948, Churchill observed: "Events
happen from day to day but they all happen as a result of long
chains of causation which one must bear in mind if one is to see
where the next link comes in or closes."[51] History for the statesman
is put to work much as the soldier uses his crude handwritten map
for practical and common-sense purposes, not as the philosopher or
scientist marshals data in support of grand *a priori* principles. In
Churchill's eyes, England's finest tradition was its heroic struggles
against tyranny:

You have no doubt noticed in your reading of British history—and I hope
you will take pains to read it, for it is only from the past that one can judge
the future— . . . that we have had to hold out for quite a long-time:
against the Spanish Armada, against the might of Louis XIV, when we led

50. London *Times*, November 10, 1951, p. 6.
51. *Parliamentary Debates*, Vol. 458, December 1, 1948, pp. 2019–20.

Europe for nearly twenty-five years under William III and Marlborough, and a hundred and fifty years ago, when Nelson, Pitt and Wellington broke Napoleon, not without assistance from the heroic Russians of 1812. In all these world wars our Island kept the lead of Europe or else held out alone. And if you hold out alone long enough there always comes a time when the tyrant makes some ghastly mistake which alters the whole balance of the struggle.[52]

Outside the England of Churchill and Edmund Burke, some present-day leaders display a certain morbid self-consciousness about reexamining the past for political purposes. Some moderns insist that the novelties of the present have rendered the lessons of the past obsolete. Churchill himself acknowledged: "In the modern world everything moves very quickly. Tendencies which two hundred or three hundred years ago worked out over several generations, may now reach definite decisions in a twelve-month."[53] Yet even in an era of vast and accelerated change, knowledge of a people's history and culture remains an essential requirement. Within England, Churchill called on his countrymen to remember the wise words of Lord Beaconsfield (Disraeli): "In a progressive country change is constant and the great question is not whether you should resist change, which is inevitable, but whether the change should be carried out in deference to the manners, the customs, the laws, the traditions of the people, or in deference to abstract principles and arbitrary and general doctrines."[54]

Internationally, despite all the immense technological changes of our day, Western civilization survives. Recognizing this, the liberal Catholic journal *Commonweal* commented editorially: "It is certainly true that Mr. Churchill formed his speaking and writing habits in another century, but it does not follow that he views the current world less clearly because of that. To Mr. Churchill, the forms of Western Civilization are still recognizable and his language

52. London *Times*, May 14, 1945, p. 5.
53. *Parliamentary Debates*, Vol. 474, April 24, 1950, p. 623.
54. Quoted in Churchill, "Hope for 1945: Speech to the Primrose League," December 31, 1945, *War Speeches, 1940–1945* (London: Cassell and Company, 1946), 228.

still applies."[55] Policymakers immersed in the present may overlook
the tides of history. Speaking to a Scottish Union meeting, Churchill
warned: "Great events are happening. They happen from day to day
and headlines are never lacking. But we must not allow the ceaseless
click and clatter which is the characteristic of our age to turn our
minds from these great events."[56] For this British traditionalist,
America's present is best apprehended through its history: "Americans should not fear to march forward unswervingly upon the path
to which Destiny has called them, guided by the principles of the
Declaration of Independence, all written out so carefully and so
pregnantly, in the balanced, well-shaped language of the 18th century, by the founders of the greatest State in the world. All is there,
nothing can be abandoned; nothing need be added, nothing should
be denied."[57] One of the grave risks for every nation and people is to
abandon what they have, in a vain quest for what might be. Futurist
schemes may lead nations to be indifferent to present urgencies, especially in world affairs. Early in World War II, Churchill cautioned: "Do not let spacious plans for a new world divert your energies from saving what is left of the old."[58]

Tradition, then, both illuminates the future and enriches the
present; it is indispensable to the art of statesmanship. Yet tradition
is more than a call to action and assurance of progress; it is also a
reminder of tragedy, which is an unchanging dimension of human
existence. At the core of international politics is a tragic element
from which there can be no escape. Sometimes shifts and reversals
in fortune decree that final tragedy will be averted. A *Times* (London) editorial writer discovered in Churchill's history of the war a
recurrent theme of tragedy. The editorial explained: "The volume,
sub-titled 'The Hinge of Fate,' is clearly central to his conception of

55. "Churchill's European Union," *Commonweal*, LXVI, (May 30, 1947), 155.
56. Churchill, "Scottish Unionist Meeting," May 18, 1950, *In the Balance*, ed.
Randolph S. Churchill, 280.
57. London *Daily Telegraph and Morning Post*, April 12, 1947.
58. Churchill, "Prime Minister to Minister for Works and Buildings," January 6,
1941, *The Second World War*, Vol. III, *The Grand Alliance* (Boston: Houghton
Mifflin, 1950), 723.

the war as high tragedy, in that grandest sense of high tragedy which can work itself out, like the Oresteia, to a happy ending; and also it is rounded off as a complete tragedy in itself. The essence of tragedy lies in reversal of fortune." [59]

The nature of international politics with its unceasing conflicts of interests and clash of wills gives it a tragic coloration which no social engineering or institutional reforms can change. Almost alone among Western statesmen, Churchill preserved a sense of the tragic proportions of life and politics. Even President Roosevelt, great-hearted political genius that he was, lacked this capacity. Perhaps the depth of Churchill's politics derived from recurrent experiences of heroism and shame, of darkness and light. It has been said that however exalted the words Churchill uttered, his spirit remained a denizen of inner worlds where both joy and sorrow intermingle as part of the whole. In this regard, Churchill stands in a long and honorable line of statesmen of which Lincoln is the finest American expression. The sense of the tragic dimension of politics was shared by another of Churchill's cohorts, the chancellor of the Exchequer, R. A. Butler of Saffron Walden, who quoted a classical nineteenth-century statement on politics in a speech in Parliament on October 22, 1946: "This abyss of iniquities which we call politics is vainly covered with a tissue of brilliant phrases. It is easy for anyone of the least intelligence and whose heart is in the right place to see through this tissue and recognize that in spite of evangelical treaties, and in spite of a reign of justice, it is always the weaker who are sacrificed to interests of the more powerful." [60]

Tragedy results from the fact that politics often involves the choice of lesser evils. In reviewing allied military strategy, Churchill maintained that while "unconditional surrender" was an unsatisfactory policy, other alternatives were still worse. He explained:

My principal reason for opposing, as I always did, an alternative statement on peace terms, which was so often urged, was that a statement of the actual conditions on which the three great Allies would have insisted and

59. London *Times*, August 3, 1951, p. 5.
60. *Parliamentary Debates*, Vol. 427, October 22, 1946, p. 1528.

would have been forced by public opinion to insist would have been far more repulsive to any German peace movement than the general expression "unconditional surrender." I remember several attempts being made to draft peace conditions which would satisfy the wrath of the conquerors against Germany. They looked so terrible when set forth on paper, and so far exceeded what was in fact done, that their publication would only have stimulated German resistance. They had in fact only to be written out to be withdrawn.[61]

The tragic choices in politics and the disparity between abstract justice and the rewards accorded the strong and the weak are factors few democratic leaders school themselves to understand. Perhaps only someone who has known the meaning of tragedy in his own life can cope with the tragic moral ambiguities of politics.

Statesmanship and the Future

Alongside the issues of tradition and tragedy in politics is the problem of political prediction. The great perturbations of human events in the twentieth century make political prediction the most hazardous of all "sciences." Yet statesmen like businessmen are driven to make crude estimates or forecasts of the future. No other phase of a statesman's task is more perilous and uncertain, for deep hopes and profound emotional involvement becloud issues and obscure vision. The four demons who pursue the leader who is called upon to forecast the future are sentiment and passion, ignorance of the facts, indeterminate consequences, and the influence of fortune or chance. These problems were the causes of deep anxiety for Churchill, who feared that while techniques and the raw material for political forecasting had improved and multiplied, so had the problems to be comprehended. The enormous scope of the world context caused him to declare in the spring of 1947: "The scene which we have to contemplate and try to measure at this moment is enormous. It comprises all the passions of mankind, all the policies and anxieties of the victorious Powers, and upon a correct judgment

61. Churchill, *The Hinge of Fate*, 689.

of it depends the peace and future of mankind."[62] There is a whole vast sphere in which individuals and states act from emotions and fears.

It has been said that if men wish strongly enough for the goal they seek, they will realize it whatever the obstacles. At another pole of political experience, others maintain that nothing as destructive as war and tyranny is possible in the benign universe of modernity. Such projections of sentiment and passion stand in the pathway of accurate prophecy. If passions confound the political leader, it is ignorance that limits his judgment. In Churchill's words: "The facts may be unknown at the time, and estimates of them must be largely guesswork, coloured by the general feeling and aims of whoever is trying to pronounce."[63] This is the most crucial problem of political prediction, for "in considering the future, one is on much less certain ground . . . because we do not know all the facts, and it is foolish to prophesy unless they are known."[64]

Infinitely more complicated than knowing the facts of the case, tenuous as that may be, is perceiving the possible consequences of action. The supreme irony of history is the fact that rational and well-conceived policies have produced evil results while faltering and uncertain policies have brought success. Churchill called attention to this truth, saying: "The majestic events of history and the homely incidents of daily life alike show how vainly man strives to control his fate. Even his greatest neglects or failures may bring him good. Even his greatest achievements may work him ill."[65] The mystery and fullness of life constitute its drama, causing Churchill to reflect: "How little can we foresee the consequences either of wise or unwise action, of virtue or of malice! Without this measureless and perpetual uncertainty, the drama of human life would be destroyed."[66] When some social scientists are reminded of the limits of knowledge, they grow irate and impatient; their attempts to factor

62. London *Daily Telegraph and Morning Post*, April 14, 1947.
63. Churchill, *The Gathering Storm*, 319–20.
64. *Parliamentary Debates*, Vol 434, March 12, 1947, pp. 1352–53.
65. Churchill, *Marlborough*, V, 157.
66. Churchill, *The Gathering Storm*, 201.

out the imponderables of life, however, have added little to human understanding.

All the other difficulties inherent in forecasting political developments are capped by the baffling role that fortune and chance play throughout history. The fate of whole peoples may be suspended on a mere thread of history; even a mild wind of chance may transform a nation's destiny. During the war Churchill commented on France's fate: "The manner of the fall of France was decided on June 16 by a dozen chances, each measured by a hair's breadth." [67] These four factors—passion, ignorance, consequences, and chance—forced him to the conclusion:

It is not given to human beings, happily for them, for otherwise life would be intolerable, to foresee or to predict to any large extent the unfolding course of events. In one phase men seem to have been right, in another they seem to have been wrong. Then again, a few years later, when the perspective of time has lengthened, all stands in a different setting. There is a new proportion. There is another scale of values. History with its flickering lamp stumbles along the trail of the past, trying to reconstruct its scenes, to revive its echoes and kindle with pale gleams the passion of former days. What is the worth of all this? The only guide to a man is his conscience; the only shield to his memory is the rectitude and sincerity of his actions. [68]

Many Western thinkers, whether liberals or modernists, religionists or rationalists, reject Churchill's conception of the future. They insist that the statesman must have a clear vision of the future if he is to lead and not follow. On March 14, 1945, the *Christian Century* quoted Churchill as saying: "It is a mistake to look too far ahead. Only one link in the chain of destiny can be handled at will." [69] His attitude incited the religious editiorialist to write:

The world of imponderables at which Mr. Churchill permitted himself to take one awe-struck glance provided the real explanation why both his address and that of the President contained so little real news. Each filled in details concerning the agreements reached at the Crimean conference. Each pointed toward the next step to be taken at San Francisco. But nei-

67. Churchill, *Their Finest Hour*, 221.
68. *Parliamentary Debates*, Vol. 365, November 12, 1940, p. 1617.
69. "Decision in the Dark," *Christian Century*, LXII (March 14, 1945), 328.

ther asked or answered the great questions on which the future of civilization depends. Their silence can mean only that neither knows what to expect as the nations they lead take one stride after another down an unknown road. They lead, but are themselves led.[70]

Yet when historians look back to developments since 1945, who would question whether Chruchill or the editorial writer best understood the future?

Furthermore, the unreliability of predictions is greatest in proportion to the vastness of the problem being surveyed. In 1939, Churchill, in weighing the prospects of war, sought to narrow analysis to three basic factors contributing to the likelihood—or unlikelihood—of war. By reducing the scope of the question, he was enabled to judge with greater accuracy the likelihood of war, but significantly he had little to say about the timing of the outbreak of conflict:

During the present year, three things have become evident: First, the two dictators cannot long go on as they are; second, they cannot reform or submit to a rebuff without exposing themselves to mortal internal danger, and, third, they are henceforth going to be confronted with organized resistance. Here again there is a conjunction of facts and tendencies from which it is rather difficult to see any outcome.

While all those processes are visibly in train, it is still not possible to predict at what point they may actually explode.[71]

In World War I, Churchill put forward two reasoned estimates of the military situation, unceremoniously rejected at the time, but widely recognized today as masterpieces of political and military clairvoyance. Well-known professional military strategists predicted that Germany's offensive would go unchecked during the first week of fighting. By the second week, France's counterattack would break the backbone of Germany's offensive and force her to retreat sometime between the ninth and thirteenth days. Churchill, whose views were dismissed by professional strategists as those of a dilettante of the Boer War, took exception to these overly sanguine views. He forecast instead that on the twentieth day France would be en-

70. *Ibid.*
71. Winston S. Churchill, "War Now or Never," *Collier's*, CIII (June 3, 1939), 53.

gaged in a full retreat from the Meuse toward Paris and the Germans would be transferring a part of their strength to meet a Russian attack at their rear. In his "silly memorandum" which was roundly denounced by the general staff, Churchill maintained that the French could strike back no earlier than the fortieth day. Looking back, no other document in the archives of World War I predicted so accurately the course of events. By the twenty-first day, France was heavily in retreat which was not reversed in the offensive of the Marne until the forty-first or forty-second day.[72] An "utterly amateur legend" was therefore either a fortuitous accident or a brilliant evaluation in the science of estimating military situations.

On yet another occasion in the war, Churchill prepared a secret memorandum on the commitments and casualties of the Battle of the Somme. Circulated among military authorities by his friend Lord Birkenhood, Churchill's estimate of enemy losses was dismissed by responsible leaders as fatalistic amateur guesswork. He estimated that losses were in the ratio of 1 German to 2.23 British. In contest, the commander-in-chief, Sir Douglas Haig, claimed German losses far exceeded those of the Allies. It was later disclosed through the use of official German figures that the ratio was 1 to 2.27. British Headquarters estimated 130,000 Germans were casualties; Churchill estimated 65,000 losses. He further estimated fifteen German divisions were engaged in battle; historians found sixteen divisions had been in action. Subsequently, Churchill's memorandum was employed in a military training exercise at Sandhurst as a model in the use of the deductive process in military calculation.[73]

The same deductive process proved successful in anticipating certain probabilities and tendencies in the political field. As early as September 5, 1943, the prime minister forecast that it was "inevitable that Russia will be the greatest land power in the world after this war, which will have rid her of the two military Powers, Japan

72. Rene Kraus, *Winston S. Churchill: A Biography* (Philadelphia: J. B. Lippincott, 1940), 163–64.
73. *Ibid.*, 224–25.

and Germany, who in our lifetime have inflicted upon her such heavy defeats."[74] Churchill evidently had a kind of sixth sense on political issues, or more likely the same comprehension of the underlying sources of conflict that guided one of his followers in a prediction about Korea. On October 23, 1946, Brigadier Fitzroy Maclean revealed: "I have just come back from a visit to Korea, and I must say that I found the situation there singularly disquieting; even by present-day standards. Korea has been the occasion of at least two wars in the last half century and it is now . . . well on the way to becoming, once again, a powder magazine which the slightest spark will set off."[75] In less than four years, Maclean's prediction came true.

On September 23, 1949, a presidential announcement from Washington announced that an atomic explosion had occurred in the Soviet Union. Most American leaders had confidently predicted that Russian scientists were unlikely to produce the bomb until well in the 1950s. On November 7, 1945, in concluding a speech before Parliament in which he had assessed the deterrent effect of the United States monopoly of the atomic bomb, Churchill had predicted: "How long, we may ask, is it likely that this advantage will rest with the United States? In the Debate on the Address, I hazarded the estimate that it would be three or four years. According to the best information I have been able to obtain, I see no reason to alter that estimate."[76]

No one should imagine that Churchill's clairvoyance was consistently maintained or that his judgments were always without errors. On political questions outside the ken of his experience where the novelties were greater, he was frequently wholly mistaken. He predicted on March 6, 1947, that Nehru and his followers in India would be unable to carry on for more than a year or two, warning: "In handing over the Government of India to these so-called politi-

74. Churchill, "Prime Minister to Field Marshal Smuts," September 5, 1943, *Closing the Ring*, 129.
75. *Parliamentary Debates*, Vol. 427, October 23, 1946, pp. 1697–89.
76. *Parliamentary Debates*, Vol. 415, November 7, 1945, p. 1297.

cal classes we are handing over to men of straw, of whom, in a few years, no trace will remain."[77] He also guessed that the refugee problem in Israel would present few difficulties, proclaiming: "I do not think we shall find—I make this prediction—that there will be, once fighting stops and some kind of partition is arranged, any difficulty in the great bulk of the present refugees returning to do work essential to the growing prosperity and development of the Jewish settlement in Palestine."[78]

Nevertheless, measuring his record against that of his contemporaries or judging him alongside those who gaily anticipated an easy and harmonious postwar relation with the Soviet Union, we find that he towers above them all. The most instructive of his opinions is the estimate he advanced on September 5, 1943, concerning the type of balance-of-power arrangement that would be essential in the postwar world for the maintenance of peace. During an era of unprecedented good feeling with the Russians, he warned: "I hope, however, that the 'fraternal association' of the British Commonwealth and the United States, together with sea and air power, may put us on . . . balance with Russia at least for the period of rebuilding."[79]

Statesmen may well be blinded by national biases and prejudices when it comes to forecasting their own future. A final test of Churchill's political judgment requires the assessment of his prophecy that:

The British nation will rise again, if not to its former pre-eminence, at least in solid and lasting strength.

As I said at Fulton: "Half a century from now, there will be at least 80,000,000 of Britons spread about the globe, united in defence of our traditions, our way of life, and of the world themes to which we and the United States have long been faithful."[80]

77. *Parliamentary Debates*, Vol. 434, March 6, 1947, p. 174.
78. *Parliamentary Debates*, Vol. 460, January 26, 1949, p. 960.
79. Churchill, "Prime Minister to Field Marshall Smuts," September 5, 1943, *Closing the Ring*, 129.
80. London *Daily Telegraph and Morning Post*, April 15, 1947.

PART THREE

Statesmanship, Public Opinion, and

Politics

"Circumstances alone decide whether a correct conventional manoeuvre is right or wrong. The circumstances include all the factors which are at work at the time; the numbers and quality of the troops and their morale, their weapons, their confidence in their leaders, the character of the country, the condition of the roads, time, and the weather: and behind these the politics of their states, the special interests which each army has to guard, together with many other complications. And it is the true comprehension at any given moment of the dynamic sum of all these constantly shifting forces that constitutes military genius.

"The problem can seldom be calculated on paper alone, and never copied from examples of the past. Its highest solution must be evolved from the eye and brain and soul of a single man, which from hour to hour are making subconsiously all the unweighable adjustments, no doubt with many errors, but with an ultimate practical accuracy."

CHAPTER FIVE

The Tradition of Statesmanship

Churchill's conception of international politics was rooted, as we have seen, in the tradition of nineteenth-century diplomacy and statecraft. Equally, his opinions of the proper role of the individual statesman and leader revealed an attachment to the traditions and values of aristocratic world politics. For him, however, this approach had different consequences than commonly accompany veneration of the past. Loyalty to history's heroes, culture, and decorum characteristically generate attitudes of weary indifference toward the present and paralysis of the capacity to act. Because Churchill's sympathy for the past centered not on the accidents of nineteenth-century leadership and letters but on the fundamentals of international politics, he never yielded to disillusionment with the present. Churchill viewed political leadership in the tradition of the British philosopher Edmund Burke. For Churchill as for Burke, the tasks of the leader are practical and immediate. His first duty was to the nation. He must strive to safeguard the national interest, whatever the means required. In deciding whether or not to create and strengthen political alliances or abandon them, his sole standard must be whether or not his actions served the national interest. To be effective, statesmanship must rest on established principles and constraints rather than on passion or sentiment. One such principle is the axiom that nations have no permanent friends, only permanent interests, a principle that often offends popular democratic sentiments.

The aristocratic conception of politics is at its core eminently practical and prudential. Its first rule is that the practice of politics cannot be equated with the principles of philosophy. Whereas the ideals of political philosophy may sometimes be approximated in politics, they are never fully realized or attained. Although the principles of the philosopher and precepts of the statesman are not the same, the traditionalist learns to live in both realms. This is the clue to Churchill's success in an alien political environment. It would be a counsel of despair to maintain that contemporary society is intolerable and that modern man has no choice but to remain self-alienated and estranged from it. Inspired by a desire for public awards and public attainments, the British aristocracy, whatever its philosophical preferences, fiercely resisted succumbing to political isolation. The aristocratic conception of politics has been so flexible that many British aristocrats have accepted as a high calling participation in politics even under the most unfavorable conditions. They never ceased to regard the stakes of public life as potentially capable of bringing them to the summit of personal attainment. For this reason, leaders drawn from the British aristocracy played the game of politics seemingly with abandon and oftentimes with unrivaled skill. At their best, they judiciously blended political expediency with solicitude for the welfare of other groups. Some of their success, while denounced by critics as desperate and cynical opportunism, provides striking examples of the union of political wisdom and moral judgment. Both Disraeli and Churchill's father, Lord Randolph Churchill, helped fashion the essential doctrines of Tory democracy, with its principles of liberal conservatism by which the Tory gentry in England sought to beguile the proletariat away from the liberal middle class and more recently the working class from the Socialist party. Their policies were inspired by the facts of the immediate political situation. The enactment of practical programs of social reform and unemployment assistance illustrates the prudent magnanimity of the Tory gentry and their calculated concern for the mass of common men. The more effective Conservatives were led to take the broadest and most liberal view of their own rational self-interest. The aristocratic preference for politics by the gifted and talented few and their basic aversion to mass government by clerks, economists, and calculators kept them close to the marketplace of British domestic politics.

This rather antiquarian conception of politics has implications for the theory of leadership which go beyond the behavior of the British gentry. The concept of the leader in modern democratic societies is epitomized in the sensitive yet half-tragic figure of the present-day "practical politician" who takes soundings of the swift-running tides of public opinion in order to discover whither he is going to lead the people. What such a conception of popular leadership gains in responsiveness to rapid shifts in public opinion, it can lose in the quality of bold and creative leadership. To make the leader an impersonal instrument whose movements do no more than register successive waves of public sentiment is to run the risk of transforming the statesman, whose politics comprise the whole man, into the less noble figure of the crafty politician whose talents and virtues remain at least partly dormant and unused. It may be that this is the inevitable price of modern mass politics. If so, the cost of the tradeoff should not go unnoticed.

One concrete manifestation of the deterioration of personal political leadership in our day has been the disappearance of private memoirs written with a sense of intellectual growth, moral cultivation, and high literary taste. If contemporary public figures tell their story at all, they do so in the form of notes containing gossip and racy disclosure. Even the best of them seem aimed at disclosing the worst in their colleagues and adversaries and the best in themselves. It is not unfair to say that men whose full character and personalities have been fragmented and obscured in politics are unlikely to rediscover themselves in writing their memoirs. Churchill, as a member of that school of statesmen who traditionally conceived of themselves as representing an aristocracy of talents, suffered fewer inhibitions in chronicling history. The distinguished British novelist C. S. Forester appraised Churchill's contributions as leader and historian in a review for the *Atlantic Monthly*, noting:

Mr. Churchill occupies a special position and is under a special responsibility as a writer of English prose. In millennia to come, his work will be studied as we now study Thucydides and Tacitus, as source books of incomparable value. He is happily devoid of the almost morbid self-consciousness which restrains most of his contemporaries from employing eloquence, for fear lest they fall into rhetoric, and he will use on occasion an exalted phrasing entirely compatible with his theme and with the emotions both of himself and his reader. The sheer beauty of some of his passages is admirably set off by the directness and common sense of his parallel commentary.[1]

1. C. S. Forester, "Winston Churchill, Leader and Historian," *Atlantic Monthly*, CLXXXII (July, 1948), 95.

Such talents, which even Churchill's critics recognized, were realized and strengthened in the "school of the leader." In classical theory, it was postulated that political wisdom was attainable through the arduous process of moral and intellectual self-development. Churchill's development illustrates such an evolution. As a subaltern in India, he absorbed the stately prose of Gibbon and Macaulay, conceived his ideas of the state and its leaders from Plato and Aristotle, evaluated the profound social implications for our time of Darwin and Malthus, and blended them all into a version of man and politics that became uniquely his own. His words brought back echoes of master stylists, but the sonorous notes and surging tides of his grand public pronouncements also created new images meaningful in the present instead of merely reflecting memories of the past. Few leaders in the aristocratic tradition possess the qualities of the statesman in the same generous proportions as Churchill.

The sources for evaluating his political philosophy are therefore more ample and trustworthy than most private papers and public statements. We take it for granted that what he said on major issues is more than a rationalization of private interests. Therefore, we can take him at his word when he declared:

Again I rely upon the series of my directives, telegrams and minutes, which owe their importance and interest to the moment in which they were written, and which I could not write in better words now. These original documents were dictated by me as events broke upon us. As they are my own composition, written at the time, it is by these that I prefer to be judged. It would be easier to produce a series of afterthoughts when the answers to all the riddles were known, but I must leave this to the historians.[2]

Nevertheless, Churchill was unwilling to describe his volumes of *The Second World War* as true history. Instead, he preferred to regard them as his "contribution." It was characteristic of the ancients that their discourses on abstract principles took the form of a

2. Winston S. Churchill, "Prime Minister to Dominions Secretary," March 4, 1942, *The Second World War*, Vol. IV, *The Hinge of Fate* (Boston: Houghton Mifflin, 1950), *v.*

dialogue. In this form, philosophy was cast in direct and personal comments by private individuals. As the vertical dimension of general principles crossed and intersected the horizon of concrete personal experiences, truth was revealed and illuminated. Thus Churchill's narrative and his analysis of grand political events has followed the thread of men's personal experiences. For him, the dimension of existence called politics was concrete and heroic. In his chronicle on World War II forces and laws of history and politics appear, but they take form and derive their meaning from the individual's experiences. In his defense, Churchill would have argued that the one realm about which he was best informed was his own experience. So he wrote a dramatic account in which he stood forth as the chief actor.

In commentary on domestic and international politics, Churchill expressed opposition to those powerful forces and tendencies that have reduced the leader to a bit of hapless driftwood tossed about on the tides of public opinion. In domestic politics, he repeatedly confessed his personal disagreement with both historic parties. He referred with pride to his disdain for the pacifists during the great wars and his contempt for the jingoists after the conflicts. His strategy changed with each successive challenge. In war, his motto was resolution and unflagging courage; in victory, magnanimity; and in peace, goodwill. These standards were as personal and concrete in their implications as Wilson's fourteen principles were impersonal, abstract, and remote. Churchill's public and historic policies expressed the central commitments of his being and character moreso than most American and Western contemporaries. His version of international statesmanship presumed a broad public mandate in the conduct of diplomatic affairs with discretion to serve himself and his people as wisely as he could and not simply mirror their every fleeting impulse. In his tasks, the statesman must display certain fundamental moral virtues—to a consideration of which we now turn.

Moderation has long been seen as a traditional virtue of the statesman. Only when all sides give evidence of self-restraint can the political process flow on without untimely interruption. Therefore, one test of the statesman is his capacity for saying less than he might have said in a given crisis. After the Quebec Conference in 1943, Churchill reflected upon the content of a radio report he prepared, saying: "There was so much to say and not to say in the broadcast."[3] A dictum that the statesman must cherish is epitomized in the slogan "don't say everything" on the vital issues of the day. Shortly after the British elections in 1951, *The Times* editorialized: "If Mr. Churchill did not try to deal with the obvious weaknesses in the plans of the North Atlantic Treaty Organization or with the criticism made by General Eisenhower in Rome, no doubt he wishes to wait until his meeting with President Truman and the American defense chiefs in Washington."[4] Such a posture was novel for Americans, who have come to expect a steady stream of *ex cathedra* proclamations by prominent leaders on every aspect of vital current issues. Churchill maintained a carefully considered reticence on many of the most important issues of the day. In part, his political practice can be explained by the maturity and sanity of British politics. It may also reflect aristocratic politics, which recognizes more clearly than liberalism the subtleties and ambiguities of politics. Another more fundamental cause is the precarious and uncertain place of the leader in mass international politics. The nature of the relationship in modern democracies between the leader who must act on the basis of political realism and mass public opinion buffeted by the irrational pressures of sentiment and emotions creates a dilemma—the dilemma of realist foreign policy steering a course against the impulses and volatility of contemporary public opinion.

3. Winston S. Churchill, "Thoughts on the Fall of Mussolini," *The Second World War,* Vol. V, *Closing the Ring* (Boston: Houghton Mifflin, 1951), 119.
4. London *Times,* November 7, 1951, p. 7.

CHAPTER SIX

Public Opinion and the Dilemma of Realist Foreign Policy

What makes the relationship of realist statesmanship and public opinion so perilous for the future is the compelling force of widespread popular attitudes on foreign policy. It is widely assumed, for example, that the people are more reasonable than their governments. Are not the great mass of the people in every country unalterably opposed to war? The crux of the problem, however, is that popular reactions have little to do with the peace-loving traits of the great mass of the people. Public opinion in the short run tends to be corrupted by purveyors of deceptively simple and attractive slogans and panaceas or by the influence of politicians who mislead by identifying their selfish interests with the aspirations of the whole nation. The credo of Western liberal democracy that truth will ultimately win out in the marketplace of ideas is limited in two crucial respects in international issues. First, the liberal faith anticipates that this victory will be won as truth proves its superiority in the long run. However, the crises of international politics follow close on the heels of one another and special-interest groups force decisions by pressing for immediate action and short-run solutions. Second and more fundamental, the nature of truth in international affairs has its own peculiar dimensions. The brave and innately wise masses of the people must reach decisions within a sphere where the characteristic supports of the democratic system are absent. On issues in foreign policy, the people must make choices in a realm in which law is weak and ineffective, whereas domestic experience is grounded in the relative certainties of Anglo-American law. Moreover, there are no common moral standards in world politics, whereas domestically rivalries are blunted, limited, and resolved through the acceptance of common values. The broad outlines of a tragic dilemma are visible in the differences between the two situations. In foreign affairs, the great, good-hearted and collectively shrewd public is thrust abruptly into a strange new environment. It can succeed in distinguishing the truth only with immense difficulty. Realist answers are poor competitors in such a marketplace—complicated, morally ambiguous, and easily distorted. The recipes and formulas of utopians and demagogues are bold, militant, emotional, and, as a rule, emotionally satisfying. Panaceas offer immediate salvation to desperate souls who in their craving for certainty are susceptible to simple solutions which appear to dispose of all their problems.

How is the statesman whose proposals for the nation are realistic in character to deal with this dilemma? He may offer his policies on their merits and trust that the people will accept them. If he hopes for their early adoption, he usually is driven to some form of idealistic appeal to the people. In coming to terms with a public whose resistance to realistic policies can be overcome only by casting them in moralistic molds, the statesman is driven to new modes of popular diplomacy which in previous eras were not required.

If these impressions about the dilemma of political realism are substantially true, their test ought to come with the statesmanship of Churchill. For if anyone dared to confront the public with unpalatable truths and to challenge popular illusions, it was obviously Churchill. If anyone could remain immune to the ravages of the tyranny of the majority's way of looking at world affairs, one would expect it would have been Churchill. Indeed, there is good and ample evidence that frequently he espoused unpopular causes and championed programs that were wholly out of tune with public sentiments. He repeatedly warned the British people as early as 1945, on the eve of their great victory, that Britain's postwar position would have to be subordinate to the United States. He challenged and criticized the diplomatic make-believe and self-satisfied idolatry of the United Nations by those who imagined that the new organization had overnight replaced world politics. And he preached untiringly that peace could not be preserved by pious sentiments embodied in universal documents like the Charter of the United Nations or the Pact of Paris (the Kellogg-Briand Pact outlawing wars of aggression). At the same time, he recognized the value of documents such as the Atlantic Charter in temporarily uniting allies in war.

On the defense of vital policies for which he was responsible and whose acceptance hinged on his skill and tactics, he hesitated not for one moment in appealing to the public in moralistic terms. No better illustration can be offered than the debate concerning the Yalta Agreement, particularly as it concerned Poland's eastern boundary. In that debate we can observe, stripped of all side issues or extraneous points, the real and inevitable conflict between political realism and the need for public support. This crisis graphically illustrates the dual aspect of the problem. It provides a sample of Churchill's moralistic formulation of a policy whose sole justification was to be found in realistic terms. And secondly, it illustrates the counter arguments, on the one hand, of those utopians who found his idealism too mild and, on the other hand, of fellow realists who disapproved of his use of moralistic justifications.

Yalta: The Clash of Moralism and Realism

In his opening speech in the first debate over Yalta, Churchill, as Britain's responsible executive, endeavored to show that Yalta was a political settlement grounded in moral principles which assured the rights of every party to the agreement. He said: "The Russian claim has always been unchanged for the Curzon Line in the East. . . . I have never concealed from the House that, personally, I think the Russian claim is just and right. If I champion this frontier for Russia, it is not because I bow to force. It is because I believe it is the fairest division of territory that can in all the circumstances be made between the two countries whose history has been so intermingled."[1] He added that the Curzon Line had been drawn at a time when Russia had few friends among the Allies. It had been drawn in 1919 by an expert commission on which one of Britain's most distinguished diplomats, Sir Eyre Crow, had served. (Stalin had de-

1. *Parliamentary Debates* (Hansard) House of Commons, Fifth Series, Vol. 408, February 27, 1945 (London: His Majesty's Stationery Office, 1950), 1275.

fended the Yalta settlement with a similar claim.) The circumstances at the time and personalities involved made it unlikely that the Russians were shown any undue favor. Therefore, Churchill concluded his defense:

Finally, under the world organization, all nations great and small, victors and vanquished will be secured against aggression by indisputable law and by overwhelming international force. The published Crimea Agreement is not a ready-made plan imposed by the great Powers on the Polish people. It sets out the agreed views of the three major Allies on the means whereby their common desire to see a strong, free, independent Poland may be fulfilled in co-operation with the Poles themselves, and whereby a Polish Government which all the United Nations can recognise, may be set up in Poland.[2]

If Churchill expected to allay what *The Times* frequently called the hagridden fears of the problem of power of the more utopian members of Parliament, his hopes proved short-lived. Sir William Beveridge of Berwick upon Tweed rose immediately to condemn the prime minister's approach:

We have to stick to principle. We have to stick to principle in international affairs, and if it happens that one cannot both stick to one's friends and stick to principle, one must stick to principle; because principles even if they appear for the moment to be unreasonable, may change and become reasonable. Opportunism, appeasement, self-regarding policies, power politics, all lead to the grave of all our hopes.[3]

Other members charged that Britain as the trustee of Poland must not make concessions to the Soviet Union. If expediency were to guide foreign policy, Britain would be no better than Nazi Germany; World War II would have been fought in vain. Commander Sir Archibald Southby sought to bring his wayward colleagues back to moral principle when he declared: "With much of the Yalta Agreement I am in accord, but if our foreign policy is to be based upon expediency and not upon principles then it is bound to fail,

2. *Ibid.*, 1278.
3. *Ibid.*, 1315.

and I cannot in honour express my confidence in it . . . I hold that there is a greater loyalty than that which we owe to any one man, Government or party—the loyalty to those fundamental ideals of justice, liberty and honour to uphold which we have twice in our lifetime seen the British sword drawn."[4]

Churchill came under fire from critics in another camp. The British statesman whose views we cited at the beginning of our study challenged Churchill within the framework of the prime minister's own philosophy. Captain Thorneycroft, whose operative approach to international politics was an exact replica of his leader's, asserted:

I do not regard the Polish settlement as an act of justice. It may be right or wrong, it may be wise or foolish, but at any rate it is not justice as I understand the term. It is not the sort of situation . . . [before] a disinterested body . . . in which the strength and power of one of the parties is never allowed to weigh in the balance. The sooner we recognize that we are a long way from that sort of thing happening the better.[5]

And Lord Dunglass of Lanark, continuing along on a similar course, declared:

the Prime Minister is right about the territorial settlement. The Russians have never receded for one moment, from the view that what they have taken, they will keep. . . . I feel rather different from some other members about this territorial matter. I believe that if you try to force what is an act of power, within the framework of the Atlantic Charter, you will not whitewash the act but you will break the Charter. When the Prime Minister says that he accepts this as an act of justice, I must take a fundamentally opposite view. We have dozens of times in our history accepted this kind of an arrangement as a fact of power.[6]

Another member, Mr. Raikes (Essex, South-East), said:

The most eloquent speech [by Captain Thorneycroft] . . . did not base it on justice; with great honesty he said he thought it was an unjust settle-

4. *Ibid.*, February 29, 1945, p. 1437.
5. *Ibid.*, 1456–57.
6. *Ibid.*, February 27, 1945, p. 1300.

ment. . . . [Mr. H. Nicolson] in rather gentler language agreed with him. One thing is certain; however great the vote may be to-day, it will not be able to go out that all who voted for the motion voted for it because they believe that the motion was just. Well may the Prime Minister say, like Channing, "Save, oh save me, from my candid friends."[7]

Lord Dunglass supplied the kind of profound political analysis which Churchill might himself have offered had he been cast in a different role:

It would be comfortable to believe that relationships between different communities of men were always governed by reason, but the reality as history reveals it, is that the governing principle is that of power. Power has not been destroyed in this war; it has been redistributed. It is still there. It is still used. . . . Any settlement at this time must take account of it.

I think a valid criticism of the peace settlement of 1919 was that it allowed too much for the triumph of reason, and too little for the fact of power. While all that is true, yet it is also true to say that the world can never pass from the old order of the rule of force to the new order of the rule of law, except by way of a period during which the Great Powers themselves are willing, and are seen to be willing, to exercise restraint in the use of power. The position in post-war Europe will be a state of great power and great weakness side by side, and that does not lead to stability. One reason why there is world concern over the differences between Russia and Poland, is because it is the first case, a test case, in the relationship between a Great Power wielding great military might and her smaller and weaker neighbour.[8]

Such exchanges in a brilliantly instructive debate if taken together dramatize the tensions which exist between realism, idealism, and public opinion.

The Yalta example also demonstrates that policies which are founded on realistic principles but require support by large groups of people for whom they are alien concepts must be reformulated in simple moralistic terms. The impact of public opinion on the realistic conduct of foreign policy takes on a dual character. The influ-

7. *Ibid.*, February 28, 1945, p. 1491.
8. *Ibid.*, February 27, 1945, p. 1305.

ence of domestic public opinion is well known and we have considered some of its implications. In addition, pressures from public opinion in other countries play an important role. Churchill has been confronted repeatedly with attacks from moralistic critics and detractors not only in England but also in the United States and the Soviet Union. Criticisms of his Fulton speech developed despite his effort to anticipate them by forming, as he said, his propositions in mild, mellifluous, carefully shaped, and guarded statements. The kind of general criticism that originated overseas and especially in the United States was illustrated in a *Christian Century* article which concluded: "No one doubts that his magnificent courage will continue to be equal to whatever demands are made upon it, but the situation into which the world is now passing so swiftly demands more than courage. It requires a contemporary mind, not a mentality steeped in the imperial ideology of the eighteenth-century. More than all else, it calls for principles which place people above politics, humanity above the vanishing glories of empire." [9] From the opposite pole in the East-West struggle, *Pravda* in 1948 assailed him for the destruction of abstract moral principles: "He openly proclaims power politics, which must be realized by any Anglo-American military alliance. To whom is it not clear that all of this, as a matter of fact, means nothing else than the liquidation of the United Nations Organization? So with another stroke he settles with an organization which he in his capacity of an ardent defender championed." [10] Within Britain, Ernest Bevin declared: "As atomic energy evolves . . . the necessity of its use as a weapon will have disappeared by reason of the new world organisation. . . . I have already said that power politics, spheres of influence, and that kind of approach to world affairs do present great difficulties." [11]

In a certain sense, the need to justify policies in crusading and semi-religious language is demeaning for the statesman. To think of foreign policy as a commodity which must be sold to the public

9. "A Future Without Churchill," *Christian Century*, LXII (January 31, 1945), 134.
10. *Pravda*, March 11, 1948, quoted in New York *Times*, March 12, 1946, p. 4.
11. *Parliamentary Debates*, Vol. 415, November 7, 1945, p. 1337.

hardly accords with the tradition of leaders as stewards of the public interest. Yet there is truth in the proposition that foreign policy must be marketable. The necessity of rallying domestic support and of answering overseas critics required Churchill, more than once, to defend himself and his nation in the most resounding moralistic tones. In January, 1945, he declaimed:

We seek no territory; we covet no oil fields; we demand no bases. . . . We do not set ourselves up in rivalry of bigness or might with any other community in the world. . . . We have given, and shall continue to give, everything we have. We ask nothing in return except that consideration and respect which is our due, and if that were denied us we should still have a good conscience. Let none, therefore, in our own Commonwealth or in the outside world misname us or traduce our motives. Our actions are no doubt subject to human error, but our motives in small things as in great are disinterested, lofty and true. I repulse those calumnies, wherever they come from, that Britain and the British Empire is a selfish, power-greedy, land-greedy, designing nation obsessed by dark schemes of European intrigue or colonial expansion. I repulse these aspersions whether they come from our best friends or worst foes.[12]

He answered the critics of Britain's policy in Greece in similiar tones:

What do we seek in Greece? Do we want anything from Greece? What part do they play in our so-called power politics? How much does it matter to us from a national point of view, what form their government takes? I repeat: we want nothing from Greece but her friendship, and, to earn that and deserve that, we have to do our duty. . . . Whatever they decide, Monarchy or Republic, Left or Right, that shall be their law, as far as we are concerned. When I see all the fury expended on this subject, and when we are abused, without one shadow of truth, as if we wanted some islands or bases from Greece, as if we needed their aid to keep ourselves alive, I feel added anxiety for the future.[13]

Lest anyone concluded that this euphemistic statement regarding Greece represented Churchill's considered view of Greece's impor-

12. *Parliamentary Debates*, Vol. 407, January 18, 1945, pp. 426–27.
13. *Ibid.*, 407–408.

tance to Britain, we need only remember that the same British leader negotiated a percentage agreement with Stalin which gave Britain a 90 percent influence in Greece. Greece was essential to Britain in securing lines of communication in the eastern Mediterranean. In December of 1944, when Churchill and Sir Pierson Dixon visited Greece, communist forces (ELAS) had engulfed the whole of Greece outside Athens. When Britain intervened, Stalin remained passive in recognition of the sphere-of-influence agreement.

Of all his appeals to the moral sense of the ordinary citizen, none was more successful than Churchill's drawing on the wellsprings of British patriotism. No one displayed more consummate skill in tapping the sources of nationalism. By his inspiring wartime leadership, he wrote an enduring chapter in Britain's long history indelibly etched on its people's memories. No Englishman of the time could ever forget his description of the British effort in World War II: "With blood and tears they will bear forward faithfully and gloriously the ark that enshrines the title deeds of the good commonwealth of mankind." [14] No Western leader has been more successful in merging the moral commitments and political interests of a nation than Churchill in Britain's "finest hour."

Unconditional Surrender and the Balkans

Modern social science has thrown into question the belief that mere words are a key to a man's standards and motives. Socioeconomic theories derived from Karl Marx and Max Weber question the value of examining the words of a leader because words are said to be little more than rationalizations of private or group interests. This fashionable social science view obscures a profoundly subtle relationship between political rhetoric and ultimate beliefs. A leader who engages in serious political thought is unlikely wholly to obscure his deeper convictions. Specifically, in the present study we may find embedded in commonplace statements by Churchill the best clues to his philosophy and his thinking. This is not to deny

14. Winston S. Churchill, "War Now or Never," *Collier's*, CIII (June 3, 1939), 54.

that however important a man's words may be, his deeds remain the most enduring test of his philosophy. There is often a yawning gulf separating what statesmen say and what they do. In Churchill's wartime policy, we discover two striking examples of the inescapable tension between theory and action or between responses to the demands of realism and public opinion.

Unconditional Surrender. The first example of a seeming contradiction between theory and practice in Churchill's foreign policy is on the question of "unconditional surrender." The wisest students of international politics have long maintained that the most basic problem in Soviet-American relations was the problem of Germany. The lack of stable political conditions in the heart of Europe has provided a continuing invitation to powerful neighbors with expansionist policies. With the deterioration of German power following World War II, a power vacuum developed alongside the massive concentration of Soviet and satellite power. Historically, the juxtaposition of great power and great weakness has always produced conditions making for potential world tension. In the past, executors of foreign policy have sedulously sought to avoid political vacuums. Throughout the history of modern international relations, policy makers have tried to anticipate what nation was most likely to constitute the next threat to the peace. World War II, it is frequently said, was not waged in this spirit. Historians point to the policy of "unconditional surrender" as the most convincing evidence that Allied leaders were not sufficiently aware of the political consequences of the elimination of German power as an historic counterforce to Russian expansion. The war was fought exclusively for military objectives, and General Omar Bradley in all candor declared: "We were less concerned with postwar political alignments than destruction of what remained of the German Army. . . . As soldiers we looked naïvely on this British inclination to complicate the war with political foresight and non-military objectives."[15]

In England the criticism of unconditional surrender began with

15. General Omar Bradley, *A Soldier's Story* (New York: Henry Holt and Company, 1951), 528, 536.

the Labor party's charge that this policy eliminated all German leadership and authority and left the allies without anyone with whom they could deal in Germany. As late as July 21, 1949, the foreign secretary, Ernest Bevin, declared:

> It began [the policy for Germany] with the declaration at Casablanca of unconditional surrender on which the British Cabinet, or any other Cabinet, never had a chance to say a word. But it did leave us a Germany without a law, without a Constitution, and without a single person to deal with, and without a single institution to grapple with the problems. We have had to build absolutely from the bottom with nothing at all. We have had to build a state with 20,000,000 displaced persons scattered about.[16]

There were three parts to Bevin's criticism. He appeared to be saying: (1) the policy of "unconditional surrender" was the cornerstone of a policy for Germany which created a political vacuum; (2) no British cabinet was asked to approve or reject this policy; and (3) by implication, the Allies had alternatives that were more desirable and rational than this ill-fated policy.

Churchill, responding to the attack, set about answering his critic on all three counts both in public and parliamentary speeches and in his history of the war. At first he replied to Bevin, admittedly on the spur of the moment, saying:

> The first time I heard that phrase [unconditional surrender] used was from the lips of President Roosevelt. . . .
>
> It was made by President Roosevelt without consultation with me. I was there on the spot, and I had very rapidly to consider whether the state of our position in the world was such as would justify me in not giving support to it.
>
> I did give support . . . but that was not the idea which I had formed in my own mind. . . . If the British Cabinet had considered that phrase, it is likely that they would have advised against it, but working with a great alliance and with . . . friends from across the ocean we had to accommodate ourselves.[17]

Hence his first answer was that while a policy of "unconditional surrender" was hardly one he would himself have contrived, he was

16. *Parliamentary Debates*, Vol. 467, July 21, 1949, p. 1585.
17. *Ibid.*, 1585–86.

forced to go along in the interests of Allied unity when it was presented to him by President Roosevelt. Later he reviewed the argument that this phrase prolonged the war by compelling the enemy to forego thoughts of surrender in resistance to tyranny. As part of a general defense of Allied Policy, he rejected this hypothesis. He found support from Allen W. Dulles (the author of *Germany's Underground*), who undertook to show that resistance movements within Germany were disorganized, uncoordinated, and unable, because of the extent of totalitarian controls, to launch successful opposition to the Nazis. However, there were many in the Parliament, including members of both parties, who found Churchill's answer unconvincing.

Bevin mounted his attack in the early summer of 1949. By late autumn, Churchill had reconsidered his first, hastily formulated reply. On November 17, 1949, he explained:

The right hon. Gentleman raised this matter . . . and on the spur of the moment I said that the first time I heard the words "unconditional surrender"—in regard, of course, to the late war—was when the President used them in his speech to the Press Conference at Casablanca. This was the impression which had been left in my mind and which I had expressed to Mr. Robert Sherwood three years before when he raised the point with me in connection with his biography of Mr. Harry Hopkins. This impression was confirmed in my mind by what President Roosevelt said himself on the point, which is quoted in the Hopkins biography. This is the quotation: "Suddenly the Press Conference was on, and Winston and I had no time to prepare for it, and the thought popped into my mind that they had called Grant 'Old Unconditional Surrender,' and the next thing I knew, I had said it." [18]

It should be noted that Sherwood did not accept this casual explanation. He argued that the formula had been discussed and accepted by the American Chiefs of Staff in Washington a week before the start of the Casablanca Conference. Historians discovered evidence in the account Churchill subsequently provided that this was the case. He revealed on November 17, 1949, that the "unconditional surrender" had been mentioned at a luncheon with President

18. *Parliamentary Debates*, Vol. 469, November 17, 1949, p. 2217.

Roosevelt and Harry Hopkins and that at the time he had apparently approved:

I have now looked up the telegrams and records of the occasion, and I find that undoubtedly the words "unconditional surrender" were mentioned, probably in informal talks. At any rate, on 19th January, 1942, five days before the end of the Conference, I sent the present Prime Minister, then the Deputy Prime Minister, the following message as part of a long telegram on other matters:

"We propose to draw up a statement of the work of the conference for communication to the Press at the proper time. I should be glad to know what the War Cabinet would think of our including in this statement a declaration of the firm intention of the United States and the British Empire, to continue the war relentlessly until we have brought about the 'unconditional surrender' of Germany and Japan. The omission of Italy would be to encourage a break-up there. The President liked this idea, and it would stimulate our friends in every country."[19]

By the exclusion of Italy from the formula, the prime minister had intended to hasten the overthrow of Mussolini by other Italian forces. On January 21, 1942, Anthony Eden replied for the cabinet, announcing their support of the statement. But in his reply, Eden expressed the sense of the cabinet that Italy should not be excluded from the statement, for the morale of the Italians was more likely to deteriorate if they knew that there would be no slackening of Allied attacks. The cabinet's willingness not only to approve but to extend the concept of unconditional surrender dampened Churchill's enthusiasm for the policy. He recalled:

I have the strong feeling that I cooled off on the point because I did not want to bring Italy into this sphere; and I thought that that would influence the President too. This is borne out by the agreed communiqué which was drafted by the Combined Chiefs of Staff and approved by both of us and which contains no mention of unconditional surrender.[20]

In his history of the war, Churchill further explained that under the pressure of events, especially the vexing problem of relations between the two French leaders Giraud and de Gaulle, Roosevelt and

19. *Ibid.*, 2218.
20. *Ibid.*, 2219.

he turned their attention from any further consideration of "unconditional surrender." And the official communiqué which was prepared by members of their staff made no mention of the phrase. It is significant, Churchill asserted, that the document which contained no reference to "unconditional surrender" was considered and approved by President Roosevelt, the War Cabinet, and himself. The president, however, apparently assumed that his formula had been fully approved; for before the famous press conference at Casablanca he drafted the following statement: "The President and the Prime Minister . . . are more than ever determined that peace can come to the world only by a total elimination of German and Japanese war power. This involves the simple formula of placing the objective of this war in terms of an unconditional surrender by Germany, Italy and Japan."[21]

Churchill reported that on January 24, 1942, the president made his "startling declaration" at the press conference that "unconditional surrender" would be enforced upon all the enemies. It was alleged that this came as a complete surprise to the British and, referring to the document prepared by the members of the staffs as well as the Chiefs of Staff, Churchill explained:

It was natural to suppose that the agreed communiqué had superseded anything said in conversation. General Ismay, who knew exactly how my mind was working from day to day, and was also present at all the discussions of the Chiefs of Staff when the communiqué was prepared, was also surprised. In my speech which followed the President's, I of course supported him and concurred in what he said. Any divergence between us, even by omission, would on such an occasion and at such a time have been damaging or even dangerous to our war effort.[22]

If Churchill accepted the phrase without enthusiasm at the time solely in order to preserve Anglo-American unity, the chronology which followed indicates that it became a program of action that he

21. Quoted in Robert E. Sherwood, *Roosevelt and Hopkins: An Intimate History* (New York: Harper and Brothers, 1948), 696.
22. Winston S. Churchill, *The Second World War*, Vol. IV, *The Hinge of Fate* (Boston: Houghton Mifflin, 1950), 686–87.

never repudiated or abandoned. On June 30, 1943, he referred in a speech at Guild Hall in London to "unconditional surrender" as the essence of the Allied demands upon the Nazi, Fascist, and Japanese tyrannies. He was careful to point out that while this phrase meant that the will of the enemies must be completely broken, it did not mean they would be treated with inhumanity or dealt with from "the lust of vengeance." Moreover, in practice, when Mussolini was defeated Churchill urged that an early effort should be made to reach a general settlement with the Italian nation in order to avoid creating chaos and anarchy. He was anxious that the rescuing powers, Britain and the United States, not dismantle the structure and unity of the Italian state so drastically that there would be no responsible authorities with whom to deal.

One of the most significant statements by Churchill on "unconditional surrender" was his admonition on August 14, 1943, to the foreign secretary that the formula be used with discretion and prudence. There had been frequent mention of it and to this he objected. He observed: "All this is quite true, but it might better have been left unsaid. The displacement of Ribbentrop by von Papen would be a milestone of importance, and would probably lead to further disintegration of the Nazi machine. There is not need for us to discourage this process by continually uttering the slogan "Unconditional Surrender."[23] A gradual breakdown of unity in Germany would mean a weakening of their resistance and a consequent saving of thousands of Allied lives. This should be the supreme object of Allied policy even in pursuing "unconditional surrender."

On several occasions in 1944, Churchill sought to make the distinction between treatment which the Germans would receive as a "right" and that which would be meted out to them by virtue of their humanity by the Allies. On January 14, 1944, he addressed a note to all members of the Big Three, explaining: "By 'unconditional surrender,' I mean that the Germans have no *rights* to any particular form of treatment. For instance, the Atlantic Charter

23. Winston S. Churchill, "Prime Minister to Foreign Secretary," *The Second World War*, Vol. V, *Closing the Ring* (Boston: Houghton Mifflin, 1951), 663.

would not apply to them as *a matter of right*. On the other hand, the victorious nations owe it to themselves to observe the obligations of humanity and civilization."[24] Some critics maintained that an appeal to justice was impossible in warfare. Where there is no mutuality of rights and duties, there could be no true justice. Churchill's conception of the Atlantic Charter was that the members of the Grand Alliance had assumed certain rights and responsibilities essential to the preservation of at least a provisional unity throughout the war.

In concrete terms, Churchill was hopeful of publishing a list of fifty to one hundred German outlaws of first notoriety who would be held for capital punishment at the end of the war. This would serve to reassure the rank and file in Germany that "unconditional surrender" in no way implied mass executions. However, opposition developed, especially from Marshal Stalin, who challenged this stipulation on the grounds that it was far too lenient. The British war leader observed that he was not at all certain that Stalin was serious in his objection or what his motivation might be. (Stalin in fact qualified his opposition in appeals to the Germans.) Again on February 22, 1944, Churchill defined even more specifically what was meant by the phrase "unconditional surrender":

Unconditional surrender means that the victors have a free hand. It does not mean that they are entitled to behave in a barbarous manner, nor that they wish to blot out Germany from among the nations of Europe. If we are bound, we are bound by our own consciences to civilisation. We are not to be bound to the Germans as the result of a bargain struck. That is the meaning of "unconditional surrender."[25]

At the time of this statement, hope persisted that the General Staff, though at that time fully supporting Hitler, might eventually break with him. In January of 1943, a movement surfaced of leading German generals on the Eastern Front to denounce Hitler, but with the announcement of the doctrine of "unconditional sur-

24. Churchill, *The Hinge of Fate*, 689–90.
25. *Parliamentary Debates*, Vol. 397, February 22, 1944, p. 69.

render," their resistance did not mature. If Churchill's personal formulation of the policy was politically inspired, his motivation had
the dual purpose of encouraging moderates abroad without inviting
complacency or slackening of efforts at home. On this point, he
struggled for coherence: "I must find the narrow line between re-
proof of complacency at home and encouragement of the enemy
abroad. . . . Moreover, this should be remembered. There was a
time when we were all alone in this war and when we could speak
for ourselves, but now we are in the closest relation on either side
with our great Allies; every word spoken has to be considered in
relation to them." [26]

In the conduct of war, therefore, the dual aspects of public opinion, about which we have already commented,[27] are present in a
particularly complex and troublesome form. In this case, not general world opinion but the attitudes of the enemy's population were
a limiting factor in determining the appeal to the British population. A balance had to be struck. In rallying the members of the
British Commonwealth to action, Churchill had pledged them to
continue the struggle until "every trace of Hitler's footsteps and
every stain of his infected and corroding fingers had been sponged"
and if necessary, as he said, "blasted from the face of the earth." [28]
Yet even the faintest possibilities of a political convulsion within
Germany led him to reformulate his declarations in order to encourage vital segments of German public opinion. It would, however, be
untrue to leave an impression that Churchill at any time was optimistic or sanguine over the chances of any significant political up-
rising in Germany. His opinion, which he expressed frequently to
Allied authorities, was that the iron control of all German life by
storm troops and secret police had deadened if not destroyed most
of the normal reactions of public opinion. To place much hope or
dependence in popular political uprisings would be to misread the
pulse of the civilian population which through the pervasiveness of

26. *Ibid.*, 699.
27. See pages 119–21.
28. London *Times*, June 13, 1941, p. 4.

totalitarian techniques had by now been plunged into a coma of dull apathy and submission.

It is clear from the debates and from memoirs which have subsequently been published that both Roosevelt and Churchill were under considerable pressure to reconsider their policy of "unconditional surrender." In the United States, psychological warfare experts urged its review and modification and asked that a new version should be communicated immediately to the German people. They maintained that a policy framed in less absolute terms would shorten the war. Even General Eisenhower appeared sympathetic with this effort. His biographer and aide, Harry C. Butcher, reported that Ike revealed that:

Ed Stettinius told me the President was far from well and that he is becoming increasingly difficult to deal with because he has changed his mind so often. There have been discussions with him as to the meaning of "unconditional surrender" as applied to Germany. Any military person knows that there are conditions to every surrender. There is a feeling that, at Casablanca, the President and the Prime Minister, more likely the former, seized on Grant's famous term without realizing the full implications to the enemy.[29]

Butcher added that the psychological experts and General Eisenhower supported a general review and modification of the policy which might then be communicated to the German people proposing something short of this "absolute" concept. Butcher indicated that the general and the experts felt this might shorten the war.

In the same manner, certain members of Parliament asked for a reconsideration of the policy, which they said was stiffening the resistance of the German people and needlessly prolonging the war. Pressed in particular by Rhys Davies, the prime minister stubbornly if testily responded: "I am not of opinion that a demand for unconditional surrender would prolong the war. Anyhow, the war will be prolonged until unconditional surrender has been obtained."[30]

29. Harry C. Butcher, *My Three Years with Eisenhower* (New York: Simon and Schuster, 1946), 518.
30. *Parliamentary Debates*, Vol. 407, January 16, 1945, pp. 21–22.

However, two days later, he offered assurances to the German people which amounted substantially to a reformulation of the policy he had so recently defended when he announced: "Peace, though based on unconditional surrender, will bring Germany and Japan an immense, immediate amelioration of the suffering and agony which now lie before them. We, the Allies, are no monsters, but faithful men trying to . . . raise . . . a structure of peace, of freedom, of justice and of law, which system shall be an abiding and lasting shelter for all." [31]

Moreover, at about this time, he set forth certain practical conditions under which the policy could be defended. He insisted that the justification of "unconditional surrender" should be conceived of in practical and realistic terms. Essentially, it was the lesser of two unhappy alternatives, for if the Allies should be driven to specify in detail the terms of surrender, the effect would be even more ominous than this vague and general formula. The prime minister maintained: "There is another reason why any abrogation of the principle of unconditional surrender would be most improvident at the present time. . . . We should have to discuss with the enemy, while they still remained with arms in their hands, all the painful details of settlement which their indescribable crimes have made necessary for the future safety of Europe and of the world, and these, when recited in detail, might well become a greater obstacle to the end of the struggle than the broad generalization which the term 'unconditional surrender' implies." [32] Among the minimum terms which would have had to be set down were the disarming and disbanding of all German armed forces, the dissolving of the General Staff, the removal or destruction of all German military equipment, the elimination or control of all German industry capable of use for military production, the trial and swift punishment of all war criminals, the liquidation of Nazi political, legal, and cultural institutions, and the purging from all phases of public and private life of the evil effects of this tyranny. In Churchill's opinion, these

31. *Parliamentary Debates*, Vol. 407, January 18, 1945, p. 425.
32. *Ibid.*, 424.

requirements could hardly have seemed less onerous to the Germans than "unconditional surrender."

Therefore, as we have seen, Churchill's response to his critics was to demonstrate: (1) the British War Cabinet was consulted on the issue of "unconditional surrender," approved it and in fact went beyond Churchill in the application they favored; (2) while there were alternatives to "unconditional surrender," none gave any promise of being less offensive to the German people; but (3) once adopted and set forth, the policy of total surrender had to be tempered with mercy and political wisdom. In one final classic statement contained in his "Review of the War" before Parliament on January 18, 1945, Churchill presented the essence of what might be called a realist's conception of "unconditional surrender" and the manner in which its severity could be mitigated:

What . . . should be our attitude towards the terrible foe with whom we are grappling? Should it be unconditional surrender, or should we make some accommodation with them through a negotiated peace, leaving them free to regather their strength for a renewal of the struggle after a few uneasy years? The principle of unconditional surrender was proclaimed by the president of the United States at Casablanca. . . . I am sure it was right at the time it was used, when many things hung in the balance against us. . . . Should we then modify this declaration . . . made in days of comparative weakness . . . now that we have reached a period of mastery and power?

I am clear that nothing should induce us to abandon the principle . . . or to enter into any form of negotiation with Germany or Japan . . . until the act of unconditional surrender has been formally executed. But the President . . . and I . . . have repeatedly declared that the enforcement of unconditional surrender upon the enemy in no way relieves the victorious Powers of their obligations to humanity, or of their duties as Christian and civilized nations. I read somewhere that when the ancient Athenians, on one occasion, overpowered a tribe in the Peloponnesus which had wrought them great injury by base, treacherous means, and when they had the hostile army herded on a beach naked for slaughter, they forgave them and set them free, and they said: "This was not because they were men; it was done because of the nature of Man." Similarly, in this temper, we may now say to our foes: "We demand unconditional surrender, but you well know how strict are the moral limits within which our action is confined. We are not extirpators of nations, or butchers of people. We make no bargain with you. We accord you nothing as a right. Abandon your resistance unconditionally. We remain bound by our customs and our nature.[33]

The Balkan Invasion. No single phase of wartime strategy evoked greater controversy than the question of the proposed Allied invasion through the Balkans or Southeastern or Central Europe. In the long history of Anglo-American differences on World War II strategy, no other question was debated more often or was the occasion of so much division and bitterness between Allies. From December 7, 1941, until August of 1944, before the invasion of southern France, the Americans staunchly defended the concept of a full-scale invasion of Western Europe while the British persistently demanded an alternate or supplementary thrust into the "soft underbelly" of Europe. From a purely military point of view, there were serious disadvantages to the British maneuver. It called for operations in difficult terrain and in coastal areas where naval action would be greatly restricted. It anticipated operations which might have called for action across "army lines" of major nations. It appeared at first glance to be a revival of Churchill's eccentric "Dardanelles fiasco" in World War I which he always believed had been soundly conceived but improperly executed and which, it was said, he now sought to vindicate. Moreover, some American critics like Secretary of War Henry Stimson suggested that this was merely a device and a stratagem to save British lives. Yet the various reasons given by critics for Churchill's proposal were contributory at best. The fundamental basis for a Balkan diversion in Churchill's mind was strategic.[34] It was strategic within a larger pattern of politicomilitary objectives and it was the first part of this compound word that American policy makers frequently overlooked in the conduct of the war. America fought to win the war and expressed ideas concerning the peace in the vaguest

33. *Ibid.*, 423–24.
34. For a different view on Balkan strategy, see Samuel Eliot Morison's important work, *Strategy and Compromise* (Atlantic Monthly Press, 1958).

of general principles, such as affirmations contained in the Atlantic Charter or in declarations concerning the United Nations. The British and the Russians both had grand designs and overall conceptions of the peace and their military strategy was guided and influenced by these considerations. The Australian historian Chester Wilmot, who was often ridiculed but seldom answered by apologists for American strategy, wrote: "The Americans liked to suggest that they were 'only concerned with the winning of the war,' as if war was merely an international tournament fought to decide who was the best exponent of the military art. But war is waged for political and economic objectives which must always be kept in view by the directors of grand strategy. Otherwise, as has so often happened, the war may be won but the peace will be lost."[35] John R. Deane described the situation at the time of Teheran in his history:

Stalin appeared to know exactly what he wanted at the Conference. This was also true of Churchill, but not so of Roosevelt. This is not said as a reflection on our President, but his apparent indecision was probably the direct result of our obscure foreign policy. President Roosevelt was thinking of winning the war; the others were thinking of their relative positions when the war was won. Stalin wanted the Anglo-American forces in Western not Southern Europe; Churchill thought our postwar position would be improved and British interests best served if the Anglo-Americans as well as the Russians participated in the occupation of the Balkans.[36]

With respect to the Balkan invasion or diversion, the British position was realistically founded on politicomilitary interests, its American detractors notwithstanding. Not irrelevant is the fact that the British saw in the approach a means of preserving their vital interests in the Mediterranean and the Near East which were the result of over a century and a half of British foreign policy. Historically, they had succeeded in checking the southeastward expansion of Russia by bolstering and encouraging friendly forces in Greece, Turkey, and the Balkans. They had blocked Russia's expansion into

35. Chester Wilmot, *The Struggle for Europe* (New York: Harper and Brothers, 1952), 130.
36. John R. Deane, *The Strange Alliance* (New York: Viking Press, 1947), 43.

the Mediterranean by supporting Turkey's control of the Dardanelles. It was understandable, therefore, that in World War II they
perceived the political importance of central and southern Europe
and urged military action which would secure their own interests
against Russian or German expansionism. In a word, the British
proposal was grounded in more than military logic, however reti-
cent they were in articulating their underlying assumptions, especially in the high-level, three-cornered talks which, it must never be
forgotten, involved participation by the Russians.

All this being true, Churchill's role in the development of the
concept of a Balkan invasion was, at the same time, both logical and
enigmatic. He was not only the foremost architect of the concept of
a Balkan campaign but he defended and reintroduced it in wartime
conferences time and again. Yet in his history of the war, he rejected
the view that he ever looked upon a Balkan diversion as a substitute
for the more fundamental cross-channel invasion. Indeed, the two
tests we have selected of the political realism in Churchill's policy
lead us in opposite directions. In the case of "unconditional surrender," the policy enunciated and put into effect by Roosevelt and
Churchill was hardly as realistic as the reinterpretation given it by
Churchill. On the contrary, in the question of military action in
Southeastern and Central Europe, the strategy as introduced in important wartime conferences proved more realistic than American
strategy. Yet if Churchill's Balkan policy was more realistic, his subsequent words disavowing political intentions with which both his
wartime associates and their biographers have credited him are directly the opposite. In the case of "unconditional surrender" what
Churchill said was more realistic than what he or, more accurately,
the Allies did. In the present example, his Balkans policy was wiser
than the subsequent interpretation he gave it. Thus we are left with
confusion worse confounded unless our inquiry can provide us with
new evidence to clarify these issues.

In seeking to find our way through the morass of seeming contradictions, we shall consider Churchill's scheme for the Balkans
from two points of view. First, we have the task of finding out precisely what he proposed, a question on which there is little agree-

ment even today; and secondly, we must consider the chronology or timetable of his policy statements.

The concept of a Balkan invasion was an intrinsic aspect of Churchill's general Mediterranean policy. From one point of view, the idea of Balkan invasion merely provided the capstone for a policy designed to safeguard the British lifeline in the Mediterranean. When British strongholds in Egypt, North Africa, and Italy had been safeguarded and defended through successful military campaigns, it was a logical extension of the same strategic thinking to consider means for securing Britain's remaining crucial outposts in Greece, Turkey, and the other Balkan countries. The policy for the Balkans, in other words, was but the first phase in a progression of steps in a politicomilitary strategy aimed at safeguarding historic British interests. Reporting the trend of his thinking in 1942 in the fourth volume of his history, Churchill recounted: "If we could end the year in possession of North Africa we could threaten the belly of Hitler's Europe, and this operation should be considered in conjunction with the 1943 operation. That was what we and the Americans had decided to do. To illustrate my point I had meanwhile drawn a picture of a crocodile, and explained to Stalin with the help of this picture how it was our intention to attack the soft belly of the crocodile as we attacked his hard snout."[37] These words, to which Stalin is reported to have exclaimed "may God prosper this undertaking," are significant on at least two counts. First, they show that Churchill as early as 1942 had no illusions about the Balkans operation providing a substitute for a cross-channel invasion. But secondly they show how seriously he had misunderstood what the "Americans had decided to do."

At the time, Churchill was anxious to demonstrate that his strategy was aimed primarily at creating a threat to Germany in the south. He commented: "President Roosevelt and I had long sought to open a new route to Russia and to strike at Germany's southern flank. Turkey was the key to all such plans."[38] According to this design, Turkey was to enter the war on the side of the Allies. Yet when

37. Churchill, *The Hinge of Fate*, 481.
38. *Ibid.*, 696.

the foreign secretary incautiously remarked on May 31, 1943, that once Italy had been knocked out of the war and Allied "troops had reached the Balkan area," the Turks would prove more friendly and cooperative, Churchill intervened to correct this impression. He gently admonished Mr. Eden for his indiscretion by saying: "Eden and I were in full agreement on the war policy, but I feared that the turn of his phrase might mislead our American friends. The record states: 'The Prime Minister intervened to observe emphatically that he was not advocating sending an army into the Balkans now or in the near future.'"[39] Taking his cue from the prime minister, Eden agreed that once British power had been victorious in Italy, its mere existence there would constitute enough of a threat to the Balkans that Turkey would be encouraged to cooperate. In 1943 the Soviet Union was not unsympathetic with this objective.

There is one point that Churchill felt compelled to emphasize and to reiterate over and over again. He formulated his policies for Western Europe and the Balkans under the cloud of criticisms and suggestions that he harbored hidden motives to dynamite the plans for "Overlord," the invasion of Western Europe. In the fifth volume of his history, he cited a passage from one of his Canadian radio broadcasts to show that this had never been his design: "Personally, I always think of the Third Front as well as the Second Front. I have always thought that the Western democracies should be like a boxer who fights with two hands and not one."[40] And in the same volume he went on to explain: "While I was always willing to join with the United States in a direct assualt across the Channel on the German sea-front in France, I was not convinced that this was the only way of winning the war and I knew it would be a very heavy and hazardous adventure."[41] He remained convinced in his heart that Germany was vulnerable on its southern flank. It is reported that in an emergency conference at the Fuehrer's headquarters on September 25, 1943, representatives of the German army and navy strongly urged the evacuation of Crete and other points in the Aegean be-

39. *Ibid.*, 826.
40. London *Times*, September 1, 1943, p. 4.
41. Churchill, *Closing the Ring*, 582.

cause they were indefensible. Hitler overruled this action because of its political consequences, but the very fact that the controversy had arisen confirmed for Churchill his belief of "how deeply the Germans were alarmed at the deadly threat which they expected us to develop on their southeastern flank."[42] Possibly the determining factor in Churchill's strategy was his conviction that the Germans, if hard-pressed enough in the Balkans and the Mediterranean, would have to divert forces from Western Europe.

However firm and deep-seated Churchill's beliefs may have been, he apparently never felt free to press them to a showdown. Critical problems emerged growing out of the nature of the unnatural and tenuous Big Three alliance. Difficulties arose as a result of the differences in mental processes with which the British and Americans approached foreign policy. The conflict over policy in the Balkans placed a grave strain upon Allied unity. Reflecting on his Balkan strategy, Churchill said: "It . . . constitutes . . . the most acute difference I ever had with General Eisenhower."[43] It also evoked far-reaching differences with General Marshall, and of its possible effect on his partnership with Roosevelt, the prime minister commented: "When so many grave issues were pending, I could not risk any jar in my personal relations with the President."[44] Therefore, to avert a rupture in present or future Anglo-American relations, Churchill conscientiously denied that his plan for a "right hook" as part of the overall Allied military effort against Europe ever implied the abandonment or even the curtailing of plans for invading western France. In his history of the war, he departed from his design of allowing events and episodes to speak for themselves in regard to the Balkans. By summarizing the meaning of the chapter in which telegrams about his various Balkan proposals are included, he appeared concerned that the events and episodes might speak only too clearly. Some might say "he protests too much" when they read his words: "The reader of the telegrams presented in this chapter must

42. *Ibid.*, 207.
43. *Ibid.*, 218.
44. *Ibid.*

not be misled by a chance phrase here and there into thinking: (a) that I wanted to abandon "Overlord"; (b) that I wanted to deprive "Overlord" of vital forces; or (c) that I contemplated a campaign by armies operating in the Balkan peninsula. These are legends. Never had such a wish entered my mind."[45]

Moreover, his strategy for the Balkans at first met stronger resistance from President Roosevelt and the American Chiefs of Staff than from Premier Stalin, whose opposition grew proportionately with Soviet strength. Churchill attempted to meet these objections by explaining in considerable detail how much Allied strength he proposed to divert to the various projects. General Marshall had warned that Italy and other possible diversions might become a vacuum into which the resources for "Overlord" would be dissipated. The prime minister countered:

> This was the triple theme which I pressed upon the President and Stalin on every occasion not hesitating to repeat the arguments remorselessly [which were for strength in the proportion of 6/10 Overlord, 3/10 Italy, and 1/10 Eastern Mediterranean]. I could have gained Stalin, but the President was oppressed by the prejudices of his military advisers. . . . Our American friends were comforted in their obstinacy by the reflection that "at any rate we have stopped Churchill entangling us in the Balkans." No such idea ever crossed my mind.[46]

In much the same terms, he proposed to Stalin the deployment of seven divisions from Italy and North Africa for use in "Overlord." This would have left twenty-two divisions in the Mediterranean for use in Italy or for what he chose to call other objectives. These might have included "an operation against Southern France or for moving from the head of the Adriatic towards the Danube."[47] But these or any other operations would have to be timed to conform with "Overlord." Before that major effort was launched, he felt it would not be too costly or difficult to spare two or three divisions to take control of the islands in the Aegean.

45. *Ibid.*, 254.
46. *Ibid.*, 346.
47. *Ibid.*, 354.

The arguments Churchill presented in discussions at the Cairo Conference in November of 1943 supply the best guide to his conception of strategy in its broad outlines. At Cairo, he proposed two concrete military efforts. First, he urged that "Overlord" or the invasion of western France be launched sometime between May and July of 1944. Secondly, he proposed that the West exploit opportunities for assisting its Soviet ally in the east not only with a second but a third front. The second operation should be undertaken in two parts, with an option reserved for the second step in the strategy. He recommended that the Allies capture Rome as the first step, secure the airfields north of the city (from which air attacks on Germany could be launched), but resist every temptation to advance on the ground beyond the Pisa-Rimini line. At this stage and as a second step the Allies would be free to decide whether to advance into southern France from the Riviera to Marseilles and Toulon and from there up the Rhone River *or* to move from the right-hand of their power in northern Italy up the Istrian peninsula gap.[48] Churchill from the beginning was himself more attracted to the latter alternative for reasons that went beyond military considerations. At least one American military man, General Mark Clark, agreed that such an action, if successful, would place the Western Allies in a much stronger position at the end of the war to meet the challenge of the Soviet Union. In a letter to Hanson W. Baldwin, General Clark explained: "To have taken advantage of Tito's situation with the opportunity of landing a part of our forces across the Adriatic, behind protected beachheads which Tito could have provided, with the bulk of our forces in Italy attacking through the Ljubljana Gap would, if successful, have placed the Western Allies in a much stronger position at the end of the war to meet the ever increasing challenge of Soviet world domination."[49] Variations on this theme included discussions of landings further south along the Dalmatian coast near Zara or Split. For reasons to be considered, Churchill's

---

48. *Ibid.*, 344–45.
49. Hanson W. Baldwin, *Great Mistake of the War* (New York: Harper and Brothers, 1950), 40.

strategy was not adopted. In his writings after the war, Churchill did not hesitate to say: "I regard the failure to use otherwise un-employable forces to bring Turkey into the war and dominate the Aegean as an error in war direction which cannot be excused by the fact that in spite of it victory was won." [50]

To summarize, our review makes clear that there were two as-pects to Churchill's theory of a Balkan operation. The one that was military in character was obvious and was often articulated. The other, which was politically inspired and resulted from his forecast of the postwar world balance of forces, was hidden and left vague and obscure. The object of his policy in purely military terms was to strike at the German army from the rear, open a wide avenue up the Danube to Germany and coordinate and facilitate the resistance efforts of the peoples of the Balkans. It envisioned in minimum terms sending supplies and equipment and conducting commando operations. There were twenty-one German divisions and nine Bul-garian ones against whom an Allied thrust would have to be di-rected. In justifying this policy as the one best designed to stretch enemy resources to the breaking point, Churchill hinted at other motives to which the Russians might take exception. For example, he wrote:

We ourselves had no ambitions in the Balkans. . . . Monsieur Molotov, Mr. Eden, and a representative of the President should meet together and advise the conference on all the political points at issue. For example, did our Soviet friends and Allies see any political difficulty in the course advo-cated? If so what? . . . From the military point of view there was no ques-tion of using large forces in this area. [51]

For most Americans, it was solely as military projects that Churchill's schemes were to be judged. The secretary of war, Henry L. Stimson, wrote with a kind of furious self-righteousness about what he called that wholly erroneous view which held that opposi-tion to Russian expansion guided the British strategy. Stimson ex-plained that he had never been present at any conversations be-

50. Churchill, *Closing the Ring*, 346.
51. *Ibid.*, 367.

tween the three nations in which political objectives had in any way been broached. He assumed, therefore, that the Balkan campaign was merely an effort by Churchill to vindicate his long-held strategic conceptions.[52] General Eisenhower's biographer reported that Stimson told the general "that the Prime Minister was obsessed with the idea of proving to history that invasion of the Continent by way of the Balkans was wise strategy and would repair whatever damage history now records for Churchill's misfortune at the Dardanelles in the last war."[53] General Eisenhower himself suggested this was one of the two considerations that motivated Churchill but added that he was also concerned as a political leader with the future of the Balkans.[54] In his own account, *Crusade in Europe*, the general as the military man, ironically enough, demonstrated greater sensitivity than Stimson, the political leader, to the claims and demands of the political problem At the same time he showed his inability to do anything about his judgments on nonmilitary matters. Eisenhower observed:

Although I never heard him say so, I felt that the Prime Minister's real concern was possibly of a political rather than a military nature. He may have thought that a post war situation which would see the Western Allies posted in great strength in the Balkans would be far more effective in producing a stable post-hostilities world than if the Russian armies should be the ones to occupy that region. I told him that if this were his reason for advocating the campaign into the Balkans he should go instantly to the President and lay the facts, as well as his own conclusions on the table. I well understood that strategy can be affected by political considerations. . . . But I did insist that as long as he argued the matter on military grounds alone I could not concede validity to his arguments.[55]

The key to the political aspect of Churchill's plan comes most candidly from the lips of another great statesman in the Western tradition. Churchill from his youth enjoyed a comradeship with

52. Henry L. Stimson and McGeorge Bundy, *On Active Service in Peace and War* (New York: Harper and Brothers, 1948), 447.
53. Butcher, *My Three Years*, 373.
54. Dwight D. Eisenhower, *Crusade in Europe* (Garden City, N.Y.: Doubleday, 1948), 194–95.
55. *Ibid.*, 283–84.

Field Marshal Smuts of the Union of South Africa that was more cordial and intimate than his association with almost any other Western statesman. Their minds were in tune on most of the great issues and Churchill commented on Smuts's approach to the Balkans by saying: "I always found . . . great comfort in feeling that our minds were in step."[56] It was significant that on August 31, 1943, Smuts wrote to the prime minister: "Surely our performance can be bettered and the comparison with Russia rendered less unflattering to us. To the ordinary man it must appear that it is Russia who is winning the war. If this impression continues, what will be our post-war world position compared with that of Russia? A tremendous shift in our world status may follow, and will leave Russia the diplomatic master of the world." On September 3, 1943, Smuts followed with a second communiqué, saying: "We should immediately take Southern Italy and move on to the Adriatic, and from a suitable point there launch a real attack on the Balkans and set its resurgent forces going. This will bring Turkey into the picture."[57] To this Churchill replied: "I have always been anxious to come into the Balkans. . . . We shall have to see how the fighting in Italy develops before commiting ourselves beyond Commandos, agents, and supplies, but the whole place is aflame, and . . . it may well be that the Germans will be forced to retire to the line of the Save and the Danube."[58]

Churchill's exchange with Field Marshal Smuts should make it abundantly clear that something besides the natural human desire to stand vindicated before the bar of history inspired him. Only if it is recognized that his policy was the result of a political-military approach which had two dimensions can we evaluate it properly. He aimed at pursuing the most economical and efficient military strategy but efficiency depended, in the long run, on proper discretion regarding political objectives. It would be fair to paraphrase Stimson and say that Churchill was indeed obsessed but not with self-vindication alone but with winning the war and more importantly

56. Churchill, *Closing the Ring*, 125.
57. *Ibid.*, 126, 128.
58. *Ibid.*, 128–29.

the peace. This obsession drove him to give attention to political as well as to military objectives. For that reason, he proposed a Balkan campaign as one useful instrument in such a policy.

The Chronology of the Balkan Controversy. Now that we have considered the British or, as some Americans labeled it, the Churchillian scheme for operations in the Balkans, it remains to examine the timing of his proposals. The proposal for an invasion of western France was, in Stimson's words, the "brain child of the United States Army." [59] This invasion was originally planned for 1943, but a token landing to assure the Russians of our good faith was to be undertaken in 1942. The date for the "sacrifice landing," as Churchill derisively termed it, was first set for September of 1942. In his opposition especially to the earlier invasion, Churchill consistently pressed for a series of strategic thrusts around the fringe of the Mediterranean. At that time the goal was to offer rational alternatives to a cross-channel invasion whose price was too costly at the time. But they also reflected a strategic outlook in which a relatively higher priority was given to the Mediterranean and the Near East than the Americans could accept. The immediate British goal was to oppose precipitate action on the Continent in 1942. The ultimate goal was to force an offensive via Belgrade to Warsaw. This goal appears never to have been seriously contemplated by American military leaders, who advocated the landing in southern France as soon as possible—constituting in their minds the shortest route to Berlin. From their point of view the invasion of the Balkan peninsula meant the prolongation of the war. Even if the Anglo-American forces could have occupied Belgrade, Soviet troops would have been able to reach the English Channel through the North European plains.

As early as January 29, 1941, Churchill, in communicating with the secretary of state for war disclosed his long-range objectives:

We must however contemplate as our main objective in this theatre the bringing into heavy action of the largest possible force from the Army of

59. Stimson and Bundy, *On Active Service*, 419.

the Nile to fight in aid of Greece or Turkey or both. How many divisions, or their equivalent, do you contemplate being available by July for action in Southeast Europe? I should have thought four Australian, one New Zealand, one of the two South Africans, the three British, and three of the six Indian divisions, should be available—total twelve. Those troops should be equipped on the highest scale.[60]

In the same message, Churchill suggested that the total British forces be distributed to include five British divisions at home as a mobile task force, ten and eventually twelve in the Middle East for "action against the Germans in Greece or Turkey on the highest scale,"[61] four in Egypt, and four African colonial divisions. By December 18, 1941, he defined Western policy in southern Europe as one of liberation "by the landing at suitable points, successively or simultaneously, of British and American armies strong enough to enable the conquered population to revolt."[62] There are signs that throughout 1941 and 1942 a guiding principle in Churchill's policy was the desire to bring Turkey into the struggle. Every inducement and attraction was considered and the prime minister, according to Butcher, "even suggested equipping forty-five Turkish divisions."[63]

It followed that Allied policy for North Africa—Italy—Sicily and the Balkans was viewed as a unity by Churchill. He wrote to Stalin on January 27, 1943, that "the breaking down of Italy would lead to contact with the Western Balkans and with the highly hopeful resistance" there.[64] Once Italy were eliminated, the effect in the Balkans would be to release patriots and nationalist leaders held in check up to then by Axis forces. The resistance forces would include at least twenty-five Italian divisions. Such a situation would present the Germans with two alternatives, the first being to withdraw and the other to call back large forces from the Russian or ultimately

60. Winston S. Churchill, "Prime Minister to Secretary of State for War," January 29, 1941, *The Second World War*, Vol. III, *The Grand Alliance* (Boston: Houghton Mifflin, 1950), 787.
61. *Ibid.*
62. *Ibid.*, 656.
63. Butcher, *My Three Years*, 230.
64. Churchill, "Prime Minister to Premier Stalin," January 27, 1943, *The Hinge of Fate*, 708.

the western front. Either alternative would serve the Allies and strengthen their position on all fronts. For anyone who imagined that Churchill's Mediterranean strategy was fragmentary and piecemeal and not all a part of a larger design, he confided: "When in the summer of 1943, we broke into Sicily and Italy, the Balkans and especially Yugoslavia never left my thoughts." On July 22, 1943, in a letter to General Alexander, he explained: "Before leaving for Quebec, I decided to pave the way for further action in the Balkans by appointing a senior officer to lead a larger mission to the partisans in the field." [65] The reputation, character, and daring of Fitzroy Maclean, the appointee, suggest the importance Churchill assigned to the task. In August of 1943, he acknowledged: "When the tremendous events of the Italian surrender occurred, my mind turned to the Aegean islands, so long the object of strategic desire." [66] At every stage along the way in his attempt to strengthen the Turks and the partisans, Churchill assessed possible Soviet attitudes and made political judgments as to their reactions, saying: "The Russians' preponderance of strength is so great that trifling improvements we are making in the Turkish forces need not, and I believe will not, disturb them." [67]

In 1943, such efforts would have to be pursued with commando forces, who represented "troops of the highest order and the only ones we are likely to be able to spare for the Balkans this year." By September, 1943, Churchill speculated on whether once the defensive line in northern Italy has been stabilized, "it may be possible to spare some of our own forces assigned to the Mediterranean theatre to emphasize a movement north and northeastward from the Dalmatian ports." On October 7, 1943, he set forth the major assumptions undergirding his strategy for the Balkans in a letter to President Roosevelt: "I believe it will be found that the Italian and Balkan peninsulas are militarily and politically united, and that really it is one theatre with which we have to deal." [68] Thus if it is

65. Churchill, *Closing the Ring*, 463, 465.
66. *Ibid.*, 205.
67. *Ibid.*, 661.
68. *Ibid.*, 662, 136, 210.

claimed that Churchill's Balkan design was something separate and apart from his Italian strategy, his own exposition would seem to expose the ignorance of his critics. Each link in the chain from Sicily at the outset to the operations on the Italian peninsula, to the seizure of air bases at Foggia, to the vigorous action against Rome and to plans for the Balkans as a whole were stepping-stones along the pathway of his deeply cherished but ill-fated Balkan "Grand Design."

The timetable of invasion plans up to November, 1943, had included the operation in North Africa in 1942. This action met in part the demand for operations in the European–North African theater as an earnest of the West's military engagement alongside the Russians. But this alternative, rather than the invasion of western France, constituted a rational military action in which the calculable costs did not exceed the tactical advantages the Allies hoped to gain. At the Casablanca Conference in January, 1943, the British once again, to the ill-concealed distaste of the Americans, tried to put off the operation on the continent at least from the spring until the autumn of 1943. In retrospect, and based on the lessons of the North African campaign, the perils of a cross-channel operation in 1942 or 1943 now appear obvious. A successful landing in France in 1942 or 1943 appears not to have been in the cards. The Allies in 1942 were as weak in trained divisions, landing craft, and equipment as the Germans were proportionately stronger. This ratio was to shift rather decisively by the time "Overlord" was actually launched.

British resistance to the strategy of "Overlord" diminished as American power became fully mobilized. In August, 1943, at the conference in Quebec, the British agreed, albeit reluctantly, that "Overlord" must be given priority. Significantly, however, the British at the Moscow Conference of Foreign Ministers in October 1943, and at Cairo and Teheran in late November sought to reopen the question. General Eisenhower's biographer reported that a few days before the Cairo Conference: "the Prime Minister and the British are still unconvinced as to the wisdom of *Overlord*, and are persistent in their desire to pursue our advantages in the Mediterranean, especially through the Balkans."[69] Not for the first or last time, Churchill found himself isolated as Roosevelt and Stalin sided with one another on a series of crucial issues. When Roosevelt proposed that the Russians could hardly conceive of a Balkan invasion as comprising a true "second front," Stalin heartily agreed. As Soviet capacities to liberate its Balkan neighbors increased, it was natural that Stalin would favor an invasion of southern France instead of a trans-Adriatic operation into the Balkans. The attraction of two strong personalities for one another was strengthened and cemented by the unfailing unanimity of American military advisors opposed to any tactic which diverted from the principal objective. Describing his feelings in December, 1943, Churchill commented: "When I thought of the dull, dead-weight resistance, talking no account of timing and proportion, that I had encountered about all Mediterranean projects, I awaited the answer with deep anxiety."[70]

Despite his commitments at the wartime conferences in late 1943, Churchill continued openly to press for broader, more inclusive interpretations of military objectives. He foresaw at each stage in the unfolding of the war contingencies and new developments which might require new policies and actions. On the basis of the military situation in the Aegean, he sought to keep at least token strength in the Mediterranean. He proposed holding in the Mediterranean some of the L.S.T.'s which would eventually be assigned for use against western France. He argued his case on a week-to-week basis, saying: "The only solution was to hold up most of those in the Mediterranean for another three weeks. There was good hope that this could be done without injury to 'Overlord.'"[71] In the long run, there was always the possibility that "Overlord" would prove abortive. On February 19, 1944, he wrote to General Ismay regarding troops still in the Mediterranean: "In the event of 'Overlord' not being successful or Hitler accumulating forces there quite beyond our power to tackle, it would perhaps be necessary to adopt the

69. Butcher, *My Three Years*, 442.
70. Churchill, *Closing the Ring*, 440.
71. *Ibid.*, 430–31.

flanking movements both in Norway and from Turkey and the Aegean in the winter of 1944–45. In view of such contingencies I am reluctant to liquidate this force. It could surely meanwhile be employed in the Balkans or in exterminating the German garrisons in the islands off the Dalmatian coast."[72]

Moreover, actual strategy would be determined by the outcome of the Italian campaign. As late as February 22, 1944, he proposed in Parliament that when conditions had been stabilized in the struggle for Rome, at that point Britain and the United States should take a "new view" of strategic objectives. In General Eisenhower's account of discussions, Churchill's concern for the Balkans as late as August 15, 1944, had not diminished. The general reported: "The Prime Minister wants Alexander to have enough force not only to hold the line but to continue into the Balkans, through the Ljubljana gap, in Yugoslavia, to reach Germany through Austria."[73]

In only one way were Churchill's policy proposals changed during the period. At a certain point, he apparently abandoned any hope he may have had that the Balkans could be saved from Russian domination. Yet the same political principles which had inspired his early concern led him to champion every military action which offered some prospect that Central Europe might be safeguarded against Russian control. The best chance of achieving this political objective would be to invade Germany via Austria and the Ljubljana Gap. In the summer of 1944, Churchill made a last-ditch attempt to influence the postwar distribution of power. Some American military men like General Ira Eaker, then commanding the Mediterranean air forces, at first sympathized with the plan. But opposition from the highest military level soon silenced their views. General George Marshall is reported to have told General Eaker: "You've been too damned long with the British."[74] Overwhelmingly the most powerful voices among American military authorities favored a diversion to supplement "Overlord" not in southeastern Eu-

72. *Ibid.*, 694–95.
73. Butcher, *My Three Years*, 644.
74. Quoted in Baldwin, *Great Mistake*, 39.

rope but in southern France. Through this diversion, the retreating German forces would be trapped and destroyed in the field. By the time the action in the south had been launched, the German troops had already escaped. Churchill was impatient with the strategy in southern France primarily because he thought that better use could be made of the troops. He was not alone in this judgment, for in his book *Calculated Risk*, General Mark Clark, commander of the Fifth Army, argued:

A campaign that might have changed the whole history of relations between the Western World and the Soviet Union was permitted to fade away. . . . Not alone in my opinion, but in the opinion of a number of experts who were close to the problem, the weakening of the campaign in Italy in order to invade Southern France, instead of pushing on into the Balkans, was one of the outstanding political mistakes of the War. . . . Stalin knew exactly what he wanted in a political as well as military way; and the thing he wanted most was to keep us out of the Balkans. . . . It is easy to see, therefore, why Stalin favoured Anvil at Teheran. . . . There was no question that the Balkans were strongly in the British minds, but . . . the American top-level planners were not interested. . . . I later came to understand, in Austria, the tremendous advantages that we had lost by our failure to press on into the Balkans. . . . Had we been there before the Red Army, not only would the collapse of Germany have come sooner, but the influence of Soviet Russia would have been drastically reduced.[75]

By contrast, General Eisenhower assumed that the British prime minister was piqued because he held that a better alternative would be to drive forward in Italy and from there into the Balkans against Germany's southern flank. After one of the general's visits with Churchill, his aide reported: "Ike told me later that the Prime Minister gave him hell for insisting on the ANVIL operation, the British Premier still being wedded to pursuit of the Germans in Italy and to possibilities in the Balkans."[76] The reactions to Churchill's position, whether by General Eisenhower, Robert Sherwood (the author of *Roosevelt and Hopkins*), or President Roosevelt's son Elliott, were

75. Mark Clark, *Calculated Risk* (London: Harrap Publishers, 1951), 348–51.
76. Butcher, *My Three Years*, 607–608.

unanimous and give us a picture of Churchill's viewpoint as he articulated it in wartime conferences.

Some military historians have suggested a distinction between two periods in the history of military operations in World War II, namely 1942–43 and 1944. They argue that in the first period an invasion of the Balkans was impossible without Turkey's cooperation. (Churchill and Stalin agreed on this point.) But the Turks followed a policy similar to that of Spain vis-à-vis Hitler. They asked for enormous military supplies the Allies were unable to deliver. As the records of the Second Cairo Conference, December 2–7, 1943 (*Foreign Relations of the United States*, 1943, Conference at Cairo and Teheran, pp. 655–832) make clear, Turkish leaders such as President Ismet Inönü refused to intervene as long as the Germans were able to retaliate.

Churchill's "grand design" for military operations in 1942 and 1943 was formulated in three memoranda which he shared with Roosevelt on a visit to Washington on December 22, 1941. The invasion of French Northwest Africa was decided on at an Anglo-American Conference in July, 1942. A decision to continue the Mediterranean strategy was reached at the Casablanca Conference in January, 1943. On both occasions, the American military leaders argued against a Mediterranean involvement.

At Teheran, Roosevelt raised the possibility of an operation across the Adriatic for a drive into Rumania to effect a junction with the Red Army. Churchill supported this plan but Stalin thought that it would be unwise to disperse the Anglo-American forces in the eastern Mediterranean and suggested instead that after the capture of Rome, allied forces in Italy should be transferred to southern France. With strong support from General Marshall and Admiral King, this strategy was eventually adopted.

Military historians who questioned Churchill's Balkan strategy in 1942–43 found his proposal for action in the summer of 1944 more specific and militarily feasible. Churchill's plan for Anglo-American forces to advance through the Ljubljana Gap into Austria moving in the direction of Vienna and possibly into Western Hungary was defended by some of the same strategists who opposed the earlier proposal. But President Roosevelt and General Eisenhower opposed the plan on grounds that a decision had been reached at Teheran to invade southern France. But that invasion was delayed for technical reasons until August 15, and by then the Normandy invasion had achieved a measure of success and the second invasion had little military significance.

Certain conclusions are supported by this lengthy survey of Churchill's Balkan strategy. First, his policy was a natural by-product of traditional British aims and objectives in the Mediterranean. It was more understandable for the inheritor of historic British foreign policy to conduct the world struggle against Germany with an eye on the probable effects upon the distribution of world power of military strategy than it was for the newcomers who so recently had been thrust onto the European scene. British power was a function of its influence in the Mediterranean and of its success in limiting Russian expansion into the Bosphorus and the Straits. From the beginning it was predetermined that Britain's historic interests should be a factor influencing proposals for military steps against Germany.

Secondly, there is little doubt that Churchill constructed his numerous plans of action in North Africa, Sicily, Italy, and the Istrian peninsula as parts of one policy making up, as it were, a shroud to envelop the menace of German aggression and at the same time prepare the most auspicious political conditions for a future of international peace and order. There is good evidence that Churchill's strategic thinking was all of a piece on this issue, while the same is not true of all phases of American policy. If Churchill refused to make explicit the inevitable relationship between a military campaign in North Africa or Italy and his future objectives in Southeastern or Central Europe, it was probably because of a keen sense of the contingencies of history. Few Western statesmen have been more aware of the essentially tentative and provisional character of military and political strategy. Few leaders have sensed as clearly that every action is limited by circumstances. It was hardly surprising, therefore, that he looked upon military strategy as comprising actions to be taken one step at a time. If he said less than others did about the future, it was because over a long lifetime he had traveled an uncertain course achieving less than he might have projected in any ideal or rational plan. He was prepared to settle for as much as the immediate situation would warrant.

Finally, Churchill gave every sign of being moved instinctively by a profound anxiety over the prospects of future Russian expansion. It is understandable that his aims should have been concealed and obscured in order to preserve the wartime alliance. It may be true that in his concern for future Anglo-American-Russian relations, Churchill felt concerned to hide some of his objectives from historians and scholars even in his history of the war. On several occasions, he disavowed being in any sense guided by plans to contain the Soviet Union following the war. His protests, however, were not supported by his actions and policies nor reflected in the reactions of his wartime associates.

There are probably three explanations which account for the discrepancies between Churchill's words of self-justification and the inherent logic of the policies he set forth. In the first place, he envisioned a number of concrete actions of a limited character which could have been taken in the Balkans. If we assume that nationalism in the Balkans was sufficiently inflammable so that a modest infusion of Allied arms, equipment, and Commando aid could have touched off an explosion against which German military power would have proved ineffective, then Churchill's claim that he had never contemplated large-scale Allied military action is persuasive. To the extent that he believed his own claims, Churchill undoubtedly conceived of the Balkan campaign as requiring only limited commitments.

Another factor that obviously influenced Churchill's approach is the paramount importance that he gave from the outbreak of World War II to Anglo-American unity. In Parliament he again and again assigned an inferior position to all other interests as compared with this aspect of British foreign policy. It was natural, therefore, that he never pursued his emphasis on Balkan strategy beyond the point where it could have jeopardized this fundamental relationship. In his communication of September 11, 1943, to Field

Marshal Smuts, who had proposed that a Balkan strategy be substituted for plans to strike at western France, Churchill was utterly candid in enunciating this principle: "There can be no question whatever of breaking arrangements we have made with United States for 'Overlord' (crosschannel). . . . I hope you will realise that British loyalty to 'Overlord' is keystone of arch of Anglo-American co-operation. Personally I think enough forces exist for both hands to be played, and I believe this to be the right strategy."[77]

A final element that offers a clue to Churchill's reluctance to draw the same conclusions from his own proposals that some objective observers have drawn involves the whole problem of Anglo-Russian relations. No one who has read his wartime correspondence can imagine for one moment that he was insensitive or unaware of the view that Soviet leaders were taking of his policies. On several occasions Premier Stalin challenged Churchill's sincerity about establishing a second front in the West. One of these instances is reported in the fifth volume of the history of the war:

Before we separated, Stalin looked at me across the table and said "I wish to pose a very direct question to the Prime Minister about 'Overlord'. Do the Prime Minister and the British Staff really believe in 'Overlord'?" I replied, "Provided the conditions previously stated for 'Overlord' are established when the time comes, it will be our stern duty to hurl across the channel against the Germans every sinew of our strength." On this we separated.[78]

On yet another occasion, Churchill displayed anxiety regarding the Soviet attitude and reaction to the goals of his Balkan strategy. On October 20, 1943, he advised Eden on his mission to Moscow: "You should try to find out what the Russians really feel about the Balkans. Would they be attracted by the idea of our acting through the Aegean, involving Turkey in the war, and opening the Dardanelles and Bosphorus so that British Naval forces and shipping could aid the Russian advance and so that we could ultimately give

77. Churchill, "Prime Minister to Field Marshal Smuts," September 11, 1943, *Closing the Ring*, 131.
78. Churchill, *Closing the Ring*, 373.

them our right hand along the Danube? . . . It may be that for political reasons the Russians would not want us to develop a large
scale Balkan strategy." [79] What were the Russian attitudes toward
Britain's interests in Leros and its objective of capturing Rhodes?
Did they oppose these programs because they promised to open
up the Black Sea? These questions and thoughts, Churchill warned
the foreign secretary, were only for his private meditation and
reflection.

In all his statements on the Balkan strategy Churchill accepted
without qualification that wise policies to establish a balance of
power against future Russian expansionism would have to respect
Russian vital interests. For this reason, and not from idle curiosity
or the desire to put something over on the Russians, he made repeated inquiries such as the one posed to Mr. Eden. At the same
time that his policies were directed toward establishing substantial
Western spheres of influence, he was never unwilling to recognize
the extent of the Russian sphere. In this spirit he declared: "It seems
to me that Rumania must primarily make its terms with Russia . . .
at whose mercy they will soon lie. . . . The same applies to Bul-
garia. . . . The whole of Europe is heading, irresistibly towards new
. . . foundations." [80] The main reason for Churchill's reticence about
the purpose of his Balkan strategy may be the fact that he hoped
someday to do business again with the Soviet Union. (For an opposing view of strategy, see Samuel Eliot Morison, *Strategy and
Compromise.*)

79. *Ibid.,* "Prime Minister to Mr. Eden," October 20, 1943, p. 286.
80. *Parliamentary Debates,* Vol. 402, August 2, 1944, p. 1483.

CHAPTER SEVEN
Progress, Politics, and Leadership
in the Western Tradition

To conclude our discussion of Churchill's statesmanship, we turn to the historical tendencies of his era. In few periods of history have men found in repeated tragedies, conflicts, and failures the bright signs of inevitable progress within an ever benign universe as in the modern era. During and after each of two great world wars, a vague messianic belief arose that man stood on the threshold of a glorious new epoch in history. Belief in the twin forces of science and man's prospects of moral and rational perfection have stirred contemporary prophets to forecast that the poisons and evils by which the body politic of Europe had for so long been ravaged would be banished with the birth of a new world order. Wherever men turn in the present age, they confront some version of this prevailing world sentiment. We are reminded on every hand that we have harnessed the forces of nature. We are told that the same techniques by which the physical universe has been conquered can be the means of controlling a massive and complicated social order. With the increase in the tools and materials of social knowledge, mankind has the ability to gauge so precisely the trends of the social order and the forces which move it that only an accident will upset its harmony or disturb the perfect functioning of new institutions.

Mankind's faith in modern science as the key to all progress and development was for Churchill one of the banes of contemporary society. Science for him was essentially an amoral and neutral force, while the great issues with which men were confronted were intellectual, moral, and political. "It is . . . a fact that science has come to us in many other forms than those of blessing and healing and convenience. Great powers have been wrested by man from nature, and unless the quality and spirit and vision of the human race in many lands, in all the strongest lands, narrows the gap between these powers and the qualities and standards of human intelligence and virtue, what might take the form of immeasurable blessings may become the cause of our total destruction."[1] Whereas the consequences of science in the exploiting of natural resources are automatic and determinate, the results which flow from plans and policies in the social order are always ambiguous, beclouded, and uncertain. Inevitably, the requirements of politics and society are utterly unlike those of scientific inquiry. Modern thinkers have insisted, however, they were easily and readily equated. Yet in politics there is no effective substitute for political wisdom nor any sound way of preempting moral judgment. If physical resources and scientific data can be accumulated, classified, and stored, men have discovered no comparable way that wisdom can be stockpiled. Primarily because he was so profoundly aware of the essence and enduring nature of politics, Churchill was loath to entrust public responsibilities to scientific experts and administrative specialists. He commented: "On many occasions in the past we have seen attempts to rule the world by experts of one kind or another. There have been the theocratic, the military and the aristocratic and it is now suggested that we should have scientific—governments."[2]

The school of the statesman is not the physical world but the network of social relations in which conflicts emerge and must be adjusted. There is a nonscientific dimension to life which has its own formulas and calls for its own inventions. Churchill's recipe for educating mankind for politics was well stated in a speech at the University of Miami:

This is an age of machinery and specialisation but I hope, none the less—indeed all the more—that the purely vocational aspects of university study will not be allowed to dominate. . . . Engines were made for men, not men for engines. Mr. Gladstone said many years ago that it ought to be part of a man's religion to see that his country is well governed. Knowledge of the past is the only foundation we have from which to peer into and

1. London *Times*, July 17, 1948, p. 4.
2. *Time*, November 19, 1945, p. 29.

measure the future. Expert knowledge, however indispensable, is no substitute for a generous and comprehending outlook upon the human story with all its sadness and with all its unquenchable hope.[3]

From one point of view, Churchill attributed many of the ills and shortcomings of society to the role of modern science. Instead of viewing science as a touchstone for the relief of painful divisions and rivalries in society, he often implied that some of the fault for their remaining unsolved lay with science and democracy. Mass society has found no place for the art, as distinct from the science, of politics. More precisely it has no room for that small number of well-trained professionals whose skill, to paraphrase Churchill, was the beautiful intricacy of diplomatic and military maneuver, not the symmetry of geometric propositions. Science, in fact, frequently threatened and sometimes destroyed the qualities of humanity and chivalry which, in Churchill's scale of values, constituted the glory of a less troubled Europe. Without those qualities which the humanities and not the sciences best supply, man could scarcely prove worthy of the stewardship of the weapons and secrets wrested from nature. The virtues he deemed so important were the property of a mind informed by history and philosophy. As this was the highest attainment for man in the world of the ancients, so the paramount task of the university should be to inculcate clear thinking on the main themes of government and society. It was not only that science offered few clues to the relief of tensions in society. More important, present-day technology placed in jeopardy those intrinsic qualities of individuality by which humanity had advanced. Paradoxically, scientific techniques, from which many expected salvation, have produced a mechanical order in which the individual has been alienated from himself. Powerful weapons of destruction and new tools of industrial production which this mechanical order have made possible turn on their creator to threaten and destroy him. To arrest this threat, one hope remains of recovering those human resources through which mankind has progressed over the centuries. The highest demand is for autonomous and independent individu-

3. Winston S. Churchill, "University of Miami," February 26, 1946, *The Sinews of Peace*, ed. Randolph S. Churchill (London: Cassell and Company, 1948), 92.

als, for: "On all sides we see the organisations and machinery of life and government growing stronger and more formidable. Man must, by his personality and individuality, at least keep pace with the mechanical developments; and must be sure that he uses his institutions and is not the mere expression of their workings."[4]

Men live by values and the spirit. There have recently been significant rediscoveries of this as students of society have turned from futile and ill-fated toils in constructing value-free sciences of society. In the broad range of politics, scholars and statesmen are abandoning their illusion that values are irrelevant. A government by scientists, Churchill found, would be as intolerable as a government by theocrats or by any group whose preoccupation was something other than seeking the best government—not the best government *a priori* but the best under the circumstances. But he reserved his sharpest criticism for those who would substitute science not only for politics but for society itself. As a principal speaker at the celebration of the founding of a great scientific institution of learning, the Massachusetts Institute of Technology, he spoke out:

> In his introductory address, Dr. Burchard, the Dean of Humanities spoke with awe of "an approaching scientific ability to control men's thoughts with precision." I shall be very content if my task in this world is done before that happens. Laws just or unjust may govern men's actions. Tyrannies may restrain or regulate their minds with falsehood and deny them truth for many generations of time.
>
> But the soul of man thus held in a trance or frozen in a long night can be awakened by a spark coming from God knows where and in a moment the whole structure of lies and oppression is on trial for its life. . . . Science no doubt could if sufficiently perverted exterminate us all; but it is not in the power of material forces in any period which the youngest here tonight need take into practical account, to alter the main elements in human nature or restrict the infinite variety of forms in which the soul and genius of the human race can and will express itself.[5]

Churchill's opposition to the uncritical admiration of everything scientific was rooted in his comprehension of the fundamental

4. London *Times*, July 17, 1948, p. 4.
5. New York *Times*, April 1, 1949, p. 10.

nature of politics. Present-day efforts to reduce all politics to an exact science in which every political development could be foreseen and predicted err by neglecting three of its most basic characteristics. Whatever the goals and extrinsic character of politics, its intrinsic qualities are everywhere the same. In the first place, politics, especially on the international scene, while not identical with force, supplies a rational alternative, as well as a basic deterrent, to force. It is true and even axiomatic that politics is a struggle for power. Some have interpreted this to mean that politics was a war by proxy for military forces. But force or military strength and its use are only incidents. The problems of politics are endless. Force and warfare are those expressions of power in which the strength of individuals and nations are tested and decided. The problems of politics endure and know of no decisive solutions. In human affairs, the best man can hope for is to discover some kind of relatively stable equilibrium of power through which insight and steadiness may be wisely adapted in the interest of peace. Force is so ambiguous as a determinant of political power because it is always relative to somebody else's potential means of force. And the baffling and difficult prospect of comparing the elements of strength makes politics something other than an exact science. Churchill reflected on these more subtle aspects of politics when in 1951 he wrote: "It is said that we are getting stronger, but to get stronger does not necessarily mean that we are getting safer. It is only when we are strong enough that safety is achieved; and the period of the most acute danger might well arise just before we were strong enough."[6]

Therefore, the capacity to use force effectively is decisive as an element of political power only if that capacity is as significant in relative terms as it is in itself. That is, nations whose power is sufficient to warn any ambitious or aggressive friend or foe that a test of military strength would be more expensive in lives and resources than other alternatives can encourage the use of a peaceful alternative to force. Politics is an alternative to force because both are in

6. *Parliamentary Debates* (Hansard) House of Commons, Fifth Series, Vol. 487, May 10, 1951 (London: His Majesty's Stationery Office, 1950), 2161.

practice overt expressions of conflicts and rivalries that underlie and produce them. Force will be employed as the expression of conflict when politics has failed in its mission. Politics presumes that individuals and groups through checks and balances will be led to refrain from a use of violence if in so doing they would jeopardize their own interests.

Recent foreign policy in the West is intelligible only to the degree that this principle is comprehended. Policies designed to deter the Russians derive from this principle and the fate of the nation is intimately bound up in its validity. Many Americans, and indeed some Europeans, under the spell of the liberal illusion about power politics have judged the rearmament program in Europe and America in exclusively military terms. For example, we have often been told that a rearmament program could be justified because at a certain date in the foreseeable future we would be able to turn back the Russians at some line or other, or conversely, that it should be rejected because the chances of success or a military victory at any time in the foreseeable future did not exist. Yet there is an alternative to both these propositions and it is the one on which responsible leaders base their thinking. In a word, it is the conception that a deterrent to Russian expansion can be created which will invite them not to abandon but to seek their objectives through means other than military expansion. Such a concept remains essentially meaningless unless the inseparable relationship of force and politics to their source in political rivalries and struggles for power is fully comprehended. In general, even for aggrandizing states, politics will be chosen as a means to the end of domination and control only if there are sufficient deterrents to the use of force to make the peaceful the more rational alternatives; as Churchill expressed it: "I have always held the view that the maintenance of peace depends upon the accumulation of deterrents against aggression."[7]

Peace for Churchill, then, was seen in a political light, leading him to proclaim: "I am looking for peace. I am looking for a way to stop war, but you will not stop it by pious sentiments and appeals.

7. *Parliamentary Debates*, Vol. 339, October 5, 1938, p. 44.

You will only stop it by making practical arrangements."[8] Such practical steps require not simply the use or threat of force nor merely the profession of good and peaceful intentions. They are steps which aim at erecting an edifice of political power. At the present moment in history such a goal required as one of its pillars the growth of Anglo-American unity; for in Churchill's mind: "Neither the sure prevention of war, nor the continuous rise of world organisation will be gained without what I have called the fraternal association of the English-speaking peoples. This means a special relationship between the British Commonwealth and the Empire and the United States."[9] It also included the emergent power of Western Europe, and its nations joined together without dogmatic and inflexible ideological tests. As Churchill viewed the Soviet threat, for the present and the foreseeable future the best deterrent remained the power of the United States. "We must be under no delusion that it is not American armed force which preserves the peace of the world at the moment."[10]

With these Churchillian proposals, we are in the presence of little that is new or unusual from a concrete or specific point of view. The steps and measures that he urged have been recommended by others. It was the overall theory undergirding his recommendations which was novel or at least which was often misunderstood or misrepresented and therefore overlooked. It is precisely an understanding of the nature of politics that presents the most serious theoretical difficulty for many contemporary analysts. The prevailing errors which result, on the one hand, from disregarding the intimate relationship of politics and force or, conversely, the mistakes which arise from equating the two were avoided by Churchill. To him it was axiomatic that they were both merely alternate expressions of the unceasing struggle for power among nations. Because politics is so intimately related to force on the international scene, only the effective balancing of power can postpone or prevent perilous resorts to force.

The second aspect of politics of which Churchill in his concept

8. *Parliamentary Debates*, Vol. 310, March 26, 1936, pp. 1529–30.
9. New York *Times*, March 6, 1946, p. 4.
10. London *Times*, April 22, 1948, p. 6.

of statesmanship has reminded us is its provisional and prudential character. The tactics of politics are immediate and tentative. The measures that nations take can be identified with more general causes than their own interests only at grave risk of failure, hypocrisy, and vacillation. For those who espouse broad and lofty humanitarian objectives, it is inevitably true that nations in their policies pursue programs on this level only when their own national interests are not jeopardized thereby. Symbolic of the practical aspects of politics was Churchill's approach to the problem of Spain. On September 19, 1945, when no immediate and overwhelming threat from the East was apparent, he bluntly rejected General Franco's requests: "It is out of the question for the British Government to support Spanish aspirations in future peace settlements, nor do I think it likely that Spain will be invited to join a future world organisation."[11] By May 12, 1949, however, the changing conditions of international politics and the increasing menace of Russian imperialism having become apparent, he felt called upon to say: "The absence of Spain from the Atlantic Pact involves, of course, a serious gap in the strategic arrangements for Western Europe. I was glad to hear . . . [the favorable expression for] the return of ambassadors. I do not ask more than that at the present time."[12] Yet in another and earlier period, he had questioned whether Spain was properly considered part of the NATO region.

If it were not for the practical requirements of politics, these shifts and turns in policy, at least in emphasis if not in substance, could be properly denounced as blatant inconsistencies. Since politics are preeminently practical and provisional and grounded in changing circumstances, political adjustments in the interest of the objectives of states are essential. Therefore, we must look for consistency not in each concrete political action but in the more general principles which inspire the conduct of foreign policy. For Churchill, the principle which informed all others was the broad concept of the national interest. It is here, in what is general to all international action, that consistency can be found. The steps nations take in the

11. New York *Times*, September 19, 1945, p. 18.
12. *Parliamentary Debates*, Vol. 464, May 12, 1949, p. 2027.

conduct of policy are by the nature of contemporary international politics limited and prudential. Only as they contribute to national security and survival are measures justified and clarified.

A third characteristic of politics must be noted which differentiates politics most vividly from other spheres with which it is frequently confused and confounded. Politics is qualitatively different from philosophy. Its guides are relative and the absolutes it knows are those which can be associated with successful political action. One such principle is the rule of the balance of power. Another is the precept that compromise, while impossible on matters of principle, is essential for issues involving political interests. It is the virtue of political action that the actor in politics remains free to negotiate and explore so long as he is guided by a sense of his nation's true interests.

In sum, the realm of politics is one in which the participants must choose among options made legitimate not by abstract principles but by their relation to the viability and survival of the nation at any given time. It is mandatory that certain lines of action be followed on particular occasions and others pursued under other conditions. No absolute principle provides ready-made answers to these painful choices. It was conceivable to a British archpatriot that a way could be found through novel arrangements to relate Britain, despite historic policies of freedom of action in Europe, to some proposed plan for Western European union. If politics is looked at in absolute terms with respect to the forms in which the traditional interests of nations have expressed themselves, Churchill's changing attitude toward Europe could be interpreted as a political stratagem. If we assume that the relative character of political action makes possible a variety of practical responses, then what he declared on June 27, 1950, expressed political wisdom: "Although a hard-and-fast concrete federal constitution for Europe is not within the scope of practical affairs, we should help, sponsor, and aid in every possible way the movement towards European unity. We should seek steadfastly for means to become intimately associated with it."[13]

13. *Parliamentary Debates*, Vol. 476, June 27, 1950, p. 2157.

Once we have comprehended, as Churchill did, the nature of the political environment within which all statesmen must function, the actual role and behavior of the political leader become clearer and more understandable. Churchill had a good deal to say about political leadership. Yet many of his most striking affirmations were found in the relation between his words and his deeds and in the inferences to be drawn from his comments on the actions of well-known contemporaries. It was one of Churchill's maxims that: "Men in power must be judged not by what they feel, but by what they do. To lament miseries which the will has caused is a cheap salve to a wounded conscience."[14] It is helpful to observe that he attributed to the leader as human being certain qualities distinct from other requirements he established for the leader as political actor. If we acknowledge there are general human virtues and concrete political or practical virtues, this observation may serve to distinguish what Churchill had in mind. The leader, as man, must possess the general virtues of wisdom, courage, judgment, moderation, and moral conviction. As political actor, he must also have the capacity to concentrate on essentials, to choose in the light of changing circumstances and to act in the face of a torrent of fast-moving events. In this distinction, Churchill's vision of the statesman is further differentiated and defined.

14. Winston S. Churchill, *Marlborough: His Life and Times* (6 vols.; New York: Scribner's, 1938), I, 59.

PART FOUR

War

"Force, like peace, is not an abstraction; it cannot be understood or dealt with as a concept outside of the given framework of purpose and method. If this were better understood, there could be neither the sweeping moral rejection of international violence which bedevils so many Americans in times of peace nor the helpless abandonment to its compulsions and its inner momentum which characterizes so many of us in times of war."—George F. Kennan

CHAPTER EIGHT
The Nature of War

The peril of another general world war confronts society with terrors of unparalleled magnitude. The extent of awareness of the hideous and hopeless character of modern war is not the same for different generations. For the oldest generation among us whose memories go back to World War I, the scene persists of men locked in grisly, indecisive combat, huddled together in cold, muddy trenches, harassed and pinned down by artillery and facing death from machine gun fire. For the succeeding generation, the grim sense of tragedy is more violent and terrible. An image flashes through their minds of vast metropolitan areas laid waste, of millions of defenseless victims, of human cogs in armored machines lunging across enemy lines, of the human and material debris of indiscriminate bombings, and of burnt flesh and melting steel structures seared by the absolute weapon. Finally, the youngest generation sees its existence imperiled by a Damoclean sword of total atomic destruction. For any one of these generations, it comes as no surprise that for Churchill war constituted the ultimate human problem. In the twilight of his career, the Conservative leader only too vividly remembered what two generations were striving to forget and what another was seeking to avoid. He had seen war firsthand in its various manifestations both as a participant and an observer and he feared the ultimate destruction of a third world war.

Only those who reflect on its historical background can appreciate fully the most terrifying aspects of contemporary twentieth-century war. One can comprehend present-day warfare only through comparing it with forms of conflict fundamentally unlike it. Throughout history wars were fought for concrete and limited objectives. Kings and emperors did battle for strategic frontiers, important towns and castles, or other territorial objectives. War and diplomacy were two sides of one reality, and successes in one were registered in agreements in the other. The story is told of diplomatic negotiations in the Middle Ages conducted under a sacred elm tree which stood on the boundary line separating the hereditary estates of the kings of France from the estates of the Plantagenet rulers who governed England and certain western provinces in France. By custom, the sovereigns of the two states met here to negotiate. Often discussions were interrupted by reports of victories or defeats, and when talks were resumed, the negotiators recognized the new power situation that war had created. War and diplomacy were inseparable from one another and were carried on amidst the continual ebb and flow of conflict over limited territorial or dynastic objectives.

War in the modern European era in the fifteenth and sixteenth centuries grew more extensive and intensive. With the breakdown of medieval Christianity and the release of loyalties and emotions of religion into political channels, the nature and conduct of war intensified. Contemporary warfare underwent a fourfold transformation characterized by outright revolutions in the objectives of war, the ratio of participants to total population, the rules regarding noncombatants, and the moral and spiritual fervor which inspired the warring states. First, the objectives of war in the feudal period were localized for practical political reasons. Regional or continental ambitions awaited the flowering of the nation-state. The absence of a money economy set limits to the potentialities for aggrandizement by rulers and princes. Wars consisted essentially of skillful maneuver and tactical artifices in which prisoners and positions counted but human lives were not carelessly sacrificed.

Second, the proportion of soldiers which governments were willing and able to support dropped as low as 1 percent of the total population in the last part of the eighteenth century. Under feudalism, the warrior had been a permanent factor, but not the army. Radical individualism characterized warfare growing out of attempts by feudal nobility to preempt for themselves all military prerogatives. Nevertheless, the nature of militarism in early modern European history placed sharp limits on wars' duration. The common foot soldiers, while more numerous, remained mercenaries whose livelihood depended on the existence of enemies with whom they could make war. Under these circumstances, an eighteenth-century military leader, the Marshal of Saxe, declared: "I am not at all in favor of battles, especially at the beginning of a war. I am even persuaded that an able general can wage war all his life without being compelled to give battle."

Beneath the surface, however, new forces were stirring. The Age of the Enlightenment did not leave the military system untouched. Pacifist currents of thought in the Enlightenment opposed war as such, and antagonism appeared to warfare as it was practiced. Voltaire described paid mercenaries as murderers for hire and the scum of the earth. Quesnay singled out the standing army as the most unproductive of any military system. Rousseau spoke of such armies as the pest that was fast depopulating Europe. In their place, he urged the creation of nonprofessional militias in which every citizen would serve his country. In the name of the Enlightenment a ferment of romantic ideas against the caste-ridden standing army spread. Although the recruitment and leadership of the great mass of common men as soldiers began late in the eighteenth century, the strategic concept of victory through wars without battles lived on. Even that iron disciplinarian Frederick the Great was wont to refer to a battle as an unpleasant emetic necessary only at periodic intervals. Any large-scale emergence of citizen armies awaited the American and French revolutions.

Thus the seeds of the Enlightenment, which were planted at the beginning of the eighteenth century, did not bear fruit until the end of that century. At the time of Frederick the Great, two-thirds of the Prussian army was comprised of foreign mercenaries. Against the armies of France recruited in the French Revolution as the result of conscription, the Prussian troops, of whom one-third were mercenaries, and the English army, described by the Duke of Wellington as mere scum of the earth, suffered a decisive and melancholy fate. Until the French Revolution, *esprit de corps* among the officer-nobility was judged more important than nationalist sentiment among the rank-and-file, and war was interpreted as a noble art appropriate to standing armies and their quasi-feudal array. In practice, during much of the eighteenth century casualties through desertion ex-

ceeded those in battle; and to keep his army intact Frederick the
Great offered bonuses to deserters who returned to their units after
six months. In the words of the historian Toynbee: "About the middle of the eighteenth century, war was in much the same condition
as slavery: it was an ancient social evil which was manifestly on the
wane."[1]

However, war as a temperate and well-mannered contest proved
incapable of withstanding the impact of the social forces set in motion by the French Revolution and the Industrial Revolution. It was
a portent of future developments that, at a time when prudent Federalists like Alexander Hamilton were formulating principles of foreign policy for the United States, Mirabeau warned the French National Assembly that representative governments might prove more
bellicose than absolute monarchy. These warnings were to be realized by the mid—twentieth century. Industrialism provided the pro-
tagonists in war with new and more terrible equipment; democracy
gave them that emotional fervor and lethal drive which only a righteous and popular cause provides. From a quantitative and qualitative viewpoint, developments with their genesis in the eighteenth and
nineteenth centuries wrought havoc in the twentieth century. Wars
grew in number, duration, and objectives. In an earlier era, substantial intervals of peace followed extended and costly wars. When wars
or sets of wars had lasted for from ten to twenty years, as much as a
century passed before another general war occurred. Extended
periods of peace followed the imperialism of Spain in the sixteenth
century, the wars of Louis XIV in the eighteenth century, and the Napoleonic Wars in the nineteenth century. From the Battle of Waterloo
to the Battle of the Marne, casualties in civil wars were greater than
those from international wars. It remained for the twentieth century
to bring about a change to this recurrent pattern. If there are precedents for two "knockout blows" of two world wars which followed
so sharply on the heels of one another, they must be found in ancient
not modern history. The double wars of the Romans and Carthagi-

1. Arnold J. Toynbee, *A Study of History* (10 vols.; London: Oxford University
Press, 1939), IV, 142.

nians and the two struggles of the Peloponnesian War by which Greek civilization was wrecked come closest to World War I and II.

War in the twentieth century is also unique in a qualitative sense. The spiritual and material aspects of international conflict have caused it to become "total war." The customary distinctions between civilians and combatants painfully worked out over nearly four centuries of trial and error have been obliterated. The legal status of the great mass of the people as civilians and noncombatants no longer gives assurance they will be spared destruction. Through universal military conscription foreshadowed in the French "levee en masse," active participants in war have increased, whether by coercion as in totalitarian states or through the voluntary enlistment in democratic societies. Qualitatively, war has been altered in the attitude of the participants who now seek, and, through modern technology, have the means of pursuing victory through the wholesale destruction of the enemy rather than through the avoidance of costly battles. Quantitatively, the change is characterized by the magnitude and uninterrupted nature of wars and in the numbers of individuals who both conduct and are imperiled by war. From the sixteenth to eighteenth centuries, the size of armies was numbered in tens of thousands.[2] In World War I, they reached a million; the Second World War found military establishments numbering ten million. In the seventeenth and eighteenth centuries, no more than 1 percent could be mobilized for military service. By World War I, the proportion for major European nations was 14 percent. Whereas the ratio dropped during World War II to a figure no greater than 10 percent in all but three cases—the exceptions were the United States, the Soviet Union, and Germany—twelve men are needed for military preparedness on the home front for one man engaged in actual military combat.

Churchill's public statements as early as 1901 make clear that he had studied, comprehended and pondered the influence of the great forces by which war was being transformed. His biographer, Rene

2. Hans J. Morgenthau, *Politics Among Nations* (5th ed.; New York: Alfred A. Knopf, 1978), 372.

Kraus, quotes a statement by Churchill in 1901 which is prophetic. He wrote then: "Now when mighty populations are impelled on each other, each individual embittered and inflamed, when the resources of science and civilization sweep away everything that might mitigate their fury, an European war can only end in the ruin of the vanquished and the scarcely less fatal commercial dislocations and exhaustion of the conquerors. The wars of the people will be more terrible than the wars of the kings."[3] In 1939, he further explained that the irrational qualities of mass societies in modern nation-states had become a major source of world conflict:

Why does the moth go to the candle? Its wings have been singed already. It has felt the bite of the flame. It would no doubt like to live its brief life and yet it flies to the burning candle with universal and almost automatic resignation. All nations are now moving forward abundantly and blindly, as if in a trance, toward the infliction upon one another of indescribable horrors. Such a contrast between the will of man and his actions seem to spring only from madness or from a seizure of herd passion.[4]

The passions of the herd gave contemporary nationalism its irrational and uncontrollable force despite boasts that this was the "Age of Reason." The changes that occurred were so unlike those that optimistic spokesmen of the Enlightenment had prophesied that Churchill reflected: "In 1900 a sense of moving hopefully forward to brighter, broader and easier days was predominant. Little did we guess that what has been called the century of the common man would witness as its outstanding feature more common men killing each other with greater facilities than any other five centuries together in the history of the world."[5]

In retrospect, the nineteenth century was an era of remarkable political attainment in the avoidance of war. Churchill described the second half of the nineteenth century and the first decade of the

3. Rene Kraus, *Winston S. Churchill: A Biography* (Philadelphia: J. B. Lippincott, 1940), 120–21.
4. Winston S. Churchill, "War Now or Never," *Collier's*, CIII (June 3, 1939), 9–10.
5. New York *Times*, April 1, 1949, p. 10.

twentieth century in these words: "For more than forty years there had been no major war in Europe. Indeed since the Civil War in the United States, there had been no great struggle in the West. . . . For several generations Britannia had ruled the waves—for long periods at less cost annually than that of a single modern battleship."[6] Throughout much of the nineteenth century the relative monopoly of sea power which the British enjoyed was a sacred trust in the service of the general interest of the world. In Churchill's words: "That was a marvellous story of British majesty and serenity in the days of calm and peace, when Britain stood armed as a trustee of the great power of the sea for all the world. Those were the days in which we sustained the American Monroe Doctrine, protecting all that vast world which had grown up in the West and now, with its vast might and strength, came to rescue the peoples of the old world."[7] Enlightened societies made the transition to the twentieth century in a spirit of unqualified optimism. At least one British twentieth-century statesman, its wartime prime minister, was frank enough to say:

But we entered this terrible Twentieth Century with confidence. We thought that with improving transportation nations would get to know each other better. We believed that as they got to know each other better they would like each other more and that national rivalries would fade in a growing international consciousness. We took it almost for granted that science would confer continual boons and blessings upon us. . . .

In the name of ordered and unceasing progress, we saluted the Age of Democracy expressing itself ever more widely through parliaments freely and fairly elected on a broad, universal franchise. We saw no reason why men and women should not shape their own home life and careers without being cramped by the growing complexity of the State, which was to be their servant.[8]

Yet the twentieth century became an era of total war. Churchill described the consequences of the two great wars and of the objectives

---

6. *Ibid.*
7. London *Times*, December 12, 1950, p. 4.
8. New York *Times*, April 1, 1949, p. 10.

of present warfare in a melancholy phrase: "What a terrible century this twentieth century has been. Two frightful world wars have shattered almost every institution."[9] He went on to say:

It is established that henceforth whole populations will take part in wars, all doing their utmost, all subjected to the fury of the enemy. It is established that nations who believe their life is at stake will not be restrained from using any means to secure their existence. . . .

Mankind has never been in this position before. Without having improved appreciably in virtue or enjoying wiser guidance, it has got into its hands for the first time the tools by which it can unfailingly accomplish its own extermination.[10]

Wars were no longer, as in the days of feudalism or the eighteenth century, to be won through an avoidance of conflict nor was moderation preserved by clever artifices and stratagems. Instead, it can be said, as Churchill remarked on the final German breakthrough in World War II:

Harsh as it may seem to say, a terrible thing to say in dealing with our own precious flesh and blood, it is our interest and the American interest that the whole Western front, and the air everywhere . . . should be in continuous action against the enemy, burning and bleeding his strength away at every opportunity and on all occasions, if we are to bring this horror to an end. I think it was not necessarily a bad thing, indeed it was a good thing, that large parts of the Western front were thrown into counter battles in open country by the enemy, counter battles in the forests, undulations and hills of the Ardennes, rather than that all our troops should be compelled to advance at this season of the year across great rivers and seas of mud against lines of concrete fortifications. It suited the Allies that there should be as much fighting as possible in the open country rather than that the whole front should be crashing up against pillboxes.[11]

It is the quality of his insights into the essential characteristics of contemporary warfare which entitles Churchill to respect as a stu-

---

9. London *Times*, June 29, 1950, p. 3.
10. Winston S. Churchill, *The Second World War*, Vol. I, *The Gathering Storm* (Boston: Houghton Mifflin, 1948), 40.
11. *Parliamentary Debates* (Hansard) House of Commons, Fifth Series, Vol. 407, January 18, 1945 (London: His Majesty's Stationery Office, 1950), 419.

dent of warfare. Out of respect for these insights, his contemporaries have listened not only to his words about particular wars and their effect upon the larger world crisis but also to his judgments about the future of warfare in general. In 1939, he had few serious doubts that war as a policy for the Allies could serve a rational purpose, or that they would emerge united and intact from the struggle. At that time he predicted: "Nor need there be fear about the final result, although the sufferings of the assaulted nations will be as great in proportion as they have neglected their preparations. There is no reason to suppose that they will not emerge, living and controlling, from the conflict." [12]

Yet during the course of World War II, he had begun to think that the prospects of survival from a third great struggle were infinitely more dubious: "After the experiences which all have gone through, and their sufferings, and the certainty that a third struggle will destroy all that is left of the culture, wealth, and civilisation of mankind and reduce us to the level almost of wild beasts, the most intense effort will be made by the leading Powers." [13] From his repeated statements, we must conclude that in his mind war, which at one time played a rational role as an instrument of national policy, had been undermined in its purposes. He made this concern explicit in many of his speeches in the postwar period and, even when speaking in mythological terms, he made plain his anxiety and fear: "But be careful . . . to keep them from colliding with each other, for, if that happens, both Gog and Magog would be smashed to atoms and we should all have to begin all over again—and begin from the bottom of the pit." [14]

The burden of our historical survey would seem to indicate that because, and not in spite of, the various material and political advances and developments, war had become absolute in character. Democracy and science, which had been heralded as solutions to war, have increased its intensity and ferocity. Thus society, having

12. Churchill, "War Now or Never," 54.
13. Winston S. Churchill, "Prime Minister to Dominions Secretary," March 4, 1942, *The Second World War*, Vol. IV, *The Hinge of Fate* (Boston: Houghton Mifflin, 1950), 711.
14. London *Times*, November 10, 1951, p. 6.

witnessed war's decline as a rational alternative in foreign policy, is now imperiled by a new era of barbarism and destruction if through some means or other war cannot be averted. Churchill summarized the peril in one concluding phrase:

How astonishing it is that present day civilisation should be exposed to dangers from which it was believed the labors of the seventeenth, eighteenth and nineteenth centuries had permanently rid the world; and that we, with all our vast delicate scientific structure of economics and finance upon which so many new millions get their bread, be exposed to potential strokes far more sudden and immediately decisive than any which could be dealt by the Cimbri and the Teutons, the Parthians, the Visigoths and the Gauls. . . . Many communities have been plunged back into a state of insecurity hitherto only associated with barbarism.[15]

Nevertheless, it is not without hope or significance that a dawning awareness of the destructiveness of contemporary warfare has brought forth new discussions concerning the inevitability of war. In past centuries, the question lacked the urgency and relevance it possesses today. Generally, throughout history, war has been accepted as inevitable because of the nature of man and human existence. Today, war appears to have lost its qualities as a rational instrument of diplomacy or as a means to any valid end. At one time, legitimate aspirations and goals for which nations had striven by traditional diplomatic techniques might, at the dictate of expediency, be pursued by exchanging war for diplomacy. In practice, the avowed ends of the state, whether honor, independence, or security, were sufficient to compensate for the sacrifice and suffering that warfare entailed. In earlier times the burden of war fell heavily on only a limited few. As we have seen, combat in the eighteenth century was a monopoly of mercenaries who fought for hire under the leadership of once-powerful noblemen who retained only the military vestiges of their power. The price of limited war, despite the brutality of all forms of group strife, was not so great that nations and individuals could not be persuaded to overlook the repulsive-

15. Winston S. Churchill, "Europe's Peace," February 5, 1937, *Step by Step, 1936–1939* (New York: Putnam's, 1939), 81.

ness of employing such means to attain the noble ends they sought. War was construed as a means of pursuing the objectives of diplomacy "by other means" because the risks were slight that either the objectives of war or the belligerents would be mortally damaged in the strife.

The new modes of war in the twentieth century have altered the connection between war and diplomacy fundamentally. No one can any longer argue convincingly that a rational relationship exists between the brutal instrumentalities of war and the political goals toward which they can be directed. War, far from being an alternative to diplomacy, has become the *reductio ad absurdum* of statecraft. Both militarists and pacifists have declared that in any future world struggle, mankind would witness the destruction of victors and vanquished alike and neither would be assured of a viable social and economic existence. Among the past objectives in war, only national survival still remains a legitimate basis for engaging the enemy. Even here the alternative is more apparent than real, for both war and capitulation threaten the modern nation-state with destruction. Through capitulation, the nation gives up its present sovereignty and future existence and thereby its national tradition which past generations have secured. Through war, the nation imperils its freedom, general welfare, and moral purpose, insofar as modern warfare inevitably makes imperative measures and operations for which only the garrison state is equipped. The most tragic phase of the present crisis, therefore, is the narrowing down of the alternatives available in foreign policy. When a state is confronted with worldwide conflict against major aggressors, the alternatives are no longer national suicide or war. Under certain conditions, the real alternatives may be nothing less than two different kinds of national suicide, one through surrender and the other by war and even victory itself.

At the same time that far-reaching changes in technology, transportation, and scope have fundamentally altered the nature of war, profound human forces have transformed the intensity of national loyalties and thereby the psychological aspects of war. It is hardly surprising that these revolutionary changes should have preoccupied Churchill and come to the fore in his appraisals of the nature of war.

Nowhere have the changes that affect contemporary warfare been more far-reaching than with respect to transportation and communication. As Hans J. Morgenthau demonstrated,[16] from the beginning of recorded history throughout at least half of the nineteenth century, man's greatest speed on land or water was ten miles an hour. Until as late as the mid–nineteenth century, the time required to travel between two distant centers in Western Europe had not radically changed from the era of the Roman Empire. Whereas modern man by the mid–twentieth century could circle the globe in a few days, in 1790 a similar time was required to go from Boston to New York, a distance of approximately two hundred miles.

In other words, the world has witnessed the shrinking of a large-scale map into a small-scale globe. While men are now able to circle the globe with greater speed than ever before, there is little evidence these changes have brought greater human or political understanding. Ironically: "In the first half of the twentieth century, fanned by the crimson wings of war, the conquest of the air profoundly affected human affairs. It made the globe seem much bigger to the mind and much smaller to the body!"[17] Man's physical conquest of the globe has not been matched by similar intellectual or moral triumphs. Churchill pointed out: "In the Nineteenth Century Jules Verne wrote 'Round the World in Eighty Days.' It seemed a prodigy. Now you can get round it in four; but you do not see much of it on the way."[18]

In war, as Morgenthau demonstrated, mechanical developments resulted in unprecedented increases in the numbers of people destroyed by a single weapon. In an early era of warfare, a strict ratio existed of one thrust or one mechanical operation of a weapon for every victim. The first revolution which transformed this ratio was

16. Hans J. Morgenthau, *In Defense of the National Interest* (New York: Alfred A. Knopf, 1951), 53.
17. Churchill, New York *Times*, April 1, 1949, p. 10.
18. *Ibid.*

that brought about by the machine gun. One burst of fire was potentially destructive of hundreds of victims. The second revolution came with obliteration bombing in World War II threatening a thousand lives. The third revolution was by far the most portentous. The destruction caused by atomic bombs at Hiroshima and Nagasaki was a mere token of the destructiveness of atomic and hydrogen bombs capable of destroying and disabling millions of people. As a result of the three revolutions, a man or a small group of men acquired the power of destroying life up to a million-fold beyond past destructiveness. Even in World War II, weapons and material became more important than the human component of warfare, which led Churchill in 1941 to declare: "In the last war the U.S. sent two million men across the Atlantic. But this is not a war of vast armies, firing immense masses of shells at one another. We do not need the gallant armies which are forming throughout the American Union. . . . But we do need most urgently an immense and continuous supply of war materials and technical apparatus of all kinds."[19]

Technological changes also affected the importance of relatively permanent elements of national power such as geographic location. Churchill observed: "In all previous wars control of the sea had given the Power possessing it the great advantage of being able to land at will on the enemy's coast, since it was impossible for the enemy to be prepared at every point to meet seaborne invasion. The advent of air-power had altered the whole situation."[20] In World War II, the Germans were able to move their air force any place in France or the Low Countries as threats to the coastline might arise. Therefore, the chances of daring moves against one point or another were vastly diminished. In World War III, if it should come, the fighting would be influenced by contemporary Soviet technological developments. Or, as Churchill saw it: "In the event of war with Soviet Russia, two dangers would menace the defence of free Europe and our own life here. The first is the large number of U-

19. London *Times*, February 10, 1941, p. 7.
20. Churchill, *The Hinge of Fate*, 332–33.

boats, far more than the Germans had at the beginning of the late war, of an improved . . . type. . . . The second is, of course, the mining peril at all our ports and all free European ports."[21]

If the nature of war in the second half of the twentieth century reflected far-reaching technological changes, it was also influenced by profound social psychological developments. Within the modern state system, there had been power struggles for most of four centuries. Also present were recurrent rivalries and competition among political philosophies or pseudoreligions. The novelty of international politics in the contemporary Western world arises from the joining of the two conflicts into a single worldwide struggle. The centers of power in the United States and the Soviet Union are the shrines of universal democracy and world communism. In one respect, communism is the antithesis of religion and sees religion as the primary obstacle to progress. Yet as early as 1936, when most observers looked on communism as an economic system pure and simple, Churchill was saying: "The wars of Religion, we were told, have ended. Perhaps the wars of rival Irreligions have begun. Fascism and Communism each vaunt their themes, and neither will lack champions or martyrs."[22]

Thus communism, while maintaining that salvation through traditional religion is a deceit and an illusion, affirms its own true bolshevist faith by which all men can be redeemed. Because of the breakdown of universal moral standards, the efforts of bolshevism to elevate its own principles and standards to a worldwide level is the most far-reaching attempt at conversion through fire and the sword that Western society has witnessed. It should be noted that a chain of events since World War II has weakened the evangelical appeal of communism. Events in Hungary (1956), Czechoslovakia (1968), Afghanistan (1979), and Poland (1981) demonstrate that *Machtpolitik* and force, not the revolutionary dynamism of communism, are the ultimate weapon of the Soviet Union.

Although the aims of worldwide communism and the political

21. *Parliamentary Debates*, Vol. 486, April 19, 1951, p. 2017.
22. Churchill, "The Spanish Tragedy," August 10, 1936, *Step by Step*, 37.

instruments through which it pursues them are different in degree, they are not different in kind from some political systems in the West. In warfare, the aims of democratic societies have been enlarged in the struggle to involve total victory. The means through which such ambitions are being pursued are the agencies of the modern democratic state. The birth of national self-consciousness and the organization of vast national communities have made possible the administration of enterprises of war and destruction on a scale not envisaged before. Or, as Churchill put it: "All the noblest virtues of individuals were gathered together to strengthen the destructive capacity of the mass. Good finances, the resources of world-wide credit and trade, the accumulation of large capital reserves, made it possible to divert for considerable periods the energies of whole peoples to the task of devastation."[23] In the realm of the mind and the spirit, comparable forces were at work. National education provided the means of unifying national purpose, while the press through perpetual stimulation assured the constant attention of multitudes of people to a country's all-consuming effort. Finally: "Religion, having discreetly avoided conflict on the fundamental issues, offered its encouragements and consolations, through all its forms, impartially to all the combatants."[24] All these changes whereby the moral principles that had restrained nations were transformed into political ideologies equated with national interests and justifying virtually any political practice destroyed all the ancient and historic contraints that had influenced the conduct of nations. War became more brutal and ruthless because of the fusion of profound technological changes and the fervor of mass societies. In Churchill's grim portrait: "In the sombre wars of modern democracy chivalry finds no place. Dull butcheries on a gigantic scale and mass effects overwhelm all detached sentiment."[25]

23. Churchill, *The Gathering Storm*, 38.
24. *Ibid.*, 39.
25. Winston S. Churchill, "Prime Minister to General Ismay," April 29, 1941, *The Second World War*, Vol. III, *The Grand Alliance* (Boston: Houghton Mifflin, 1950), 200.

It should be obvious that Churchill was deeply aware of the profound revolutions in technology and nationalism by which warfare was being transformed. However, this knowledge in no way beclouded his grasp of certain timeless principles for the conduct of war which remain constant. These principles concern national unity, the role of chance and accidents, and the effects of moral constraints. They provide continuity in Churchill's outlook on war, even as his grasp of technological revolutions led him to understand the place of change. First, victory in war demands that primary emphasis be placed on national unity in misfortune and adversity alike. In the dark days before the war, Churchill concentrated on this principle saying: "War is little more than a catalogue of mistakes and misfortunes. It is when misfortune comes, however, that allies must hold more firmly together than ever before. Here in Britain, and I doubt not throughout the British Empire and Commonwealth of Nations, we always follow a very simple rule, which has helped us in maintaining the safety of this country: 'The worse things get, the more we stand together.'[26] In practice, victory may come through the conquest of space or the defeat of an enemy, but it may also result from the gains made possible in strength and power through a breathing space before actual conflict. A nation's territorial gains or losses may be paid for through bartering time against power. In 1941, Churchill counseled: "A vast scene can only be surveyed as a whole, and it ought not to be exposed and debated piecemeal, especially at a time when operations which are all related to one another are wholly incomplete. Into the general survey of the war come all sorts of considerations about the gain and loss of time and its effects upon the future."[27]

Churchill never forgot a second characteristic of warfare and politics, the role played by chance. Accidents may occur at any stage in a campaign or social program. However far-sighted the planners, blueprints yield to chance and to developments that no one could have foreseen. In military planning, Churchill observed that:

26. *Parliamentary Debates*, Vol. 481, November 30, 1950, p. 1338.
27. *Parliamentary Debates*, Vol. 372, June 10, 1941, p. 140.

Very few set-piece battles that have to be prepared over a long period of time work out in the way they are planned. . . . The unexpected intervenes at every stage. The will-power of the enemy impinges itself upon the pre-scribed or hoped-for course of events. Victory is traditionally elusive. Acci-dents happen. Mistakes are made. Sometimes right things turn out wrong, and quite often wrong things turn out right.[28]

In the human drama, the will and determination of the actors can never be anticipated or controlled. Indeed: "There is only one thing certain about war, that it is full of disappointments and also full of mistakes."[29] Whatever the uncertainties, man must act despite the vast unknown into which he is forever plunging: "There are some arguments which deserve to be considered before you can adopt the rule that you have to have a certainty of winning at any point, and that if you have not got it beforehand you must clear out. The whole history of war shows the fatal absurdity of such a doctrine. Again and again, it has been proved that fierce and stubborn resistance, even against heavy odds and under exceptional conditions of local disadvantage, is an essential element in victory."[30]

The third principle affecting the liberal democracies in their conduct of war arises from the moral limitations within which states operate. For democracies, there are moral boundaries in war. Certain actions which might serve a democracy's objectives are ruled out by its own moral principles. No democracy, for example, could exterminate a whole people even if its strategic aims would be facilitated in this way. The irreducible moral limits for democracies are rooted in such unchanging values as respect for the individual. What Churchill said about British tactics might be said with equal force for other Western democracies:

[It would be] impossible for us [the British] to imitate the mass extermina-tion methods of the Germans. . . . The idea that general reprisals upon the civil population and vicarious examples would be consonant with our whole outlook upon the world of affairs and with our name, reputation

28. *Parliamentary Debates*, Vol. 376, December 11, 1941, p. 1688.
29. London *Times*, April 27, 1941, p. 4.
30. *Parliamentary Debates*, Vol. 372, June 10, 1941, p. 148.

and principles, is, of course, one which should never be accepted in any way. We have, therefore, very great difficulties in conducting squalid warfare with terrorists.[31]

These three principles, concerning the primacy of national unity, the role of fortune, and the moral limitations that restrict democracies in war, constitute a common law of warfare for free peoples in the modern era. It is a sign of Churchill's wisdom that he should make them explicit to his countrymen, just as it was a mark of understanding that he appreciated so well the revolutions which had transformed mid–twentieth-century conflict.

The unwritten law on which any enduring peace must be founded is that war must be conducted for both military and political objectives. Present-day Western society has learned that wars waged solely for military victory can plant the seeds of a new conflict. In recent times, the most serious error in the conduct of war has been the failure of leaders to foresee and resist the newest and most likely threat to the peace emerging after World War II. More than professionalism in the techniques of warfare was required to anticipate the new threat. For this reason, Churchill resolutely maintained that military strategists even in war must be subject to political direction. On May 20, 1943, he explained: "Modern war is total, and it is necessary for its conduct that the technical and professional authorities should be sustained and if necessary directed by the Heads of Government, who have the knowledge which enables them to comprehend not only the military but the political and economic forces at work, and who have the power to focus them all upon the goals."[32] Peace must take firm root in political and economic soil. In war as in politics, a nation must define its objectives and priorities; its military decisions cannot be made without an eye to political objectives. No nation can do everything in war; every country must make choices. In 1941, the prime minister addressed the Parliament, elaborating on an ancient maxim:

The House has been reminded of Frederick the Great's maxim, ". . . that it was pardonable to be defeated, but that it was not pardonable to be sur-

31. *Parliamentary Debates*, Vol. 432, January 31, 1947, p. 1343.
32. New York *Times*, May 20, 1943, p. 4.

prised. . . ." It is . . . evident, I think, that you would not solve your problem, as Frederick the Great's maxim and his remarks seem to suggest, by being prepared at every point to resist not only what is probable but what is possible. In such circumstances, upon which there is no need to enlarge, it is not possible to avoid repeated rebuffs and misfortunes, and these, of course, we shall very likely have to go through for quite a long time.[33]

The establishment and maintenance of peace required the wise definition of interests as well as shrewd judgment in the use of scarce men and resources. On February 9, 1941, Churchill observed in a radio broadcast: "Next to cowardice and treachery, over-confidence, leading to neglect or slothfulness, is the worst of martial crimes."[34] Peace is a product of clarity about peacetime objectives and the prudent choice of means and ends in wartime. It may be a truism, but one which has had limited circulation in some Western democracies, to say that peace is established in warfare through the simultaneous pursuit of both military and political aims and the conduct of the war by the victors.

33. *Parliamentary Debates*, Vol. 371, May 7, 1941, p. 942.
34. London *Times*, February 10, 1941, p. 7.

CHAPTER NINE
Three World Wars

The overall philosophy underlying most of the statements set forth above comprehends the major principles in Churchill's approach to war. It is possible to analyze and evaluate further his conception of war and of its causes by looking at his views of specific wars. If we choose as examples of warfare the two worldwide struggles and select as a third the possible conflict which Churchill hoped might be averted, we can trace the evolution of his thinking over a significant historical period.

World War I

The First World War falls, in one sense, outside of the limits of this study. Yet in this war may be found the origins of all rational reflection on contemporary war and its prevention. It provides a picture of scene one in a modern Greek tragedy which has continued to unfold irresistibly until this very moment. For some historians, the two worldwide conflagrations represent two parts of a single great holocaust. Churchill would appear to support this interpretation when he declared:

One must regard these 30 years or more of strife, turmoil and sufferings in Europe as part of one story. I have lived through the whole story since 1911. . . . In its main essentials it seems to me to be one story of a 30 years' war, or more than a 30 years' war, in which British, Russians, Americans and French have struggled to their utmost to resist German aggression at a cost most grievous to all of them, but to none more frightful than to the Russians, whose country has twice been ravaged.[1]

All the major dimensions of the post–World War II crisis by which peace and order are threatened have their origin in this conflict. The

---

1. *Parliamentary Debates* (Hansard) House of Commons, Fifth Series, Vol. 408, February 27, 1945 (London: His Majesty's Stationery Office, 1950), 1276–77.

passing of the European age, the emergence of communism in Russia, the creation of power vacuums in Central and Eastern Europe and the sickness in mind if not in body of once stable, conservative Germany have largely shaped the 1950s, 1960s, 1970s, and 1980s. Therefore, all lines of inquiry into mankind's current predicament carry us back to World War I.

This is the diagnosis upon which Churchill has proceeded in formulating his views on the consequences of the First World War. The fires of ruthlessness and destruction of the war roared on undeterred until they had burned themselves out. Their ashes caused mortal wounds in the international body politic. In reviewing the world crisis from 1911 to 1918, Churchill wrote: "Events passed very largely outside the scope of conscious choice. Governments and individuals conformed to the rhythm of the tragedy, and swayed and staggered forward in helpless violence, slaughtering and squandering on ever-increasing scales, till injuries were wrought to the structure of human society which a century will not efface, and which may conceivably prove fatal to the present civilization."[2] Churchill could discern few signs of the West recovering fully from its wounds.

If the conflict was as tragic and its results as ominous as these passages portend, one would suppose that Churchill in some form or other had examined its causes. It may be sufficient to note that he wrote in *The World Crisis* that the real source of the conflict was the deterioration of the European political situation after 1870.[3] That evaluation was based on a firm belief that changes in the character of the balance of power and the weight of certain nations on the scales produced political circumstances that made the great conflict likely. His political orientation even in this earlier period led him to argue that the provisions of the Treaty of Utrecht were constructive in sustaining French national power, which was to serve as a deterrent to the ascendancy of Germany. Others had claimed the terms of Utrecht were too lenient for the defeated French, but Churchill evaluated the treaty in the light of the European balance of power.

2. Winston S. Churchill, *The World Crisis, 1911–1918* (New York: Scribner's, 1931), 1–2.
3. *Ibid.*, 1–30.

His analysis of the European situation after 1870 was based upon his appraisal of important shifts in the balance of power. In *The World Crisis*, he enumerated the aims underlying Bismarck's foreign policy. He maintained that Bismarck sought German ascendancy against France because he assumed France would sooner or later act against Germany from feelings of *revanche*. He was unable to conceal his admiration for the diplomacy of Bismarck, not so much for the skill with which the Triple Alliance was founded, but for the manner in which Bismarck, through the Reinsurance Treaty with Russia, sought to ameliorate the clash of Russian and Austrian interests in the Balkans. Through this arrangement, Germany was relieved of the threat of a concentration of French and Russian power, while Russia was reassured that a hostile combination of Austria and Germany would not imperil its interests in the Balkans. Bismarck's policy encouraged Great Britain to retain friendly relations with a power who was not a naval rival and who was sedulously cultivating good relations. France in such a world remained isolated, but Germany sought to encourage the extension of France's overseas interests. The delicate and intricate structure depended, however, on the wisdom and sagacity of German statesmen.

Prudence disappeared with the fall of Bismarck and the accession of the young kaiser with his band of intemperate advisors. The older political constellation had been one which potentially assured the predominance of Germany. It is also guaranteed a rational balance of forces not only through the reinsurance clause but the reluctance of its architect Bismarck to employ it aggressively in overextending German power. However, the new regime brashly set about jettisoning the Reinsurance Treaty and speeding German naval preparedness. The abandonment of the reinsurance clause drove the Russians into the arms of France; German naval preparedness led somewhat later to the British entente with Japan and France. The massive concentration of power in the hands of the Germans, which the wisdom of Bismarck had prevented from becoming an open threat to all Europe, led now to belated attempts to establish a new balance of forces when it became obvious that the executors of German foreign policy were no longer moderate but reckless men.

For England this threat remained vague and remote until Germany deliberately embarked on a policy of naval supremacy or the attainment of a naval position second only to England. The concentration of power in one state with the greatest land forces and the second most important naval forces in Europe endangered the whole European system. Until this point, Europe had enjoyed the protection of England's vastly superior navy, greater, in fact, than the next two largest European navies. By delaying its efforts to construct a new balance in Europe, England waited longer than its interests dictated. The force that might have balanced Germany in the East was eliminated, if only for the moment, with Russia's defeat at the hands of Japan in 1904. Such conditions of political instability provoked an arms race and a most dangerous state of mind on both sides. As mutual fears were intensified with the growing power of the Triple Entente, speculation grew that its expanding power in comparison with Germany's made the risk of conflict ever greater. It was doubtful indeed that the new and reckless German leaders would tolerate the possibility of such restraints on its power being established. This was the key to German foreign policy in the period immediately before World War I.

Therefore, the advent of World War I occurred in the shadows of a bitter, increasingly inflamed and essentially tragic struggle between one great constellation of powers and another arising to threaten it. In popular imagination, these brutal facts of the struggle for power were not generally recognized. Churchill commented that many Englishmen lived in two worlds, that of domestic politics as usual and of the tragic international struggle for power. In his words to the British people: "There was the actual visible world with its peaceful activities and cosmopolitan aims; and there was the hypothetical world, a world 'beneath the threshold,' as it were, a world at one moment utterly fantastic, at the next seeming about to leap into reality—a world of monstrous shadows moving in convulsive combinations through vistas of fathomless catastrophe."[4]

This "hypothetical world" was plainly the real world for Church-

4. *Ibid.*, 14.

ill, and attempts to obscure the urgency of creating a balance by which peace might have been maintained was to be untrue to the interest of the country. In fact, if peace could be preserved at all, it would only be through delicate adjustments and rectifications in the balance such as oftentimes had been worked out in the past. There was a chance that a system of combinations of power in equipoise in which violence was contained by counter-checks and balances might be established by the "cryptic phrases" of a polite and discreet diplomacy. However, "The vials of wrath were full" and even this marvelous system was to prove insufficient to restrain national passions. In practice, Germany was unable to restrain its ally Austria (some authorities maintain to the contrary that Austria-Hungary could not and would not have started a war without Germany's encouragement), and in the chain of events following Sarajevo the West witnessed the utter breakdown of the existing balance of forces.

The antidote to such a struggle, if it existed at all, was neither simple nor foolproof. For example, it was in the interests both of Americans and British that a balance be sustained in Europe. Yet England responded hesitantly and reluctantly when it perceived the great perils to the system. The gradual shift of power from Austria-Hungary to Germany was a threat which no one could minimize. Until well into the war itself, many Americans, and among them President Wilson, denied all responsibility for confronting the causes and objects of war within the complicated power politics of Europe. Had the United States played a more positive role, developments might have taken another course. The New York *Times* on November 8, 1945, quoted Churchill as saying with respect to the Truman declaration of October 27, 1945, which outlined postwar American responsibilities: "If such a statement had been made in the summer of 1914 . . . the Kaiser would never have launched an aggressive war over a Balkan question. All would have gone to a great parley between the most powerful governments of those days. In the face of such a declaration the World War of 1914 would not have occurred."[5] What antidote there was for the First World War

5. New York *Times*, November 8, 1945, p. 4.

resided in such alternatives for Churchill as he looked back on the origins of the conflict and its grave consequences for the future.

World War II

Churchill reported in his history of the Second World War a conversation with President Roosevelt about the nature of that struggle. The latter had inquired what would be the best name for the conflict then in progress. Churchill repeated in his history the answer he gave at the time: "I said at once 'The Unnecessary War.' There never was a war more easy to stop than that which has just wrecked what was left of the world from the previous struggle."[6] What he implied in his answer was more illuminating than the well-known title he gave the war. By referring in his statement to the scars which were visible upon "what was left of the world from the previous struggle," he indicated specifically that the threat of a second great conflict was implicit in the outcome of the first. A kind of remorseless logic inherent in the political arrangements following World War I carried the nation-actors from one crisis to another and eventually into war itself. Austria-Hungary had been dismembered and no new state or coalition of states had taken its place as a buffer against German expansion to the southeast. Moreover, the balance which had existed earlier against Germany in the east had been upset by an uncertainty over Russia's political role in the face of its apparent antagonism to capitalist states. Both England and France were war weary, grievously weakened in influence and power, and fatally lacking in bold and courageous leadership. The one power at the center of Europe that remained a united people, smarting from defeat and uneasy as a consequence of deep social unrest, was Germany.

The Versailles Treaty, which brought about this state of affairs, was a tragic settlement fraught with future hardships of every kind, regardless of the moderate character of its individual provisions. Peace on the European continent had been founded on a balance of

6. Winston S. Churchill, *The Second World War*, Vol. I, *The Gathering Storm* (Boston: Houghton Mifflin, 1948), iv.

power with many nations as factors on the scales. After the settlement at Versailles, the weakening of some states left others stronger and more dangerous than they had ever been in the past. The gradual shift of power from Austria-Hungary to Germany was responsible for shattering the equilibrium of Europe and for tempting the Germans to embark brazenly and feverishly upon an arms race with nations who preferred to blind themselves to the new threat. Looking back in 1937, Churchill observed: "As an independent Conservative member I felt bound to give the alarm when, five years ago, the vast secret process of German re-armament, contrary to Treaty, began to be apparent. . . . My only regret is that I was not believed. I can quite understand that this action of mine would not be popular in Germany. Indeed, it was not popular anywhere. I was told I was making ill will between the two countries."[7]

Despite ominous clouds on the horizon, Churchill nurtured the hope that German power might be balanced and contained primarily by the strength of the French army. He hoped the preoccupation of the Soviet Union would prevent the combining of Soviet strength with other forces opposed to the status quo. In 1932 he observed: "At the present time, and until, or unless Germany is re-armed . . . I put my confidence, first of all upon the strength of the French Army; secondly, upon the preoccupation of Russia in the Far East, on account of the enormous increase in the armaments of Japan; and thirdly, I put it, in a general way, upon the loathing of war which prevails."[8] Even then the reasons for concern were unmistakable. If the Germans were not to remain disarmed, then the natural supremacy of that country was bound to assert itself. In Churchill's terse warning: "A stationary population of 40 millions under-inhabiting the fairest portion of the globe, in contact, along hundreds of miles of land frontier with a multiplying, progressing German race and state of 60 or 70 millions, is a proposition inherent with explosive quality."[9] He repeatedly stressed that while talk-

7. Winston S. Churchill, "Friendship with Germany," September 17, 1937, *Step by Step, 1936–1939* (New York: Putnam's, 1939), 141.
8. *Parliamentary Debates*, Vol. 272, November 23, 1932, p. 88.
9. Winston S. Churchill, *The Aftermath* (New York: Scribner's, 1929), 222.

ing of peace, Europe should understand the causes of war as they had always existed. The fear which hung over Europe was that an immense imbalance of power would tempt the Germans to become the aggressor. For those who remained innocent of the peril, Churchill explained: "I should very much regret to see any approximation in military strength between Germany and France. Those who speak of that as though it were right, or even a question of fair dealing, altogether underrate the gravity of the European situation."[10]

Of those who would endorse arms parity between France and Germany, Churchill asked: "Do you wish for war?" Once France as the leader of nations favoring the status quo had lost its position of equality, to say nothing of its preponderance of power, the nations commited to upsetting the status quo would interpret the change as a clear invitation to test the peace structure. The changes beneath the surface were far more important than an occasional triumph or defeat at one of the many disarmament conferences. They specifically included the disappearance of France's military ascendancy, the acceleration of German rearmament, and evidence as a consequence that the scales of the European balance of power were decisively tilting in Germany's favor.

The margins of initiative for states who sought peace after World War I were substantially diminished. Earlier circumstances had cut a swath within which all nations were compelled to move. The European system was so unstable, the imbalance of power between nations like Germany and Russia on the one hand and the infant states of Eastern Europe was so extreme, and the war weariness of England and France was so overpowering that it is tempting to say that World War II was inevitable.

It nonetheless remains true and is a fact of politics that certain things are possible in spite of the tragic circumstances in which states find themselves. If the nations who supported the status quo had remained armed and united, the prospects of peace would have been enhanced. As Churchill commented: "I have no doubt whatever that firm guidance and united action on the part of the Vic-

10. Churchill, *The Gathering Storm*, 72–73.

torious Powers would have prevented this last catastrophe."[11] The best time for effective action came before Hitler's rise to power. At that time, the Allies could have supported and strengthened the moderate forces within the Weimar Republic in the period before 1933. So far as political and legal forms are concerned, it is difficult to indict the West. The peace treaty which the United States accepted for Germany was hardly vengeful or punitive. Yet the best policy for Germany was defined as rigorously noninterventionist and more active measures were called for. Germans were treated with undisguised contempt and the prestige on which societies thrive was denied them. The weakness of German society in general was further aggravated by the international community's doing nothing to return the new Germany to a respected place in the society of nations. The story is told by George F. Kennan that, as late as 1926, no German was accepted on the golf links at Geneva, a slight by the participants in the new international organization (the League of Nations) which left deep and tragic scars. As Churchill observed: "If the Allies had resisted Hitler strongly in his early stages . . . a chance would have been given to the sane elements in German life . . . to free Germany of the maniacal Government . . . into . . . which she was falling."[12] It ought to be remembered that the German people by a majority twice voted against Hitler, but the allies and the League of Nations were so indecisive that once he ascended to power his aggressions were a triumph over every moderate and restraining force in Germany.

We may notice, if only in passing, that whenever Churchill refers to those acts which might have been expected of the League, he does so in terms of the roles of its member states, not of the League as a vague corporate abstraction. Thus he declared: "If the United States had taken an active part in the League of Nations, and if the League of Nations had been prepared to use concerted force, even

11. Winston S. Churchill, "A Speech to the Joint Meeting of the Senate and Chamber: Brussels," November 16, 1945, *The Sinews of Peace*, ed. Randolph S. Churchill (London: Cassell and Company, 1948), 41.
12. *Ibid.*

had it only been European force, to prevent the re-armament of Germany, there was no need for further serious bloodshed." [13] In a day and age when it has been fashionable to promote the fiction that existing international organizations have lives apart from member national governments, this honest statement of political realities is as wholesome as it is true.

From 1934 to 1939, while the margins of choice for the nations had dramatically narrowed, they still allowed for the resolution of certain important conflicts. For one thing, not until 1934 was German supremacy seriously challenged. Churchill commented regarding that period: "There was no moment in these sixteen years when the three former allies, or even Britain and France with their associates in Europe, could not, in the name of the League of Nations and under its moral and international shield, have controlled by a mere effort of the will the armed strength of Germany." [14] The control of events remained in the hands of England and France until the middle of 1934, in so far as they were able to act in concert. But the moment was swiftly passing when military advantage lay with the members of the League. The policy of German rearmament was launched on precisely the date that British Prime Minister MacDonald was pressing for the disarmament of France. By 1935, Churchill still remained confident that firm action could arrest the Germans and prevent war or at least delay it indefinitely. He observed: "Germany either could have been brought to the bar at Geneva and invited to give a full explanation and allow inter-Allied missions of inquiry to examine the state of her armaments and military formations in breach of the Treaty; or, in the event of refusal, the Rhine bridgeheads could have been reoccupied until compliance with the Treaty had been secured, without there being any possibility of effective resistance or much likelihood of bloodshed." In Churchill's mind, failure to resist German remilitarization and reoccupation of the Rhineland in 1936 (which were both contrary to the treaties of Versailles and Locarno) meant the Allies had "lost

13. *Ibid.*
14. Churchill, *The Gathering Storm*, 15–16.

irretrievably the last chance of arresting Hitler's ambitions without a serious war."[15] It advanced the detrainment points from which the German army could invade France by one hundred miles, weakened the position of the German General Staff which would have forced Hitler to withdraw if there had been resistance, and practically handed over to Hitler the Danubian area.

In summary, it was possible that a stiffer and more resolute attitude against Hitler's adventures might have caused the Nazis to delay attempts to realize their timetable and have led to division within that regime. If there had been firmness in 1936 when Germany sought to reoccupy the Rhineland, the chances for peace would have improved. Another fateful event in the years from 1933 to 1939 was the unsuccessful attempt by President Roosevelt to initiate high-level negotiations among Germany, Italy, France, Britain, and the United States looking toward a general settlement. Churchill had this to say of President Roosevelt's proposals of January 11, 1938: "No event could have been more likely to stave off, or even prevent, war than the arrival of the United States in the circle of European hates and fears. To Britain it was a matter almost of life and death."[16] The acceptance of these overtures might even at the eleventh hour have prevented the events so shortly to follow in Austria and Munich. Churchill concluded: "We must regard its rejection— for such it was—as the loss of the last frail chance to save the world from tyranny otherwise than by war."[17]

In the dark hours of 1938 there came a moment when war might have been shortened and made less costly if the conflict had been joined at that time. Not war's prevention but its amelioration, providing it had to come, was the question Churchill examined, saying: "There was sense in fighting for Czechoslovakia in 1938 when the German Army could scarcely put half a dozen trained divisions on the Western Front, when the French with nearly sixty or seventy divisions could most certainly have rolled forward across

15. *Ibid.*, 145–46, 195.
16. *Ibid.*, 254.
17. *Ibid.*

the Rhine or into the Ruhr. But this had been judged unreasonable, rash, below the level of modern intellectual thought and morality."[18] Yet when war did take place, the two leading Western democracies were forced to stake their lives with far graver risks on the safeguarding of Poland's territorial independence. Looking back, Churchill reflected: "History, which we are told is mainly the record of the crimes, follies, and miseries of mankind, may be scoured and ransacked to find a parallel to this sudden and complete reversal of five or six years' policy of easy-going placatory appeasement, and its transformation almost overnight into a readiness to accept an obviously imminent war on far worse conditions and on the greatest scale."[19]

Even as late as 1939, there was still a chance, however slight and fleeting, that peace might be secured. At any rate, Churchill expressed the opinion that: "The alliance of Britain, France, and Russia would have struck deep alarm into the heart of Germany in 1939, and no one can prove that war might not even then have been averted. The next step could have been taken with superior power on the side of Allies."[20] A union of the three powers would have placed the Nazis in a most difficult position. German forces in being at the time hardly made possible a full-scale war on two fronts, nor could Hitler afford to run the risk of a major setback. It was a pity, Churchill suggested, that Allied diplomacy had not succeeded in placing the Nazis in this awkward position.

By August 27, 1939, however, there was no doubt, if there had been any after 1936, that war was inevitable, and Churchill awaited his task as a war leader: "In these hours I knew that if war came— and who could doubt its coming?—a major burden would fall upon me."[21] Five days later the bitter, grinding, seemingly hopeless struggle began. Yet the melancholy chain of events leading up to September, 1939, on which we have Churchill's running impressions, sug-

18. *Ibid.*, 347.
19. *Ibid.*
20. *Ibid.*, 363.
21. *Ibid.*, 401.

gest that World War II was not inevitable but that the poisons which caused it had antidotes which might have been used more than once along the way.

World War III?

We enter a realm of speculation and current history when we turn to examine Churchill's views on the prospects of a third worldwide conflict. Even views about the last war are not yet fully crystallized. With a possible third world war, we embark on a history which has no ending. If we compare the present with the past and the time span of postwar developments with the interwar period—a dubious comparison at best—Churchill's comments in the late 1940s and 1950s correspond, it seems, to the position of the West in 1926. In strictly chronological terms, the opinions that Churchill offered on the prospects of World War III are roughly equivalent to those he set forth between 1919 and 1926 on the chances of a second major struggle. In retrospect, his comments in 1926 were not especially important for events that took place in 1937. For this reason, some would maintain it was much too early to give serious attention to his pronouncements about the future. Yet current history has unfolded with such speed and rapidity and long-range prophecies by Henry Adams and de Tocqueville forecasting the rise of Russia and the United States as the great world centers of power have been realized so decisively that a mere chronological comparison is virtually meaningless. For example, the estimates Churchill offered about the perils of continuing the "Cold War" without a settlement are marked by an urgency without parallel in any events of the post–World War I period. Thus his comments on a third world war are not remarks about some remote possibility but deal with impending conflicts that from one standpoint are already upon us. The same principles for evaluating national power and interests by which Churchill has always been guided were invoked for the cold war. His manner of reasoning, applied with such consistency and rigor, may assist in better understanding the present crisis. For this reason, we have chosen to trace in some detail the estimates commencing in 1945 by Churchill on the likelihood of a third general conflict.

What were the prospects of war in the autumn of 1945? This was the question Churchill addressed to the government on October 22, 1945. The answer he gave to his own question was that the West could look forward to an interlude of peace unless the political situation was more critical than intelligence available to private citizens would indicate. In an early debate over demobilization he declared:

I must, however, make one very serious reservation. In my calculations and estimates I have definitely excluded the possibility of a major war in the next few years. If His Majesty's Government considers that this is wrong, then it would not be a case of demobilisation at all but of remobilisation, because what has taken place and is going on has already woefully impaired the immediate fighting efficiency of the enormous forces we still retain. I believe, however, it may be common ground that this possibility of a major war may rightly be excluded, and that we have an interlude of grace in which mankind may be able to make better arrangements for this tortured world than we have hitherto achieved. Still I make that reservation.[22]

Less than five months after this debate, Churchill reminded his listeners that the spirit of boundless hope and confidence which had prevailed after the First World War was conspicuously missing in the aftermath of World War II. However, in the warning he raised at Fulton, Missouri, Churchill was able to say that war was in no sense imminent: "I repulse the idea that a new war is inevitable; still more that it is imminent. It is because I am sure that our fortunes are still in our own hands and that we hold the power to save the future, that I feel the duty to speak out now."[23] His warning at Fulton was concerned with the disequilibrium in world power which, if allowed to continue unchecked, would imperil the peace and make war inevitable.

If men felt less confidence in 1946 than in the third decade of the century, one cause was the devastation which warfare had wrought.

22. *Parliamentary Debates*, Vol. 414, October 22, 1945, p. 1696.
23. New York *Times*, March 6, 1946, p. 4.

All Asia was in turmoil and Europe had proved unable to arrest the trend toward its decline among the world regions. Churchill observed: "The problems of the aftermath, the moral and physical exhaustion of the victorious nations, the miserable fate of the conquered, the vast confusion of Europe and Asia, combine to make a sum total of difficulty, which, even if the Allies had preserved their wartime comradeship, would have taxed their resources to the full."[24] These profoundly troubled and unsettled conditions made the spector of war an ever-present reality. On Septmeber 19, 1946, Churchill cautioned: "I must give you a warning. Time may be short. At present there is a breathing-space. The cannon have ceased firing. The fighting has stopped; but the dangers have not stopped."[25]

On October 23, 1946, in calling for discussion in Parliament on the military strength of the Soviet Union, Churchill, while rebuking a Labor backbencher who had charged that the opposition had resigned itself to preparing for war, frankly stated: "I cannot pretend that it would be possible to conduct discussions with any sense of reality at the present time without the occasional use of that odious and tragic word [war]."[26] Yet on numerous occasions in 1946 Churchill took pains to declare that whereas the outlook for peace was less promising than in 1919, the solemn duty of statesmen was, with courage and imagination, to supply new and more solid ground on which hope could be founded. It was the responsibility of Western leaders to seek more enduring security arrangements through which peace might be preserved. One novel factor which encouraged his hope for peace was the American monopoly of the atomic bomb. Despite his anxiety regarding the power of the Soviet Union, Churchill consistently maintained that war was unlikely so long as the West enjoyed a monopoly in this crucial sphere. But on a later occasion, he went further and predicted that even with the passing of its monopoly, a relative advantage for the West in atomic production, so long as it was substantial in character, would

24. *Parliamentary Debates*, Vol. 423, June 5, 1946, p. 2012.
25. London *Times*, September 20, 1946, p. 4.
26. *Parliamentary Debates*, Vol. 427, October 24, 1946, p. 1686.

contribute to peace. In discussing the American monopoly of the atomic bomb on November 7, 1945, and speculating on how long it could hold this advantage, he declared: "In the debate on the address I hazarded the estimate that it would be three or four years. According to the best information I have been able to obtain, I see no reason to alter that and certainly not to diminish it. But even when that period is over, the progress made by the United States scientists—and I trust by our own—both in experiment and manufacture, may well leave us and them with the prime power and responsibility for the use of these dire, superhuman weapons."[27]

In 1947 and 1948 Churchill spoke in more somber tones about the risks of war. On January 4, 1947, he compared the situation then to the crisis in 1938: "Certainly the scene we survey . . . bears many uncomfortable resemblances to that of 1938. Indeed, in some respects, it is even darker. The peoples of Europe have fallen immeasurably deeper into the pit of misery and confusion. Many of their cities are in ruins. Millions of their homes have been destroyed."[28] And on January 24, 1948, he made a more general statement:

I am often asked "will there be war?" It is a question I have often asked myself. Can you wonder that this intrudes itself when the Lord President of the Council [Herbert Morrison] speaks as he did ten days ago of the risk of war with Russia. . . .

When I spoke at Fulton I said I did not believe the Soviet Government wanted war but the fruits of war. I overwhelmingly hope and pray that the view I have expressed is still correct. I cannot tell. I should not blame His Majesty's Government if, even with all the information at their disposal, they were also not able to come to a definite conclusion.[29]

However, there were reasons for hope in spite of these perils, and the foremost was the American atomic bomb monopoly. He reminded the British: "We must not be in any doubt as to what is pre-

27. *Parliamentary Debates*, Vol. 415, November 8, 1945, p. 1297.
28. Winston S. Churchill, "The Highroad of the Future," *Collier's*, CXIX (January 4, 1947), 11.
29. *Parliamentary Debates*, Vol. 446, January 23, 1948, p. 558.

serving the peace and security of the world at the present time. It is the power and strength of the United States." [30]

Moreover, although the threat of the Soviet Union hovered ominously over the scene of the quivering European balance of power, the general world picture was one in which, potentially at least, the West had important advantages. In discussing what might be expected if the Soviet Union and its satellites should resign from the United Nations, Churchill observed on October 14, 1947: "Great wars come when both sides believe they are more or less equal, and when each thinks he has a good chance of victory. No such conditions of equality would be established if the Soviet Government and their Communist devotees were to make a separate organization of their own." [31]

However, the fact such equality was more nearly in being by 1948 must be counted as one of the reasons for Churchill's increasingly somber attitude. Notwithstanding, the most profound change on the world scene was the new role of the United States. Whereas it had attempted with indifferent success to withdraw from all European affairs after World War I, the aftermath of World War II witnessed its participation to the extent of outright guaranties of the European system. On December 10, 1948, as plans for a North Atlantic Treaty Organization were beginning to unfold, Churchill contrasted the two American approaches to world peace and concluded: "We gather from what the Foreign Secretary said yesterday that the United States may well now be prepared to do what they have never done before, or dreamed of doing before, namely, give a guarantee to Western Europe against aggression coupled with practical measures of military collaboration. It is a tremendous event. . . . If such an event had occurred in 1940, or in 1939, the whole tragic history of the world might well have been changed, and possibly a catastrophe might have been prevented." [32]

30. Winston S. Churchill, "Speech to Women's Advisory Committee of the Conservative Party, Albert Hall," April 21, 1948, *Europe Unite*, ed. Randolph S. Churchill (London: Cassell and Company, 1950) 296.
31. New York *Times*, October 15, 1947, p. 4.
32. *Parliamentary Debates*, Vol. 459, December 10, 1948, p. 707.

In 1949, the first clear indications of the revival of strength of the European community enabled Churchill, however cautiously, to forecast:

As I have said on former occasions, we are dealing with absolutely incalculable factors in dealing with the present rulers of Russia. No one knows what action they will take, or to what internal pressures they will respond. He would be a bold, and I think, an imprudent man who embarked upon detailed prophecies about what will be the future course of events. But it is absolutely certain that the strengthening by every means in our power of the growing ties which unite the signatories of the Atlantic Pact, of the Brussels Treaty, and the signatories of the Statute of the Council of Europe . . . is our surest guarantee of peace and safety.[33]

And on June 2, 1949, he postulated with increasing emphasis the doctrine of peace through strength: "I have a growing hope that by the strength of our united civilization, and by our readiness and preparedness to defend our freedom with our lives, we may avert forever the horrible vision of a third world war."[34]

In 1950, Churchill's opinions fall naturally into views he expressed before and after the outbreak of war in Korea. At the year's beginning, he urged that all haste must be made in strengthening the West and in reconciling the German people with France and England. The programs for the dismantling of German industries were being carried beyond the point of diminishing return. If continued, the West would have squandered what precious time still remained in which war might be averted. Yet there were deterrents to war more substantial than generally realized. In a passage from a speech before the House of Commons on March 28, 1950, impregnated with wisdom about the nature of contemporary warfare, Churchill expressed his views on this issue:

I will begin by stating the reason why I do not believe that another war is imminent or inevitable, and why I believe that we have more time, if we use it wisely, and more hope of warding off the frightful catastrophe from our struggling, ill-informed and almost helpless human race. Here is the reason. There never was a time when the deterrents against war were so

33. *Parliamentary Debates*, Vol. 464, May 12, 1949, pp. 2025–26.
34. London *Times*, June 2, 1949, p. 2.

strong. If penalties of the most drastic kind can prevent in our civil life crime or folly, then we certainly have them here on a gigantic scale in the affairs of nations. The penalties have grown to an extent undreamed of; and at the same time, many of the old incentives which were the cause of the beginning of so many wars, or features in their beginning, have lost their significance. The desire for glory, booty, territory, dynastic or national aggrandisement; hopes of a speedy and splendid victory with all its excitement . . . are now superseded by a preliminary stage of measureless agony from which neither side could at present protect itself.[35]

He examined specifically the events which might be expected if war came about:

Another world war would begin by both sides suffering as the first step what they dread most. Western Europe would be overrun and Communised, with all the liquidation of the outstanding non-Communist personnel of all classes, of which . . . elaborate lists have already been prepared. . . . That is one side. On the other hand, at the same time, Soviet cities, air fields, oil fields and railway junctions would be annihilated; with possible complete disruption of Kremlin control over the enormous populations who are ruled from Moscow. These fearful cataclysms would be simultaneous, and neither side could at present, or for several years to come, prevent them.[36]

And he added, as his private opinion, that these practical if negative foundations, which moralists found ignoble, were from his point of view effective and real and therefore should be publicized and developed as a basis for peace. He declared: "Moralists may find it a melancholy thought that peace can find no nobler foundation than mutual terror. But for my part, I shall be content if these foundations are solid, because they will give us the extra time and the new breathing space for the supreme effort which has to be made for a world settlement."[37]

The crisis in Korea occurred at approximately the mid-point of 1950 and provided a new departure for Churchill's reflections. Events and developments up to this date had reflected the grave ten-

---

35. *Parliamentary Debates*, Vol. 473, March 28, 1950, pp. 197–98.
36. *Ibid.*, 198.
37. *Ibid.*

dencies of which we have spoken. But the postwar situation of great concentrations of power alongside enfeebled and unstable nations and resources had been gravely damaged by the struggle that was merely a portent of a wider conflict which broke out in Korea. The principal change which occurred with Korea was the transition from a "hypothetical struggle" that had been hidden and obscured, to one that became actual and self-evident. Indeed, this phase in the course of events had the important advantage of rallying the West to a more genuine common effort which offered the best hope of peace. On June 28, 1950, Churchill announced: "It may well be that the action which the United States has taken, with which we have associated ourselves today, placing a fleet equal to the American at their side, and showing the fraternal association of the English speaking race all over the world, may in the end be found to be effective in warding off from us the infinite horrors of a third world war."[38] The cornerstone of this common effort was the unity of the English-speaking world: "I do not myself think there is a greater war imminent. . . . But I am sure of this that if there were any weakness or division in the English-speaking world, if it were not for the great and courageous championship of the cause of freedom by the mighty United States, if outside the iron curtain there were not strong and loyal supporters of the maintenance of peace, then there could be no limit to the miseries which the whole world would have to undergo."[39] Specifically, the prospects of cementing the ties among free peoples everywhere had been enhanced by the measures undertaken in Korea. He explained on July 15, 1950: "I do not say that what has happened and is happening in Korea has made the dangers of a third world war greater. They were already grave, but it has brought them nearer. It has made them more apparent, and I trust indeed that the great masses of peoples throughout the free world have been made more aware and more alive to where they stand."[40]

Yet more was required than unity and good intentions in the

38. London *Times*, June 29, 1950, p. 3.
39. *Ibid.*, July 21, 1950, p. 3.
40. *Ibid.*, July 17, 1950, p. 2.

West. The need was for resolute action. Churchill went so far as to compare the situation in the summer of 1950 with the summer of 1940 but explained: "By this I do not mean that war is imminent. We cannot tell, but I do not think it is imminent. But I must ask you not to suppose that time is on our side: that we have only got to go on with our party quarrels and close our eyes and stop our ears to the facts of the situation to find that all will work out all right in the long run."[41] To drift along in the conduct of domestic and diplomatic affairs as if the present situation could go on indefinitely would be to invite destruction.

In 1950 Churchill enumerated additional reasons for suspecting that war might be prevented. On August 11, 1950, in an address to the Council of Europe at Strasbourg he asserted: "There is another reason why the general armed assault by the Communists against the Western democracies may be delayed. The Soviet dictator has no reason to be discontented with the way things have gone. Since the World War stopped in 1945, they have obtained control of half Europe and all China without losing a single Russian soldier, thus adding nearly 500 million people to their own immense population."[42] Furthermore, if war came, it would be initiated by one and only one of the antagonists: "They [the S.U.] have repeatedly been assured that the United States would not fight what is called a 'preventive' war. The United States have expressed the general opinion of the civilised world upon that aspect. On this basis the war, if ever it comes—which God forbid—will come at the moment of their choice."[43]

As 1950 was drawing to its close, Churchill answered the argument of some critics that any vigorous program of European rearmament would provoke the Russians into launching their own form of "preventive" war:

Dangerous as it may be to make such a prediction . . . I would venture to express the opinion that a major attack by Russia in Europe is unlikely in

41. *Ibid.*
42. New York *Times*, August 12, 1950, p. 8.
43. *Parliamentary Debates*, Vol. 481, November 30, 1950, p. 1332.

the near future, and that it will not be provoked or produced by the modest measures of defence now so slowly, so tardily and ineffectively developed up to the present day by the Atlantic and Western powers. Even if our preparations developed more rapidly, a long period must elapse before they could offset the Russian superiority, even if the Russian strength itself were not increased meanwhile.[44]

In 1951 and indeed into 1952, Churchill indicated that, from one standpoint at least, the chances of peace appeared to have substantially improved. The massive rearmament program in the West, so tardily and reluctantly undertaken, was the basis for faith that the risk of war had somewhat lessened. On February 15, 1951, in an exchange with Minister of Defense Emanuel Shinwell, Churchill expressed the following view:

The Minister of Defence said yesterday that the danger of war had become more acute in the last few months. I follow these matters as closely as I can, and I am not aware of any facts which justify this assertion. On the contrary, I think that the gigantic measures for rearmament adopted by the United States—the declaration of a state of emergency, 10,000 million dollars additional taxation, 27 months military service and the appointment of General Eisenhower—have all improved the chances of . . . the formation of a European front which will be a real deterrent upon Soviet Communist aggression in Europe; they have all improved the chances of this being achieved before the vast American superiority in the atomic weapon has been overtaken by the Russian stockpile.[45]

Under conditions of protracted tension, wars sometimes come about through accidents even when no one really wants them to take place. Churchill believed that war for the Soviets would probably be a matter of calculated design and on May 10, 1951, in the House of Commons he removed any doubts as to the reasoning he was employing:

Of course, it is always very dangerous, and never more so than at the present time, to predict anything that may happen in the future. But in my view, a Soviet attack will not arise because of an incident. An incident may

44. *Ibid.*, 1333–34.
45. *Parliamentary Debates*, Vol. 484, February 15, 1951, p. 640.

be a pretext, but the moment will be fixed by the result of long, cold calculations, or miscalculations, and among the factors which will play a potent part the season of the year, including harvest time, will be extremely important. I do not, therefore, consider that the question of our doing our duty . . . should be overclouded by all the statements that may be made that this will bring on a general war. Nobody knows what will bring on a general war except those who have the supreme power in the Kremlin.[46]

Yet no one, let alone a wise statesman like Churchill, could ignore the play of fortune in world politics. Indeed, when he considered the prudence of the foreign policies of various nations or of their action within the United Nations he betrayed his anxiety about the effects of an impulsive diplomacy originating on America's side of the Iron Curtain. On October 8, 1951, he dealt with this problem when he exclaimed:

I do not believe that a third world war is inevitable. I even think that the danger of it is less than it was before the immense rearmament of the United States. In any case it will not be a British finger that pulls the trigger of a third world war. It may be a Russian finger or an American finger, or a United Nations organisation finger, but it cannot be a British finger. Although we should certainly be involved . . . the control and decision and the timing of that terrible event would not rest with us.

Our influence in the world is not what it was in bygone days. I could wish indeed that it was greater, because I am sure it would be used as it always has been used to the utmost to prevent a life and death struggle between the great nations.[47]

Again, at the lord mayor's banquet, he expressed his concern that the precarious nature of the present situation might send the foes tumbling into grave conflict: "What is the world scene as presented to us to-day? Mighty forces, armed with fearful weapons, are baying at each other across a gulf which, I have the feeling to-night, neither wishes and both fear to cross; but into which they may tumble and drag each other to common ruin."[48] What of the 1980s?

46. *Parliamentary Debates*, Vol. 487, May 10, 1951, p. 2167.
47. London *Times*, October 8, 1951, p. 2.
48. *Ibid.*, November 10, 1951, p. 6.

As 1951 came to an end the hopes of Western statesmen that war might be averted rose almost universally. The true and firm grounds for this hope was enunciated most clearly in a broadcast to the nation by Mr. Churchill.

If we can stave off a war conflict for even five or ten years all sorts of things may happen. A new breeze may blow upon the troubled world. I repudiate the idea that a third war is inevitable. The main reason I remain in public life is my hope to ward it off and prevent it. The desire of mankind in this tragic twentieth century can be seen and felt.[49]

The chances of a respite from open conflict had their roots in American power and endeavor, for: "A tithe of the efforts now being made by America would have prevented the second world war and would have probably led to the downfall of Hitler, with scarcely any blood being shed except his own."[50]

With this prediction, we leave our discussion of Churchill's concepts of the inevitability of war. He appeared to conclude that the risks of a temporary and uneasy peace in which a reckless move by either side might plunge all parties into general conflict could never be wholly removed. But at year's end, Churchill held out the hope, based upon developments over the last seven years, that war might be averted at least for five to ten years. On December 7, 1951, a date which a decade before had spelled tragedy, it is significant that Churchill should announce: "Looking back over the last few years, I cannot feel that the danger of a third world war is so great now as it was at the time of the Berlin air lift crisis in 1948. . . . Of course, no one can predict the future, but our feeling, on assuming responsibility, is that the deterrents have increased and that as the deterrents have increased, the danger has become more unlikely."[51]

But the hopes he cautiously expressed were more modest than the millennial dreams of eternal peace which others proffered. His wise warning of June 30, 1943, was no less apposite for the dangers today. "Wars come with great suddenness, and many of the deep,

49. *Ibid.*, October 9, 1951, p. 2.
50. *Ibid.*, November 10, 1951, p. 6.
51. *Ibid.*, December 7, 1951, p. 4.

slow courses which lead to the explosion are often hidden from, or only dimly comprehended by, the masses of the people, even in the region most directly affected."[52]

The framework he used in considering the crisis of March 10, 1936, is equally relevant as a model for thinking about the present cold war: "Wars do not always wait until all the combatants are ready. Sometimes they come before any one is ready, sometimes when one nation thinks itself less unready than another, or when one nation thinks it is likely to become, not stronger but weaker as time passes."[53] These words tell us what we have most to fear. The Soviet Union, sensing that by 1954 the West's strength might eclipse its own could plunge the world into a fearful struggle. And Churchill sought to make it crystal clear that he had never promised this could not happen.

Therefore, in conclusion, the issue of whether war is inevitable or perpetual peace is a possibility is a topic unworthy of serious thought when it is formulated in these terms. For it is unfortunately true that "the history of the human race is a history of war, and the records of thousands of years show only a few uneasy intervals of peace."[54] In the present crisis, the fine thread on which peace is suspended possesses two strands. First it is surely well known that what has deterred the Soviet Union has been the strength of the West which in the early years of the cold war was expressed in the atomic bomb. But it is equally important to note that for Churchill there were other factors which have restrained the United States as well from the danger of its own precipitate action. On these two points, Churchill observed:

There are two factors which we cannot measure, let alone control, either of which may prove decisive. They are the following: first, the calculations and designs of the Soviet autocracy in the Kremlin, and secondly, the anger of the people in the United States at the treatment they are receiving and the burden they have to bear. Neither of these is within our control.

---

52. Churchill, "Before the Autumn Leaves Fall," June 30, 1943, *Onwards to Victory*, compiled by Charles Eade (Boston: Little, Brown, 1944), 160.
53. *Parliamentary Debates*, Vol. 309, March 10, 1936, p. 2009.
54. Churchill, "War Now or Never," *Collier's*, CIII (June 3, 1939), 9.

It is my firm conviction that while there is a real, solid hope of building up an effective European army the United States will forbear, and that while American superiority in atomic warfare casts its strange but merciful shield over the free peoples the Soviet oligarchy will be deterred.[55]

In short, Churchill considered the issue of the inevitability of war in relative rather than absolute terms. Whereas romanticists look upon war as inevitable and fulfilling and idealists speak of the possibility of perpetual peace, neither alternative had meaning for Churchill. His approach was to look upon wars as more or less imminent while peace, paradoxically, was the product of wars averted. This realistic approach of gaining peace through the avoidance of war by the amelioration of sharp rivalries from which warfare might otherwise emerge was the basis on which Churchill could say in the 1950s that war was less likely than it had been in 1946. The same may be true in the 1980s. In any event, this diagnosis is the essence of political realism.

55. *Parliamentary Debates*, Vol. 478, September 12, 1950, pp. 986–87.

PART FIVE

Peace

"A war postponed may be a war averted. Circumstances change, combinations change, new groupings arise, old interests are superseded by new. Many quarrels that might have led to war have been adjusted . . . and have, in Lord Melbourne's phrase, 'blown over.'"

CHAPTER TEN

A Survey of Historic Approaches

Five approaches to the problems of international peace and world order have prevailed in modern international society. They are the balance of power, disarmament, world government, international organization, and diplomacy. Each has been identified with a particular philosophy of international politics; each has conceived the resolution of the world's troubles as being dependent upon particular methods or agencies without which international conflict would be inevitable. Often two or more approaches have been combined as essential ingredients of one approach. Indeed, when any one approach has been conceived of in isolation from the others, it has been the result of the pressures of popular opinion. Critics have charged that certain traditional methods have always culminated in war. They have attempted to demonstrate that only one approach would guarantee peace.

The classical approach to the unchanging problems of rivalry and war has been the balance of power. It provides that in any constellation of mutually independent and separate political entities there is a dynamic principle which operates to infuse order and stability into the system through the tendency of political units to establish and reestablish conditions of equilibrium. In the play of political forces, each group and nation strives to promote a situation in which no single nation by achieving overwhelming power can threaten at will the survival of all the others. In pursuing its ends, every nation attempts to increase its own power through internal and external policies aimed at combining its efforts with strong and faithful allies. Any given balance of power is temporary and uncertain, for no phase of life can long be held in permanent equilibrium. But a rough stability has often been attained in society through the persistent efforts of its members in maintaining a balance of power with an ever-changing content.

The balance of power has witnessed both success and failure in its long history, but its greatest contributions have been as an instrument of international order. Because of its effects as a principle of political dynamics, no one state in modern times has permanently acquired such power that the independence of all others were placed in jeopardy. The modern state system through a system of pressures and balances has operated to prevent universal imperium. The contributions of the balance of power to world peace, on the other hand, although sometimes spectacular, have been erratic and unpredictable and in general unsuccessful for any extended period of time, as the painful procession of ever more destructive wars tragically attests. The balance of power, while maintaining international order and the independence of the members of international society, has failed to preserve the peace. There have been exceptions, as in the nineteenth century when the practice of the balance of power was faithfully and sedulously cultivated. But nations in general have failed to avert wars through this approach either because they abandoned its principles or misjudged and miscalculated the elements required in its wise application.

Disarmament as an approach to international order and peace has been emphasized increasingly as war has become the scourge not of a handful of mercenaries but of all men everywhere. Moreover, a concomitant of the brutalization of war has been the growth of practical morality and respect for human life as expressions of the Age of the Enlightenment and political liberalism. The spirit of a more liberal age was responsible for the social and political reforms in which criminal law was transformed, prison changes initiated, and electoral reforms concluded. Beyond these critical changes, the greatest humanitarian task of all was the outlawing of war. To the rational man, the path to this goal was to be found in the one simple and unambiguous step of outlawing or reducing the means of destruction and violence. The assumption underlying disarmament was that men fight because they have arms. Yet the history of attempts at disarmament is a melancholy story of numerous failures and few successes. On those rare occasions when temporary agreements have been reached, an increase instead of a reduction in armaments has subsequently resulted. This was the case with the

Washington Treaty of 1922 by which American, British, and Japanese production of capital ships was restricted, only to free their energies and resources for an armaments race in cruisers, destroyers, and submarines. Only in those extraordinary instances where the underlying political problems were first adjusted or resolved has disarmament or the regulation of armaments resulted in any substantial pacification. In American experience, the Rush-Bagot Agreement concluded in 1816 between the United States and Canada, which until its revision during World War II allowed each nation three naval vessels of equal tonnage and armament for use on the Great Lakes, remains the outstanding example of the positive function disarmament can play. But its success was dependent upon the sequence in which political settlement and disarmament were achieved. Political agreement provides the only foundation from which arms control agreements can evolve and prosper. Therefore, the disarmament approach to peace can be effective only when nations have taken the first step of working out viable political understandings. So long as they continue advancing mutually contradictory claims in the struggle for power, their demands for national armaments must remain unresolved and contradictory. We must conclude that disarmament or rearmament are merely symptoms of the struggle for power. When nations have arrived at a tolerable understanding about the distribution of power among them, an arms pact will reflect the easing of the burden of competition and rivalry which this accommodation has brought about. At that moment, moreover, the relaxing of the arms race can have the result of contributing still further to the lessening of political tensions and to the heightening of mutual confidence among nations.

However, the movement which has eclipsed all others in popular and moral appeal is that of world government. It has had immense appeal in spite of its failure to advance beyond the discussion stage. Its aims and high purposes have imparted to large bodies of people a deeper sense of urgency than has resulted from any of the other approaches. It has found supporters in Europe and America, Asia and Africa. One may ask what has accounted for the attractiveness of world government as a doctrine of political salvation among peoples and nations from such diverse backgrounds. Some would say that its force rests on three factors or conditions which, in varying degree and at different times, have been persuasive to different groups and peoples. Since the age of the Stoics and the first followers of Christianity, the sense of the moral unity of mankind in the West has expressed itself in programs and visions for universal political institutions. Men of many colors and creeds have conceived of themselves as members of one human race. In practice, every effort to create an institutional framework commensurate politically with the range of these moral sentiments, whether the Roman or Napoleonic empires, has been corrupted, sometimes at birth, has faltered and disappeared. But the residual belief in the essential unity of mankind has been perpetuated in innumerable world government movements.

The second basic factor is technological in character. Through vast and massive changes in transportation and communication, the separate parts of the world have been knit together in one economic universe. Yet this interdependence of the world's people wrought by the industrial revolution has not altered the conditions of international anarchy which have been a characteristic of the political scene. The economic argument for world government holds that since there is one economic world, it must follow inevitably that a single political universe can be created. In consequence of modern technology, the interdependence of nations in peace is matched by their close proximity in war. Thus rivalries have been intensified and wars made more absolute. These conditions of present-day warfare and virtual elimination of distance as a limitation on strategy have stirred men to seek some kind of remedy from the toils of unending wars.

Finally, the experiences of nation-states in achieving harmony and order domestically have encouraged men to attempt to adapt national institutions to the conditions existing on the world scene. In doing so they have reasoned as follows. War exists internationally alongside conditions of international anarchy; peace obtains within the nation-state side by side with its organs of government. Therefore, since national societies owe their peaceful condition to states endowed with supreme power and authority, the transference of sovereignty from national states to a world state offers the best hope for achieving peace and order. The logic of this threefold argument for world government is unexceptionable so far as it goes. But unfortunately it does not go far enough. For the unresolved dilemma upon which every concrete plan has been impaled is the issue of whether what is necessary and desirable is therefore possible and acceptable. The aggregate of experience in the modern state system would indicate that up to now no sovereign nation-state has shown itself willing or able to pay the price that would be essential for the creation of a supranational system. Later we shall discover in Mr. Churchill's own words some of the reasons that this has been so.

In addition, history offers examples of actual experiments in harmonizing and integrating the manifold relations among sovereign nation-states. At least three international organizations have devoted themselves to the maintenance of international order and peace. The Concert of Europe was an informal expression of the "European System" whose members met periodically to consult upon problems for safeguarding the status quo established by the Congress of Vienna in 1815. The League of Nations, created in 1919, and the United Nations, in 1945, have been full-fledged international agencies with permanent locations and secretariats. It has been customary to consider them the only international organizations. Yet if peace and order are the real purposes of international organization, the lessons to be gained from nineteenth-century practice are no less vital than those from the twentieth century. For the nineteenth was a century of almost uninterrupted peace in which the five leading nations engaged in general war with one another for only eighteen months, if we exclude the Crimean War as a semicolonial struggle.

It was during this century of peace that the fifth approach was more assiduously cultivated and respected than in any subsequent period. Diplomacy is the ancient technique whereby two nations whose conflicting interests appear irreconcilable seek to discover if their vital interests are also incompatible and how far they can compromise on nonvital interests. If we were to apply this general concept to British foreign policy, we would find that England had been willing to compromise on secondary issues in the Far East or in Africa but on vital interests, such as the territorial integrity of the Low Countries, it has been unyielding. In an unorganized international society, diplomacy continues to be the one indispensable approach to world peace. In practice its success depends on prudent judgments regarding the balance of power. The activities of any international organization must rest upon the foundations that diplomats have established. If in international politics, compromise and accommodation are wanting, competing states within or outside an international government have but the one recourse of war itself.

CHAPTER ELEVEN

The Balance of Power as Law or Alternative

The balance of power as a cardinal principle of international politics has probably had a longer and more venerable tradition than the other major approaches to order and peace. Of its early presence as a general social principle David Hume remarked:

> In all the politics of Greece, the anxiety, with regard to the balance of power is apparent. . . . Thucydides represents the league which was formed against Athens, and which produced the Peloponnesian War, as entirely owing to this principle. And after the decline of Athens, when the Thebans and Lacedemonians disputed for sovereignty, we find the Athenians (as well as many other republics) always threw themselves into the lighter scale, and endeavored to preserve the balance. They supported Thebes against Sparta, till the great victory gained by Epaminondas at Leuctra; after which they immediately went over to the conquered, from generosity, as they pretended, but in reality from their jealousy of the conquerors.[1]

For our own time, Churchill stated unequivocally the principle of British foreign policy:

> For four hundred years the foreign policy of England has been to oppose the strongest, most aggressive, most dominating power on the Continent. . . . [Therefore] we always took the harder course, joined with the less strong Powers, made a combination among them and thus defeated and frustrated the Continental military tyrant whoever he was, whatever nation he led.[2]

We have the word of the contemporary British historian Arnold J. Toynbee that "the Balance of Power is a system of political dynam-

---

1. David Hume, *Essays and Treatises on Several Subjects* (Edinburgh: Bell and Bradfute, and W. Blackwood, 1925), I, 331 ff.
2. Winston S. Churchill, *The Second World War*, Vol. I, *The Gathering Storm* (Boston: Houghton Mifflin, 1948), 207–208.

ics that comes into play whenever a society articulates itself into a number of mutually independent local states."[3] In all societies composed of autonomous members, the separate units owe their autonomy primarily to the success of the balance of power. But if it is true that the function it serves has been ubiquitous in the affairs of Chinese, Sumerian, Greek, and Western civilizations, the conceptions men have held of its role and importance have seldom been precisely the same. Nowhere is this seen more dramatically than in the two basically divergent outlooks which prevail in the mid—twentieth century. There is, first, a popular and widely held view of many writers and publicists which assumes that the statesman has a choice between policies that are founded on the balance of power and those which reflect a better and more desirable kind of international relations. The supporters of this view can be expected to approve of the balance of power as, at best, a temporary expedient whose usefulness is limited and whose principles and application need not be accorded continuing thought or attention. By contrast, a second less popular conception has served as the common law of diplomatists and statesmen over much of the past four centuries. It views the principle of equilibrium as an indispensable foundation for any political decision. Unless one state is prevented from gaining ascendancy over the others, the system itself, with its multiplicity of members, will ultimately be shattered and destroyed. It is common to human existence and to animal life in general that when any species or group seeks to increase its independence and power beyond the point where equilibrium with its competitors can be preserved, either its competitors will give way and disappear or else, by combining, will keep the aggressor in his place. Among animal species this process is often unconscious and automatic, but in diplomacy its effectiveness depends on those sharp discriminations and informed calculations by which the statesman perceives and anticipates crucial changes in the balance of power. The first philosophy of balance of power, by considering the whole process as only a

3. Arnold J. Toynbee, *A Study of History* (10 vols.; London: Oxford University Press, 1939), III, 301.

passing and inferior operation, is hardly conducive to its development. The second philosophy, viewing the necessity of balance as
permanent and enduring, calls for serious reflection upon its history, its function, and its nature.

The "Law" of the Balance of Power

Churchill, it should be obvious, has tried to dispel any doubts as to
which of these theories was superior. Indeed, it is quite obvious that
in the controversy over the balance of power, we are once again
in the presence of the fundamental clash between the two philosophies of political realism and political idealism. There are important groups of Western idealists for whom the balance of power is
merely the most sinister expression of the whole evil panoply of
techniques and principles associated with power politics. Alliances,
spheres of influence, and balance of power are all concrete signs of
the degradation and corruption of moral political behavior into immoral power politics. The leader of this school of thought in the
United States immediately after the Second World War was Henry
Wallace. He consistently opposed what he called Churchill's war
doctrine and holy crusade and in an editorial of January 13, 1947,
he reported in the *New Republic*: "Churchill is an incurable be-
liever in Anglo-Saxon destiny. . . . I argued with him once against
an . . . Anglo-American bloc . . . as he sought to persuade a skeptical Roosevelt. I am opposed to all such alliances."[4]

Outside America, certain British liberals espoused concepts of
foreign policy which, if less beclouded than their American counter-
parts, were hardly any better equipped to translate current principles of international politics to accord with new problems and
alignments. Consider, for example, the statement of the man who
following the death of Harold Laski was generally considered the
intellectual leader of British socialism. Richard Crossman (Coven-
try, East) declared in Parliament on January 23, 1945: "I noticed the

4. Henry A. Wallace, "Churchill's Crusade," *New Republic*, CXVI (January 13,
1947), 23.

suggestion in the speech of the Foreign Secretary yesterday that we were discarding the balance of power in our foreign policy. We cannot discard something which ended years ago. In 1942 the European balance of power ceased to mean anything at all."[5] There is, of course, a significant blending of truth and untruth in Crossman's comment. The statement is incontestable that the European balance of power as it was known for almost four centuries was destroyed sometime during World War II. But the political idealist falls prey to illusions about a principle whose enduring purposes he only dimly understands when he maintains with such finality that the balance of power "ended years ago." The confusion of form with substance and of a particular historic expression of the balance of power with its existence is a sign of the weaknesses inherent in liberal thought on foreign policy. Because of its denial of the brute facts of power, modern liberalism is almost completely deficient in the intellectual tools essential for assessing international political situations.

Obviously the perspective from which the observer views the balance of power influences the specific content he gives it. Some observers conceive of the balance of power as an absolute parity or equality between nations occupying the two scales of the balance; others maintain that nations pursuing a foreign policy of the status quo must enjoy a margin of strength which will deter the imperialist power from reckless adventures. In the 1930s, Churchill appeared more in agreement with the latter view. On July 13, 1934, he explained: "If you wish to bring about war, you bring about such an equipoise that both sides think they have a chance of winning. If you want to stop war, you gather such an aggregation of force on the side of peace that the aggressor, whoever he may be, will not dare to challenge."[6] Throughout a large part of the interwar period, the powers whose interests clashed with those of the Axis could have combined together and created conditions of equilibrium by means of which Nazi expansionism might have been forestalled. In-

---

5. *Parliamentary Debates* (Hansard) House of Commons, Fifth Series, Vol. 446, January 23, 1945 (London: His Majesty's Stationery Office, 1950), 565.
6. *Parliamentary Debates*, Vol. 292, July 13, 1934, pp. 730–31.

stead of capitulation at Munich, England and France had the alternative of establishing a viable balance of power through combining their power with the Soviet Union and the smaller or intermediate powers. On October 5, 1938, Churchill lectured the Parliament on this point: "France and Great Britain together, especially if they had maintained a close contact with Russia, which certainly was not done, would have been able in those days in the summer, when they had the prestige, to influence many of the smaller states of Europe; and I believe they could have determined the attitude of Poland. Such a combination, prepared at a time when the German dictator was not deeply and irrevocably committed to his new adventure, would, I believe, have given strength to all those forces in Germany which resisted this departure, this new design."[7]

Certain developments in the period between the world wars were detrimental to the maintenance of any balance of power. Two events in particular in 1935 combined to deal a heavy and ominous blow to world peace. In that year, England suffered the loss of parity in air strength with the Germans. Simultaneously, Italy, which had acted historically as a counterforce to German expansion in Southeastern Europe, marched into the camp of its historic rival. This critical and far-reaching shift imperiled the European balance of power and provoked Churchill's comment that: "We have seen how helpful Mussolini had been in the protection of Austrian independence, with all that it implied in Central and Southeastern Europe. . . . The gravity of this downward turn in the balance of safety oppressed my mind."[8] In consequence of the transference of a crucial weight in the balance of power, Germany was enabled to pursue without fear its policy of annexing Austria with all the grave and strategic consequences for Central Europe. By means of this policy, Germany succeeded in isolating Czechoslovakia and the other nations falling within its sphere. The success of the Nazi aggression in Austria was an extension of earlier changes in the distribution of power in Europe.

7. *Parliamentary Debates*, Vol. 339, October 5, 1938, p. 363.
8. Churchill, *The Gathering Storm*, 165.

In the spring of 1939, one means existed for redressing the balance of power. If one asked what novel force could be introduced to establish a new balance of power, there could be only one answer. Only if Russia were joined with the West could the overwhelming power of the Nazis and Fascists be balanced and a rough equilibrium established. On May 4, 1939, Churchill observed: "We do not know at present what proposals have been made by the Russian Government to Great Britain and France. There is reason to believe that they are bold, logical, and far-reaching. If so, it is of enormous consequence that they should be promptly dealt with."[9] In any event, every Russian overture should be examined on its merits. Peace might yet be saved, Churchill reflected, through the redressing of the balance of power in Central and Western Europe. And if the prospects of peace should deteriorate and war become inevitable, Russian power as a counter to German strength in the East was the best assurance of an active and effective front engaging the Nazis throughout Eastern Europe. This objective of an Anglo-Franco-Russian entente was founded on the one sure guide of all foreign policy, the national interest. Russia's role in this alliance would be in accord with its own interests for "Russian interests are deeply concerned in preventing Herr Hitler's designs in Eastern Europe."[10]

Churchill in his policies was true to his words concerning the mutuality of Britain's and Russia's interests. In 1941 when the Germans were advancing into Russia, he once more proclaimed that a military combination of power from every available source was essential to redress the superior military might of the German "Wehrmacht." "Any man or state who fights on against Nazidom will have our aid. Any man or state who marches with Hitler is our foe. . . . It follows, therefore, that we shall give whatever help we can to Russia and the Russian people."[11] This was no class or religious war, he said, but what was at stake was the independence of England, the

9. Winston S. Churchill, "The Russian Counterpoise," May 4, 1939, *Step by Step 1936–1939* (New York: Putnam's, 1939), 318.
10. *Ibid.*, 319.
11. New York *Times*, June 23, 1941, p. 1.

British Commonwealth, and the numerous small states of Europe. What was at stake, in other words, was the European balance of power. Because this was an issue, the British war leader was able to promise: "If Hitler imagines that his attack on Soviet Russia will cause the slightest division of aims or slackening of effort in the great Democracies who are resolved upon his doom, he is woefully mistaken."[12] Had only abstract moral principles or universal ideological goals guided Churchill in his formulation of war strategy, historians would look in vain for a declaration of this kind. But since the searchlight by which he was guided along the murky paths of war and peace was the instrument of the balance of power, his words and deeds were dependent upon shifts in the political situation and necessary responses.

Implementing the Balance of Power

The balance of power has worked most effectively whenever there has been some nation that was the "holder" of the balance. Such a nation, by staying aloof from the major coalitions and blocs of nations, has retained its freedom of action to affect substantially the prospects of war or peace through joining with the weaker nations threatened with domination and control. For Churchill this policy of siding with the weaker group represented the "wonderful unconscious tradition of British foreign policy." Venice pursued a similar policy founded on essentially the same principles in the world of the north Italian city-states. Churchill in characterizing British foreign policy made a point of contrasting it with other foreign policies during the interwar period: "England in accordance with her foreign policy of 300 years, sustained the weaker side. France found an ally in the Russia of the Czars and Germany in the crumbling empire of the Hapsburgs. The United States, for reasons which were natural and traditional, but no longer so valid as in the past, stood aloof and expected to be able to watch, as a spectator, the thrilling, fearful drama unfold from across what was then called 'the broad

12. *Ibid.*

Atlantic.'"[13] Britain for nearly four hundred years had played the role of "balancer," joining with the weakest coalition of powers to frustrate any threat to the European balance of power from whatever direction it might arise.

The immediate question emerging from this historical review is whether there is at present any nation on the political horizon willing and able to perform this ancient function. Following World War II, Churchill reaffirmed the belief of practically every other informed observer that the chances of Britain's playing its traditional role were practically nil. Even its position at the geometric center of its famous three orbits of interest could not assure that England was able to serve as the historic balancer. Indeed, the burden of Churchill's conclusions was that England must more and more adjust itself to a new role, that of playing a minor partner alongside the United States. At the same time, he rejected the even more popular concept that Western Europe, if united, might act as a "Third Force." That suggestion, however promising at first sight, hardly stands the test of searching examination. The only immediately practical way of pursuing such an objective would be by adopting the policy Hitler sought to impose on all Europe. That is, only a Europe restored to its prewar status and forcibly united could on any conceivable basis prove a match in war potential for either the United States or the Soviet Union. And at the moment of Europe's partition following the war, this possiblity became remote. In truth, the weight of European power in Churchill's time was probably no more than a feather on the scales of the world balance of power. Europe's destiny rested largely on the knees of the giants from east and west. In comments which illuminate his thinking on the nature of the problem, Churchill on November 30, 1950, spoke to Parliament on European rearmament. He referred to the argument frequently made that a European army, and especially one containing a German contingent, would be provocative to the Soviet Union. Some observers claimed that the Soviet leaders might interpret these policies as an invitation to attack while their military advantage was still substantial. Churchill rejected this view, saying:

13. New York *Times*, April 1, 1949, p. 10.

"It does not seem likely, however, that anything that we can do in the next two years in Europe will reverse the balance of military power. We may be stronger, but not strong enough in that time to deter, still less to prevail. There is plenty of room for us to get much stronger without altering the situation in Europe decisively."[14] The steps which might be taken to strengthen Western Europe might assist the separate nations in protecting themselves from revolutions and upheavals at home, but they could hardly affect in any appreciable way the great gulf between European and Russian power.

So Western Europe hardly qualifies as the "holder" of the balance of power, for it has neither retained its freedom of choice between East or West nor does its power weigh sufficiently in any world balance of power to decisively influence the calculations of the superpowers. As for the other candidates for this ancient and vital task, they all appear deficient on some count or other. Some have maintained that China or India because of their vast territories, great populations, and plentiful resources could qualify. In the critical period lying immediately ahead, however, Churchill considered this most unlikely since they gave little evidence of having suddenly acquired the capacity to exert their latent strength effectively.

There is one respect in which Churchill considered England's role in the balance of power to be decisive. It concerned the intra-European balance of power. The paramount European problem in the aftermath of both world wars had been to combine the dual aim of restoring a healthy and prosperous Germany without creating a Germany that would constitute a serious threat to European security. The effective pursuit of these twin objectives in the period following World War II was dependent upon the success of Britain and France in combining in any intra-European balance of power to offset the emergence of the naturally most powerful European state. Either France or Britain if isolated from one another would inevitably be overshadowed by Germany with its skilled population, superior resources, and advanced technology. But: "France and Britain, both sorely distressed, can combine together and, thus joined, have

14. *Parliamentary Debates*, Vol. 481, November 30, 1950, p. 1333.

the superior power to raise Germany, even more shattered, to an equal rank and to lasting association with them."[15]

These general beliefs and convictions reminiscent of the statesmanship of the concert of Europe in the nineteenth century were given concrete and graphic expression in Churchill's response to the following situation. On June 27, 1950, he belabored the government for its "hands-off" policy in discussions concerning the Schuman Plan. The burden of his criticism was not that England should commit itself to full-fledged involvement on the continent. What he found most offensive was that England by boycotting the conference had dealt a deathblow to the balance of power within Europe. "The absence of Britain deranges the balance of Europe. I am all for a reconciliation between France and Germany, and for receiving Germany back into the European family, but this implies, as I have always insisted, that Britain and France should in the main act together so as to be able to deal on even terms with Germany, which is so much stronger than France alone. Without Britain, the coal and steel pool in Western Europe must naturally tend to be dominated by Germany, who will be the most powerful member."[16]

The nature of politics demands tireless zeal in perceiving the need for effective equilibriums of power on the municipal and regional levels as well as on the world scene. For the realist in politics the idea of the balance of power comprises an operating principle which must never be abandoned or overlooked. In every sphere of political and military life, the greatest of western statesmen have lived by its precepts in situations like the one that involved the fate of the French navy during World War II. Following France's collapse on June 23, 1940, its naval vessels remained in the waters of North Africa. In this way their capture and control by German authorities was temporarily averted and in the spring of 1941 Churchill warned against the consequences of their falling to Germany. While some had suggested that the loss would not be too serious in absolute terms, he warned: "[The] movements of French war vessels

15. *Parliamentary Debates*, Vol. 473, March 28, 1950, p. 193.
16. *Parliamentary Debates*, Vol. 476, June 27, 1950, p. 2153.

from Africa to France would alter the balance of naval power, and would thus prejudice the interests of the United States as well as our own. Therefore, I trust that such incidents will be avoided."[17] In this warning, the application of a basic political principle was clearly stated. In these terms the French navy was vital. The principle of the balance of power is folly for those who make their judgments on the basis of simple absolutes or merely quantitative evaluations which in this case would have permitted the observer to ignore the relative importance of the French naval units in relation to world balance of power.

The New Balance of Power

During the greater part of the history of the modern state system the main weights in the balance of power have been predominantly in Europe. Expansion of major political importance was confined in practice to the European countries that were bounded by the Atlantic Ocean and the North Sea in Western and Central Europe. No Far Eastern countries played an important role until the signing of the Anglo-Japanese entente of 1902. Until the termination of the Napoleonic Wars in 1815, the significant factors in the balance of power were all European nations, with Turkey the one notable exception. However, the century from 1815 to 1914 witnessed the expansion of the European into a worldwide balance of power system. If one can point to a single dramatic event which heralded this transition it would be the proclamation in 1823 by President Monroe to the American Congress of the doctrine which bears his name. Once the mutual political interdependence of Europe and the Western Hemisphere was recognized, the foundations for the transformation of a European into a world balance of power system was laid. The changing character of the relationship of the New World to the Old World reflected in the balance of power did not escape the nineteenth-century British foreign secretary, George Canning. He had been criticized for not grasping the opportunity of redressing the

17. *Parliamentary Debates*, Vol. 370, April 9, 1941, p. 1595.

balance of power which France had upset by its invasion and intervention in Spain. He was urged to declare war against France in Europe. But Canning maintained that war against France was only one of the methods for restoring the balance of power. The British policy of recognizing the newly independent Latin American republics was another means of pursuing the same end, for now the weights in the balance of power were found in both continents. Canning asked: "Is the balance of power a fixed and unalterable standard? Or is it not a standard perpetually varying as civilization advances, and as new nations spring up and take their place among established political communities?"[18] While the balance of power has been in principle everywhere the same, the means of applying and adjusting it have been varied and the active elements comprising it almost constantly changing.

In the seventeenth century, the weights were France, Spain, Austria, the Netherlands, and England. Then Russia and Prussia were added to the scales. When one nation upset the equilibrium of power, the means of restoring it were either by limiting and checking the power of the expanding nation or by compensating the others by increasing their strength commensurately elsewhere in the world. Canning asked the question: "What if the possession of Spain might be rendered harmless in rival hands—harmless as regarded us—and valueless to the possessors. Might not compensation for disparagement be obtained . . . by means better adapted to the present time?"[19] Canning discovered these means to be inherent in the new situation of the Western Hemisphere. He concluded that by dividing Spain from its one-time possessions and preventing France from increasing influence abroad, the balance of power could be restored by means other than war: "Contemplating Spain, such as our ancestors had known her, I resolved that if France had Spain, it should not be Spain '*with the Indies*'. I called the New World into existence, to redress the balance of the Old."[20] In his recognition of the passing of

18. R. Therry (ed.), *Speeches of the Right Honourable George Canning* (3d ed., 6 vols.; London: J. Ridgway and Sons, 1836), VI, 109–10.
19. *Ibid.*, 111.
20. *Ibid.*

the countries within the Western Hemisphere from a passive to a more active role in world politics, Canning was merely one of the first Western statesmen to anticipate the new universal character of the balance of power.

The general trend toward universalizing the balance of power continued throughout the course of World War I. Before the conflict was ended, practically every nation in the world had participated on one side or the other. Significant is the fact that historians should describe the struggle as a world war. Following the war, the decline in the strength and vitality of the European countries made it almost inevitable that the pivotal areas in the balance of power would lie outside of Europe. In practice, however, for various reasons the full implications of these deep-seated changes were not perceived in this period. It was of course true that the historic relationship of the non-European to the European world had been drastically altered. No longer were the non-European nations subject to domination or subordination by European powers. No longer did they serve as sources of power and wealth in the struggle for power. Instead, the historic movement toward great non-European centers of power reached its highest expression during World War I and was consummated in World War II. Yet the tragic element in international politics throughout the interwar period was the outright failure of the United States actively to pursue its interests within some concept of the world balance of power. It was Churchill's opinion that if the United States in time of peace had thrown its weight resolutely into the scales of the balance of power, the far-reaching disequilibrium which proved Europe's undoing might have been significantly alleviated. The most grievous upset was the breakdown of the fragile and delicate balance which previously existed in Central and Eastern Europe. Any talk of a balance was no more than talk once the annexation of Austria was complete. Thereafter, any counterforce to Germany's expansion southward was out of the question. Finally, the whole fabric of France's security system in the West was shattered decisively by the agreement at Munich. On October 4, 1938, Churchill observed: "The position of all states outside the German system, and particularly that of France and England, will have to be adjusted to these new dominating facts. It would be affectation to deny that the whole basis of French foreign policy in Central and Eastern Europe has disappeared."[21] To restore an equilibrium, the military cooperation of two major powers who were non-European in whole or in part proved essential. It was primarily the industrial might of the United States and the numerical superiority of the Soviet army which swayed the balance and led to victory in World War II.

At the same time, another result of World War II was to emancipate Europe's colonies in Asia just as its American colonies had become independent in the eighteenth and early nineteenth centuries. Their emergence as independent factors in international politics had the effect of extending still further the active limits of the balance of power. Instead of continuing as pawns in the European struggle for colonial advantage, the Asian newcomers began more actively to determine the part they would play in the balance of power. Indeed, the most far-reaching transformation in the balance of power has been in the locus of the struggle for power. The centers of world power in Europe, which had played out their rivalries in the vast half-occupied colonial areas of the world, now were made subject to a reversal of this historic relationship. Europe, the former center from which influence and power radiated, became the foremost political theater and the most likely battlefield in the struggle between east and west. Thus the first characteristic of the "new balance of power" is its universal or global character. Along with that change, however, the operation and practice of the balance of power has been transformed. The areas which at one time were the scene of extra-European rivalries today are active centers of power, pursuing their own independent aspirations and national policies and adding to the complexity of the new balance of power.

Yet these changes taken together are not as new or disturbing as the factors responsible for the destruction of the modern state system itself. That system had survived vast social upheavals since the beginning of the sixteenth century. Its principal characteristics had been a system of self-generating restraints including those pro-

21. Churchill, "France After Munich," October 4, 1938, *Step by Step*, 250.

duced by the approximate equality of a multiplicity of states, none of whom was sufficiently powerful to control all the rest. The operation of the balance of power in a multiple-state system of near equals meant that no state could venture too far without assurances of support from others. Because this support was seldom unequivocal, nations were required to proceed cautiously so that advances would never rule out strategic retreats and the nation might take no position which left it without a path along which it could retrace its steps. The uncertainty of alliances and counter-alliances among numerous states relatively equal in strength and the effect any nation might exert on the balance through shifting its power from one group to another served to restrain nations from measures of a reckless and hazardous character. Indeed, the utter unreliability of commitments by nations whose survival could be placed in jeopardy by their peers encouraged prudence and circumspection by the nations.

Today all this has changed radically. Nations in the aftermath of World War II are no longer approximately equal. Their capacity to affect the outcome of major struggles is dependent on the role of the superpowers. If the nations in question are the United States or the Soviet Union, they are able to determine the outcome of the struggle. However, the power of these giants in comparison with their allies has become so overwhelming that no shift in alignments among other powers can decisively affect the balance. Thus the traditional restraints by which nations have been controlled for the past two or three centuries are no longer effective.

Moreover, the immense disparity in power between the superpowers and every other nation has lessened if not destroyed the flexible qualities of the balance. The minor powers are at one and the same time powerless to affect in any fundamental way the distribution of power and yet able to shift their weight from one side to the other with unhampered freedom as their interests dictate. The Western European powers aligned with the United States have had little viable choice but to remain in their present camp. The line that separates east and west is not only military and spiritual in character but political as well. The cold war is responsible for the fact that the claims and policies of both sides have become inflexible and the Iron Curtain resembles more than anything else a battle line along which both sides must hold their ground but cannot easily advance or retreat. The practice which was common in the eighteenth and nineteenth centuries of crossing over from one side to the other through concluding new alliances with former enemies is no longer feasible. Nations have lost their traditional freedom of maneuver, and Churchill with regard to England was keenly aware that: "We have to give our hand generously, whole-heartedly to our allies across the Atlantic Ocean, upon whose strength and wisdom the salvation of the world at this moment may well depend. Joined with them . . . we may save ourselves and save the world." [22]

The growth of influence and power of the United States which was inevitable was accelerated by the conduct of two world wars. Developments which would otherwise have taken half a century were hastened and speeded up by the consequences of the two wars. Because he recognized the narrow and restricted area within which British foreign policy had to be conducted, Churchill seized every opportunity to urge that British policy be harmonized with that of the United States. He inspired the words of his foreign secretary: "If Russia were to succeed in splitting the Anglo-American alliance, the whole of the free world would lie open to forcible subjection by Communism. That is the supreme consideration which must ever be present in our minds." [23] The Conservative prime minister spoke for himself on the vital issue of Britain's ties with the United States: "There is another reason why we should be very careful not to indulge in criticisms of the United States or their commanders, or do anything which could weaken, even by gusts of opinion, the vital ties that bind our fates together. . . . [For] in Korea and the Far East the burden falls almost entirely on the United States." [24] As long as England cherished its independence and its political institutions, it had no choice in the orientation of its foreign policy.

22. London *Times*, October 24, 1951, pp. 7, 4.
23. *Parliamentary Debates*, Vol. 481, November 29, 1950, pp. 1185–86.
24. *Parliamentary Debates*, Vol. 481, November 30, 1950, pp. 1336–37.

There was, therefore, a threefold deterioration of the balance of power affecting its flexibility, multistate membership, and inner freedom of maneuver leading to the popular view that the balance of power was useless and should be abandoned. Obviously, the bipolar character of the present balance of power was hardly the ideal form of self-regulating mechanism by which equilibrium historically had been maintained. The moral consensus among European powers which enhanced its functioning for over three centuries has vanished from the world scene. Not only is the system bereft of the living spirit by which it was sustained and fortified but its structural features are no longer adequate to its unhampered operation. The older European system had its "safety valves" in the struggle for power. Geographic areas located on the periphery of the European world were less highly prized and the major powers could deflect their rivalries from common frontiers to the vast empty spaces of the world where concessions could more readily be made at the expense of other peoples' interests. The most radical contemporary change has been the fusing of the center or core of the balance of power with its periphery and the empty spaces surrounding it. The geographical limits of the balance of power encompass the world, and the superpowers appear able to pour their resources into every corner of the world. Their goals have become less the avoidance and postponement of disputes or the deflection of rivalries into areas where the tensions were less acute but the drastic augmenting of their own power through lining up every ally unconditionally and requiring the whole world to choose sides.

These structural and spiritual changes have led to a new type of perspective on foreign policy. For over three hundred years, with a few important exceptions, the diplomatic mind found a place for its accommodating methods, its intellectual virtuosity, and its shrewd but subtle political judgments. However, these modes of action and forms of judgment today find no place in the conduct of the cold war. What each side must fear and oppose is not the emergence of a serious rival who has arisen unnoticed until it has become powerful enough to tip the scales of the balance of power. The supreme threat which both great powers unceasingly resist is the military challenge that the other's substantial increase in armaments would inevitably create. In confronting this threat, the qualities of mind which are called for are those of the military mind. The virtues of finesse and of subtlety which played so crucial a role when important variables outside of the competence of the principal participants could alter and upset the balance are now much less visible. The military mind has become indispensable since both sides are forced to increase their military potential in order to deter the other or, if necessary, to strike a decisive blow in a war where the first action might be conclusive. In a word, the art of diplomacy has been transformed into a form of warfare itself. The one way to maintain the balance of power is by keeping pace in an unrelenting arms race; the only way to restore the balance once it has been disturbed is by increasing the military strength of one or the other superpower.

This primitive spectacle of a bipolar balance of power, devoid of every traditional restraint except for the self-restraint of the two major powers, has led some observers to the conclusion that the system no longer offers hope and that war is in fact inevitable. Others have imputed to the mechanism of the balance itself a peculiar responsibility for all the world's troubles. Yet the political situation confronting us is not the result of the balance of power as such. Those who would cast out the balance of power as an imperfect mechanism for maintaining international order and occasionally international peace must examine the alternatives and weigh their prospects in comparison with the workings of an admittedly imperfect system. Whereas a system in which equilibrium rests on the opposition of two supremely powerful states is fraught with grave hazards, such a system is likewise capable of producing inestimable benefits. The philosopher of the French court of Louis XIV and advisor to his grandson conceived of a balance between two equal powers as the most ideal form of the balance of power. Thus Fénelon counseled: "The fourth system is that of a power which is about equal with another and which holds the latter in equilibrium for the sake of the public security. To be in such a situation and to have no ambition which would make you desirous to give it up, this is indeed the wisest and happiest situation for a state. You are the common arbiter; all your neighbours are your friends, and those that are not make themselves by that very fact suspicious to all the others."[25] However, the success of this form of the balance of power is dependent on qualities of moderation and self-restraint. If finesse and intellectual virtuosity are less evident today, wisdom and moderation are the preconditions for the continuation and success of an equilibrium. Fénelon cautioned: "You get stronger every day; and if you succeed, as it is almost inevitable in the long run by virtue of wise policies, to have more inner strength and more alliances than the power jealous of you, you ought to adhere more and more to that wise moderation which has limited you to maintaining the equilibrium and the common security. . . . Yet since one cannot hope that a power which is superior to all others will not before long abuse that superiority, a wise and just prince would never wish to leave to his successors, who by all appearances are less moderate than he, the continuous and violent temptation of too pronounced a superiority. For the very good of his successors and his people, he should confine himself to a kind of equality."[26] These words of wisdom are no less essential toward the end of the twentieth century than in the eighteenth century as the successors of the present Soviet regime await their opportunity or as one administration follows another in the United States.

There is no disputing that Churchill saw the practical wisdom of such precepts as did few contemporary statesmen. His comments made clear that while apprised of the changes the system of the balance of power had undergone, he believed it might yet be an instrument of good. He considered that moderation and wisdom in the maintenance of a state of equilibrium allowed the West collectively to preserve a margin of strength but not one of transcendent superiority. He never conceived of the balance of power as one requiring absolute equality and parity. In 1947, for example, there was already speculation over what might result if the Soviet Union were to break with the United Nations. Some prophesied that war would

25. Fénelon, *Oeuvres* (Paris, Garnier Frères, 1870), III, 160.
26. *Ibid.*, 160–61.

become inevitable if there were "two worlds." Churchill disputed this point and reasoned: "We should all be sorry to see that, but if one of these worlds is far more powerful than the other, and is equally vigilant and is also sincerely desirous of maintaining peace, there is no reason why a two-world system should lead to war. Great wars come when both sides believe they are more or less equal, when each thinks it has a good chance of victory. No such conditions of equality would be established if the Soviet Government and their Communist devotees were to make a separate organization of their own."[27] Therefore, if the West, or more precisely the United States, retained a slight margin of power, the bipolar system might conceivably preserve the peace for a long time. Yet, to attain it a measure of realism and moderation joined with decisiveness, commitment, and boldness was required. He warned: "I must not lead you to suppose that time is on our side; and that we have only got to go on with our party quarrels and close our eyes and stop our ears to the facts of the situation to find that all will work out all right in the long run."[28] The demands for the safeguarding of peace do not reside in a single political mechanism with all its defects and failings. They rest instead on statesmen who pursue their separate national policies and who, in the use they make of the system, may be prudent or foolish, moderate or reckless, realistic or utopian. The role of statesmanship, which has been discussed elsewhere,[29] remains the indispensable prerequisite both for the success of the traditional and no less the contemporary balance of power system.

We may leave this discussion of the new balance of power with one further comment. Observers disagree whether or not the balance of power that existed immediately after the war has been changed or altered. Some declare that the fall of Czechoslovakia was decisive to a change in the balance; others contend that the loss

27. New York *Times*, October 15, 1947, p. 4.
28. Winston S. Churchill, "The Plymouth Fair," July 15, 1950, *In the Balance*, ed. Randolph S. Churchill (London: Cassell and Company, 1951), 328.
29. Chapter Two, p. 25.

of China by the West was the most decisive change, which in turn the Sino-Soviet split has altered; still others point to Korea as an example of far-reaching political changes. Others see a multipolar world resulting from the rise of the Third World and the revival of Europe and Japan. Churchill was nowhere explicit on this point, but clearly he believed that the most radical change to which future historians would point was the explosion of an atomic bomb in 1949 by the Soviet Union. Soon after the initiation of the Korean action, he observed: "I do not know of any great change in the balance of world power or the imminence of world danger that has occurred since the dark day when the Government informed us that the Russian Communist Government had gained possession of the secret of the atomic bomb and led us to believe they had produced it. . . . It is quite true that the Soviet-impelled aggression in Korea and the vehement and valiant action of the United States . . . had made everyone realize and pay attention to dangers. . . . [But] the dread balance has not been changed." [30] If Churchill had lived, he might have modified this judgment with the rise of an independent China, a strengthened Europe, and a more powerful Japan. However, the greater likelihood is that he would have continued, in respect to war and peace, to emphasize the bipolar world.

Alternatives to the Balance of Power

What most distinguished Churchill from the majority of Western statesmen was not his view that peace and order were still possible by means of the system of a bipolar balance of power. The nature of total war and the aspirations inherent in contemporary crusading nationalism made it unlikely that a secure world would soon be realized. Practically, the real difference between the views espoused by Churchill and those of the great body of his contemporaries come into focus with their attitudes as to whether or not there are any clear and available alternatives to the balance of power. If we take the philosophy of Churchill as a whole, it is clear that he shared few

30. *Parliamentary Debates*, Vol. 478, September 12, 1950, p. 976.

of the general misconceptions of idealists and popular writers. Nowhere did he say that statesmen had a choice between balance of power policies and a better kind of international relations. If he indulged himself the luxury of suggesting in words that new forms of international politics might be on the horizon, his deeds invariably betrayed his deeper convictions. Churchill would probably concur wholeheartedly with Toynbee who, after an extended roundtable conference in which liberal and utopian scholars had again and again asserted that the balance of power was outmoded and archaic, offered the following sardonic comment: "That is comforting; I can go to sleep again. All the same, I rather mistrust this argument that such a thing as 'the balance of power' does not exist."[31] For Churchill the balance of power clearly existed and was a lasting if not permanent feature of international society.

31. Arnold J. Toynbee, "After Munich: The World Outlook," *International Affairs*, XVIII (January-February, 1939), 9.

CHAPTER TWELVE

The Disarmament Dilemma

When you have peace you will have disarmament. . . . Europe will be secure when nations no longer feel themselves in danger as many of them do now. Then the pressure and the burden of armaments will fall away automatically.[1]

The second historic approach to the problem of international peace and world order is the disarmament approach. In the aftermath of World War I, programs for disarmament, whether general or local, quantitative or qualitative, aroused massive popular approval and support in the West. Following that great conflict a widespread belief emerged that war was an atavism and that men fought primarily because of mutual fears engendered by armaments races. Men of good will accustomed to quick results in their business and professional endeavors rallied round to "solve" the armaments problem. They brought to the problem the same energy they would have employed in resolving an efficiency problem in the economic world. One disarmament conference followed another and Geneva was the scene of an uninterrupted procession of attempts to reduce international tensions. The compelling logic of disarmament led to the organization of the moral energy and dedication of people everywhere who threw themselves into the task with passionate and unqualified devotion. Churchill described this response by reflecting: "We all desire to see peace and goodwill established among nations, old scores forgotten, old wounds healed. The peoples of Christendom united to rebuild their position in the world, to solve the problem of their toiling masses, to give a higher standard of life to the harassed populations. We can all expatiate upon that."[2]

---

1. *Parliamentary Debates* (Hansard) House of Commons, Fifth Series, Vol. 292, July 13, 1934 (London: His Majesty's Stationery Office, 1950), 733.
2. *Parliamentary Debates*, Vol. 276, March 23, 1933, p. 539.

However, it has been in the implementation of these sentiments that the adherents of disarmament have been beset with the most baffling and perplexing obstacles and problems. For Churchill: "The differences which arise are those of method. They arise when our sentiments come into contact with baffling and extremely obstinate concrete obstacles."[3] Moreover, success or failure to achieve the reduction of armaments has been dependent upon the contriving of practical steps for dealing with political problems. The best of good intentions have not been enough. At approximately the mid-point in the interwar period Churchill advised: "I have a sympathy with, and respect for, the well-meaning, loyal-hearted people who make up the League of Nations Union in this country, but what impresses me most about them is their long suffering and inexhaustible gullibility. Any scheme of any kind for disarmament put forward by any country, so long as it is surrounded by suitable phraseology, is hailed by them, and the speeches are cheered, and those who speak gain the need of their applause. Why do they not look down beneath the surface of European affairs to the iron realities which lie beneath?"[4] The iron reality in the interwar European situation was the unresolved character of the major political disputes and the dependence of Europe for its security on the strength of the French army. In 1933, Churchill commented: "If Europe enjoys peace in this year it has been under the shield of France."[5] To press for disarmament by France under these conditions would have been tantamount to a conspiracy aimed at undermining the security of Europe. Yet in practice this was the policy of British left-wing circles to which Churchill took strong exception.

The Case for Disarmament

A brief survey of the conditions which led to an increase in popular concern with the problem of arms limitation helps illuminate Churchill's philosophy. It was no accident that the disarmament

3. *Ibid.*
4. *Parliamentary Debates*, Vol. 272, November 23, 1932, pp. 79–80.
5. *Ibid.*, 87 ff.

movement should have received its great stimulus in the aftermath of World War I. Spokesmen of other ages and different countries obviously conceived of disarmament as one of the great practical measures for attaining world peace. Yet in the eighteenth century, war was sufficiently temperate and indecisive that few statesmen or publicists could argue convincingly that nations must either accept restrictions and controls on their modes of warfare or fall prey to their own violence and destructiveness. The toll taken by wars was not great. Since World War I, the spirit of indifference which was understandable in the past was replaced by a new sense of urgency manifested in one effort after another to promote and achieve disarmament. The heightened resolve following World War I was overshadowed following World War II by the vastly more intensified energy and fervor of prominent leaders laboring under the ominous cloud of ultimate atomic destruction. Some urged that, failing armament agreements, statesmen from East and West should pledge never to use the final and "absolute weapon." Churchill addressed himself quite specifically and directly to this view. He examined the argument that no civilized people ought to use the bomb first unless it had been used against them. What this would mean in practice, he declared, was that nations would agree never to fire until they had been first shot dead. "That seems to me undoubtedly a silly thing to say and a still more imprudent position to adopt. Moreover, such a resolve would certainly bring war nearer. The deterrent effect of the atomic bomb is at the present time almost our sole defence."[6] However, to the popular mind preoccupied with the increasing danger and immediacy of the threat, disarmament became a vital and personal issue. So did "no first use" appeals in the 1980s.

The arguments for disarmament have been threefold, based on assumptions underscored in varying degrees of emphasis by its leading proponents. Disarmament is necessary because of the threat of universal destruction, the risk of economic deterioration, and the importance of reducing tensions in the world. The first of these arguments is plainly the one given highest priority in contemporary Western society. The profound and far-reaching revolutions in war-

6. *Parliamentary Debates*, Vol. 482, December 14, 1950, p. 1368.

fare have changed the purpose of war. The earlier ratio of one shot to one victim which prevailed in the past was superseded by the ratio of one atomic bomb for hundreds of thousands if not millions of possible victims. Revolutions in technology and in warfare have brought with them changes in the alternatives for the policy makers. Instead of a choice between disarmament and limited warfare, the real alternatives have ultimately become disarmament or suicide. Such choices, while terrifyingly real, were not compelling enough to induce Churchill to abandon the fateful weapons of suicide. Paradoxically enough, such weapons of destruction were also the chief weapons of security. He counseled: "It would nevertheless be wrong and imprudent to entrust the secret knowledge or experience of the atomic bomb, which the United States, Great Britain and Canada now share, to the world organisation, which is still in its infancy. It would be criminal madness to cast it adrift in this still agitated and un-united world."[7] Because international society is only imperfectly organized, states still are required to safeguard their separate independence. In the long run he was hopeful that the engines of destruction might contribute to peace. Thus: "This revelation of the secret of nature, long mercifully withheld from man, should arouse the most solemn reflections in the mind and conscience of every human being capable of comprehension. We must indeed pray that these awful agencies will be made to conduce to peace among the nations, and that instead of wreaking measureless havoc upon the entire globe they may become a perennial fountain of world prosperity."[8]

The second argument for disarmament is based on the calculation of practical men of affairs that the continued diversion of great sums of money for military expenditure will sooner or later exhaust a nation's economic strength. Students of comparative civilizations have discovered that past societies fallen into a state of decline have displayed an unmistakable tendency to devote ever increasing proportions of their resources to military preparations. In

7. New York *Times*, March 6, 1946, p. 4.
8. London *Times*, August 7, 1945, p. 4.

the early 1930s, the League of Nations secretariat reported that the average military expenditures of sixty-one leading countries over a period of the last four years had reached the unprecedented sum of four billion dollars. They forecast that such expenditures would contribute to the gravest economic crises and even to eventual bankruptcy. Therefore, disarmament had become a compelling economic necessity. Churchilll's response was again unconventional. No one was more vigilant in attempts to assure maximum military efficiency for a minimum of military expenditures. His method of meeting the challenge of economic collapse was not by trimming the essential objectives of his country through arms reductions. Instead he sought, through the husbanding of national resources, to maintain essential national security objectives. As for the contribution of disarmament conferences to the economy, he observed: "If by any means an abatement of expense and sacrifice involved in maintaining large armies and navies could be achieved, we should not look back to the legal reasons which have brought the Conference into being. What we have to consider is whether any useful result is actually obtained or has been obtained. I confess I have always doubted the utility of these conferences on disarmament in the present condition . . . of the world."[9]

A third line of reasoning in support of disarmament holds that tensions among nations mount in direct proportion to increases in armaments. If arms were reduced, tensions would be eased and accommodation facilitated. Proposals presented to the members of the Sixth General Assembly of the United Nations by the American secretary of state, Dean Acheson, provided for a policy embodying the steps inherent in this sequence. Arms were to be reduced and tensions alleviated in order to make possible political discussions. Suffice it to say, Churchill considered these proposals merely representative of one of the fatal errors that were made between the wars in which leaders insisted on putting the cart before the horse. He was in full accord with the United Nations correspondent of *The Times* who characterized the American and Soviet proposals say-

9. *Parliamentary Debates*, Vol. 265, May 13, 1932, p. 2347.

ing: "At the same time there is a marked suggestion of the market place—perhaps of an Oriental bazaar—about these rival proposals of East and West, and most observers comment on their air of unreality, seen against the present international background." [10] Churchill frequently charged that the interwar disarmament conferences had the effect of stimulating new tensions so that harmony actually began to ebb as soon as discussions were resumed. He wrote: "there has been during these recent years a steady deterioration in the relations between different countries, a steady growth of ill-will, and a steady, indeed a rapid increase in armaments that has gone on through all these years in spite of the endless flow of oratory, or perorations, of well-meaning sentiments, of banquets, which have marked this epoch." [11] Thus we may conclude regarding the three arguments for disarmament, that the first laid most heavily upon Churchill's mind especially since World War II, but he was skeptical about most approaches to the other two.

National Interest and Disarmament

The fundamental problem which has beset every program for universal disarmament has been the issue of divergent national interpretations of the consequences of disarmament and of the weapons that should be restricted. The sources of each nation's security are dependent on such factors as its geographic position and its relations with neighboring countries. In armament programs, nations traditionally have been dependent first and foremost upon themselves. For: "All history has proved the peril of being dependent upon a foreign State for home defense instead of upon one's own right arm." [12] Therefore, the first duty of every responsible statesman is to assess objectively the means of safeguarding his country's independence based on its national interest and its available and po-

10. London *Times*, November 20, 1951, p. 4.
11. Winston S. Churchill, *The Second World War*, Vol. I, *The Gathering Storm* (Boston: Houghton Mifflin, 1948), 102.
12. *Parliamentary Debates*, Vol. 286, March 8, 1934, p. 2066.

tential material resources. For these reasons, to conceive of universal disarmament is an intellectual and moral accomplishment; to work out concrete practical policies which are consonant with national interests is an infinitely more baffling and challenging political task. Not surprisingly, in view of his philosophy, Churchill measured the various disarmament proposals of his time in the light of the national interests of particular sovereign states, especially in the period between the two world wars.

Churchill wrote at a crucial stage in the interwar period: "I am very doubtful whether there is any use in pressing national disarmament to a point where nations think their safety is compromised, while the quarrels which divide them and which lead to armaments and their fears are still unadjusted."[13] This observation was nowhere more relevant than for France's foreign policy between the two wars. In 1932, Churchill declared in Parliament: "As Lord Grey has recently reminded us, France, though armed to the teeth is pacifist to the core. All the countries associated with France have no wish to do anything except to maintain the *status quo*."[14] France was primarily a land power and opposed policies which limited its sources of strength while not altering the elements of naval power in which other states were supreme. To take but one example, a program offered at the World Disarmament Conference by Hugh Gibson, the American delegate and noted diplomatist, provided for a kind of qualitative disarmament. Aggressive weapons, so-called, such as tanks, mobile guns larger than 155mm., and gas were to have been outlawed. The response in the French press, which was typical of French reactions to most disarmament programs, was highly critical of this attempt to prohibit types of armament that were of vital interest to land powers like France while leaving essentially untouched the naval strength of countries like the United States and Great Britain.

In the interwar period, France sought consistently to explore the implications for its security of each projected disarmament program. For example, French reactions to the Hoover Plan should

13. *Parliamentary Debates*, Vol. 276, March 23, 1933, p. 540.
14. *Parliamentary Debates*, Vol. 272, November 23, 1932, p. 87.

have been foreseen. That dramatic proposal provided for a general overall one-third reduction in armaments. It was met by French fears and anxiety about what actions the United States would take in the event of a breach of the Kellogg-Briand Pact. When, as French leaders feared, Hugh Gibson proved unable to offer guaranties of any kind, French rejection of the plan was assured.

Furthermore, France's policy toward disarmament remained the same regardless of the government in power at any particular time. In 1932, for example, it was widely believed that France would display a new and more cooperative spirit toward disarmament when Monsieur Herriot assumed office. Delegates to the disarmament conferences soon discovered, however, that French policy was unchanged and was in practice not primarily dependent upon its spokesmen at any particular moment in history. Neither Paul Boncour, who represented France in the conversations at Geneva, nor Monsieur Herriot at Lausanne could hold out any hope of substantial concessions in the absence of substantial guaranties of French security. Churchill observed at the time: "No plan for stopping war at this present late hour is of any value unless it has behind it force, and the resolve to use that force. Mere passive resistance by some nations would only precipitate the disaster if others, or their leaders, stood ready to take advantage of it." [15]

The policy of Great Britain at successive disarmament conferences was similarly founded upon the British national interest. For a British statesman to acknowledge this was more difficult than for the British scholar or historian. Thus the historian Arnold Toynbee in 1932 could observe: "It was natural . . . that each of the Governments . . . should bear its own national interests in mind." [16] By contrast Churchill explained: "I have formed the opinion that none of the nations concerned in the Disarmament Conference except Great Britain has been prepared willingly to alter . . . its ratio. . . . [or] impair their factor of safety." [17] Yet neither Toynbee nor Churchill

15. Churchill, "How to Stop War," June 12, 1936, *Step by Step 1936–1939* (New York: Putnam's, 1939), 26.
16. Arnold J. Toynbee, *Survey of International Affairs* (London: Oxford University Press, 1933), 237.
17. *Parliamentary Debates*, Vol. 272, November 23, 1932, p. 83.

would have disputed the fact that the British proposals for naval disarmament tended to emphasize particular restrictions on the building of submarines. No objective observer would claim the British delegates remained unaware that such a policy which suited their interests would be entirely unacceptable to smaller naval powers under existing conditions of relative naval strength. Almost every British proposal contained some kind of reference to the elimination of the submarine. In practice, Britain was unwilling to sacrifice and abandon the production of key elements in its own naval strength for only minor concessions by the smaller naval powers.

On one point in particular, the American delegation to disarmament conferences between the two world wars found itself in accord with British policy. The same principle of restriction on submarine construction which the British had emphasized was contained in several of Hugh Gibson's draft-proposals. For the United States as for Britain, such proposals were unlikely to injure relative positions of power. Nor was the United States placing its national interest in jeopardy when it set forth a plan for disarmament based on the restriction of armaments to a specific proportion of each nation's budget. No one was unmindful of the fortuitous coincidence of this basic principle with the superior wealth of the United States. The fact that the spectacular Hoover Plan for one-third disarmament was introduced without warning shortly before a crucial domestic election drew comments from the best-informed political analysts. These practical realities as described by Churchill and others whose thinking places them in the realist tradition were meant to take nothing away from the genuine idealism which inspired American efforts at arms reduction. It is well to remember, however, the important connection between ideals and the conditions under which they would have been implemented, as well as the effects on disarmament proposals.

In the present cold war, the same play of national interests has influenced and molded disarmament policies of the various nations. The Soviet Union, whose knowledge and production of the atomic bomb was from the outset qualitatively and quantitatively inferior to the United States, urged the outlawry of that deadly weapon, prompting Churchill's statement: "I can quite understand the Com-

munist propaganda about barring the atomic bomb, for such a decision would leave the civilization of the world entirely at their mercy
even before they had accumulated the necessary stockpile themselves."[18] The one area in which the United States was supreme until
September 29, 1949, was the atomic bomb. On October 11, 1948,
Churchill observed: "Of one thing I am quite sure, that if the United
States were to consent, in reliance upon any paper agreement, to destroy the stocks of atomic bombs which they have accumulated,
they would be guilty of murdering human freedom and committing
suicide themselves. . . . Nothing stands between Europe to-day and
complete subjugation to communist tyranny but the atomic bomb
in American possession."[19] The national interest of the United
States and the interests of its allies or "clients" required that its relative advantage in production be safeguarded. Once the American
monopoly was broken, its advantage lay in its superior techniques
of atomic production, and Churchill repeated on August 26, 1950,
as in 1948: "It is indeed a melancholy thought that nothing preserves Europe from an overwhelming military attack except the
devastating resources of the United States in this awful weapon.
That is at the present time the sole deterrent against an aggressive
Communist invasion. No wonder the Communists would like to
ban it in the name of peace."[20]

Major Issues and Problems of Disarmament

Thus Churchill viewed the problem of disarmament not as a profound moral issue but as a baffling political problem. References to
four aspects of the problem recurred so frequently in his public
statements as to merit special discussion. Taken together, they provide a composite picture of his overall thinking on disarmament.
The first issue or problem concerns the methods best adapted to
achieving agreements on disarmament. More specifically, he asked:

18. *Parliamentary Debates*, Vol. 477, July 5, 1950, p. 501.
19. London *Times*, October 11, 1948, p. 4.
20. *Ibid.*, August 28, 1950, p. 2.

are attempts to achieve general or local disarmament more likely to succeed? If we take state practice in contemporary international society as our guide and accept the assumptions underlying successive attempts to bring about disarmament since World War I at face value, the case for general disarmament conferences appears convincing to almost all moderns. Yet every attempt at general disarmament conferences, including the two Hague Conferences, the Geneva Conference of 1932, and successive disarmament commissions under the aegis of the United Nations, has failed. As a rule these failures have been dismissed by disarmament enthusiasts by pointing to procedural defects such as insufficient diplomatic preparation, inadequate personnel, or an unfortunate combination of circumstances. However, almost no one has questioned the underlying approach.

Churchill was a prominent dissenter from this prevailing viewpoint. For him, the spectacular multilateral conferences could not have succeeded even under the most ideal circumstances. The continuation of the struggle for power among the principal participants made it virtually inevitable that they would fail. In 1934, he proposed, in criticizing the widespread popular emphasis given to the Geneva Conference, other more desirable alternatives. Nations could pursue: "private interchanges in secret diplomacy between the Foreign Offices of the different countries of a friendly character—'if you will not do this, we shall not have to do that,' 'If your program did not start so early, ours would begin even later,' and so on—such as have always gone on, and may perfectly legitimately go on. I believe a greater advance and progress towards a diminution of expenditure on armaments might have been achieved by these methods than by conferences and schemes of disarmament which have been put forward at Geneva."[21] Churchill would have reduced disarmament efforts, in method and objectives, to more modest proportions. For the grand spectacle of general disarmament conferences, he would have substituted discussions through normal diplomatic channels. Because of knowledge that lasting ac-

21. *Parliamentary Debates*, Vol. 276, March 23, 1933, p. 541.

cords have rested on agreements of a local character between two or three nations, he placed his hopes in limited arrangements between a small number of states among whom the power conflict was reduced or who preferred a regulated instead of an unregulated competition for power. If his approach ignored the worldwide character of the arms race, it did not overlook the grave issues that separate the two main adversaries in the cold war.

The second issue Churchill examined dealt with the consequences of disarmament conferences. It is a fair question to ask whether in practice arms agreements, even when successfully concluded, have ever led to a reduction of arms. The tendency to continue to seek disarmament would seem to indicate that the approach had successes and constructive achievements to its credit. Yet what from a logical point of view would seem to follow was not true historically. It is worth remembering that in international politics we are dealing with a dominant philosophy which has proven almost impervious to the lessons of experience. Leaders have proceeded on the assumption that if the Hague Conferences, the London Treaty of 1930, and the Geneva Conference of 1932 were all spectacular failures, another such conference should be organized immediately. The frame of mind of rigorous self-examination which dictates for every business enterprise and professional establishment, for example, that unsuccessful approaches and methods should be abandoned and replaced has not applied to the conduct of international affairs.

On the contrary, Churchill argued that: "the holding of these conferences over the last seven or eight or nine years has . . . actually prevented the burden from being lightened . . . [through] the normal working of economic and financial pressures. But these conferences have focused the attention of the leading men in all nations upon the competitive aspects of armament. . . . [and] intensified the suspicions and the anxieties of the nation."[22] He based his conclusions on the unmistakable results of the interwar conferences. The Washington Naval Agreement of 1922 provided that the strength in capital ships of the American, British, and Japanese navies should be reduced by approximately 40 percent. Although such limitation

22. *Parliamentary Debates*, Vol. 272, November 23, 1932, pp. 83–85.

was temporary and although the five signatories foresaw a period of regulated competition from 1931 to 1942, by which time the parties would have reached a ratio of 5:5:3:1.67:1.67 [the proportions accorded the United States, Britain, Japan, etc.], a reduction in battleships appeared assured. However, the decline in importance of battleships as sinews of warfare was the more basic reason for their successful limitation. A growing number of naval experts believed that the future lay with small, fast vessels with heavy fire power. The acceptance by the signatories of limits on production of larger but outmoded battleships was less a recognition of the principle of disarmament than a formalizing of an action that the nations would have taken anyway. Moreover, the arrangement with respect to capital ships was the signal for an intensified competition in vessels which had already been accepted as most important in current naval warfare. So the reduction in armaments which resulted in 1922 had only accidentally a connection with the procedures for disarmament. In practice it proved merely the first stage in a more serious armaments race. Nevertheless, it can be argued that some reduction of armaments was achieved in this case.

The London Treaty of 1930 is a striking example of an agreement in which even so modest an accomplishment as this was denied. It sought to place limits on the tonnage of cruisers, destroyers, and submarines. The agreement, which recognized the supremacy of Britain and the United States, trailed by Japan with two-thirds the capacity of the others, had the practical effect of establishing maximum limits which the United States, because of public opinion, and Japan, due to the limits of its building capacity, were unable to reach in the near future. Therefore, instead of reducing the armaments of the three powers, the London Treaty presented two of the three with maximum limits allowing for increases considerably beyond their present capacity. Churchill considered such armament agreements as contributing to the outbreak of war. Speaking of them, he wrote: "Thus both in Europe and Asia, conditions were swiftly created by the victorious Allies which in the name of peace, cleared the way for the renewal of war."[23] His reference here was to

23. Churchill, *The Gathering Storm*, 14.

the London Treaty of 1930, and the different conferences involved numerous complicated political and technical problems, including those of France and Italy. Admittedly, no brief discussion such as that outlined above can do justice to all the complexities. Nevertheless, when he referred to the period of disarmament conferences as the epoch of oratory, banquets, and well-meaning sentiments, Churchill's words reflected a deep-seated conviction. In his mind such undertakings contributed not to a reduction but to a rapid increase in armaments that was marked by a deterioration in relations among countries and a steady development of suspicion and ill-will.

The third problem of disarmament is perhaps best illustrated in a fable recounted by the Spanish diplomatist and scholar Salvador de Madariaga. At the February 25, 1932, meeting of the General Commission on Disarmament at Geneva, he commented sardonically on the many diverse national outlooks on disarmament. With particular reference to the proposal for universal disarmament by the Russians, he wrote:

The animals had met to disarm. The lion, looking sideways at the eagle, said: "Wings must be abolished." The eagle, looking at the bull, declared: "Horns must be abolished." The bull, looking at the tiger, said: "Paws, and especially claws, must be abolished." The bear in his turn said: "All arms must be abolished; all that is necessary is a universal embrace." [24]

One of the most popular interwar approaches to disarmament was the conception that arms reduction could be achieved on a qualitative basis. Some weapons were conceived of as aggressive while others were defensive. By outlawing the production of aggressive weapons, it was believed that the means and the sources of aggression would disappear. Yet each nation in practice has construed as defensive those weapons in which it enjoyed an advantage. Conversely, weapons that were the most unsuited to its own needs and which it had no intention of constructing anyway were classified as aggressive. To mention a few important examples, England and the United States insisted that the battleship was a purely defensive

24. Quoted in Toynbee, *Survey of International Affairs*, 208.

weapon and that the only weapon which was clearly aggressive was the submarine. Japan considered neither the battleship nor the submarine as offensive weapons but preferred that aircraft carriers, a possible threat to Japanese security, be classified as aggressive. All small naval powers considered large battleships to be offensive while Germany maintained that all vessels already forbidden to Germany by the Versailles Treaty were offensive. By way of contrast, the Germans claimed that "pocket battleships" which had been permitted by the treaty ought to be considered defensive in character.

The sole grounds on which the popularity of the qualitative approach can be explained is in terms of its relative simplicity and clarity. Only because of its simplicity did it exert a powerful appeal upon world opinion. In opposing the government's disarmament program proposed in May of 1932, Churchill maintained that it was easier to expose its fallacy than to convince the members of Parliament of its folly. He asserted: "The Foreign Secretary told us that it was difficult to divide weapons into offensive and defensive categories. It certainly is, because almost every conceivable weapon may be used in defence or offence; either by an aggressor or by the innocent victim of his assault."[25] The distinction between offensive and defensive weapons depended entirely on the circumstances and they could not be forecast or written into a policy in advance. Churchill believed it was an absurdity and self-deception to contrive impressive formulae for qualitative disarmament. The issue was merely one aspect of a more fundamental and baffling problem of deciding on the standards for allocating types and quantities of weapons to the nation seeking to arrive at an agreement. As the history of attempts to give concrete meaning to equality between France and Germany in the 1930s indicates, or with present-day attempts to achieve agreement between the United States and the Soviet Union, such ventures in disarmament create problems so baffling that no commission or conference has yet discovered practical and effective solutions. Armaments are considered an instrument of defense and security; experience has taught that any attempt to produce a quan-

25. Churchill, *The Gathering Storm*, 71–72.

titative measure of security is extraordinarily difficult and practically impossible. Considered during the interwar disarmament era were such perplexing and uncertain factors as risks, intentions, natural frontiers, and anticipated policies as were standards of allocation for particular armaments. We need hardly remind ourselves that such issues remain insoluble so long as the political problem remains unresolved.

The final question or problem that Churchill raised was that of inspection and control. The facts of particular national arms programs and the means of controlling and enforcing an agreement are dependent on facilities for inspection. "What is called war talk will be swept away by an interchange of actual military facts, supported by equality between all powers, great and small, which are involved. That will be a great step forward in itself and may lead the way to others."[26] This comment was made on November 1, 1946, and reflected a certain optimism and buoyancy which later disappeared from Churchill's declarations. One reason was the failure of the United Nations to find a way of establishing an arms agreement with provisions for effective inspection. Sovereign nations in general and the Soviet Union in particular foster and defend the concept of the impenetrability of their national borders. A system of reciprocal inspection which would be difficult at any time became nearly impossible in the case of the Soviet government, which maintains its power through holding before its people the specter of a continuing external threat.

The Real Issue Underlying Disarmament

In June of 1934, the Standing Commission of the Disarmament Conference at Geneva was, because of limited effectiveness, adjourned indefinitely. On July 13, 1934, Churchill emphatically declared in the House of Commons: "I am also very glad that the Disarmament Conference is passing out of life into history. . . . It is the greatest mistake to mix up disarmament with peace. When you

26. New York *Times*, November 1, 1946, p. 15.

have peace you will have disarmament."[27] He went on to describe and evaluate the steady deterioration of relations among nations which had accompanied the efforts of successive disarmament conferences. He concluded: "Europe will be secure when nations no longer feel themselves in great danger, as many of them do now. Then the pressure and the burden of armaments will fall away automatically, as they ought to have done in a long peace, and it might be quite easy to seal a movement of that character by some general agreement."[28] With these remarks, Churchill appeared to approve the French conception of disarmament more than he did that of the British government in power. The British view, advanced frequently during the period by Sir Arthur Henderson, was based on the assumption that security and disarmament were so closely interdependent that progress in one inevitably facilitated progress in the other. What mattered was not where one started but what was accomplished wherever an effort was made. The French view, by contrast, which enjoyed the support in particular of the Rumanian and Polish governments, was that progress toward disarmament was entirely and exclusively dependent on the prior attainment of security. Time and again Aristide Briand repeated the French thesis that there were three successive stages to the disarmament problem: arbitration, security, and disarmament. One must precede the other and, failing to make progress, nations would be obliged to seek security through armies and national defense. Churchill was constrained to speak disparagingly of Western policy toward France: "It was argued in odd logic that it would be immoral to disarm the vanquished unless the victors also stripped themselves of their weapons. The finger of Anglo-American reprobation was presently to be pointed at France, deprived alike of the Rhine frontier and of her treaty guarantee, for maintaining, even on a greatly reduced scale, a French Army based upon universal service."[29]

Such examples reveal Churchill as opposed to disarmament

27. *Parliamentary Debates*, Vol. 292, July 13, 1934, p. 733.
28. *Ibid.*
29. Churchill, *The Gathering Storm*, 13–14.

pursued in isolation from the underlying problems of the power struggle. He maintained that attempts in the interwar period were not directed at the real problems. He observed: "If you wish for disarmament, it will be necessary to go to the political and economic causes which lie behind the maintenance of armies and navies. There are very serious economic and political dangers at the present time, and antagonisms which are by no means assuaged."[30] Disarmament was intelligible only when it was taken as the crowning achievement, and not the first step, of a general political settlement, which might be culminated by "the broad general reduction of the hideous burden of armaments."[31] So long as the contest for power and security were unresolved and tensions not relaxed, it was in the nature of things that rival nations would advance conflicting claims leading to the maintenance of armies and navies. There could be but one adequate precondition for a disarmament agreement, namely, a political settlement. One aspect of such a settlement, in Churchill's opinion, would be the reduction of political grievances. "Here is my general principle. The removal of the just grievances of the vanquished ought to precede the disarmament of the victors. . . . Nobody keeps armaments going for fun. They keep them going for fear."[32] Another aspect of disarmament is the traditional goal which diplomacy has always pursued: "the patient and skillful removal of the political causes of antagonism which a wise foreign policy should eventually achieve."[33] Unless nations arrive at some form of settlement respecting the relative distribution of power between them, no nation can afford to reduce its arms program. In a brilliantly written and wisely reasoned editorial entitled "Disarmament" in *The Times* of December 1, 1951, the real issue concerning disarmament was stated in a single cogent sentence: "Disarmament will come, if it comes at all, only when the two leviathans have in fact achieved a rough balance of power, when they realize that they do

30. *Parliamentary Debates*, Vol. 265, May 13, 1932, p. 2352.
31. Churchill, "The Choice for Europe," May 9, 1938, *Into Battle* (London: Cassell, 1941), 20.
32. *Parliamentary Debates*, Vol. 272, November 23, 1932, p. 89.
33. *Parliamentary Debates*, Vol. 265, May 13, 1932, p. 2353.

not mean to attack each other, and when this balance and this realization can at last lead to written agreement on the debatable areas of the world." [34] Only with a political settlement is disarmament possible; only then can disarmament contribute to the lessening of tensions and the pacification of relations among major powers. A settlement must interact with disarmament to ameliorate the conditions of continuing rivalry among the great powers.

34. London *Times*, December 1, 1951, p. 7.

CHAPTER THIRTEEN

The World State and International Law

I cannot bring myself to visualise, in its frightful character, another world war, but none of us knows what would happen if such a
thing occurred. It is a sombre thought that, so long as the new world
organisation is so loosely formed, such possibilities and their consequences
are practically beyond human control.[1]

As a practical politician and statesman, Churchill
obviously did not give sufficient attention to many of the fundamental problems which lay beyond his range of immediate experience.
There are certain issues which the political philosopher feels obliged
to evaluate and discuss which Churchill hardly considered. The philosopher's conception of the simply or ideally best or the best attainable political system, to say nothing of any theoretical formulation of ideas of world order, were not his preoccupations. He
conceived of the world state and a world legal order as desirable in
the long run, but he was silent about the logical connection or practical significance of these ultimate ends for the immediate international situation. Such silence on the nature of world institutions and
their relation to existing national governments by a practical statesman whose political wisdom and sagacity were so widely acclaimed
would encourage the belief that these questions were not politically
relevant in Churchill's mind. Nonetheless, his insights on the issue
of a world state deserve attention.

Functions of the World State

The world state for Churchill had a triple function. First, it provided the warring and troubled nations with an ultimate political

1. *Parliamentary Debates* (Hansard) House of Commons, Fifth Series, Vol. 415,
November 7, 1945 (London: His Majesty's Stationery Office, 1950), 1293.

goal. The arguments of those who advocate world government is logically and theoretically unassailable. No peace of a lasting nature can be achieved unless there are actual political institutions corresponding in scope to the confines of a vast and interdependent world. In the same way that parts of the United Nations Charter, in particular the articles of the preamble, constitute for any reasonable U.N. supporter no more than a set of moral desiderata toward which nations ought to aspire, the principle of world government *a fortiori* is a goal or ideal and not an immediate practical possibility. In his celebrated MIT speech Churchill reflected on the role of world government as an ultimate aim when he declared: "There remains, however, a key of deliverance. It is the same key which was searched for by those who labored to set up the World Court at the Hague in the early years of the century. It is the same conception as animated President Wilson and his colleagues at Versailles, namely the creation of a world instrument capable at least of giving to all its members security against aggression."[2] It is Churchill's view of such a vision to which we now turn.

Hans J. Morgenthau in his classic *Politics Among Nations* found that peace on the domestic scene is maintained as a consequence of three factors not present in any comparable degree on the international scene. Morgenthau observed: "Peace among social groups within the state reposes upon a dual foundation: the disinclination of the members of society to break the peace and their inability to break the peace if they should be inclined. Individuals will be unable to break the peace if overwhelming power makes an attempt to break it a hopeless undertaking."[3] The world order Churchill described achieved the first goal of assuring that members were "unable" to break the peace by erecting a "reign of law supported . . . by overwhelming force."[4] The two additional conditions Morgenthau considered which were responsible for the disinclina-

2. New York *Times*, April 1, 1949, p. 10.
3. Hans J. Morgenthau, *Politics Among Nations* (5th ed.; New York: Alfred A. Knopf, 1978), 392.
4. *Parliamentary Debates*, Vol. 317, November 5, 1935, p. 311.

tion of individuals to break the peace were their loyalties to society as a whole surpassing those to any of its parts and their expectations founded on experience that their claims and demands would be satisfied by society with some approximation to justice. Churchill did not doubt for one moment that three such factors existed on the domestic scene. Loyalty to the nation above loyalties to a multiplicity of regional and social groups is the wellspring of modern nationalism. Patriotism is a virtue and the source of cohesion within the state: "where it means love of country and readiness to die for country, where it means love of tradition and culture and the gradual building up across the centuries of a social entity, dignified by nationhood."[5] Yet the primacy of national loyalties are in part the result of the conflicts and antagonisms involved in the individual's commitments within the state. For example, his loyalties as a member of a political party remain partial so long as he also remains a faithful member of other religious, economic, and social groups. Each group puts a claim on his loyalty, and while acting as a member of one, he cannot be unmindful of his responsibilities to the others. Moreover, if his economic interests place him in opposition to particular men, he is likely to be a co-believer with them by virtue of a common religious affiliation. The pluralism of social groups and their overlapping with one another mitigate and neutralize the strivings of individuals within them. The individual must play his role as a member of different groups simultaneously and can succeed only by restricting the intensity of his separate loyalties. The one loyalty which includes and subsumes all the others, however, is loyalty to the nation itself. It has no rivals or competitors. All other unities are ultimately embedded in the fabric of national unity. Whatever issues arise among social groups, they must be fought out within the restraining limits of loyalty to the nation.

The other factor which restrains the anarchic tendencies within domestic societies is the expectation by most of its members that justice will be done. In the nation there are political institutions in which minorities may with confidence look forward to becoming

5. New York *Times*, May 10, 1946, p. 10.

majorities; there are judicial organs in which grievances can be heard and adjudicated and social machinery through which peaceful change can be achieved. None of these factors is effectively present on the international scene. The sole way in which small nations, whose national claims and goals are cherished more than international law and order, can assure that they will be taken seriously is through acquiring the essential elements of national power and influence alone or in concert with others. The institutional agencies and processes of social change which exist within the nation are absent or largely defective on the world scene. Because the factors which operate to make individuals unable or disinclined to break the peace within nations are absent on the international scene, the likelihood of war is increased.

The world state, moreover, served an additional purpose for Churchill. It was an ideology or rallying point for like-minded nations with compatible interests anxious to enrich and fortify the pursuit of their cause. A union of democracies was at one and the same time the most plausible and realizable supranational goal for him and the best symbol around which to gather the democracies whose interests are compatible. On October 14, 1947, he proclaimed: "I believe . . . that above all these a world instrument, in Al Smith's words, 'to weld the democracies together,' can be erected which will be all powerful so long as it is founded on freedom, justice and mercy and is well armed."[6] Through the union of democracies on as wide a basis as possible, predatory nationalism would be destroyed and the aggrandizement of certain nations by others would be eliminated. Placed alongside Churchill's basic conception of the struggle for power as the source of all rivalries, this statement can hardly be viewed as more than a slogan or ideology.

Finally, world government is an objective standard against which all partial experiments in political integration may be measured and evaluated. The British Commonwealth was for Churchill a small-scale model of the world state that eventually might be created. In truth, the full benefits of science, freedom, and peace are attainable

6. *Ibid.*, October 15, 1947, p. 4.

only when a state is established coextensive with the confines of the political world. In a statement addressed to the commonwealth states, he said: "It is our hope . . . that the tolerant, flexible, yet enduring relationship which binds us all together by ties which none could put on paper but are dear to all, may some day be expanded to cover all the peoples and races of the world in a sensible, friendly and unbreakable association, and so give mankind, for the first time, their chance of enjoying the personal freedom which is their right and the material wellbeing which science and peace can so easily place at their disposal."[7] The objective standard of world order is the basis on which the present situation must be evaluated. Indeed, the fundamental reason why international anarchy is unacceptable is that there exists a universal conception of order which some have partially perceived and understood. Man's concern for injustice proves the existence of a general conception of justice. "We are reminded how in a state of savagery every man is armed and is a law unto himself but that civilization means that courts are established, that men lay aside their arms and carry their causes to the tribunal. This pre-supposes a tribunal to which men, when they are in doubt or anxiety, may freely have recourse. It pre-supposes a tribunal which is not incapable of giving a verdict."[8] No such tribunal or the attitudes by states upon which it could base its procedures is in sight at this moment. Still, in his contrast between savagery and order Churchill assumed the ultimate existence of such a standard.

It is one thing to cherish and nurture the fond hope of an ultimate world state or to refer existing political institutions to it as to an objective standard. However, another development in contemporary thinking constitutes a positive danger. When means and ends are confounded, when world government becomes a political doctrine assumed to provide ready-made answers for every immediately pressing political problem, the consequences have been to shackle the practical wisdom and prudence of statesmen. World government as a dogma, confounded with and mistakenly applied to

7. *Parliamentary Debates*, Vol. 478, October 26, 1950, p. 2933.
8. *Parliamentary Debates*, Vol. 301, May 2, 1935, p. 601.

each painful step in everyday politics, can prove a positive detriment to security and order. In a word, fanaticism over a society's ends can rob men of their common sense about means. In the same way that communism as a political philosophy has rigidified the actions of the Soviet leader and diplomat, the doctrine of world government can blind other leaders, not excluding our own, to the everyday demands for the bitter compromises and tragic concessions required by contemporary politics.

History is starred with a thousand gleaming ideas of concrete political ideals and institutions which were assumed capable of transforming society and the world. Some have appeared more beguiling than others; many hold out only vague hopes and distant visions for the faithful believers. When conceived of too immediately as imminent steps that must be taken without delay, the fury of the intransigent crusader supplants the tentative and compromising spirit of the diplomatist. Thus individuals and nations run the risk of reckless self-destruction before their vaunted goals are within sight of attainment. It is necessary to point out that if enthusiasts for the world state base their case on analogy, which is a common tool of intelligent thinking, the one pathway for achieving their aims is the spirit of compromise that influenced the founding fathers. The constitution of the United States which, with the Swiss system, is often taken as a model for the world state, was written by men inspired by the libertarian views of the French Enlightenment and imbued with the tradition of English liberties. Whatever his strengths, the rabid crusader is hardly the man most likely to possess these virtues.

World Law and International Practice

Most grand designs and blueprints for world government have included some concept of an omnipotent world law. Such plans have called for a lawgiver and law executor in the form of an executive and legislature able to make *de novo* principles of universal law that would be widely accepted. However, while the dreamers and planners have traveled the high road of world transformation, diplomatists and statesmen have stumbled along with the shambles of international law as it existed. Many tireless workers for the establishment of more effective international law have claimed that, given an enlightened spirit, it would be strengthened rather than dismantled. A natural evolution can be traced from self-redress to arbitration to judicial proceedings. Progress was being made in moving from the second to the third of these stages. However, the kind of optimism which existed before the two world wars has today largely receded set back by the assaults of new technological conditions and profound underlying political forces. Whereas the publicist W. E. Hall could assert in 1895, "we see international law at the close of each fifty years in a more solid position . . . it has taken firmer hold, it has extended its sphere of operations, it has ceased to trouble itself about trivial formalities, it has more and more dared to grapple in detail with the fundamental facts in the relations of states,"[9] most contemporary observers now acknowledge that this same international law, at least with regard to the laws of warfare, has been weakened and largely destroyed in the conduct of World War II. In his account of that war, Churchill lamented: "Now in the Second World War every bond between man and man was to perish. . . . The hideous process of bombarding open cities from the air, once started by the Germans, was repaid twenty-fold by the ever-mounting power of the Allies, and found its culmination in the use of atomic bombs which obliterated Hiroshima and Nagasaki."[10] The steady decline of international law in practice is seen by the contrast with World War I, in which "the laws of war had on the whole been respected. . . . Vanquished and victors alike still preserved the semblance of civilised states. A solemn peace was made which, apart from unenforceable financial aspects, conformed to the principles which in the nineteenth century had increasingly regulated the relations of enlightened peoples."[11] During that war, however, the Germans set up a sea res-

9. W. E. Hall, *A Treatise on International Law* (3rd ed.; London: Oxford University Press, 1895), ix.
10. Winston S. Churchill, *The Second World War,* Vol. I, *The Gathering Storm* (Boston: Houghton Mifflin, 1948), 17.
11. *Ibid.,* 16–17.

cue service and employed German transport planes marked with the Red Cross symbol. When they were shot down by the British, the complaint was lodged that this was contrary to the Geneva Convention. To this charge, Churchill replied: "But all German air ambulances were forced or shot down by our fighters on definite orders approved by the War Cabinet. . . . There was no mention of such a contingency in the Geneva Convention, which had not contemplated this form of warfare. The Germans were not in a strong position to complain, in view of all the treaties, laws of war, and solemn agreements which they had violated without compunction whenever it suited them."[12] Both sides violated international law and the violations increased in World War II.

Despite these serious and unmistakable defects, present-day international law provides a practical expedient and a necessary set of procedures. Hence, though Churchill envisaged world law as a goal for the future coterminous with the achieving of a world state, he looked toward practical international law and its procedures as something to engage the statesman's attention in his immediate conduct of policy. The narrowness of the span of effective rules of international law indicates the division among the world's peoples on their ends and purposes and the means they would employ in pursuing them. Yet existing international law may serve to fill some of the gaping crevices that separate peoples without any moral consensus. Where justice and respect for general principles of international conduct are lacking, Churchill would use international law as a wedge or a practical expedient to prod miscreants into more responsible behavior: "I wish . . . to identify His Majesty's Government and the House of Commons with the solemn words which were used lately by the President of the United States, namely, that those who are guilty of the Nazi Crimes will have to stand up before tribunals in every land where these atrocities have been committed in order that an indelible warning may be given to future ages, and that successive generations of men may say, 'so perish all who do the like again.'"[13]

12. Winston S. Churchill, *The Second World War*, Vol. II, *Their Finest Hour* (Boston: Houghton Mifflin, 1949), 322–23.
13. *Parliamentary Debates*, Vol. 383, September 8, 1942, p. 97.

Churchill gave special emphasis to one sphere of practical international law. It was the international law of recognition. What most concerned him here was the political implications of recognition. His guiding rule was: "Recognition does not mean approval. One has to recognize and deal with all sorts of things in this world as they come along. After all, vaccination is undoubtedly a definite recognition of smallpox. Certainly I think it would be very foolish, in ordinary circumstances, not to keep necessary contacts with countries with whom one is not at war."[14] Paradoxically, recognition is most essential when the legal and moral standing of the other side may be open to question. "Ambassadors are not sent as compliments but as necessities for ordinary daily use. The more difficult relations are with any country in question, the more necessary it is to have the very highest form of representation on the spot."[15]

In several concrete cases in recent diplomatic history, Churchill demonstrated that he took seriously such general principles of law. One instance involved the withdrawing of ambassadors by members of the United Nations from Spain. Churchill was hardly a friend of the immediate postwar Spanish government and at Potsdam he opposed their admission to the United Nations. However, he maintained that the idea of treating Spaniards as pariahs would only be taken as a national affront and lead to the rallying of patriots to the government of that country. He observed: "I think it is better to have ambassadors than to carry it all on through the back door, as it all has to be carried on—a sort of black market diplomacy. Also, I do not think it is a good thing to appear to treat with lack of ceremony a people so proud and haughty as the Spaniards, living in their stony peninsula, have always shown themselves to be."[16] The net effect, he argued, of the West's policy had been to assist General Franco in consolidating his position, which might otherwise have been gradually weakened. It was a serious mistake to allow the legitimate objections to Franco and his form of government to impair relations with Spain. Strategically and militarily,

14. *Parliamentary Debates*, Vol. 487, May 10, 1951, p. 2157.
15. *Parliamentary Debates*, Vol. 459, December 10, 1948, p. 720.
16. *Parliamentary Debates*, Vol. 464, May 12, 1949, p. 2027.

Spain was a part of Europe, and the West's trade with Spain was valuable, including Spain's export of products ranging from iron ore to oranges. How was this trade to be maintained and supervised in the future? Churchill commented: "I suppose that when we have withdrawn our ambassador we shall have to have commercial counselors. . . . in order to remain in fruitful contact with one of the oldest and now least aggressive of the nations of Europe. I suppose there would be a kind of diplomatic black market whose agents would go in the back door instead of through the front. We may be sure that the 28,000,000 living in that great peninsula would be in some contact with the outer world, even if there were no Ambassadors. . . . I should have thought we had enough trouble on our hands without getting into such futile and fatuous entanglements." [17]

A comparable issue involved a dispute over the recognition of Israel. On December 10, 1948, Churchill urged that envoys be sent without delay to Tel-Aviv. The Israelis had established a government which was functioning effectively. They enjoyed the support of a victorious army. Therefore the government could not be ignored or treated as if it did not exist. Opponents of recognition held that Israel's boundaries had not yet been established, but Churchill countered: "*De facto* recognition has never depended upon an exact definition of territorial frontiers. There are half-a-dozen countries in Europe which are recognised today whose territorial frontiers are not fully settled. Surely, Poland is one. It is only with the general Peace Treaty that a final settlement can be made." [18] England in particular had special reasons for according early recognition to the new state. "The Russians have a very large representation and America is fully represented and altogether nineteen countries have recognised the Palestine Government either *de facto* or *de jure*. The setting up of this Government is an event in world history. It would surely be most foolish, with all these countries represented, that we, who still have many interests and duties and memories in Palestine and the Middle East, should be left to maintain a sort of sulky boycott." [19]

17. *Parliamentary Debates*, Vol. 423, June 5, 1946, pp. 2017–18.
18. *Parliamentary Debates*, Vol. 460, January 26, 1949, p. 951.
19. *Parliamentary Debates*, Vol. 459, December 10, 1948, p. 720.

Finally there was the most contentious dispute over diplomatic recognition, that involving Communist China. Here we can do no better than to allow Churchill to speak at length on this issue in words set forth at the time. On November 17, 1949, he declared in Parliament:

Now the question has arisen also of what our attitude should be towards the Chinese Communists who have gained control over so large a part of China. Ought we to recognise them or not? Recognizing a person is not necessarily an act of approval. . . . The reason for having diplomatic relations is not to confer a compliment but to secure a convenience.

When a large and powerful mass of people are organised together and are masters of an immense area and of great populations, it may be necessary to have relations with them. One may even say that when relations are most difficult that is the time when diplomacy is most needed.

We ought certainly to have suitable contacts with this large part of the world's surface and population under the control of the Chinese Communists. We ought to have them on general grounds, quite apart from all the arguments—and they are very important arguments—about the protection of specific British interests. Again I would say it seems difficult to justify having full diplomatic relations with the Soviet Government in Moscow and remaining without even *de facto* contacts with its enormous offshoots into China.[20]

He insisted at the same time that no steps should be taken without close consultation with the United States and within the British Commonwealth. On May 10, 1951, he reminded the Parliament of this issue, saying: "In November, 1949, I was in favour of the recognition of Communist China, provided that it was *de facto* and not *de jure* . . . and provided that it could be brought about as a joint policy with the United States and the Dominions."[21] His criticism of the recognition policy of the Labor government was that recognition had been accorded without prior Anglo-American agreement and without joint action by the dominions. It was timed to take place only three days before the Colombo Conference of Dominion

20. *Parliamentary Debates*, Vol. 469, November 17, 1949, pp. 2225–26.
21. *Parliamentary Debates*, Vol. 487, May 10, 1951, p. 2157.

Foreign Secretaries. Furthermore, not only was China recognized by the British but the recognition granted was *de jure*. He asked what had been the consequences of all this and on May 10, 1951, exclaimed: "The response of the Chinese Communists was very surly. They took all they could get from our recognition and gave nothing in return. They did not even recognise us. The United States were much offended by our isolated action, and that is how that part of the story ends." [22]

The field of practical international law, then, is that aspect with which Churchill was most conversant. The deep political fissures that separate national and regional societies make it quite pointless to look for the attainment of absolute standards of international law amid the billowing and turbulent clouds of the present or the immediate future. But nations in a period where numerous jagged tears have been ripped in the flimsy fabric of international law can still use some of its principles wisely and prudently to facilitate their commerce and to provide good examples for nations whose philosophy is alien to the traditional law of nations. Thus Churchill urged the allies during the war to invoke international law not in the interest of final and transcendent principles but to inspire better behavior by the Nazis: "Lots of Germans may develop moral scruples if they know they are going to be brought back and judged in the country, and perhaps the very place, where their cruel deeds were done." [23] However, to fill out the content of international law with a proliferation of empty and extravagant multilateral pacts would be to breed only cynicism and distrust about existing international law. True world law awaits a closer and more direct approach to an effective world community where common fears, shared beliefs, and a sense of togetherness will bind people to one another morally and psychologically even as technology has made them economically interdependent.

22. *Parliamentary Debates*, Vol. 487, May 10, 1951, p. 2158.
23. Winston S. Churchill, "Prime Minister to President Roosevelt and Premier Stalin," October 12, 1943, *The Second World War*, Vol. V, *Closing the Ring* (Boston: Houghton Mifflin, 1951), 297.

One reason Churchill may have said so little about the general purposes of international law was probably occasioned by the crisis of the international order. The expansion of Europe outside its own boundaries to areas untutored in the West's concepts of legal procedures and statehood produced a weakening of the law's effectiveness. The forms of international law which were indigenous to the Western countries with their residual vestiges of a moral consensus growing out of the fusion of Judaeo-Christian principles with Graeco-Roman philosophy and jurisprudence were alien to the cultures of Asia and Africa. More particularly, application of such principles to these non-European areas served primarily to clothe an imperialism with transparent legal vestments and only incidentally to instill elements of justice. In such regions it was utopian to expect groups with a vested interest in change to support the encrustments of Western legal tradition which clung like scales to their enslaved bodies. In the repudiation of existing international law by emerging non-European societies and in the reaction against the scruples of Christianity by totalitarianism within Europe, international law was undermined in the same way in peace as it was weakened in war. Churchill appeared to separate his dreams and hopes for world law and the world state from the limited, practical, and prudent uses of operating principles and practices of international law.

Regional Pillars of a World State

One of the more controversial positions Churchill espoused concerned regionalism and world government. Most advocates of world government interpret the pursuit of anything less than some kind of universal world order as a craven concession to expediency. A disposition to settle for short-run gains is viewed as more impractical both now and in the future than striving to attain the ultimate goal of an effectively organized political universe. Yet, as has appeared in the efforts to merge Canada with the United States, regional groups tend inevitably to founder on the shoals of parochialism and local sentiments. They are baffled by the complex and baffling problems of deciding what constitutes a region. Are the criteria economic, cultural, or geographic or is it required that nations who are to be wedded to one another in any regional arrangement share common political and economic institutions? Moreover, what is the likelihood of discovering separate regions which do not overlap with one another? What status should be accorded to groups of nations who prefer to pursue their national advantage without choosing sides in the struggle between major powers? Switzerland, Sweden, Belgium and, at one time, Poland and Turkey sought to profit by the natural contention among contiguously located great powers, each jealous and alert to the political consequences which might arise from the shift of buffer areas from one side to the other. How could their role of splendid neutrality be sustained if the world areas were polarized into a few great blocs or regions? Some have gone so far as to claim that regional groupings were necessarily artificial and reactionary and instead of alleviating world problems would merely aggravate them. Regions, even more than nations, would strive for economic self-sufficiency throwing up tariff barriers and trade restrictions around their boundaries. Within a formalized and integrated region, great powers could more readily dominate weaker neighbors. It was frequently said, especially by Americans, in discussions of postwar international institutions before and during World War II that regionalism would tend to crystallize and sanctify selfish parochialism and increase resistance to universalism. Regional unions were an archaism and only a reactionary and feckless policy could revive and restore their influence.

These widespread beliefs conflict directly and at almost every point with Churchill's philosophy. His views are rooted in concepts so alien to the philosophy underlying most universalist attitudes that he has not infrequently been portrayed as the chief antagonist of world government. It has been fashionable to maintain, as in an editorial in 1946 in the *Canadian Forum*, that Churchill had always been the arch-foe of all international organizations: "The fact is that Mr. Churchill has never shown much belief in international organization as such. He became enthusiastic for the League of Nations only in the 1930s when he saw the chance of using it as an alliance against Germany. He was reverting to type now in his attitude toward the UNO."[24]

If we explore the reasons for attacks of this kind, one obvious source was the superficial understanding of Churchill's conception of means and ends in building an international government. The prevailing opinion sees world government in an either/or perspective. Either nations pursue boldly and directly the ends of world government or they continue in chaos and anarchy forming alliances and creating regional groupings. In taking exception to this, Churchill asserted: "We must do our best to create and combine the great regional unities which it is in our power to influence, and we must endeavour by patient and faithful service, to prepare for the day when there will be an effective world government resting upon the main groupings of mankind."[25] No union or government can withstand the tides of aggression and hostile opinion unless it rests on durable foundations. In Europe, Asia, and the Western Hemisphere these foundations are the regional groupings present in inchoate form in the loose associations among local states. To bind these states closer together is one indispensable step in creating world unity. On October 11, 1950, Churchill sought to explain: "The creation of an authoritative, all-powerful world order is the ultimate aim towards which we must strive. Unless some effective world super-Government can be set up and brought quickly into action, the prospects for peace and human progress are dark and doubtful. Without a United Europe there is no sure prospect of world government."[26] On another occasion he stated: "If, during the next five years it is found possible to build a world organization of irresistible force and authority for the purpose of securing peace, there are no limits to the blessings which all men may enjoy and share. Nothing will help forward the building of that world organization so much as unity and stability in a Europe that is conscious of her collective personality and resolved to assume her rightful part

24. "Churchill and Russia," *The Canadian Forum*, XXVI (April 3, 1946), 3.
25. Churchill, "The Congress of Europe," May 7, 1948, *Europe Unite*, ed. Randolph S. Churchill (London: Cassell and Company, 1950), 315.
26. London *Times*, October 12, 1950, p. 4.

in guiding the unfolding destinies of man." [27] Churchill's opinion on this serious question was grounded in three assumptions, namely, that world and regional organizations are not incompatible, that no global system can survive unless it rests firmly on regional pillars, and that regional groupings can be used to increase the sense of community within particular regions and, among them, in the world community. To say that world government and strong regionalism are everywhere incompatible ignores an elementary principle of international politics.

Building a World Community

Programs which have as their objectives regional groupings are based fundamentally on recognition of common interests, values, and traditions within a limited area. The sense of community which must undergird every cooperative political institution is notably absent today from the world scene. We have only to contrast conditions on the world scene with those of the nation, where common experiences, language, and tradition assure a spiritual continuity that raises the nation above other social institutions whose aims are solely material. The nation, to paraphrase Edmund Burke's dictum, is more than a partnership in pepper and coffee, calico or tobacco. It is a partnership in all science and all art and in every social virtue. In Churchill's mind: "Law, language, literature—these are considerable factors. . . . Common perceptions of what is right and decent, a marked regard for fair play, especially to the weak and poor, a stern sentiment of impartial justice, and above all the love of personal freedom . . . these are common conceptions on both sides of the ocean among the English-speaking peoples." [28]

   Any statesman, therefore, must begin with his nation as it exists in history, a going historic entity which holds its generations together through common ethnic, geographic, historical, and linguistic ties. Burke observed concerning this community that no national leader could conceive of his society as a *tabula rasa* upon which he

27. New York *Times*, May 15, 1947, p. 11.
28. New York *Times*, September 7, 1943, p. 14.

might write what he pleased. Instead he was constrained to preserve and improve the materials with which his country presented him. The supreme test for the inchoate community of the British Commonwealth came during World War II when its people seemed to enter the very jaws of death and destruction. At that time: "It was proved that the bands which unite us, though supple as elastic, are stronger than the tensest steel. Then it was proved that they were the bonds of the spirit and not of the flesh, and thus could rise superior alike to the most tempting allurements of surrender and the harshest threats of doom."[29] The curiously intangible elements of "togetherness" which are boasted by national communities proved to be present in Britain's history as the sturdy cement holding the commonwealth together.

What are the conditions and social elements which make a group conscious that it constitutes a "we." At root and most vital are a core of common spiritual possessions cherished particularly within most democratic communities. Because of the influence and compelling force of these spiritual possessions, communities arise in spite of the diversity and pluralism of their cultures. The essential character of Europe's community, for example, is illustrated in the statement which follows: "It has been finely said by a young English writer, Mr. Sewell, that the real demarcation between Europe and Asia is no chain of mountains, no natural frontiers, but a system of beliefs and ideas which we call western civilization. In the rich pattern of this culture . . . there are many strands: the Hebrew belief in God; the Christian message of compassion and redemption; the Greek love of truth, beauty and goodness; the Roman genius for law."[30] These elements contribute to make Europe a spiritual conception which can be nurtured and sustained by all good Europeans.

What then are the specific factors which are most common as ingredients of social cohesion? What are the elements of community which are generally present in greater or lesser degree? No tidy abridgment of this question can satisfy anyone who is genuinely

29. London *Times*, July 1, 1943, p. 8.
30. New York *Times*, May 15, 1947, p. 16.

searching after truth. If community were other than a social and po-litical problem, it might be possible to reduce it to a mathematical proposition. But certain elements are always present in infinitely varied proportions; no reasonable man would claim for one moment that each was always equally essential to community. The most he would claim would be that there are certain factors which are a part of the burden in any situation where social unity is cre-ated out of anarchy. To begin with, one crucial link, and the bridge upon which a toiling political society oftentimes crosses over into a stronger community, is the element of a common language. Lan-guage has helped unite British and Americans in common purposes. In an address at the Pentagon in 1946, Churchill declared: "The pre-vailing feature of our work together was the intimacy of associa-tion. Language is a great bridge."[31] The intimacy and harmony of Anglo-American cooperation evolved at least partly from their common language, law, and literature. On July 4, 1950, Churchill proclaimed: "It was Bismarck who said in the closing years of his life that the most potent factor in human society at the end of the nineteenth century was the fact that the British and American peo-ples spoke the same language. He might well have added, what was already then apparent, that we had in common a very wide measure of purpose and ideals arising from our institutions, our literature and our common law. Since then, on the anvil of war, we have be-come so welded together that what might have remained for genera-tions an interesting historical coincidence has become the living and vital force which preserves Christian civilization and the rights and freedom of mankind."[32]

Likewise, common interests and experiences exist which bind the two European nations of France and England closely together: "Strong bonds of affection, mutual confidence, common interest and similar outlook link France and Britain together. The Treaty of

31. Winston S. Churchill, "Address to American and British Service Members," March 9, 1946, *The Sinews of Peace*, ed. Randolph S. Churchill (London: Cassell and Company, 1948), 111.
32. Churchill, "American Society in London," July 4, 1950, *In the Balance*, ed. Randolph S. Churchill (London: Cassell and Company, 1951), 309.

Alliance which has lately been signed only gives formal expression to the community of sentiment that already exists as an indisputable and indestructible fact."[33] From one point of view, the essence of community is the presence of a friendly atmosphere or climate of opinion among like-minded people. As Churchill reiterated so often in his statements, before European union could be attained and perfected these sentiments had to be fortified and strengthened. On October 28, 1948, he introduced a discussion of progress toward Western European union by suggesting: "I have always considered that our international and unofficial movement for a united Europe should have as its object the creation of an atmosphere in Europe, what Mr. Lecky called 'a climate of opinion,' among all its peoples, and of the people of this island, and of the British Empire, and of the United States, in favour of the ideal of European unity. . . . I believe that this can be achieved without injury to national traditions, sentiments and character of any states, large or small, concerned."[34]

At its foundations, community is a feeling of belonging. Other Europeans, Churchill implied, must learn, as he did from his early teachers, that Europe was a unique and separate world region. Only in this way would their membership survive the thrust of new and "scientific" propositions about Europe's location and history: "However, professional geographers now tell us that the Continent of Europe is really only the peninsula of the Asiatic land mass. I must tell you in all faith that I feel this would be an arid and uninspiring conclusion, and for myself, I distinctly prefer what I was taught when I was a boy."[35] From a moral and political point of view most of Western Europe is united by the "glorious treasure of literature, of romance, of ethics, of thought and toleration belonging to all, which is the true inheritance of Europe."[36] The seeds of

33. Churchill, "United Europe Meeting," May 14, 1947, *Europe Unite*, ed. Randolph S. Churchill, 81.
34. *Parliamentary Debates*, Vol. 457, October 28, 1948, pp. 258–59.
35. Churchill, "United Europe Meeting," May 14, 1947, *Europe Unite*, ed. Randolph S. Churchill, 77.
36. Churchill, "The Congress of Europe," May 7, 1948, *ibid.*, 312.

community are planted in the soil of the lives of vast numbers of ordinary, simple families and the dominating objective should be that "men will be as proud to say, 'I am a European,' as once they said, *Civis Romanus sum*. We hope to see a Europe where men of every country will think as much of being a European as of belonging to their native land, and wherever they go in this wide domain will truly feel 'Here I am at home.'"[37]

Beyond the European community, the arduous and painful pursuit of the goal of world community was not an objective Churchill would eliminate. Instead, he asked himself on many occasions, as he did on July 2, 1938, in a speech at Bristol University, whether nations through extraordinary diligence might not succeed in building a larger world system founded on political virtue. Then he declared: "That surely is the supreme hope by which we should be inspired and the goal towards which in the last resort must be the defence of right and reason. But it is vain to imagine that the mere perception or declaration of right principles, whether in one country or in many countries, will be of any value unless they are supported by those qualities of civic virtue and manly courage—aye, and by those instruments and agencies of force and science which in the last resort must be the defence of right and wrong."[38] The same irreducible requirements of underlying unity, the absence of which had thwarted the attainment of European union but which Churchill sought to transcend, were also present but in magnified form on the world scene. Through the steady, unspectacular pursuit of mutually compatible world interests, states might find themselves after some generations engaged in the breathtaking task of laying the foundations for an enduring world state. Thus: "The whole movement of the world is toward an interdependence of nations. We feel all around us the belief that it is our best hope. If independent, individual sovereignty is sacrosanct and inviolable, how is it that we are all wedded to a world organisation?"[39]

37. London *Times*, October 12, 1950, p. 4.
38. Churchill, "Civilisation," July 2, 1938, *Into Battle*, 36.
39. *Parliamentary Debates*, Vol. 476, June 27, 1950, p. 2158.

Gradualism and the World State

It is abundantly clear that the West has been offered world government without delay by various tyrants, the most recent being the Nazis and the Communists. But each time the West's decision has been that the price was too destructive of the values and principles essential to any enduring political system. Add to that "a thousand gleaming ideas" or plans for world unity each mirroring the age in which they were contrived. Every vision has faded because the preconditions were lacking or deficient at the time. Churchill's conception of the world state differed from most grand designs for world government. For him the world state, if it could ever be attained, would come as the consequence of a gradual evolution or because of an accident seized in the full tide of events and carried on to fruition.

Among publicists and scholars, it is generally accepted that there are two alternate ways in which world government might be achieved. They are world conquest and a voluntary world federation. The historic precedents and present signs favoring world conquest as the more likely alternative are legion. Historically, Alexander of Macedon, the Ts'in dynasty in China, and the military forces of Rome accomplished by conquest what had been impossible by federation and consent. Moreover, the tendency since 1648 has been toward a steady and consistent diminution in the number of powers. As the number of states has decreased, their size has progressively increased. Whereas in 1870 the typical state was France or Great Britain, by 1950 any state smaller than the United States or the Soviet Union was too small to maintain independently a peaceful life or to wage war successfully. Therefore, the way things have been going in contemporary international politics, it looks on the face of it as though world conquest was the line of least resistance and the easiest way for world government to come about. However, if this is the course which the West is to follow, it should be apprised of the traditional consequences of such unity. We may take it to be a historical rule of the most general application that once having taken up arms to achieve political unity, a conqueror has rarely proved capable of restraining himself in using the means by which he first sought to attain other higher ends. Sword blades as the foundation of any world empire are eternally threatening to spring to the surface in new bouts of conquest and expansion. Every universal state born in conquest achieved by a dominant minority has sooner or later broken down of its own weight or as a result of extravagant adventures in militarism. The state has become a mere shell of government and has dissipated its strength by requiring more from its members than they were able to give. Lacking in creative vitality, the conqueror's state has had to be patched up and repaired to assure even temporary survival. Its day of destruction has come by the sword in the same way it attained its towering but precarious eminence.

The alternate to such a world state is world government by agreement. Even the most outspoken of Churchill's critics would never contend that he was wedded to the alternative of world conquest. As we have seen, he favored the pursuit of a world government by consent as the final step in a long process for which the groundwork was being laid, almost imperceptibly, over an extended period of time. In such a framework, "world government policy" would call for a variety of concrete policies and techniques through which upheavals might be mitigated and moral values reinforced. If anything approximating a world state should be created in our time it would hardly comprise a neat and tidy system. Instead, the world state would contain elements both of consent and coercion, of universalism and regionalism, of planning and accident.

Moreover, special contributions of particular groups will be called for if the goal is to be reached. The British and Americans carry an especially heavy responsibility. On March 15, 1946, Churchill declared: "The progress and freedom of all the peoples of the world, under a reign of law, enforced by a world organization, will not come to pass, nor will the age of plenty begin, without the persistent, faithful and above all fearless exertions of the British and American system of society." [40] The organization and control of any

40. New York *Times*, March 16, 1946, p. 2.

society calls for an overarching purpose, and Churchill found a universalized conception of the goal in Anglo-American political philosophy. If world government were to be no more than an escape by war-weary souls from the bitter facts of reality to the gentle nirvana of peace, the chances of success would be questionable at best. Strong men are perpetually engaged in trying to alter the pattern of history and there are always those who would abandon peace for objectives they cherish beyond peace itself. For Churchill, regional associations are worth pursuing because they give to the "Pilgrim's Progress" along the highway of world government concrete goals which, though less sublime, have a specific and objective content. A world organization can have little real meaning for a people without long experience in representative government. Therefore, Churchill counseled: "We must do our best to create and combine the great regional unities which it is in our power to influence, and we must endeavour by patient and faithful service to prepare for the day when there will be an effective world government resting upon the main groupings of mankind. Thus for us and for all who share our civilisation and our desire for peace and world government there is only one duty and watch-word: Persevere."[41]

If nations are to conceive of themselves as members of a true supranational community they must have experienced some kind of political integration in units more inclusive than a nation state. Otherwise they will react, it has been said, as snapping dogs chained together in an inflexible and rigid world system. In these terms world government would become world tyranny. If world government should ever be realized it might come unheralded in the form of an unforeseen political event. This, at least, was the burden of Churchill's comment when he said: "I do not believe you will ever succeed in building up an international force in a vague and general manner, or that it can be created in cold blood. But it might well be that an international force would come into being by an alliance of national forces for a particular emergency or for particular purposes, and, once having been started, it might give the security to

41. London *Times*, May 8, 1948, p. 4.

the world which would avert the approaching curse of war."[42] Yet accidents and events can sometimes be facilitated by juxtaposing conditions which foster particular developments. As a three-fold foundation of a world community, Churchill sought to revive the profound moral insights of the Western tradition: "The supreme question is how we live and grow and bloom and die, and how far each life conforms to standards which are not wholly related to space or time. Here I speak not only to those who enjoy the blessings and consolation of revealed religion but also to those who face the mysteries of human destiny alone. The flame of Christian ethics is still our highest guide. To guide and cherish it is our first interest, both spiritually and materially."[43] The political expression of these beliefs calls for applying the stamp of democracy to political practices within many cultures and in many distant places. In his insistence on compromise, toleration, and the diversity of opinion, Churchill sought to promote the world cause while not forgetting the concept of man's priceless qualities as human individual. The social and political virtues which only a reinvigorated and universalized democracy can assure among peoples is an essential foundation of political community.

Furthermore, only an impractical and utopian mind would believe that consent without some measure of coercion or compromise without an element of force could be integral characteristics of a world system. Churchill was persuaded that even a world government would not be without the influence of the ascendancy of one or more great powers. As the nation-state has been forged out of the molten steel of strife and revolution, the sturdiness of the world state will depend on its military troops and forces. Churchill unceasingly demanded that "we must arm our world organization and make sure that, within the limits assigned to it, it has overwhelming military power."[44] As the core states within the world union must be ready to contribute political intelligence and moral principles, they

42. *Parliamentary Debates*, Vol. 287, March 14, 1934, p. 400.
43. New York *Times*, April 1, 1949, p. 10.
44. *Parliamentary Debates*, Vol. 400, May 24, 1944, pp. 785–86.

must also be prepared to provide substantial armed forces. Without a determination to fight for such an organization, states are likely to witness its destruction by others not averse to imposing their decisions by force.

In summary, the most striking and unique feature of Churchill's conception of world community was his unambiguous emphasis on gradualism. At every level, each man can contribute by pursuing certain desirable objectives within his own local community. The essence of gradualism is a determination to persevere in the long march of events. On September 6, 1943, Churchill lay down a challenge: "To the youth of America, as to the youth of Britain, I say 'You cannot stop.' There is no halting place at this point. We have now reached a stage in the journey where there can be no pause. We must go on. It must be world anarchy or world order." [45]

45. New York *Times*, September 7, 1943, p. 14.

CHAPTER FOURTEEN

International Organization: The United Nations

I spoke earlier of the Temple of Peace. Workmen from all countries must build that temple. If two of the workmen know each other particularly well and are old friends, if their families are inter-mingled, and if they have "faith in each other's purpose, hope in each other's future and charity toward each other's shortcomings" . . . why can they not work together at the common task as friends and partners. Why cannot they share their tools and thus increase each other's working powers? Indeed they must do so or else the temple will not be built.[1]

The fourth approach to the problems of war and peace lends itself to evaluation in more concrete terms. Whereas world government gains its appeal primarily from a philosophy or theory, international organization is embodied in an existing institution, the United Nations. Those present at its creation in the spring of 1946 heralded the United Nations as the last, best, and most concrete expression of a new form of international relations by which the baffling problems of foreign policy as such would be eliminated once and for all. Traditional international politics with its inevitable struggle for power would disappear with the new international organization. The same spirit of sublime and transcendent confidence in which each new political invention has been greeted and the same attitude of towering benevolence and condescension for every older form characterized the prevailing outlook on the United Nations. In consequence, opinion about the United Nations has drifted with the erratic winds of fortune. The tendency of elevating the United Nations to a point beyond history and politics possessed one unmistakable virtue. It helped to overcome public inertia and assisted in the launching of the organization. At the same time, however, it planted the seeds of deep and tragic disillusionment which periodically engulfed broad segments of Western public opinion.

1. New York *Times*, March 6, 1946, p. 4.

It is not difficult to show that the United Nations has suffered its most telling blows as a consequence of the clamor of two extremely vocal groups, active in pressing their views, especially in the United States. At one extreme are habitual critics who, displaying from the beginning the same violent distaste for the United Nations they had shown for the League of Nations, hurled epithets charging the United Nations was un-American and would bring in its wake a squandering of America's sacred blood and treasure. At the opposite pole, an equally outspoken group of defenders and apologists proclaimed its perfection with all the rabid self-confidence of moral crusaders. The practical consequence of the two viewpoints, one detecting in the United Nations a conspiracy against American patriotism and the other viewing it as a kind of incarnation of all the West's millennial hopes, has been to drown out the voices of other more mature and sober Americans. As a further consequence, a deepseated ambivalence began to appear in Western opinion. Americans have gushed paeans of praise for the United Nations when things were going right but threatened to forsake it when things were going wrong as they saw it. Most observers agree that the sole means of transcending such fateful alternations of attitudes lies in the constant and steady viewing of the United Nations as yet another political instrument which, wisely employed, can be useful to America. In fact, the strength of the United Nations depends fundamentally on conditions existing outside the United Nations. Through prudence in relating creatively to nations within and outside the United Nations, the United States contributes most to such conditions.

A Political Approach to the United Nations

The first and most grievous mistake in the growth of opinion regarding the United Nations has been the belief that it stood at the end of all the common toils and tribulations of mankind through history and politics. Its sponsors presented the United Nations in the rhetoric of those bent on "selling" it as a marketable commodity to public opinion and as something entirely unprecedented as a means of achieving peace. References to the defunct League of Nations dealt mainly with its organic and constitutional deficiencies when compared with the new international organization.

Churchill was among a tiny band of Western statesmen who resisted the powerful temptation of overselling the United Nations. From World War I, his attitude toward international organization was traditionalist and conservative. For him, the League of Nations was mainly an agency for continuing the purposes of the Concert of Europe. At a time when most progressive international thinkers were loath to associate the League of Nations with the procedures of the Concert of Europe, Churchill was construing the League as the most recent expression of the ancient principle of concert of power as a means of ameliorating the rivalries among nations. He said then: "Whatever way we turn there is risk. . . . But . . . the least risk and the greatest help will be found in re-creating the Concert of Europe through the League of Nations."[2]

In the postwar era, the tendency to dissociate the new international agency from earlier historic international experiments grew more pronounced. When the League of Nations was mentioned, it was primarily to illustrate the constitutional advantages of the United Nations. Because of Russian memories of expulsion from the League and, more fundamentally, because of the prevailing conception of progress which seized modern man in the nineteenth and twentieth centuries, the historic continuity of the League and the United Nations was deliberately obscured by its architects. Churchill opposed this regnant viewpoint and in advising Parliament on the nature of the United Nations, he declared: "It will embody much of the structure and characteristics of its predecessor. All the work that was done in the past, all the experience that has been gathered by the working of the League of Nations, will not be cast away."[3] It was true of the League, he said, that its constitutional structure was airy and unsubstantial, framed of a shining but too often visionary idealism. Yet essentially the same kind of structure offered the best

2. *Parliamentary Debates* (Hansard) House of Commons, Fifth Series, Vol. 281, November 7, 1933 (London: His Majesty's Stationery Office, 1950), 142.
3. *Parliamentary Debates*, Vol. 408, February 27, 1945, p. 1273.

present hope for a viable organization in 1943. In notes written to the foreign secretary, Mr. Eden, he declared: "We hold strongly to a system of a League of Nations, which will include a Council of Europe, with an International Court and an armed power capable of enforcing its decisions."[4] The real breakdown of the League was to be found in the foreign policies of its members, not its structure; the wills of the member nations had proved its "Achilles heel." On September 6, 1943, Churchill commented on the reasons for its failure, explaining: "If so, that is largely because it was abandoned, and later on betrayed; because those who were its best friends were till a very late period inflicted with a futile pacifism; because the United States, the originating impulse, fell out of the line; because, while France had been bled white and England was supine and bewildered, a monstrous growth of aggression sprang up in Germany, in Italy and Japan."[5]

These brief comments, however, are merely preliminary to the main issues that a survey of Churchill's conception of international government reveals. His attitudes, expressed at the founding and coinciding with the early activities of the United Nations, delineate his thinking. It was frequently argued, especially by Americans, that the British contributions in the preparatory stages of the founding of the United Nations were inadequate and uneven. It was sometimes said that only the Americans, and most notably Dr. Leo Pasvolsky who served with such dedication in the Department of State in drafting its preliminary structure, were armed with detailed plans and concrete programs at the conferences which went on during the autumn of 1944 at Dumbarton Oaks. If we accept these claims, it becomes important to consider what reasons if any can account for British indifference to the preparation of detailed blueprints. One clue which reflects their wartime leader's conception of the steps by which international organizations are created was his statement to Parliament on September 28, 1944, in which he urged caution

4. Winston S. Churchill, *The Second World War*, Vol. V, *Closing the Ring* (Boston: Houghton Mifflin, 1951), 282.
5. New York *Times*, September 7, 1943, p. 14.

in putting forward grandiose plans for the postwar world. More important than a network of structural arrangements for meeting postwar problems whose full nature had not yet been disclosed were the foundations to be established for Anglo-Russian-American cooperation. His words of caution were symbolic of British opinion when he declared: "Whatever may be settled in the near future must be regarded as a preliminary, and only as a preliminary, to the actual establishment in its final form of the future world organization. Those who try in any country to force the pace unduly will run the risk of overlooking many aspects of the highest importance, and also by imprudence they can bring about a serious deadlock. . . . It is right to make surveys and preparations beforehand . . . but the great decisions cannot be taken finally, even for the transition period, without far closer, calmer, and more searching discussions than can be held amid the clash of arms." [6]

The foundations of an effective international organization would rest on the predominance of the great powers. Liberals in the Western world preferred to emphasize the sovereign equality of all members; and the concept of one state, one vote, was written into the charter for the General Assembly. Churchill found the requirement that power and responsibility be kept in balance within any international organization a more immediate and practical issue. It was unreal and positively dangerous to pretend that nations inside or outside an international organization were equal in capabilities and influence. Being unequal in fact, some necessarily had to assume greater burdens than others. Churchill believed that the "Big Three" would be the trustees of peace and said: "It would be our hope that the United Nations, headed by the three great victorious Powers, the British Commonwealth of Nations, the United States, and Soviet Russia, should immediately begin to confer upon the future world organisation which is to be our safeguard against further war by effectively disarming and keeping disarmed the guilty states, by bringing to justice the grand criminals and their accomplices, and by securing the return to the devastated and subjugated countries of

6. *Parliamentary Debates*, Vol. 403, September 28, 1944, pp. 496-97.

the mechanical resources and artistic treasures of which they have been pillaged."[7] The keystone of Churchill's approach was his belief that any effective international organization must be founded on the unanimity of the great powers. To this end he instructed the House of Commons on February 27, 1943: "It is on the Great Powers that the chief burden of maintaining peace and security will fall. The new world organisation must take into account this special responsibility of the Great Powers, and must be so framed as not to compromise their unity or their capacity for effective action if it is called for at short notice."[8]

The great powers, in a word, were to be principal members of a steering committee with executive power in whom military power would be centralized: "We intend to set up a world order and organisation, equipped with all the necessary attributes of power, in order to prevent the breaking out of future wars, or the long planning of them in advance by restless ambitious nations. For this purpose there must be a World Council, a Controlling Council, composing the greatest States which emerge victorious from this war, who will be under obligation to keep in being a certain minimum standard of armaments for the purpose of preserving peace."[9] Arguments were certain to break out as to who should constitute the membership of the world council. But on this Churchill quite early expressed his willingness to compromise, especially with the wishes of the Americans. "If the United States wished to include China in an association with the other three, I was perfectly willing that this should be done; but, however great the importance of China, she was not comparable to the others."[10] The real responsibility for war and peace would rest with the major world powers who were to constitute the "Supreme World Council."

Limits on the power of the major states were recognized and were written into a formula agreed to at Yalta. It provided for the

7. London *Times*, March 22, 1943, p. 5.
8. *Parliamentary Debates*, Vol. 408, February 27, 1943, p. 1272.
9. *Parliamentary Debates*, Vol. 400, May 24, 1944, p. 783.
10. Winston S. Churchill, *The Second World War*, Vol. IV, *The Hinge of Fate* (Boston: Houghton Mifflin, 1950), 802.

right of veto by the great powers on issues concerning enforcement measures. Churchill remarked: "At the same time, the world organisation cannot be based upon a dictatorship of the Great Powers. It is their duty to serve the world and not to rule it. We trust the voting procedure on which we agreed at Yalta meets these two essential points."[11] The veto of the major world powers would not be applicable at every phase in the confronting of international problems. The drafters were to make a distinction between procedural and substantive issues with the explicit understanding that none of the superpowers could by its veto alone obstruct discussion of an issue within the executive committee.

Moreover, other world agencies within and outside the U.N. would have varied degrees of competence in alleviating international tensions. For example, the organ of the new international organization with approximately universal membership was to be the world assembly. He observed: "There must also be a World Assembly of all Powers, whose relations to the World Executive, or controlling power, for the purpose of maintaining peace I am in no position to define."[12] Moreover, undergirding the world council or executive, Churchill foresaw a network of regional councils in Europe, the Western Hemisphere, and the Far East. "The members of the World Council should sit on the Regional Councils in which they were directly interested, and I hoped that in addition to being represented on the American Regional Council and the Pacific Regional Council the United States would also be represented on the European Regional Council. However this might be, the last word would remain with the Supreme World Council since any issue that the Regional Councils were unable to settle would automatically be of interest to the World Council."[13] As many problems as possible should be settled at the regional level but when these agencies failed, the universal government should take over. Sometimes Churchill's claims were more ambitious than at other times regarding such regional bodies. On one occasion he apparently foresaw growing

11. *Parliamentary Debates*, Vol. 408, February 27, 1945, p. 1272.
12. *Parliamentary Debates*, Vol. 400, May 24, 1944, p. 783.
13. Churchill, *The Hinge of Fate*, 804.

up within the regional units "a number of Confederations formed among the smaller States, among which a Scandinavian Bloc, a Danubian Bloc, and a Balkan Bloc appear to be obvious."[14] The Far Eastern Council would likewise be comprised of members from inner regional blocs or groupings whose political interests were essentially in harmony. The regional councils in turn would supply to the steering or executive council of the international organization members who were less than major powers but who were elected in rotation from the various regional councils. They would provide further limitation on the exclusive power of the superpowers within the executive council.

Churchill's avowed objective was that the major powers not rule the whole world but that they prevent the nations from tearing themselves to pieces. The paramount task of the supreme executive council was to prevent the outbreak of war and to put it down if conflict broke out. Repeatedly Churchill spoke out against an executive council whose power in vital economic and political spheres might lead to an early derogation of national sovereignty. On May 25, 1944, he wrote in a note to Foreign Secretary Anthony Eden: "We should certainly not be prepared ourselves to submit to an economic, financial, and monetary system laid down by, say, Russia, or the United States with her fagot-vote China."[15] Other international agencies were to consider economic and social issues outside the sphere of executive council. For "the Big Three or Big Four will be the trustees or steering committee of the whole body in respect of the use of force to prevent war; but I think much larger bodies, and possibly functional bodies, would deal with the economic side."[16] The one supreme service the executive council was to render the world was in preventing the outbreak of war or bringing it to a speedy conclusion once it occurred.

On one point in particular, Churchill expressed highly unor-

14. *Ibid.*, 711.
15. Churchill, "Prime Minister to Foreign Secretary," May 25, 1944, *Closing the Ring*, 713.
16. *Ibid.*

thodox views. Not one of the United Nations' architects seriously questioned the importance of approximating universal membership within the United Nations. Indeed, its strongest claim to superiority over the League was for its supporters its expected attainment of nearly universal membership. It is a reflection of the age in which we live that the United Nations was more often than not evaluated in quantitative terms. Thus its secretariat of over three thousand staff members was compared to the staff of eight hundred employed by the League of Nations. Similar comparisons were made between the number of items on the annual agenda of the General Assembly with those of the League of Nations assembly. Such figures, together with the number of days of actual meetings in annual sessions, seemed to suggest the superiority of the United Nations. Furthermore, quantitatively in the variety and scope of the duties assigned by the charter, the United Nations had unprecedented responsibilities.

Churchill took exception to the accent on quantitative factors. His conception of a representative world assembly allowed for the importance of universal membership. But whereas many of his contemporaries ranked this consideration as *primus-inter-pares*, he conceived of universality as something for which too high a price ought not to be paid. Opinion was divided, especially in the United States, between the fervent supporters and the chronic critics of the United Nations on the question of Soviet membership. Internationalists staunchly maintained that universality was a life or death issue for the U.N.; isolationists argued that the Soviet Union ought to be expelled for its iniquitous obstructionism. Churchill, whom we have found to be neither an internationalist nor an isolationist in the popular meaning of the terms, departed from both kinds of thinking. He believed that if the Soviet Union should leave the United Nations, its absence would be a sharp blow to the fledgling organization's prestige and the prospects of negotiation on outstanding issues might be damaged. Yet he added: "We should not be unduly depressed if the Soviet-communist forces should decide to part company with the world organization. Certainly we ought not to give away anything which is essential to our security in order to persuade them to linger with us for the purpose of paralyzing the

joint harmonious action of three-quarters of mankind." Indeed, if
the Soviet Union were to depart "the two great systems might even
begin to be polite with one another and speak again in the measured
language of diplomacy."[17] Thus universal membership in the United
Nations was a value but not the highest one in Churchill's scale of
values. To the extent that the price was too high and to the degree
that diplomatic relations could be sustained and perhaps even
strengthened outside the U.N., Churchill was ready to sacrifice universality to other interests. His views and reasoning on the issue
corresponded with the views of certain political realists but with
hardly anyone else.

On one additional question Churchill stood alone, namely,
in his dogged insistence on the integral relationship between the
United Nations and its essential regional organizations. In practice,
he would have preferred a loosely formed world system in which a
general world council would operate merely to integrate the work of
three or four regional groupings. The opinion which prevailed,
however, among those who were most influential was essentially an
either/or approach. Either an international organization should be
established or regional groups, alliances, and spheres of influence
ought to continue. While regional unities were established under the
aegis of the United Nations as permitted by Article 51, regional arrangements were emergency measures to be taken only after the
international organization had ceased to function. By contrast,
Churchill envisaged a relation between international and regional
entities that was an integral one and as late as June 27, 1950, he
proposed that the U.N. should be reconstructed on the basis of
effective regional groups: "We must find our path to world unity
through the United Nations organisation, which I hope will be re-
founded one day upon three or four regional groups, of which a
United Europe should certainly be one."[18] What distinguished his
opinion from others was his flat rejection of the either/or, universal
or regional approach. For him, one purpose of regional unities

17. New York *Times*, October 15, 1947, p. 4.
18. *Parliamentary Debates*, Vol. 476, June 27, 1950, p. 2158.

would be to safeguard the larger world organization from overtaxing its resources in endless discussions of issues which concerned only a few of its members. Many vital questions can more profitably be considered at their source and as Churchill commented in 1948: "In my mind picture . . . there was the hope that each of these three splendid groupings of states and nations whose affairs of course would sometimes overlap, might have settled within themselves a great number of differences and difficulties, which are now dragged up to the supreme world organization, and that far fewer, but also far more potent figures, would represent them at the summit. There was also the hope that they might meet not in an overcrowded Tower of Babel, but, as it were, upon a mountain top where all was cool and quiet and calm, and from which the wide vision of the world could be presented with all things in their due proportion."[19] With the concentration of the world organization on a more limited and vital set of problems, the leaders who met at the highest level would be men who could speak with greater authority and prestige in behalf of their governments. For anyone familiar with the history of diplomacy and the importance of relating power and responsibility, Churchill's objective is not surprising.

The real purpose of regional entities, however, was to serve as the cornerstones for international organization. In 1950, in a speech in Copenhagen, he referred to the four main pillars of the temple of peace. "There is the United States with its dependencies, there is a wide hope—and still I will not cast aside the hope—that there is the Soviet Union, there is the British Empire and Commonwealth, and there is Europe, with which Great Britain is profoundly blended."[20] Unless these regional entities proved capable of bearing the weight imposed upon them, the United Nations would almost surely deteriorate and crumble. The sturdier the regional groups, the steadier the international organization would be. "Special associations within the circle of the United Nations, such as . . . the British Empire and Commonwealth, or like the association which prevails

19. London *Times*, May 8, 1948, p. 4.
20. London *Times*, October 12, 1950, p. 4.

throughout the Americas, north and south, far from weakening the structure of the supreme body of the United Nations, should be capable of being fused together in such a way as to make the United Nations indivisible and invincible."[21] In order to strengthen the United Nations, regional groupings would have to be integrated and subordinated within it. Instead of allowing the regional groups to eclipse the United Nations or conversely the United Nations to swallow up the natural and separate undertakings of regional units, Churchill sought a balanced system. On May 15, 1947, he affirmed: "We accept, without question, the world supremacy of the United Nations organization."[22] But: "In this great world structure . . . there will be room for all generous, free associations of a special character, so long as they are not disloyal to the world cause nor seek to bar the forward march of mankind."[23] In referring to the dependence of the greater upon the lesser groups he revealed: "Regional organisms or federations under the supreme world organisation are foreseen and encouraged in the San Francisco Charter. It is agreed they are not detrimental to the main structure. It has now to be realized as a fundamental, practical truth that without them the central structure cannot stand or function."[24] By June, 1950, he had come to doubt that regionalism was sufficiently recognized and he proposed that the United Nations be reconstituted as a federation of regional groupings.

Collective Security: Theory and Practice

Sponsors of the United Nations at its birth viewed it as an institution for collective security. Its aim was to assure that an attack on any one state would be regarded as an attack on all states. Collective security took as its standard the simple doctrine of one for all and all for one. War anywhere, in the context of Article 11 of the

21. New York *Times*, May 10, 1946, p. 10.
22. New York *Times*, May 15, 1947, p. 11.
23. *Parliamentary Debates*, Vol. 399, April 21, 1944, p. 586.
24. Churchill, "The Highroad of the Future," *Collier's*, CXIX (January 4, 1947), 11.

League of Nations, was the concern of every state. Churchill contended: "In modern wars of great nations or alliances particular areas are not defended only by local exertions. The whole vast balance of the war front is involved."[25] This was even more true of policies before wars are launched. Self-help and neutrality are the antithesis of collective security. States in the past that pursued neutrality were impartial when conflict broke out, gave their blessings to combatants to fight it out, and deferred judgment regarding the justice or injustice of the cause involved. In the eighteenth and nineteenth centuries, such a system prevailed. Wars were localized and a ring was drawn around the belligerents. In a more integrated world environment, however, any adjustment at any point in the system had an effect on the whole. A disturbance at one point upset the equilibrium at every other point.

The idea of collective security is simple, challenging, and novel. It would do for the international society what police action does for a domestic community. In municipal life if someone is killed in a neighborhood, the citizen's first impulse is to call the police. Acts of crime and violence are dealt with before they become general. This has brought relative peace and harmony to local communities. Through police or "fire brigades" on a world scale, collective security has two comparable objectives. It would *prevent* war by providing a deterrent to aggression through a multilateral treaty of mutual guaranty. It would *defend* its interest through war if it came by concentrating a preponderance of power against the aggressor. These two ends were the goals of both the League and the United Nations. If war came, all powers in the collective security system would defend its interests against the nation or alliance who threatened to overturn the security system. What was obvious to realists like Churchill was that the larger powers would play a disproportionate role in realizing this objective. It was axiomatic that: "The more closely the largest powers of today are bound together in bonds of faith and friendship, the more effective will be the safe-

25. Winston S. Churchill, *The Second World War*, Vol. I, *The Gathering Storm* (Boston: Houghton Mifflin, 1948), 274.

guards against war and the higher the security of all other states and nations."[26] The two objectives of prevention and defense had to be institutionalized. Therefore, any collective system required an organ competent to determine the merits of controversies. If an attack occurred by one state against another, someone had to sit in judgment. Someone had to decide who was the victim and who the aggressor. Governments perform such a role within states; the United Nations was to decide issues among states. From Churchill's standpoint, this would be the function of a world agency which had force at its command. He maintained: "We are all agreed that the only hope for the future of mankind lies in the creation of a strong effective world instrument, capable, at least, of maintaining peace and resisting aggression. I hope, we shall pursue . . . the idea of a United Nations armed force."[27] In its deliberations and judgments, such a world agency would seek to harness force to law and justice. The founders of the League of Nations aspired to this objective, and Churchill commented: "The League of Nations, battered though it had been, was still an august instrument which would have invested any challenge to the new Hitler war-menace with the sanctions of international law."[28] It aimed to execute its judgments by pooling the resources of all its members. "Force would clearly be required to see that peace was preserved."[29] By common action it sought to eliminate force from national policies and through pooled strength control the actions of unruly nations.

This general principle was applied in the founding of the United Nations. However, collective security for the U.N. would have required an agreement between the organization and its members respecting the minimum and maximum armed forces each would maintain: "The forces of each country might be divided into two contingents, the one to form the national forces of that country, and the other to form its contingent to an international police force at

26. New York *Times*, May 10, 1946, p. 10.
27. *Parliamentary Debates*, Vol. 480, October 31, 1950, p. 19.
28. Churchill, *The Gathering Storm*, 78.
29. Churchill, *The Hinge of Fate*, 805.

the disposal of the Regional Councils under the direction of the Supreme World Council. Thus, if one country out of twelve in Europe threatened the peace, eleven contingents would be ready to deal with that country if necessary."[30] On May 23, 1943, when this was written, Churchill appeared hopeful that success would be achieved. By 1952, the goal seemed more remote if we can judge from his public utterances.

The simple picture of collective security as theory hardly provides a perspective on the way such a system operates in practice. It is undeniable that under the United Nations the practical agencies for collective security, constitutionally or on paper, are better designed and equipped for high purposes. In contrast the agencies of collective security under the League were fragmentary and diffuse. Article 16 of the covenant provided that any member resorting to war against the covenant *ipso facto* had committed an act of aggression against all other members. It was intended that first economic measures and then overt force would be applied against any offender. However, no clear provision was made for one central enforcement agency. Each nation had full freedom to provide what troops it saw fit. The council could then advise on additional measures. In retrospect Churchill characterized that system, saying: "There was no unity. There was no vision."[31] In practice, collective security remained inoperative and: "The nations were pulled down one by one while the others gaped and chattered. One by one, each in his turn, they let themselves be caught."[32] In contrast, Article 39 of the Charter of the United Nations commissioned the Security Council to determine the existence of a threat to the peace or act of aggression and Articles 43–47 obligated the members to supply troops to the Military Staff Committee. Courts and magistrates cannot function without sheriffs and constables. In principle and theory: "It has been contemplated, surely, that formed military units should be dedicated by the different nations concerned and should,

30. *Ibid.*
31. London *Times*, June 17, 1941, p. 4.
32. *Ibid.*

as formed units, take their part."[33] On March 5, 1946, at Fulton, Churchill urged specifically that: "The United Nations Organisation must immediately begin to be equipped with an international armed force. In such a matter we can only go step by step, but we must begin now."[34] He specified:

I propose that each of the Powers and States should be invited to delegate a certain number of air squadrons to the service of the world organisation. These squadrons would be trained and prepared in their own countries, but would move around in rotation from one country to another. They would wear the uniform of their own countries but with different badges. They would not be required to act against their own nation, but in other respects they would be directed by the world organisation. This might be started on a modest scale and would grow as confidence grew."[35]

The agencies for limited collective security were even more impressive in the constitutional provisions of the North Atlantic Pact and the practical steps undertaken within NATO. Indeed, regional combinations of strength are probably the only police force upon which the world organization can depend. In the past, at one stage in the League's attempt to apply sanctions against Italy, only the British navy stood behind its enforcement decisions. Churchill referred to the role of the navy when he said: "For the first and last time the League of Nations seemed to have at its disposal a secular arm. Here was the international police force, upon the ultimate authority of which all kinds of diplomatic and economic pressures and persuasion could be employed."[36] Yet it fell short of being a full-fledged police force. Sometimes a few allies served as the backbone of attempts to create a limited security system. In March, 1936, Churchill conceded: "Let us neglect nothing in our power to establish the great international framework. If that should prove to be beyond our strength, or if it breaks down through the weakness or wrong-doings of others, then at least let us make sure that England

33. *Parliamentary Debates*, Vol. 484, February 12, 1951, p. 157.
34. New York *Times*, March 6, 1946, p. 4.
35. *Ibid.*
36. Churchill, *The Gathering Storm*, 173.

and France, the two surviving free great countries of Europe, can together ride out any storm that may blow with good and reasonable hopes of once again coming safely into port."[37] He consistently applied the same principle after World War II: "If we add the United States to Britain and France; if we change the name of the potential aggressor; if we substitute the United Nations Organisation for the League of Nations, the Atlantic Ocean for the English Channel, and the world for Europe, the argument is not necessarily without its application today."[38]

Thus Churchill's approach to collective security was primarily empirical and pragmatic in character. He was scornful of those who considered the covenant of the League of Nations sacrosanct, for he found it in large part visionary and utopian. Yet it could have provided a useful framework within which a new Concert of Europe might have grown up. On June 11, 1937, he referred to these unknown potentialities of the League and asked: "How else are we going to marshal adequate and if possible overwhelming forces against brazen, unprovoked aggression, except by a grand alliance of peace-seeking peoples under the authority of an august international body?"[39] Yet at the time his conception of the channels through which collective security might operate appeared unconventional to supporters of the League of Nations. In every emergency, he conceived of the European states as improvising the instrument and solution most appropriate for settling the conflict. For example, he maintained that the crisis precipitated by the Civil War in Spain in 1936–37 should be dealt with by a nonintervention committee made up of the major European states acting through military and diplomatic officials. On April 14, 1937, he asserted: "Is it not an encouraging fact that German, French, Russian, Italian and British Naval officers are officially acting together, however crankily, in something which represents, albeit feebly, the concert of

37. *Ibid.,* 210.
38. *Ibid.,* 211.
39. Churchill, "The Rome-Berlin Axis," June 11, 1937, *Step by Step, 1936–1939* (New York: Putnam's, 1939), 116.

Europe, and affords, if it is only a pale, misshapen shadow, some idea of those conceptions of the reign of law and of collective security which many of us regard as of vital importance?"[40] It was necessary to adjust collective security and collective self-help to the problems which confronted the world. While the formal arrangements of the League were suited to the relief of certain problems, other tensions might be eased by improvising and adapting ad hoc combinations to work outside the structure. Because certain issues fall outside the power and competence of either the League or the United Nations, nations whose vital interests were involved had no recourse but to their own strength and resources.

However, the British wartime leader did not exclude the possibility that sometime in the future responsibilities might be shouldered by the international organization. In the successive Anglo-Egyptian crises following the war, Churchill stubbornly maintained that Britain should resist all attempts at expulsion from Egypt and the Suez Canal but should steadfastly defend its strategic interests there. Yet in the long run, Britain's interests were identical with the interests of the West and on May 24, 1946, the Conservative leader observed that: "the surest resting place [in Egypt] at this time would be the 1936 Treaty and . . . we should rest there for the next five or six years in the hope that U.N.O., meanwhile, will grow up, and gather a great world army which will put so many of these strategic dangers, nightmares and calculations back into the limbo of the vanished past."[41] In the absence of a combined force, nations had no choice but to defend and safeguard their own interests.

The majority of contemporary advocates of collective security considered it attainable in the present or immediate future. By contrast Churchill believed that success in erecting a real security system would be gradual, painful, and long-range. In all probability a true collective security system could be brought about only in political crises or through a succession of piecemeal undertakings. In the interwar period, he predicted: "This process of agreements under

40. *Parliamentary Debates*, Vol. 322, April 14, 1937, pp. 1069–70.
41. *Parliamentary Debates*, Vol. 423, May 24, 1946, pp. 776–77.

the sanction of the League of Nations might eventually lead to a state which we should never exclude—namely the ultimate creation of some international force, probably particularly in aviation, which would tend to place the security of nations upon a much higher foundation than it stands on at present."[42] One way in which this might be achieved would be through the continued existence of a prolonged crisis. If nations were threatened by some mighty aggressive force which endangered their interests over an extended period, they might even following the decline of a common enemy continue to cooperate together. "If there were over a prolonged period of time, some general cause of anxiety which all nations, or many nations, felt, then possibly forces might come together for that purpose which after that danger had happily been tided over, might still subsist permanently in amity."[43] While this was not an especially original or penetrating idea, it suggested that Churchill saw the future of collective security hazardous to predict but resulting from changes in the structure of international society. Churchill was misled neither by the provisions in the charter nor the covenant which provided that members agree to support a full-blown system of collective security by pledging themselves to comply with the recommendations of international organs. While the growth and development of a true system of collective security is not a forlorn hope, the grounds for optimism for realists like Churchill were clearly different from the confidence of those who put their faith in the imposing formal structure of the United Nations.

The United Nations and Foreign Policy

Fundamental to most thinking on international affairs since the end of the nineteenth century has been a shift from the substance of international politics to the elements of international organization. Observers have tried to show that international experiments such as the League of Nations failed not because of the substantive policies

42. *Parliamentary Debates*, Vol. 292, July 13, 1934, p. 731.
43. *Ibid.*

pursued by individual members but because of some aspect of organization itself, for example, the failure to achieve comprehensive membership. The League of Nations failed, according to this view, not because of the policies of the major powers but because the United States and other nations were absent from the organization at crucial stages in its history. However, no reasonable man can seriously argue that if the United States or the Soviet Union or Nazi Germany had pursued the same policies within the League of Nations which they followed outside its jurisdiction the success of the League would have been greater or less. Its fate, which depended on the will of its members, was linked with the disastrous consequences of the nations' foreign policies.

Churchill argued that the main burden of responsibility for the League's tragic failure had to be sought elsewhere than in the particular flaws of its internal organization. Some observers looked upon organization as a substitute for rational policy or upon international organization as an alternative to foreign policy. The realist knows there is no such thing as the policy of an organization apart from the policy of its most powerful members. The actions of any major organization are the product of its members' policies and especially those of the most powerful. It is as misleading to consider the League of Nations apart from the policies of France and England as it is the United Nations apart from the policies of the Soviet Union and the United States. The process of arriving at an organization's policy, whether within public or private organizations, is a product of its members. The policies of the United States Steel Corporation help shape those of the National Association of Manufacturers, as do Macys' those of the United States Chamber of Commerce. The United States and the Soviet Union attempt to persuade the majority of United Nations' members to identify themselves with Soviet or American foreign policies. Competition goes on within the framework of an organization; individual or national policy makers shape group or supranational policies. The sharp edges of the policies of the strongest members are blunted in organizations and the aims which the larger group finds unacceptable are reformulated or accommodated. Policies which finally emerge bear the unmistakable imprint of the more influential members. Individual policies become through compromise, persuasion, and pressure the programs which take on the organization's name.

The sharpest illustration of Churchill's conception of the relation of foreign policy and international organization was expressed in his analysis of the causes for the downfall of the League of Nations. During the period betwen World War I and II, most observers explained the sickness of the League of Nations as resulting from the absence of the United States. The prevailing utopian view has been that the dramatic repudiation of the League by the American Senate sounded its death knell. It was widely assumed that if the United States had been a member, the League would have succeeded. Churchill in discussing the League of Nations both at the time and in retrospect devoted more attention to its members' foreign policies than to its structure or membership. He noted that France was committed to a rigid and intransigent status quo policy; England tried to pursue a policy of accommodation vis-à-vis Germany with a more dynamic conception of the status quo. The League depended on the unanimity of its two most consistent supporters but it suffered from the outset from the unresolved conflict between their policies. Neither was willing or able to reformulate its policy to make it compatible with the other. The unresolved conflict between the foreign policies of France and England undermined the effectiveness of the League of Nations beyond the point where it could succeed.

With current international organizations, their strength depended on the compatibility of the nations' foreign policies. In his Zurich Speech in 1946, Churchill pointed to the fact that European union was possible only if the aims and interests of France and Germany could be harmonized. Warning his hearers that he was likely to say something which would astonish them, Churchill expostulated: "The first step in the re-creation of the European family must be a partnership between France and Germany. In this way only can France recover the moral leadership of Europe."[44] No less urgent

44. London *Times*, September 20, 1946, p. 4.

was the need for adjusting German and British foreign policies. On July 9, 1951, he expressed the hope that "Germany and Britain may find a path which they can tread together along the broad lines fixed by the United Nations organisation."[45] Britain's national interests and the solvency of the United Nations were intimately bound up with Anglo-American unity. In a statement directed to Prime Minister Clement Attlee in 1951 on the occasion of the latter's impending visit to the United States at a time of cleavage over policies in Korea, Churchill asked him: "to bear in mind constantly the grave dangers which will fall upon us all should any serious divergencies occur between our policy and that of the United States, and should any serious division in the United Nations. . . . be brought about by manoeuvres which are obviously to the interest of Soviet Russia."[46] He encouraged him to adjust and to implement common interests: "The joint use of bases, the maintenance of the common staff arrangements between Great Britain and the United States, and the close integration of our foreign policies, are being pursued throughout the English-speaking world without any prejudice to the overriding and supreme status of the United Nations, which it is our solemn duty to sustain to the best of our ability, and ultimately to bring into effective reality as the sovereign instrument of world government."[47]

Moreover, another precondition of the successful operation of the United Nations was a status quo which had been recognized, formalized, and settled. A peace settlement depended on the adjustment of differences among the nations whose foreign policies had to be brought into agreement. On February 27, 1945, Churchill recommended to the Parliament that: "Many of these matters must await the time when the leaders of the Allies, freed from the burden of the direction of the war, can turn their whole or main attention to the making of a wise and far-reaching peace, which will, I trust, become a foundation greatly facilitating the work of the world or-

45. *Parliamentary Debates*, Vol. 490, July 9, 1951, p. 40.
46. *Parliamentary Debates*, Vol. 481, January 25, 1951, p. 42.
47. *Parliamentary Debates*, Vol. 446, January 23, 1948, p. 553.

ganisation."[48] The unresolved conflicts between the Soviet Union and the United States continue down to the present to be the nightmare of the life of the United Nations. The most terrible question of our time, Churchill prophesied as early as 1946, is: "What happens if the United Nations themselves are rendered by an awful schism, a clash of ideologies and passions? What is to happen if the United Nations give place, as they may do, to a vast confrontation of two parts of the world and two irreconcilably opposed conceptions of human society?"[49] If the foreign policies of the United States and the Soviet Union should prove permanently irreconcilable, the chances of success for the United Nations would be even less than the hopes of the League of Nations.

One final problem in the relationship of foreign policy to the United Nations is especially germane to the conduct of American foreign policy. Sometimes contemporary statesmen have explained their nation's foreign policy in terms of United Nations policies. President Truman repeatedly declared, as did other American leaders, that the cornerstone of American foreign policy was support for the policies of the United Nations. Yet United Nations' policies considered as abstract and independent policies are largely an imaginary quantity. In practice, supranational policies are nothing but the identical, mutually compatible or parallel policies of the major nations who constitute the international organization. The United Nations' policy for Churchill was primarily the policies of the Soviet Union and its satellites and the policies of the United States and those nations which the *Economist* (London) sometimes described as its clients. Inasmuch as it is not possible to substitute nonexisting supranational policies for those by which individual nations safeguard national interests, we may properly ask under what conditions a nation can claim to pursue a United Nations policy? In practice, nations may justify national policies by means of the ideology of international organization. When a nation is weak and its alternatives are limited and uncertain, it oftentimes tries to invoke su-

48. *Parliamentary Debates*, Vol. 408, February 27, 1945, p. 1274.
49. New York *Times*, May 8, 1946, p. 7.

pranational moral justification for its policies. On March 6, 1947, in the debate on the government's policy in India, Churchill declared: "If we, through lack of physical and moral strength, cannot wind up our affairs in a responsible fashion, ought we not to consider invoking the aid or, at least, the advice of the world international organization, which is now clothed with reality, and on which so many of us, in all parts of the House, base our hopes for the peaceful progress, freedom, and, indeed, the salvation of all mankind?"[50]

Sometimes, however, reference to United Nations policy may also be a device for concealing the absence of any positive national policy. At one point it was argued that the United States was unable to conduct bilateral negotiations with the Soviet Union because it was pledged to carrying on discussions solely within the United Nations. No one familiar with the difficulties of negotiating the outstanding differences which separate East and West inside the United Nations would construe this as anything but a refusal to have a positive policy on negotiations. For the United States to say it would not meet and negotiate with the Soviet Union except in the United Nations in its formal chambers or for a president of the United States to say he would meet the Soviet premier only at the United Nations was the same as saying he would not negotiate with the Soviet Union. British foreign policy offers its own illustrations of the use of imaginary United Nations' policies to obscure reluctance to assume national responsibilities. Before the Second World War, appeals were sometimes made to collective security policies at the same time that those who appealed were unwilling to accept the burdens of national rearmaments. Churchill's sharpest criticism of his government's policy for Palestine came with his claim on February 18, 1947, that the way the Arab-Jewish impasse had been referred to the United Nations demonstrated the substitution of a supranational technique for an effective foreign policy. He stated: "Are we to understand that we are to go on bearing the whole of this burden, with no solution to offer, no guidance to give—the whole of this burden of maintaining law and order in Palestine, and

50. *Parliamentary Debates*, Vol. 434, March 6, 1947, p. 677.

carrying on the administration, not only until September, which is a long way from February, not only until then, when the United Nations are to have it laid before them, but until the United Nations have solved the problem?"[51]

Shortcomings and Failures

In Churchill's lifetime, it was too early for a general inventory of the successes and failures of the United Nations. Its brief record at Lake Success, Flushing Meadows, and New York was obviously more limited and inconclusive than the record of the Geneva experiment, which scholars only now are reinterpreting. Yet there was one aspect of the United Nations' record of which Churchill and his contemporaries took stock, namely, its accomplishments in the sphere of peace and security. In this sphere, the claims and programs of the U.N. were most ambitious. In fact, the maintenance of peace and security stands highest in the hierarchy of aims and objectives of the United Nations. Following the war some leaders assumed that a political and legal system could be created through which the full international society would protect the victims of any armed attack. It is obvious that Churchill, especially, with his prevailing realistic viewpoint, judged the United Nations primarily in terms of its successes and failures in the political field.

One phase of the activities of the United Nations in the area of peace and security involves the functions it performs as a universal forum for discussion. The enforcement procedures of the new organization have sometimes been misinterpreted. Chapter VI of the Charter provides for mediation, conciliation, and negotiation by the members. However, in preliminary papers prepared by study groups like the Commission to Study the Organization of the Peace in the United States and in the emphasis given by the members and staff of the United Nations itself, Chapter VII, the collective enforcement chapter, received proportionately greater attention. Events from 1945 to 1952 awakened the supporters of the United

51. *Parliamentary Debates*, Vol. 433, February 18, 1947, p. 989.

Nations to the need of adapting the methods and procedures of the United Nations to political realities. The knowledge that the problems of international politics were not amenable to novel devices and techniques so long as the structure of international society remained unchanged impressed itself upon observers. Students and diplomatists began to consider ways of adapting world agencies to the time-honored procedures of negotiation and persuasion. In the autumn of 1949, the secretary general, Mr. Trygve Lie, sought to explain in his report to the General Assembly that greater effort was needed in developing the instruments and methods of Chapter VI of the Charter. In his effort to enlighten the members of the United Nations on the importance of diplomatic procedures, Mr. Lie by indirection raised the question of the adequacy of the United Nations in this traditional sphere.

While Mr. Lie was sanguine in referring to actual United Nations contributions to pacific settlements in Iran, Palestine, and Indonesia, other observers found it poorly equipped for mediation and conciliation. *The Times* in an editorial of November 9, 1951, concluded an appraisal of the United Nations as a diplomatic forum by noting that: "The United Nations Assembly has very much the same effect on the conduct of diplomacy as a General Election has on the conduct of internal politics. In each case the competition for votes and the wish to outwit one's opponents tend to blur the distinction between what is desirable and possible."[52] Even the United States and its supporters sought parliamentary triumphs within the organization when they enjoyed a permanent majority. Moreover, serious negotiation was made more difficult by the deterioration of the United Nations into essentially a propaganda platform for the major participants in the cold war. An organization that was to have become the majestic center of world security and world cooperation was in Churchill's eyes "reduced to a mere cockpit in which the representatives of mighty nations and ancient States hurl reproaches, taunts and recrimination at one another, to marshal public opinion and inflame the passions of their peoples in order to

52. London *Times*, November 9, 1951, p. 5.

arouse and prepare them for what seems to be a remorselessly approaching third world war."[53] The popular emphasis on "open diplomacy" merely accentuated the problems of East-West accommodation which would have been immensely difficult within any framework and under any conditions. Compromise and concession, which are the lifeblood of negotiations, became more difficult to achieve in the turbulent atmosphere of parliamentary diplomacy. Even in more optimistic moments, Churchill confessed that: "There was also hope that they would not meet in an overcrowded Tower of Babel but, as it were, upon a mountain top. . . . To some extent, events have moved in that direction but not in the spirit or shape which was needed."[54]

One comparison that should not escape us is the contrast between the League and the United Nations. Within the United Nations, issues have often been presented in the General Assembly without any previous discussion by subordinate committees and commissions, as was done under the League. Mr. Paul-Henri Spaak and other observers who had firsthand experience with both organizations commented that more things were prearranged under the League. Differences were threshed out in committees and agreements were arrived at through the aid of a system of rapporteurs. In the United Nations, by contrast, the tendency was for the Soviet Union to take public stands on issues which were presented to the world forum. Positions became frozen as the mass media beamed the Soviet stand to the far-flung corners of the world. In turn, the United States found itself committed to positions from which it could not gracefully retreat once the press and radio had informed the majority of the civilized world that its published terms were the irreducible minimum it could accept. At some point in the process, compromise was out of the question and concessions a luxury no righteous power could indulge itself. Thus a universal forum created for the ends of diplomacy tended to become a sounding board and

53. Churchill, "Conservative Mass Meeting," October 9, 1948, *Europe Unite*, ed. Randolph S. Churchill (London: Cassell and Company, 1950), 410.
54. *Time*, May 17, 1948, p. 28.

to serve the purposes of propaganda for the major nations. In this vein, *The Times* reported on February 28, 1949, that in a speech to the International Council of the European Movement: "Mr. Churchill pointed out that the United Nations had made a far less hopeful start than its predecessor, the League of Nations. It has already been reduced to a 'brawling cockpit.'"[55]

The decline in the adaptability of the United Nations as an effective organ for adjusting political disputes is partly the result of its membership. The League of Nations was strengthened by the fact that it remained throughout the 1920s primarily an exclusive club of liberal democracies. The United Nations, by contrast, found that its principal members from the beginning were separated by a deep and apparently unbridgeable moral and political chasm. Or in our subject's words: "It would be affectation not to notice that while the League of Nations had no United States, it was in its outset a fairly homogeneous and agreed body of associates whereas at the present time in the new U.N. we cannot be blind to the fact that there are grievous and deep-seated divisions."[56] Such divisions were aggravated by the tendency to replace traditional diplomacy with parliamentary proceedings in which the recalcitrant state, whose support was essential if important resolutions were to have any meaning, was outvoted for want of success in achieving diplomatic agreement. The price of parliamentary triumphs expressed in imaginary voting columns is too high if its consequences are the failure of all attempts to arrive at political adjustment which might otherwise have been possible.

A second serious weakness in the operation of the United Nations results from an unrealized premise on which the preservation of peace and security was founded. It was generally recognized in preparatory discussions that the great powers, and especially the Soviet Union, would never accept the principles of the Charter unless given some means of escape from military action against themselves. In what remains to this day an unfulfilled goal, collective security was predicated on the unanimity of the five great powers, the

55. London *Times*, February 28, 1949, p. 4.
56. New York *Times*, May 30, 1946, p. 12.

United States, the Soviet Union, Britain, France, and China. Belief in the possibility of consensus of the major powers proved a false premise, for the Soviet Union in practice showed that it had not in fact consented. The agreement that Churchill expected in 1945 never materialized. At that time he voiced the belief that: "His Majesty's Government's policy is firmly based on the Anglo-Soviet treaty of 1942 and considers the permanence of Anglo-Russian collaboration, within the framework of future world organization, as essential not only to her own interests but also to the future peace and prosperity of Europe as a whole."[57]

However, not only the Soviet Union but other major nations at Yalta, Dumbarton Oaks, and San Francisco displayed their reluctance to submit foreign policy to majority decisions inside the United Nations. In the United States, the veto through which these interests were expressed was defended as the only protection against international dictation and involuntary national servitude. The veto was defended as a safety valve to release energies which, if a nation were constrained to accept an international decision running counter to its own vital interests, would lead to a general military catastrophe. "As to the veto, that is a very serious matter. It is well known that Soviet Russia would not have joined the original San Francisco Conference unless they had had what they regarded as the essential security of the veto."[58] The Soviet Union had the added reason for supporting the veto without limitations because of its self-conscious position as a permanent and increasingly suspicious minority. In this position, the Soviet Union used the veto as a weapon to preserve its minority privileges. Its techniques led to abuse of the principle that had not been anticipated. Or, as Churchill put it: "I quite agree . . . that it was never contemplated at any time that the veto should be used in the abrupt, arbitrary and almost continuous manner that we have seen it used, but that it should be reserved as a last assurance to a great Power that they would not be voted down on a matter about which they were prepared to fight. That is [the Soviet abuse of the veto] certainly a great

57. *Ibid.*, September 19, 1945, p. 18.
58. *Parliamentary Debates*, Vol. 427, October 23, 1946, p. 1679.

departure from that tradition and the Foreign Secretary will be supported on this side of the House in endeavouring to secure a modification in the uses of the veto, even if he is not at this time, able to secure a very considerable restriction of its employment."[59]

The third shortcoming of the United Nations stems from its essential dualism. As we have already seen, the United Nations is an agency for collective security as well as of accommodation or conciliation. The tendency in the United States has been to stress its security functions. The British, on the other hand, have often associated themselves with the position taken in an editorial appearing in *The Times* of November 6, 1951, which declared: "However tempting it may be to concentrate on improving the collective security functions of the United Nations, it must be recognized that this can be done at present only by weakening its conciliatory functions. . . . The western Powers should first consider whether it is not better to leave defence to such organizations as the North Atlantic Council and preserve the United Nations, so far as it is possible, as a universal and conciliatory body."[60]

It would serve no purpose to consider at this point which of these conceptions was most valid. More important is the fact that twin functions of this type persisted in its early history. To neglect either purpose might be to court disaster. However: "The difficulty of combining the two functions has already been shown by the war in Korea. There the United Nations is in the strange position of being at once an impartial judge (condemning Chinese aggression), a potential arbiter and peacemaker, and an actual belligerent."[61] Through accommodation and bargaining, some degree of political consensus might be established and on this collective security depends. For in Korea: "The experience of the past year has proved how dangerous it is to leave the United Nations forces without any definition of political aims."[62]

In October 28, 1948, in the Debate on the Address, Churchill,

59. Ibid.
60. London Times, November 6, 1951, p. 7.
61. Ibid.
62. Ibid.

summarizing his views, observed: "There is always the U.N. organization, but it is still struggling for life and torn with dissension."[63] The divisions which impaired the security functions of the U.N. and weakened its structure in general could be adjusted only through traditional diplomacy. This was an opinion Churchill reflected when he said: "This new world structure will, from the outset and in all parts of its work, be aided to the utmost by the ordinary channels of friendly diplomatic intercourse, which it in no way supersedes."[64] The third defect of the United Nations will be ameliorated only when its twin purposes are fully recognized and efforts at harmonizing the actions of nations are made consonant with their security needs.

The Future of the United Nations

Many who support the United Nations consider it a long step on the road to a Parliament of Man. Frequently the United Nations is defended as a halfway house to world government. Yet for Churchill the evidence multiplied that those who would attempt to press this ultimate objective too quickly, before essential changes in the underlying structure of international society have been accomplished, would succeed only in nurturing Soviet suspicions that its minority privileges were imperiled. The Soviet Union kept watch more jealously in the beginning over Charter provisions which prescribe that great powers should deal with each other on an equal footing than over all other issues combined. It was fair to point out that the great majority of Soviet vetoes were aimed at preventing changes in procedures and structure which would alter the safeguards by which it exercised a *liberum* veto over resolutions the majority has approved. An international organization that approached more nearly the true parliament world government enthusiasts dreamed of would require the Soviet Union and any other self-conscious minority to renounce the safeguards it enjoyed. It would be required to accept in advance the will of majority rule.

63. *Parliamentary Debates*, Vol. 457, October 28, 1948, p. 250.
64. *Parliamentary Debates*, Vol. 408, February 27, 1945, p. 1273.

One would think that the overwhelming weight of earlier experience would dispel illusions that the West might have cherished that the Soviet Union, which almost daily was reminded of its minority role, would find its interests served by universalist ideals. It was appropriately said that a great deal of enthusiasm for immediate world government was explicitly anti-Russian in character. Disregarding the tentative and delicate limits of accord which had been painfully established within the United Nations, idealists wished to substitute a world government package offered to the Russians on a take-it-or-leave-it basis. If the Russians proved their ill will by refusing, it would be so much the worse for them. By contrast, Churchill showed little willingness to endanger whatever degree of minimum mutual respect existed within the present constitutional arrangements. The imperatives which may be extracted from his general conception of the United Nations emphasize the need for its wise and prudent use far more than its abrupt and radical transformation.

The first imperative which can be derived from his philosophy is that a nation ought to conduct its foreign policy *whenever possible* within the United Nations. It is part of the liberal illusion that many good people imagine that all foreign policy should be channeled through the United Nations. Beguiled by this concept, some critics attacked the Truman administration for its policies of Greece-Turkish Aid and the North Atlantic Pact, not on their merits, but because they were undertaken outside the United Nations. Churchill appeared anxious to disassociate himself from such a simple outlook when, on October 28, 1948, he asserted: "The only path of honour and duty will be for the British people to act in accordance with the principles enshrined in the United Nations organisation, and *wherever possible* through its structure and through whatever strength it may gather."[65] Churchill believed that United Nations' principles might sometimes be advanced by policies pursued outside as well as within the United Nations.

A second imperative relates to the conduct of policy within the United Nations by its members. The same set of problems which

65. *Parliamentary Debates*, Vol. 457, October 28, 1948, p. 252.

periodically confront policy makers arise for diplomatists who act inside the United Nations. The problem of timing, for example, is as vital to the success of a policy as is its wise formulation. On this basis, Churchill criticized the policy of submitting the Iranian crisis to the United Nations when the political situation had been altered by the course of events. On October 6, 1951, he expressed the opinion that: "When the Hague Court had given its decision in our favour then was the time, nearly three months ago, to lay our case before the United Nations. Mr. Attlee and Mr. Morrison have simply drifted until, after every kind of humiliation, we have been ignominiously ejected a week before our appeal to the United Nations could even be considered."[66] The United Nations, in short, was not an institution in which the requirements for political judgment could be abandoned. It merely provided the actors in international politics with a new medium in which these talents could be expressed and employed.

Thirdly, the United Nations is a means and not an end. In any immediate crisis, its paramount objective should be to remove unfounded suspicions which have tended to increase international tension. As a means to this end, the United Nations can serve as a clearinghouse for false and misleading charges and counter-charges. Through its forums and committees, in anterooms and delegate lounges, the United Nations may sift truth and falsity and distinguish tensions rooted in objective conditions from those based on unfounded suspicions. Those seated at the bar of international opinion are best able to judge in the nations' behalf. On November 1, 1946, the New York *Times* reported the following comments by Churchill on receiving the freedom of Birmingham: "We've been told that one of the great evils from which we suffer is international suspicion. There's a very good remedy for suspicions. It is the full disclosure of facts, and that simple remedy I hope will be applied to the world situation by the United Nations organization now meeting in the United States."[67] It was obvious, moreover, that reliance

66. London *Times*, October 8, 1951, p. 2.
67. New York *Times*, November 1, 1946, p. 15.

on the ideas and technique of diplomacy must supplement U.N. measures, especially when nations find themselves in conflict not because they misunderstand one another but because they perceive one another's motives only too clearly.

The fourth imperative Churchill advanced was that the United Nations provides the basis for an incipient world law and morality among nations. He declared in 1950: "We must all try our utmost to sustain the authority of the United Nations and thus lay broad and solid foundations for a world where law and freedom reign."[68] He had explained in 1946: "The purpose of the United Nations is to make sure that the force of right will, in the ultimate issue, be protected by the right of force."[69] Sometimes his hopes betrayed the realistic appraisals he had given elsewhere on the nature and limits of the new organization. Thus he predicted in 1945: "It is to this strongly-armed body that we look to prevent wars of aggression, or the preparations for such wars, and to enable disputes between States, both great and small, to be adjusted by peaceful and lawful means, by persuasion, by the pressure of public opinion, by legal method and eventually by another category of method which constitutes the principle of this new organisation."[70]

On occasion his exuberance about the moral embodiments of the United Nations led him to overlook important practical considerations. For example, it was generally agreed early in the U.N.'s history by the diplomatists of Western Europe that the "gentleman's agreement" between East and West probably entitled the Soviet Union to select one new member who would be representative of its bloc to replace the delegate from Poland on the Security Council when his term was ended. In 1949, the Soviets nominated Czechoslovakia. The United States opposed this choice, however, and successfully urged the election of a representative from neutralist Yugoslavia. Churchill on this issue strongly supported the American position. It is possible that in part he responded to the exigen-

68. Churchill, "Fifth Alamein Reunion," October 29, 1950, *In The Balance,* ed. Randolph S. Churchill, 405.
69. New York *Times,* May 10, 1946, p. 10.
70. *Parliamentary Debates,* Vol. 408, February 27, 1945, p. 1272.

cies of domestic politics, for this was a ready-made moralistic issue on which to expose the Socialists. A strong moralistic tone was present in his comment of November 17, 1949: "I cannot think of any step more likely to discourage all the forces in Czechoslovakia who are working so patiently and steadfastly to free their country from the Soviet yoke. The fact that Great Britain which has always been looked upon with so much regard by the Czechs, should give its vote for placing on the Security Council a Government which at the dictation of the Kremlin is trying to torment them into communism will be a heavy blow to all those in Czechoslovakia with whom, on both sides of the House, there is a great measure of sympathy."[71]

In viewing the United Nations, Churchill may sometimes have been misled into thinking it had already arrived at a position where law and morality were its prevailing guides and that the baffling ambiguities of the political problem required less attention than in international politics generally. On the issue of representation in the Security Council, Churchill appeared to have parted company with the vast majority of political realists who felt that in the interest of ameliorating the tensions between East and West, Czechoslovakia should have been seated. However, Churchill may have been using the issue in the same way he did support for the League of Nations in the pre–World War II era. Then he perceived in a policy of support for the League an ideological weapon whereby support for British foreign policy might be obtained especially in the United States. He explained this principle by asserting: "Strict adherence to the covenant of the League and to the [Kellogg] Pact . . . will . . . win for us a very great measure of sympathy in the United States."[72] By harmonizing British foreign policy with that of important major powers, the security of England would be enhanced. "The United Nations organisation . . . has not so far, fulfilled our hopes; it remains however . . . our citadel, and we are in full accord with His Majesty's Government in their loyal and faithful support of this in-

---

71. *Parliamentary Debates*, Vol. 469, November 17, 1949, pp. 2228–29.
72. *Parliamentary Debates*, Vol. 330, December 21, 1937, p. 1838.

stitution, whose reign and ascendancy are an earnest of the desire of the overwhelming majority of mankind."[73]

His fifth imperative casts the United Nations as an instrument of long-range goals. The U.N., in addition to serving the interests of peace and security, must deal with the underlying economic and social-psychological causes of tensions and strife. He declared: "Peace is no passive state, but calls for qualities of high adventure and endeavour. Through the United Nations we must not only prevent war but feed the hungry, heal the sick, restore the ravages of former wars, and assist the peoples of Africa and Asia to achieve by peaceful means their hopes of a new and better life."[74] The United Nations had to transcend preoccupation solely with the amelioration of current political problems by seeking to relieve the underlying sources of hatred and suffering, hunger and deprivation, alienation and bitterness. Indeed, the United Nations, Churchill might have reflected, may actually be better equipped to perform this long-run task than facilitating the accommodation of immediate international struggles for power. In his heart, Churchill was in no way overconfident that the United Nations could play much part in accommodating the differences between East and West. In the days that followed the end of World War II, he took a bold and sometimes extravagant stand about what the United Nations could do. He maintained that by invoking the authority of the United Nations on baffling international problems its strength would be tested and its capacity established. In discussing the Russian claim for a fortress in the Straits, he asserted: "If Soviet Russia still persists in putting pressure on Turkey, the matter must in the first instance be pronounced upon by the United Nations Security Council. Thus early will come a very great test for the world organization on which so many hopes are founded."[75] By mid-1947, however, the prospects for the United Nations were being more soberly interpreted, as reflected in his warning: "We must not allow ourselves to be dis-

73. *Parliamentary Debates*, Vol. 430, November 12, 1946, p. 18.
74. London *Times*, October 24, 1950, p. 6.
75. New York *Times*, March 16, 1946, p. 2.

couraged by the difficulties. Nor must we become impatient at the shortcomings of this United Nations conception in these early days. . . . If, after earnest and prolonged trial, it is found that some members of the World Organisation wish to bring it to naught or to break away from it, then those nations which remain must band themselves together ever the more strongly."[76] To the degree that the main function of diplomacy in promoting the resolution of great power rivalries has to be carried on largely outside the United Nations or at least only within certain informal U.N. channels, the fifth imperative which reserves for the United Nations the task of relieving the long-term underlying sources of tension becomes a paramount and overriding responsibility for traditional diplomacy.

76. Churchill, "The Primrose League," April 18, 1947, *Europe Unite*, ed. Randolph S. Churchill, 65.

CHAPTER FIFTEEN

New Insights on "Old Diplomacy"

The war leaders assembled in Paris had been borne thither upon the strongest and most furious tides that have ever flowed in human history. Gone were the days of the Treaties of Utrecht and Vienna, when aristocratic statesmen and diplomats, victor and vanquished alike, met in polite and courtly disputation, and, free from the clatter and babel of democracy, could reshape systems upon the fundamentals of which they were all agreed. The peoples, transported by their sufferings and by the mass teachings with which they had been inspired, stood around in scores of millions to demand that retribution should be exacted to the full. Woe betide the leaders now perched on their dizzy pinnacles of triumph if they cast away at the conference table what the soldiers had won on a hundred bloodsoaked battlefields.[1]

Approaches to international peace and order are frequently cast in exclusivist terms. It has been fashionable to speak of a choice between the balance of power and world government or the United Nations and world government. Churchill throughout his writings and public declarations tried to deflate such approaches and expose the falsity of such choices and distinctions. In particular, he attempted to show that no other approach had a chance of succeeding without the ameliorating and consensus-building role of historic diplomacy. It stands to reason that Churchill, with his first-hand experience in diplomacy throughout most of the twentieth century, would feel compelled to reassess critically the prevailing concepts of diplomacy. Moreover, since he emerges from this study as primarily a political actor and only secondarily and by accident a political theorist, we may expect his comments on the practical issues of diplomacy to be more illuminating than his sometimes unsteady attempts to pierce the philosophical obscurities of, say, the

1. Winston S. Churchill, *The Second World War*, Vol. I, *The Gathering Storm* (Boston: Houghton Mifflin, 1948), 4.

world government movement. Churchill was a practical and prudent man and since foreign policy is a practical, day-by-day adventure, he was naturally most at home in such an environment. Foreign policy is not like an eight-day clock that can be wound up and then forgotten. The only way foreign policy is successfully implemented is through the efforts of diplomats who pursue their tasks from day to day. Evolved through centuries of experience by nations confronted with the need of communicating with one another, diplomacy is a laborious and serious business which is generally lacking in the evil and mysterious features which the public frequently ascribes to it. Therefore, Churchill dealt with diplomacy not as an exercise in moral philosophy but as an issue in existing international politics.

Old and New Diplomacy

Contemporary thinking on international relations has generally proceeded on the belief that there were two patterns of diplomacy nations could follow. For some political idealists like Woodrow Wilson, diplomacy was identified with the "old dispensation" of eighteenth- and nineteenth-century diplomacy characterized by anarchy and power politics. For others, diplomacy was contrasted with the "new order" of peace under law in which the elimination of rivalry and conflict would be accompanied by the abandonment of secret diplomacy. In describing popular feelings abroad at the end of World War I, Churchill reflected: "When the war was over there was a strong feeling in favor of what is called open diplomacy."[2] Popular thinking was rooted in the belief that every diplomatic problem can be aired and settled in great open forums much as public questions are decided in town meetings or legislative assemblies within localities and nations. The formal, organizational expressions of the new diplomacy with its well-publicized diplomatic conferences are among the most spectacular technical

2. *Parliamentary Debates* (Hansard) House of Commons, Fifth Series, Vol. 272, November 23, 1932 (London: His Majesty's Stationery Office, 1950), 87.

achievements of modern civilization. Delegates from all corners of the civilized world come together in a single great metropolitan center and engage in discussions while remaining constantly in touch with their respective governments. Corps of experts accompany each delegation and the latest technical facilities for worldwide communication are skillfully employed. Yet the defects in open diplomacy are serious and far-reaching and the handicaps of the new dispensation weighed heavily on Churchill from World War I until his death.

In the period between the wars, Churchill declared: "In my experience, and interior knowledge of workings of Governments, which extends over nearly a quarter of a century, I cannot recall any time when the gap between any kind of words which statesmen used and what was actually happening in many countries was so great as it is now. The habit of saying smooth things and uttering pious platitudes and sentiments to gain applause, without relation to the underlying facts, is more pronounced now than it has ever been in my experience."[3] What he was referring to was the tendency throughout the period to revert to false and misleading devices in the practice of the new diplomacy. In many of the interwar conferences, recourse was to the diplomatic "formula." When a conference had reached a deadlock and agreement seemed out of the question, it was commonplace for some prominent political leader to introduce a simple and innocuous formula on which everyone could obviously agree. While leaving the central issues substantially unresolved, the formula, through creating an illusion of agreement, permitted the delegates to return to their respective countries pointing with pride to a well-advertised settlement they had apparently reached. The story is told of the World Disarmament Conference of 1932 which was approaching the moment of its summer adjournment. The delegates agreed on only one point, namely, that they must produce some kind of public statement before they dispersed to justify their extended labors. On July 5, 1932, Sir John Simon drew up a draft statement providing the main elements of a resolution by Mr.

3. *Ibid.*

Benes, the rapporteur. Such a practice evoked one of Churchill's most devastating criticisms of the new diplomacy when he exclaimed: "You talk of secret diplomacy, but let me tell you that there is a worse kind of secret diplomacy, and it is the diplomacy which spreads out hope and soothing syrup for the good, while all the time winks are being exchanged between the peoples who know actually what is going on."[4]

Furthermore, the pursuit of open diplomacy tended to obscure the essential and traditional function of all diplomacy. Historically, the task of diplomacy has been fundamentally different from the functions of legislation and politics within a domestic society. Politics within an integrated society is the mechanism by which the struggle for the means of authority and control are regularized and controlled. Both means and ends in the struggle for power are prescribed and determined by the will of the domestic community. Social change is facilitated by legislative organs which allow for the recognition of changing conditions through formal procedures from which violence is commonly excluded. In the absence of community and lacking an acceptable system of regularized control and effective peaceful change, international politics is from every point of view a more primitive system. For example, one essential function of diplomacy is the amelioration of rivalries from which conflict might emerge. Churchill commented: "It is customary for thoughtless people to jest at the old diplomacy and to pretend that wars arise out of its secret machinations. When one looks at petty subjects which have led to wars between great countries . . . it is easy to be misled in this way. Of course such small matters are only the symptoms of the dangerous disease, and are only important for that reason."[5] This dangerous disease is the struggle for power which requires nations to pursue their interests irrespective of legal stipulations and moral exhortations. The trifling issues with which diplomacy is preoccupied are important because: "Behind them lie

4. *Parliamentary Debates*, Vol. 275, March 14, 1933, p. 1819.
5. Winston S. Churchill, *The World Crisis, 1911–1918* (New York: Scribner's, 1931), 37.

the interests, the passions and the destiny of mighty races of men; and long antagonisms expressed themselves in trifles. 'Great commotions,' it was said of old, 'arise out of small things, but not concerning small things.' The old diplomacy did its best to render harmless the small things; it could do no more."[6]

One respected diplomatic historian, R. B. Mowat, discovered that even in its twilight period, traditional diplomacy contributed to the postponement of at least eight European conflicts which by every recognized measure ought to have broken out in wars. As we have seen, it was axiomatic in Churchill's concept of diplomacy that "a war postponed may be a war averted."[7] These truths provide the background for Churchill's endeavor to balance the old and the new diplomacy. Writing in the 1920s, he maintained: "If the nations of the world, while the sense of their awful experiences is still fresh upon them, are able to devise broader and deeper guarantees of peace and build their houses on a surer foundation of brotherhood and interdependence, they will still require the courtly manners, the polite measured phrases, the imperturbable demeanour, the secrecy and discretion of the old diplomatists of Europe."[8] Civility toward one another even on deeply divisive issues was, to reverse the saying, the tribute virtue paid to vice.

A final commentary on the old and the new diplomacy arises from the problem of the diplomatic representative. Prior to World War I, it was commonplace to send to important capitals with which a nation was entering into negotiations permanent representatives endowed with extraordinary discretion and power. Since communications were tedious and dispatching of elaborate and continuous instructions too slow paced and cumbersome, representatives were expected to act independently in safeguarding their country's interests. The revolution in communications, which made possible almost instantaneous communication from the foreign office to the representative on the scene, has found many governments restoring the power for detailed negotiations to the foreign secre-

6. *Ibid.*, 37–38.
7. *Ibid.*, 38.
8. *Ibid.*

tary. Thus ambassadors have tended to become little more than messenger boys, something that Churchill appeared to challenge when he appointed Lord Halifax, then foreign secretary, as the British ambassador to the United States upon the death of Lord Lothian. On January 9, 1941, explaining his reasons for the appointment, Churchill gave evidence of clinging to the concept of the diplomat as more than a deputy of his own foreign office. He declared: "We chose our Foreign Secretary—who had himself chosen Lord Lothian—to fill Lord Lothian's place. . . . We send to the U.S. an envoy who comes from the very center of our counsels and knows all our secrets. Although while Lord Halifax is serving as Ambassador [and] he cannot be a member of the War Cabinet, he will be . . . as it were seconded from it."[9]

Changes in the role of the diplomatic representative, traditionally that of serving as the eyes and ears, mouth and hands of foreign offices, led to excess at two extremes. The judgment and skill of the permanent envoy were shackled, his discretion about timing and tactics restricted, and his privilege of choosing the means for pursuing general objectives assumed by the secretary of state. When it is remembered that an argument's persuasiveness and the influence of a policy have depended throughout history on the diplomatic representative's skill and virtuosity, this trend became a detriment and setback to peace and order. In an opposite sense, responsibility became diffused and limited under the new mode of diplomacy. For example, machinery was set up for dealing with the unsolved problems of the Potsdam conference. Many grave questions which under the old diplomacy would have been settled at the highest level were presented to the Foreign Secretaries' Council. Grave questions remained unsolved and Churchill on August 16, 1945, reflected: "The Foreign Secretaries' Council . . . though most capable of relieving difficulties, is essentially one gifted with less far-reaching power. Other grave questions are left for the final peace settlement, by which time many of them may have settled themselves, not necessarily in the best way."[10]

9. London *Times*, January 10, 1941, p. 9.
10. *Parliamentary Debates*, Vol. 413, August 16, 1945, pp. 82–83.

The Art of Diplomacy and the Diplomat

The business of a diplomat, we remind ourselves, is unique and distinct from that of the military planner or the domestic political
leader. The art of diplomacy demands qualities which are a curious
blending of cynicism and courtesy. In one respect, diplomacy, with
its underlying objective of obtaining as much as possible for one's
country, is a grim and ambiguous calling. Since current discussions
at any given moment are merely an incident in coping with an unending series of issues arising in the future, diplomats must be cour-
teous, agreeable, and even-tempered, however committed they are
to success at any price. Thus while striving untiringly for immediate
objectives, unfailing courtesy is called for to cement good relations
in the future.

Particular qualities which are indispensable gifts and talents in
military affairs are seldom if ever likely to serve the diplomat. In
Churchill's cogent phrase: "It is alway dangerous for soldiers, sail-
ors, or airmen to play at politics. They enter a sphere in which the
values are quite different from those to which they have hitherto
been accustomed."[11] Military undertakings place a premium on the
man who can focus his attention narrowly and sharply on a well-
defined set of concrete problems. Diplomacy, on the other hand, requires intellectual gifts which enable the individual to look at a
problem from every angle, leaving no element out of account and
estimating all aspects in their relative proportions. The military
man must think in absolute terms of victory and defeat; the diplomat must approach a problem at an infinite number of halfway
points all influencing the chances of reaching distant ends and
objectives.

Numerous examples might be offered to illustrate Churchill's
opinion on this issue. In 1946, he expressed himself in the most general terms on the concrete issue of the evacuation of strategic areas
in Egypt before negotiations with the Egyptian government on a
new treaty arrangement had begun. The Socialist government had

11. Churchill, *The Gathering Storm*, 137.

ordered these areas evacuated after conferring with the Chiefs of Staff. Churchill maintained that putting a question of this kind to the Chiefs of Staff was foolish. He observed that military men were not the best judges of the most prudent diplomatic approach to a situation. "The Chiefs of Staff, in my view, were asked a question which was a political question and gave an answer which did not touch reality."[12] In the Second World War, meetings were held between the Italian General Castellano and the American envoy to Italy concerning the Italian surrender. Churchill had hoped that plans might be worked out for Italian operations against the Germans. The American representative affirmed that he was competent to discuss only the question of unconditional surrender. Churchill commented: "It is difficult to make hard-cut military negotiations fit in with flexible diplomacy."[13]

Furthermore, the tendency in democracies to hold the diplomat in low moral esteem has resulted in two simultaneous unfortunate developments. One has been the substitution of military men for diplomats with all the grave and attendant perils which we have just considered. As we have seen, it is part of the logic of the cold war that the delicate and subtle compromises and adjustments which have been the essence of diplomacy traditionally have been superseded by the military standards of advance and retreat. The most thoughtful diplomatic analysts have characterized the antagonists, the United States and the Soviet Union, as two warriors facing one another in a narrow lane in which they were able theoretically only to move ahead or to retreat. Yet, because of the crusading nature of their policies, they cannot retreat. Being engaged in a grand moral enterprise, they view all interests as vital; compromise becomes the equivalent of treason. At the same time, they cannot advance, for the threat of war accompanies the use of force of persuasion backed by force. Since the present conflict is one between two inflexible forces, the function of diplomacy has tended in practice to become obsolete. Hans J. Morgenthau put the problem in sharpest relief:

12. *Parliamentary Debates*, Vol. 418, May 7, 1946, p. 896.
13. Winston S. Churchill, *The Second World War*, Vol. V, *Closing the Ring* (Boston: Houghton Mifflin, 1951), 106.

"Under such moral and political conditions, it is not the sensitive, flexible, and versatile mind of the diplomat, but the rigid, relentless, and one-track mind of the military which guides the destiny of nations. The military mind knows nothing of persuasion, of compromise, and of threats of force which are meant to make the actual use of force unnecessary."[14] The military mind is conversant with the notion of victory and defeat and of concentrating maximum energy at the enemy's most vulnerable point, a process that is simple and unambiguous. But diplomacy counts its victories in wars that have been postponed and bitter rivalries which have been temporarily relieved and adjusted. Subtle improvements or an imperceptible deterioration in the political situation are evidence of the success or failure of a persevering diplomacy. Yet this can hardly be defined in popular language that compares with the military conditions of victory or defeat. The methods of diplomacy are relative, tentative, and conditional, and its chief distinguishing quality is patience in dissolving or circumventing obstacles which the military mind would overpower and destroy.

The nature of the contemporary crisis is not the only cause of the decline of traditional diplomacy. We have witnessed in recent times, as one phase of the reaction against power politics, the indictment of diplomacy not as a symptom but as a chief cause of power politics. General hostility to the workings of the modern state system has been expressed in particular resentment against traditional diplomacy, which has been said to endanger the cause of peace. Such a viewpoint is valid insofar as it recognizes the interconnections between the modern state system and the practice of diplomacy. No one familiar with European history would dispute the fact that the rise of the state system was paralleled historically by the growth of permanent diplomatic institutions. This coincidence demonstrates the need for creating harmony and stability in relations among states whose strongest common interest has been national security and a minimum of international order. In historic

14. Hans J. Morgenthau, *Politics Among Nations* (New York: Alfred A. Knopf, 1948), 430.

terms, diplomacy has been an expression of the need for some tolerable measure of order if international intercourse were to continue among nation-states whose rivalries were more visible than those among groups subject to the controls of effective governments and communities. However, the contemporary version of diplomacy and power politics has denied to the old diplomacy its significant if uninspiring contributions. Instead the modern viewpoint has ruled out the vital functions of which diplomacy had proven capable and has attributed to the diplomat qualities of deviousness which no righteous society could tolerate.

Notwithstanding, for Churchill, the ideal diplomat is a man of extraordinary discretion possessing deep and abundant political wisdom. His role is to conduct himself incidentally as an "Intelligent Agent" but primarily as a wise and intelligent man. In a note to Sir Alexander Cadogan, Churchill advised: "The zeal and efficiency of a diplomatic representative is measured by the quality and not the quantity of the information he supplies. He is expected to do a great deal of filtering for himself, and not simply to pour out upon us over these congested wires all the contradictory gossip which he hears."[15] Under the spell of the present version of scientific objectivity, contemporary diplomats and political leaders have seen their role as primarily that of gathering information. Some have assumed that with enough data, the answer to every problem would spring from the diplomatic pouch. For Churchill such methods have served only to obscure the real issue and have impaired the natural wisdom and common sense of men who were capable of thinking.

The Rules of Diplomacy

Skillful diplomacy also calls for the observance of certain fundamental principles and guides which Churchill was loath to see violated. One involved continuity of service. On March 19, 1944, he

15. Winston S. Churchill, "Prime Minister to Sir Alexander Cadogon," February 17, 1941, *The Second World War*, Vol. III, *The Grand Alliance* (Boston: Houghton Mifflin, 1950), 737.

wrote to Foreign Secretary Anthony Eden: "It seems to me most improvident . . . to take a man away from a post where he has gained great influence and knowledge and to send him to some entirely different atmosphere where he has to begin all over again. . . . All the great Ambassadors who have exercised influence have remained long at their post."[16] In his dispatch, Churchill ran through a list of prominent and successful diplomatists. The Russian diplomatist Maisky served his country for approximately a decade in England. Monsieur de Stael, Churchill reminisced, had become a legend among diplomats when Churchill was a boy. Some Portuguese ambassadors served their country for periods exceeding fifteen years. The tasks of diplomacy are so baffling and complicated that no diplomat is equipped to cope with them unless a particular foreign environment has become, as it were, a second home to him. "In my opinion, and I speak from long experience, the natural term of an Ambassador's mission should be six years, unless he is guilty of incompetence or divergence from the Government's policy, when, of course, he cannot be recalled too soon."[17] Diplomacy calls for continuity of service among diplomats as an indispensable precondition for its practice. Especially if diplomacy is to be carried out in accordance with Churchill's five basic rules was this the case. His first rule rested on four guides for negotiations enumerated with regard to the Iranian crisis. He warned against a diplomacy of bluff, drift, impatience, and neglect of alternatives. He began: "One such simple rule is not to parade force, or imply a readiness to use force, if there is in fact no intention to use it at need."[18] Strength is a condition of successful diplomacy because political arrangements, unsupported by situations of strength, are likely to deteriorate into mere scraps of paper. Yet the threat of force, while a weapon in successful negotiations, can, if unwisely used, be detrimental to any positive settlement. Churchill indicted the Labor government's policy in Iran for

16. Churchill, "Prime Minister to Foreign Secretary," March 19, 1944, *Closing the Ring*, 702.
17. *Ibid.*
18. London *Times*, October 5, 1951, p. 7.

tragically illustrating disregard of diplomatic precepts. In the Iranian discussions in 1951, every guide that he had mentioned was breached in some form or other. The government concentrated its naval vessels in the Persian Gulf, blustered against Iranian intransigence, and then gave in without having had any intention to use force. "Another simple rule is not to let policy be deflected by evidently precarious hopes and, especially not to postpone decisions for the sake of any such hopes."[19] He charged that the Socialist government had pursued a policy of drift in the Iranian situation awaiting the fall of Prime Minister Mossadeagh. This was a classic example for Churchill of drifting in hope that the most optimistic estimate of the situation would materialize.

"Further, it ought always to be remembered that negotiations on a difficult matter may have to be long and wearisome, more especially with an eastern country."[20] In this statement, Churchill lays bare the phase of diplomacy which has been found least intelligible in modern democratic societies with their impatience for quick solutions. Democracies have little sympathy with painful long-drawn-out negotiations. When the British broke off talks with the Iranians on September 23, 1951, Churchill condemned the Socialist government for having compromised with impatience. The virtues Churchill attributed to the diplomat indicates that he was never unaware of the need for patience. He lectured his political adversaries, saying: "If we wish to prevent the fearful tensions which exist in the modern world we must not only be cool and patient, but also firm and strong."[21] Contemporary diplomatic negotiators have shown themselves willing to break off discussions before even the groundwork for accommodation had been laid. Churchill referred with deep irony to one of the wartime conferences held in Teheran. On the afternoon of December 4, 1943, President Roosevelt announced that he would be required to leave by December 6 because of the pressure of domestic events. To this the British leader responded, "I

19. *Ibid.*
20. *Ibid.*
21. *Parliamentary Debates*, Vol. 472, March 16, 1950, p. 1297.

said that I did not wish to leave the Conference in any doubt that
the British delegation viewed our early dispersal with great ap-
prehension. There were still many questions of first-class importance to be settled."[22]

The fourth guide to action in diplomatic negotiations is the rule
of not abandoning diplomatic discussions unless some other alternative is available. In the Iranian crisis this rule was abandoned:
"Here another rule was broken—never to refuse negotiation unless
an alternative line of conduct, likely to get better results, has been
formulated."[23] The test of a prudent diplomacy is embedded in the
four criteria.

A second more general principle of diplomacy concerns timing
and its relationship to a particular stream of historical events. Certain steps might have been taken to forestall the rise of Hitler when
events were ripe in the interwar period. However: "When the situation was manageable it was neglected, and now that it is thoroughly
out of hand we apply too late the remedies which then might have
effected a cure. There is nothing new in the story. It is as old as the
Sybilline books."[24] The history of diplomacy is oftentimes the melancholy tale of measures that were ill-considered, ill-timed, and hes-
itatingly applied. Indeed: "Want of foresight, unwillingness to act
when action would be simple and effective, lack of clear thinking,
confusion of counsel until the emergency comes, until self-preservation strikes its jarring gong—these are the features which constitute
the endless repetition of history."[25] The supreme value Churchill put
upon timing in diplomacy is illustrated in his note to the foreign secretary of May 27, 1944: "It is a great pity, when an important message agreed upon between us has been sent to Stalin from me, that it
should not be delivered as fast as possible. There would always be
an opportunity for the Ambassador to give a warning if he thought
it would do extreme harm and in exceptional cases he might use his

22. Churchill, *Closing the Ring*, 409.
23. London *Times*, October 5, 1951, p. 7.
24. *Parliamentary Debates*, Vol. 301, May 2, 1935, p. 602.
25. *Ibid.*

discretion."[26] Grave international crises have been precipitated because policies were not clarified by prompt communications. "Sometimes misunderstandings arise because one sends a message and waits a long time for an answer. After it comes, one finds it is quite a nice answer, but meanwhile one has been thinking the worse of the silence. Nothing should stand in the way of prompt communication."[27]

A third general diplomatic precept Churchill advanced was that there are seldom viable substitutes for direct face-to-face negotiation. The fundamental problem of person-to-person communication by which the human predicament is everywhere complicated has its own specific application in the field of diplomacy. "[It] is so much easier to enter into arrangements by conversation than by telegram and diplomatic correspondence, however carefully phrased and however lengthily expressed, or however patiently the discussion may be conducted. Face to face, difficulties which appear really insuperable at a distance are very often removed altogether from one's path."[28] The prevailing viewpoint has been that the revolution in communications, as a consequence of which ambassadors and envoys are enabled to maintain constant contact with their foreign offices has rendered obsolete the ameliorating role of skillful face-to-face persuasion and discussion. "What an ineffectual method of conveying human thought correspondence is—even when it is telegraphed with all the rapidity and all the facilities of modern inter-communication! They are simply dead blank walls compared to personal contacts."[29] American secretaries of state such as John Foster Dulles made similar statements. In Churchill's conviction on this point, we have another example of the practical consequences of his underlying view of diplomacy.

26. Churchill, "Prime Minister to Foreign Secretary," May 27, 1944, *Closing the Ring*, 713.
27. *Ibid.*
28. *Parliamentary Debates*, Vol. 404, October 27, 1944, p. 493.
29. Churchill, "The Quebec Press Conference," September 16, 1944, *The Dawn of Liberation*, ed. Charles Eade (Boston: Little, Brown, 1945), 224.

A fourth general principle in diplomacy is to look at international politics from the position of other nations and try to recognize and understand their interests and concerns. In his history of the war, Churchill commented: "In war and policy one should always try to put oneself in the position of what Bismarck called 'the Other Man.' The more fully and sympathetically a Minister can do this, the better are his chances of being right. The more knowledge he possesses of the opposite point of view, the less puzzling it is to know what to do."[30] The taproot of diplomacy is found in defining the interests of one's nation and discovering what one's antagonist's interests may be.

Fifth, the essence of all diplomacy is compromise on nonvital and nonessential interests for assurances about national security. In practice, diplomacy depends on the willingness of each side to accept a settlement based on a *quid pro quo*. The temptation for every nation, including the United States, in creating situations of strength, is to imagine that the enemy, confronted by a true preponderance of power, will surrender. On August 16, 1945, Churchill sought to educate the Parliament: "No one of three leading powers can impose its solution upon the others and . . . the only solutions possible are those in the nature of a compromise."[31] What distinguishes true and effective diplomacy from appeasement is the nature of the bargain that is struck. In the case of concessions to Germany in the interwar period, the failure of England to gain in return concrete guaranties in the form of a *quid pro quo* made such settlements tantamount to appeasement. On January 12, 1939, Churchill declared: "The official view in Whitehall is that it was a masterstroke of policy, the first great step in the process of 'appeasement,' and an example to prove to all the world how easy it is to have working arrangements between Democratic Parliamentary nations and Totalitarian dictatorships. . . . But did he [Hitler] even in the naval sphere give up anything that he wanted, or could do in the immediate future? . . . To make the agreement gave Hitler immense

30. Churchill, *The Grand Alliance*, 581.
31. *Parliamentary Debates*, Vol. 413, August 16, 1945, p. 83.

advantages and cost him nothing."[32] In a nutshell, Churchill distinguished valid and legitimate compromise in diplomacy from worthless concessions by which no real national advantage was produced.

Secret Diplomacy

On October 22, 1946, R. A. Butler (of Saffron Walden), one of Churchill's political allies, raised in a speech to Parliament a basic and fundamental question. He asked the House of Commons to evaluate the techniques of diplomacy which prevailed in the postwar world. He warned: "I think it is true and clear to us all that there are severe limitations to the value of open diplomacy." Comparing labor negotiations with cold war diplomacy, he observed that "negotiations in front of the microphone" was not the diplomacy Foreign Secretary Ernest Bevin had employed in his long career in the Labor movement. Butler opined: "I doubt whether he would be here had he adopted such methods nor would he have been a leader of the Labour movement." The future Conservative chancellor of the Exchequer concluded a brief and pointed lecture by expressing the wish that: "While the value which publicity achieves in bringing home realities to the people of the world may be remembered, it is to be hoped that in the forthcoming discussions there will be at least some reversion to the traditional method of diplomacy which has stood us in such good stead in the past, and which, I do not doubt, the right hon. Gentleman has attempted to exercise in the limitations afforded him at the conference."[33]

So forceful a statement by Butler was obviously a conscious dissent from the popular view of diplomacy. As we have observed, a widespread belief emerged following World War I singling out secret diplomacy as a primary cause of war. It was argued that if all the mysterious and reprehensible conferences in which a handful of

32. Churchill, "The Anglo-German Naval Agreement," January 12, 1939, *Step by Step 1936–1939* (New York: Putnam's, 1939), 79–81.
33. *Parliamentary Debates*, Vol. 427, October 22, 1946, p. 1522.

clever leaders secretly plotted and carried out their evil schemes for political and military domination could be outlawed and done away with, the major cause of war would be eliminated. The most direct and effective way to accomplish such an objective was the conduct of open diplomacy in public forums and discussions. In reflecting on this opinion, Churchill said: "There was a strong feeling in favor of what is called open diplomacy."[34] If diplomacy were open and its proceedings fully publicized, it was assumed that leaders would be deterred from committing their people to policies and obligations leading to the sacrifice of human lives and sacred treasures. Since the masses were good-hearted, peace-loving people, they would be able, once they directed and controlled the processes of diplomacy, to outlaw war and guarantee that it would become an archaism.

A host of prominent and respected British statesmen accepted unreservedly the concept of open diplomacy in its period of growing popularity between the two world wars. During World War II, even Arnold Toynbee wrote: "It is the essence of this evil, war, whether the veiled war of Diplomacy or the naked war of military force, that its conduct must be secret and autocratic."[35] Lord Cecil, in arguing that all diplomatic conferences must be open and fully publicized, declared that he had never known a case in all his political experience with the League of Nations where private meetings as distinct from public forums had served any constructive purpose. He answered the criticism that delegates were less likely to make concessions in open diplomatic conferences by arguing: "If the opinion were a purely intellectual one any delegate would be as ready to withdraw it in a public as in a private meeting. If it were a question of sentiment or deep feeling he would be unready to withdraw his statement at either meeting."[36]

If we may comment, in passing, on this somewhat unorthodox

34. *Parliamentary Debates*, Vol. 272, November 23, 1932, p. 87.
35. Arnold J. Toynbee, *Nationality and the War* (London: J. M. Dent and Sons, 1915), 2.
36. Quoted in Arnold J. Toynbee, *Survey of International Affairs* (London: Oxford University Press, 1927), 61.

defense of open diplomacy, it is a curious reading of international politics to consider that foreign policies are developed from either a "purely intellectual" or a "deeply emotional and sentimental" viewpoint. In truth, policies are generally conceived, if not always defined, in terms of the objective interests of states. What is at stake, therefore, in negotiations among diplomatists who are required to safeguard their countries' interests is the power and prestige of the national community for which they speak. No nation can afford to publicize its weaknesses nor can its representative retreat from positions taken internationally in public on the basis of national principles. The embarrassment the individual would suffer from a public retreat as against a private retraction is in qualitative terms not the same as the consequences that national humiliation carries for the nation-state. The one is protected, even in humiliation, by the laws and the moral consensus of an integrated community; the other is supported at best by the fragile and uncertain restraints upon power which are currently in effect in an anarchic international world.

There are few signs in any of his public statements that Churchill shared the popular illusions of Toynbee or Lord Cecil. Nor is it difficult to demonstrate that Toynbee in his later approach thoroughly renounced them himself. In one respect, however, Churchill discovered common ground with his critics in a quite limited form of approval. On October 23, 1946, he declared in a reference to the Conference of Paris which discussed the peace treaties to be concluded with five ex-enemy states (July 29 to October 15, 1946): "As to the value of what are called the "open discussions" which have been proceeding in Paris, I can only comment that they seem to be bad diplomacy, but, none the less, valuable education."[37] If public education were the primary function of negotiations, this half-facetious, half-serious statement might be construed as a form of praise. Since compromise and adjustment in diplomacy are the goals, we can do no more than take Churchill literally.

Probably the most cogent statement of the views on open diplo-

37. *Parliamentary Debates*, Vol. 427, October 23, 1946, p. 1679.

macy of Churchill and his closest associates in the Conservative party were in the comments by Oliver Stanley (of Bristol, West) in the same foreign affairs debate in which Churchill spoke of public education before the House of Commons on October 23, 1946. Stanley warned the Parliament: "There do seem to be defects in this public, or indeed publicised diplomacy, where every speech which, in any ordinary negotiation, would be merely a preliminary to be toned down and altered afterwards, becomes a sort of standard which has to be nailed to the mast and stuck to through thick and thin, and where plain speaking, which has to take place in international as well as personal relationships, and which in the privacy of the conference room would be forgotten the next day, goes on permanent record to the perpetual poisoning of the relations of the two countries."[38] The theory of "open diplomacy" has received a fair trial in the practice of the League of Nations and especially the United Nations. Based on the lessons of these two experiments, competent observers have come to seriously question its underlying assumptions. They have maintained that open diplomacy, as with open management of a business enterprise, was nothing less than a contradiction in terms. Churchill himself asserted: "Under conditions of the fullest publicity nothing of any importance could ever be done."[39]

In roughly analogous terms, both management and diplomacy presuppose wise and judicious action by men who possess at least a minimum of discretionary power. The system of unpublicized negotiations, as is true of the practice of business management, has evolved over long centuries of trial and error. In diplomacy, history proves that systematic inquiry by private negotiators was more likely, even with many failures, to produce a common denominator wherein conflicting interests could be reconciled. The patience and resourcefulness of skillful diplomats, politically if not constitutionally responsible for the conduct of foreign policy, were more likely to produce agreement through serious discussions carried on

38. *Ibid.*, 1775.
39. Churchill, *The Aftermath: 1918–1928* (New York: Scribner's, 1929), 143.

over private conference tables. In his reflections on the peace conferences at Versailles, Churchill asked: "How could any thorny question affecting the main interests of nations, great and small, be helpfully debated by twenty-seven Powers in public?"[40] In negotiations conducted on so grand a scale, in practice only two alternatives existed: "If platitudes and honeyed words alone were used, the proceedings would be a farce. If plain speaking were indulged in, they would become a bear-garden."[41] For Churchill even the practice of delegating responsibility to a council of ten, representing the statesmen of the largest powers and convening in private sessions, was too unwieldy. The ideal unit for negotiating the peace was one which would permit "heart to heart and frank conversations between the three men on whom ultimately everything rested: Mr. Lloyd George, M. Clemenceau, and President Wilson."[42] Unless the negotiators possessed the authority and acted in behalf of the major powers they represented, the discussions at worst would prove inconclusive, or at best would result in agreements that were in conflict with the general distribution of power.

A further problem posed by the use of public diplomacy results from its essential dual nature. Negotiations in public aim at achieving some accommodation among the parties. At the same time, modern democratic nations conduct diplomacy ever alert to the movements of their nation's public opinions. Under certain conditions, negotiators may be driven by their publics to press for resolutions with importance exclusively for domestic consumption. Churchill framed his thought in the form of an aphorism: "It is always an error in diplomacy to press a matter when it is quite clear that no further progress is to be made. It is also a great error if you ever give the impression abroad that you are using language which is more concerned with your domestic politics than with the actual fortunes and merits of the various great countries upon the Continent to whom you offer advice."[43] If the objective requirements of

40. *Ibid.*, 143.
41. *Ibid.*, 143–44.
42. *Ibid.*, 144.
43. *Parliamentary Debates*, Vol. 287, March 14, 1934, p. 397.

successful diplomacy were sacrificed to placating domestic interests, public negotiations would be counter-productive in the eyes of the British statesman.

On numerous occasions, Churchill commented more broadly on the place of secrecy in international relations. The conduct of diplomacy required a setting of privacy and calm, he observed. In a wartime message to President Roosevelt he set down a guide for organizing the meetings at Cairo, Teheran, and Yalta. "In any event, I think the Press should be entirely banished, and the whole place surrounded by a cordon so that we would not be disturbed in any way."[44] In his instructions to Sir Edward Bridges, he urged that strict tenets of secrecy be imposed on British officialdom as well. It was preferable to reduce to a minimum the number of officers with knowledge about vital matters. "Ministers should be requested to restrict as far as possible the circle within which it is necessary to discuss secret matters. It is not necessary for Parliamentary Private Secretaries (unless Privy councillors) to be informed more than is necessary for the discharge of their Parliamentary and political duties."[45]

The War Cabinet in England exemplified a national body whose success depended in part on the privacy of its discussions. Its operations were characterized by its wartime leader in the following language: "It was an earnest and workmanlike body, and the advantages of free discussion among men bound so closely together in a common task, without any formality and without any record being kept, are very great. Such meetings are an essential counterpart to its formal meetings where . . . decisions are recorded for guidance and action. Both processes are indispensable to the handling of the most difficult affairs."[46] The whole problem of the arms race in the interwar period could have been more effectively controlled, in Churchill's view, by private exchanges among governments. As we have seen, Churchill conceived the best disarmament approach

44. Churchill, "President Roosevelt to the Prime Minister," October 15, 1943, *Closing the Ring*, 308.
45. Churchill, "Prime Minister to Sir Edward Bridges, General Lemay and Mr. Leal," January 1, 1941, *The Grand Alliance*, 719.
46. Churchill, *The Gathering Storm*, 452.

would have been one in which two or more countries would agree to limit their military efforts in return for concessions by the others: "I believe a greater advance and progress towards a diminution of expenditure on armaments might have been achieved by these methods than by conferences and schemes of disarmament which have been put forward at Geneva."[47]

The issue on which the greatest controversy has centered in the debate over secret diplomacy touches the question of secret clauses in peace settlements. Perhaps the most illuminating statement Churchill made on this problem came in a Parliamentary debate. The war leader was pressed by members of Parliament to disclose whether separate or secret agreements had been made at Yalta. He observed: "Otherwise [except for agreement on the Ukraine and Byelorussia] there were no secret engagements, but the conversations, of course, proceeded in a very intimate manner, and I am not prepared to say that everything discussed at Yalta could be made the subject of a verbatim report."[48] The test of responsible leadership is the willingness of the statesman to report his agreements to a fully representative cabinet. He added: "I do not accept the view that it is absolutely necessary that there should never be on any occasion a secret clause in some arrangement provided that it is reported to a wide Cabinet. It may very often be necessary to do so."[49]

A considerable body of opinion today maintains that secret diplomacy is tolerable provided that agreements arrived at in private discussions are disclosed and made public. Some modern publicists have in the light of reality revised Woodrow Wilson's dictum "open covenants, openly arrived at" to read "open covenants privately arrived at." On this precept, Churchill commented: "It would hamper very much the whole proceedings if no understandings could be made which had not to be immediately published. I should not approve of that myself, although I know that a lot of claptrap is talked about it."[50] However, in the long run, treaties ought to be made

47. *Parliamentary Debates*, Vol. 276, March 23, 1933, p. 541.
48. *Parliamentary Debates*, Vol. 411, June 7, 1945, p. 1064.
49. *Ibid.*, 1065.
50. *Ibid.*

public and private agreements be made known to the public under a
variety of circumstances. For example, when a private agreement
has been revoked, as was the case with the concrete provisions of
the wartime atomic energy accord between the United States, the
United Kingdom, and Canada, the reasons for its being kept con-
fidential usually vanish. As Churchill asserted: "The point I was
venturing to make is that the treaty—or not a treaty, the agreement—had been revoked, not that it had been maintained and kept
in secrecy. It has been revoked, and having been revoked I do not see
why the secret should not be revealed."[51] One fundamental limitation on the responsibility of a state to publish treaties and special
clauses in them which have not yet been made public continues to
exist. Private agreements are arrived at through the concurrence of
more than one party and it is essential that both parties approve
before their provisions are made public. For example, the British
leader was asked whether he intended to disclose the terms which
were reached with President Roosevelt on the subject of atomic information. Churchill replied that he had no objection to the publication of any document or agreement which he had signed on this
subject. But he added significantly: "Surely, however, this is a matter
for both the British and United States Government to settle together
in full agreement. Neither of them has the right to publish without
the consent of the other, and it would be very wrong for anyone to
try to force their hands or press them unduly."[52]

Two final spheres in which private discussions are essential
should be mentioned. At certain moments in history, grave perils
may threaten particular nations in the world. If they are ignorant
of the threats to their security, the warning must come through con-
fidential and private sources. It was a matter of pride for Churchill
that it could be said of the British "our diplomacy has never ceased
for one moment to try to apprise countries of the dangers and perils
that were coming on them."[53] Yet such warnings and alerts had to

51. *Parliamentary Debates*, Vol. 481, January 30, 1951, pp. 715–16.
52. *Parliamentary Debates*, Vol. 415, November 2, 1945, p. 1298.
53. *Parliamentary Debates*, Vol. 371, May 7, 1941, p. 371.

be made so that recipient governments might still retain the full confidence and control of their own people. Hence only subtle promptings through secret channels were helpful.

Finally, the best means for pursuing a peaceful settlement in the tragic power conflicts of the modern world have been and remain through traditional diplomatic processes. Churchill's prescription for peace in our times illustrates the importance he gave to secret diplomacy: "I believe it right to say that the best chance of avoiding war is, in accord with the Western democracies, to bring matters to a head with the Soviet Government and by formal diplomatic processes, with all their privacy and gravity, to arrive at a lasting settlement."[54] Diplomacy in private offered the greatest hope in resolving the profound differences of the cold war.

Contemporary Diplomatic Practice

Since the end of World War I, however, diplomatic practice has been conducted under a new and unfamiliar cloak. Formerly, issues had been dealt with through the direct negotiations of permanent ambassadors or envoys or else consummated and concluded in the spectacle of a full-dress international conference. Recently, however, diplomacy has proceeded on the basis of a new type of diplomatic intercourse. Issues and tensions have been dealt with not by ad hoc conferences or negotiators as they arose but rather as they appeared on the agenda for deliberation by permanent international assemblies. Opportunity has been accorded to delegates, whatever their particular interests, to make public their views on a question. After delegates have spoken, a vote is taken and the issue has theoretically been decided. In this way, diplomacy has been transferred from private negotiators to political leaders who debate the issues in open parliamentary assemblies.

One distinction between the League of Nations and the United Nations attracted the attention of Churchill. The League was but the first step in an evolving parliamentary diplomacy. It represented

54. *Parliamentary Debates*, Vol. 446, January 23, 1948, p. 561.

a less advanced stage than the United Nations in the practice of open diplomacy. More important in the long run was the reluctance of League diplomatists who labored under the spell of the fading light of traditional diplomacy to take too seriously the precepts of parliamentary diplomacy. Public debates in the council and assembly were, in Monsieur Spaak's words, prearranged and carefully rehearsed through the use of rapporteurs and committees.[55] The fact that the League was essentially a European body also encouraged the use of traditional diplomatic practice. Fewer newcomers to the international scene were engaged in the diplomatic process. Less common was the practice of justifying stratagems in the language of high moral principles.

The United Nations witnessed the full flowering of parliamentary diplomacy. Its creation heralded the substitution of the new for the old diplomacy. Equally important, its two most powerful members, the Soviet Union and the United States, viewed diplomacy from the standpoint of powerful ideological convictions. The Soviet Union and its leaders saw themselves as participating in the unfolding of an historic process and as standing watch over the dying remains of capitalist societies. In their eyes, enduring peace would become possible only when communism was established throughout the world. At that time, diplomacy, like the state, would wither away. For the present, noncommunist negotiators must be dealt with tentatively and provisionally pending the final cataclysm when communism would be everywhere established. To serve national advantage, international arrangements should be honored and diplomatic contacts preserved. However, as an instrument of the historic process, the Soviet diplomat viewed all noncommunist emissaries as fomenters of a counter-historic movement aimed at obstructing the natural unfolding of the dialectic process. Therefore, in Churchill's experience, "the post of Ambassador to the Soviets has been found extremely unattractive by all British and Americans who had been called upon to fill it, both during and after the war. During the period before Hitler's attack ranged Russia with us, our envoy had

55. New York *Times*, October 15, 1947, p. 4.

been almost entirely ignored in Moscow."[56] Ambassadors were kept at frigid arm's length and their role interpreted as the equivalent of conspirators against the forces of history. Those diplomatic accords which the Soviet Union accepted, they interpreted as performing no more than a stopgap function and everyone expected and believed that with the ripening of the historic process they would become obsolete.

The United States, for its part, tended to conceive of diplomacy as little more than a passing phase in the development of the world community. As a morally inferior stage in relations among nation-states, diplomacy was subjected to the sharpest and most indignant attacks of idealists. One aspect of the general condemnation of power politics and secret diplomacy in this country was manifest in the disposition to forswear any interest in political developments elsewhere in the world through which world power was being redistributed. Thus President Woodrow Wilson looked down with indifference on the detailed provisions of territorial settlements for the Balkans and Southeastern Europe. In place of an objective estimate of their importance, he preferred to substitute the abstract moral doctrine of national self-determination. Similarly, the American delegation at Potsdam was rarely concerned with the political consequences of particular territorial transfers. In fact, in discussions at subsequent conferences, President Truman and Secretary of State James F. Byrnes were unable even to recall what concessions had been made to the Soviet Union. Their inability to remember earned their handiwork the sobriquet of Washington correspondents "Hazy agreements—hazily arrived at." As one example, Molotov argued at the Moscow Conference in 1946 that he had asked for the return of the Turkish provinces Kars and Ardanam at the Potsdam Conference. President Truman was unable to recall that any mention had been made of these distant and alien provinces. Secretary Byrnes remembered that they had been mentioned but had no further impressions about them. In reporting this incident,

56. Winston S. Churchill, *The Second World War*, Vol. IV, *The Hinge of Fate* (Boston: Houghton Mifflin, 1950), 63.

Time magazine observed: "Whether Russia had wanted them back or not, Secretary Byrnes couldn't say for sure. Neither could he remember whether Truman, Attlee, or Stalin had happened to be around at the time."[57] American diplomacy, with few exceptions, tended to look on questions of the postwar distribution of world power with an air of supreme indifference. Since power politics were considered to be in eclipse, issues involving the distribution of power were generally viewed in a spirit of moral condemnation and disdain.

A further example of the corruption of contemporary diplomacy has been the disposition to reverse the relationship between strength and diplomacy. Historically, diplomacy had depended for its success on foundations of power and especially military strength. Yet dictatorships have frequently reversed the pattern. In the interwar period, Fascist Italy, while lacking the instruments of power to make it a true world power, sought its ends through a policy of diplomatic bluster which Harold Nicolson entitled "power diplomacy." Churchill commented in 1937: "[Mussolini] is engaged in what is called power diplomacy and so far he is getting step by step almost everything that he wishes by it. Wherever he finds himself opposed by the settled will of Great Britain and France, as at Nyon, he withdraws diplomatically and tries some new point of advance."[58] Dictatorships, without the overall essential elements of power necessary for supporting their claims, have pursued a diplomatic course aimed at the surrender of passive and indifferent foes. Power diplomacy, Churchill contended, can be met only by calling the dictator's bluff. "If perfectly plain, precise and categorical notifications are made by Britain and France together about encroachments they could not endure, it is almost certain their wishes would be respected."[59] These were Churchill's words written on October 15, 1937.

The real crisis, however, in contemporary diplomatic practice,

---

57. *Time*, March 18, 1946, p. 24.
58. Churchill, "War is not Imminent," October 15, 1937, *Step by Step*, 151.
59. *Ibid.*

with its own unique and peculiar characteristics, has resulted from the virtual breakdown of diplomatic relations between East and West. Anthony Eden, who was interpreted as speaking both for himself and Churchill, announced shortly after the Conservatives had returned to power in the autumn of 1951: "There is now virtually no diplomatic contact between east and west—either side of the Iron Curtain I mean by the phrase. That is something new and entirely to be deplored." He went on: "By this I mean, although, of course, we have missions in Communist countries behind the Iron Curtain, in all the capitals, and although they have missions here, very little business passes. Still less is there any real meeting of minds. This is something which is surely unprecedented in my diplomatic experience."[60] Such a crisis obviously is the product of more than one factor. It is an expression of profound divisions between the centers of world power in the moral and political spheres. It indicates the degree to which both sides have taken seriously their deprecation of diplomacy as at best a temporary expedient. And it suggests that the Soviet conception of the diplomat as a figure stripped of almost all discretion and acting primarily to transmit official orders and proposals has weakened if not destroyed the importance of personal qualities through which traditional diplomacy accomplished its tasks.

In earlier centuries, the appointed diplomat had the prerogative of seeking his nation's objectives through all the psychological techniques he could muster. He had discretion to modify some proposals, to emphasize others, and to meet new situations with imagination and boldness. The Soviet diplomat, as Churchill viewed him, was a cog in a pseudomilitary apparatus. His role was to transmit received policies that leaders in the Soviet Union would be willing to accept. Once such proposals were offered on a clear take-it-or-leave-it basis, the one alternative, if such policies were unacceptable, was to hope that new instructions would be sent by Moscow. Such procedures had the result of destroying, for all practical purposes, true diplomacy. Its destruction must have been in Churchill's

60. *Parliamentary Debates*, Vol. 494, November 19, 1951, p. 34–35.

mind when he wrote to President Roosevelt on November 26, 1942: "Certainly if a Russian delegation went to Cairo, which I deem unlikely, they would be so tied up that they would have to refer every point of substance back to Stalin at Moscow."[61]

The crisis in contemporary diplomatic practice has therefore been brought about by the inadequacies of parliamentary diplomacy, the weakness of American concepts of diplomacy, and the evils which arise from the authoritarian practice of Soviet diplomacy. Such conditions, strengthening and reinforcing one another, have intensified and deepened the present crisis. They make infinitely more difficult the successful pursuit of any of the five separate approaches to peace. If leaders cannot discover the means of mitigating their effects, World War III may be inevitable.

Yet the consequences of such a conflict from a moral, political, and social point of view and with respect to human survival are so appalling that anyone who is drawn toward this conclusion has a personal responsibility for making certain that every remedy or prospect has been exhausted. In this search, Churchill's wisdom may prove an intellectual and practical resource without equal. We complete our review of his world view hoping its study may close the yawning gulf which separates our problems from our ability to bring about their amelioration.

---

61. Churchill, "Former Naval Person to President Roosevelt," November 26, 1942, *The Hinge of Fate*, 662.

Acheson, Dean, 255
Adams, Henry, 206
Adams, John, 56
Anglo-American Conference, 157
Ascroft, Robert, 77
Asquith, Earl of, 90
Atlantic Charter, 23, 41, 52, 120,
  121, 133, 140
Atlee, Clement, 41

Balance of power, 30, 73, 98, 170,
  223–224, 231
Baldwin, Hanson, 146
Balkans, invasion of, 139–61
Benes, Eduard, 56
Berlin crisis (1948), 217
Beveridge, William, 122
Bevin, Ernest, 28, 125, 129, 347
Big Three, 144, 299
Bismarck, 196
Bolshevism, 188
Boncour, Paul, 258
Borgese, Guiseppe, 30–31
Bradley, Omar, 128
Burke, Edmund, 101, 113, 185
Butcher, Harry, 136
Butler, R. A., 103

Cairo Conference, 146, 153, 157
Canning, George, 239, 240
Casablanca Conference, 130, 132,
  157
Chamberlain, Neville, 8
Churchill, Winston: and alliances,
40, 41; and Africa, 43; and
atomic bomb, 208, 259–60;
and the balance of power, 73,
98; and collective security,
308–313; and conservatism,
18, 19, 20; and constitutional
idealism, 32–35; and Cuba, 43;
and cynicism, 48; and diplomacy, 3, 87, 104–10, 161–70;
and education as a young man,
61–62; and Egypt, 42; and
France, 178–79; and Fulton
speech, 5, 7, 23, 26, 125, 207,
310; and German problem, 38;
and Greece, 80–81, 126; and
history, 6; and Hitler, 37, 94,
134, 135; and human nature,
53, 78–90; and India, 43,
65–67; and international-
ism, 28–30; and isolationism,
28–30; and Israel, 279; and
Italy, 50, 131, 133; and Korea,
41; and League of Nations, 44;
and legalism, 35; and liberalism, 18; and Mediterranean policy, 142, 154, 158; and militarism, 76; and military service,
62–76; and moralism, 43, 52;
and Morgenthau Plan, 96; and
Nazi Germany, 142, 234, 281;
and Nazism 38, 92, 130, 137;
and optimism, 25–27; and pessimism, 25–27; and Poland,
121–27; political career, early,

177–78; politics and force, 166, 168; power politics, 78–98; and realism, 17, 52–58, 120; and regionalism, 282–85; and religion, 68–77; and revolution, 75; and Schuman Plan, 42; and socialism, 88–89; Soviet Union, 37, 55; Sudan, 72–74; and Western European Union, 34–35; and a scientific approach to politics, 162–71; and the tragic sense of life, 76, 90; and unconditional surrender, 128–38; and the United Nations, 297–306; and utopianism, 52–58; and world community, 285–89; and Yalta, 11, 87, 121–27
Clark, Mark, 146, 156
Clausewitz, 57
Cold War, 243
Collective Security, 306–13
Colombo Conference, 280
Concert of Europe, 227
Conference of Paris, 349
Congress of Vienna, 227
Conservatism, 18–20
Constitutional idealism, 30–35
Crossman, Richard, 231
Cynicism, 48

Dardanelles, 139–41
Davies, Clement, 27
Davies, Rhys, 85
Deane, John R., 140
de Gaulle, Charles, 131
de Madariaga, Salvadore, 264
Diplomacy, 227–28, 246
Disarmament, 224–25, 252–69

Disraeli, 18
Dixon, Pierson, 127
Dulles, Allen, 130
Dulles, John Foster, 345

Eaker, Ira, 155
Eden, Anthony, 131, 143, 161
Eisenhower, Dwight D., 95, 136, 144, 148
Enlightenment, 180, 224, 275

Fénelon, 246, 247
Forester, C. F., 115
Franks, Lord Oliver, 2
Frederick the Great, 177, 170
French Revolution, 177, 178

Geneva Conference, 261, 262
German problem, 38, 128
Gibson, Hugh, 257–59
Gradualism, 290–94

Hague Conference, 261, 262
Haig, Douglas, 108
Hall, W. E., 276
Harriman, Averell, 69
Healey, Denis, 5
Henderson, Sir Arthur, 267
Hitler, Adolf, 144, 202
Hoover Plan, 257, 259
Hopkins, Harry, 130, 131
Hull, Cordell, 48
Human nature, 24, 78–90; and ethics, 50, 53
Hume, David, 229

Industrial Revolution, 178, 226
International law, 39; and national interests, 36

International organization, 227–28
Isolationism, 19, 38, 39
Italian campaign, 155

Katyn Forest, massacre of, 37
Kellogg-Briand Pact, 258, 262
Kennan, George, 12, 13, 52, 202
Korea, 211, 212, 213, 324
Kraus, Rene, 180

Laski, Harold, 20, 21, 22
League of Nations, 87, 202, 203,
    227, 252
Legalism, 12, 35–42
Liberalism, 18, 19, 23, 79, 224
Lie, Trygve, 320
London Treaty, 262, 263–64

Maclean, Fitzroy, 100, 152
Marshall, George, 144, 145, 155,
    157
Marx, Karl, 127
Marxism, 79
McNeil, Hector, 50, 51
Militarism, 185
Monism, 54
Monroe Doctrine, 181, 239
Moralism, 42–52, 121–27
Morgenthau, Hans, 50, 186, 271,
    339
Morrison, Herbert, 21
Moscow Conference, 153
Mowat, R. B., 336
Munich agreement, 241
Mussolini, Benito, 37, 131, 133,
    233

Napoleonic Wars, 178
National interests: and disarma-
ment, 236–60; and legalism,
    36, 50; and universal constitu-
    tional commitments, 32
Negotiations: and appeasement,
    4; and strength, 4; as rational
    transaction, 19
Niebuhr, Reinhold, 75
North African campaign, 152,
    153, 158
North Atlantic Treaty Organiza-
    tion, 40, 211

Optimism, 25–27
"Overlord," 143, 145, 153, 154,
    155, 160

Pacifism, 185
Pact of Paris, 120
Pasvolsky, Leo, 298
Peloponnesian Wars, 179
Pessimism, 25–27
Politics and force, 166, 168
Potsdam, 278
Power: and conservatism, 18; fac-
    tors of, 56–58; and human na-
    ture, 79; and liberalism, 77; and
    negotiations, 3, 6; and philoso-
    phy, 113–16; and politics,
    91–98; and realism, 55; and
    strength, 3; and tradition,
    99–104; tragic predicament of,
    52

Quebec Conference, 118
Quesnay, 177

Rationalism, 54, 69
Realism, 14, 17, 52–58, 79,
    121–27

Renaissance Treaty, 196
Roosevelt, Elliott, 156
Roosevelt, Franklin Delano, 84, 85, 130, 131, 136, 141, 152, 154, 157, 199, 204, 231, 343
Roosevelt, Theodore, 18
Rush-Bagot Agreement, 225

Salisbury, Lord, 73
Schuman Plan, 238
Sherwood, Robert, 156
Shinwell, Emanuel, 56, 215
Simon, Sir John, 334
Spaak, Paul-Henri, 321
Stalin, Joseph, 134, 145, 154, 157, 160
Stanley, Oliver, 350
Stettinius, Edward, 136
Stimson, Henry, 139, 147
Streit, Clarence, 30, 31
Struggle for power, and economics, 19

Teheran, 140, 153, 157, 343
Thorneycroft, Peter, 11, 52, 123
Toynbee, Arnold, 178, 229, 230, 250, 258, 348, 349
Tragedy, 99–104
Treaty of Utrecht, 195
Triple Alliance, 196
Triple Entente, 197
Truman Doctrine, 39

Unconditional surrender, 127
United Nations, 227, 295–306, and foreign policy, 313–19; future of, 325–31
United States, foreign policy of: and atomic bomb, 145; and collective security, 317; and constitutionalism, 32; and isolationism, 27; and Monroe Doctrine, 39; and realism and idealism, 15, 16, 17
Utopianism, 52–58, 92

Versailles, Treaty of, 199, 200
Voltaire, 177

Wallace, Henry, 231
Washington Naval Agreement, 262
Washington Treaty, 225
Weber, Max, 127
Weimar Republic, 203
Wilmot, Chester, 140
Wilson, Woodrow, 48, 198, 333
World Disarmament Conference, 334
World government, 225
World state, 270–75
World War I, 194, 199
World War II, 199–206
World War III, 206–19

Yalta, 11, 87, 121–27, 300